Hinduism in America

ALSO AVAILABLE FROM BLOOMSBURY:

Buddhism in America: Global Religion, Local Contexts, Scott A. Mitchell

Hindu Worldviews: Theories of Self, Ritual and Reality, Jessica Frazier

Hinduism in America

A Convergence of Worlds

JEFFERY D. LONG

BLOOMSBURY ACADEMIC
LONDON • NEW YORK • OXFORD • NEW DELHI • SYDNEY

BLOOMSBURY ACADEMIC
Bloomsbury Publishing Plc
50 Bedford Square, London, WC1B 3DP, UK
1385 Broadway, New York, NY 10018, USA

BLOOMSBURY, BLOOMSBURY ACADEMIC and the Diana logo are trademarks of
Bloomsbury Publishing Plc

First published in Great Britain 2020

Cover design by Dani Leigh
Cover images © pamelaoliveras / Raj's Photography / Martin Holtkamp / Getty Images

A catalogue record for this book is available from the British Library.

A catalog record for this book is available from the Library of Congress.

ISBN: HB: 978-1-4742-4846-4
PB: 978-1-4742-4845-7
ePDF: 978-1-4742-4847-1
eBook: 978-1-4742-4848-8

Typeset by Integra Software Services Pvt. Ltd.

To find out more about our authors and books visit www.bloomsbury.com
and sign up for our newsletters

For the Hindu, Hindu-inspired, and Indian communities of America,
past, present, and future.

Contents

Figures

Acknowledgments

More people than I can list here have helped make this book possible. It is the product of my last twenty-five years—in other words, most of my adult life—of being involved in Hindu, Hindu-inspired, and Indian communities in North America.

I want to thank the community of the HARI (Hindu American Religious Institute) Temple, in New Cumberland, Pennsylvania, and the Bengali community of the greater Harrisburg area for providing a welcoming spiritual home and a network of good friends to my wife and myself during the last twenty years, since we moved to Elizabethtown, Pennsylvania, from Chicago.

Special warm and heartfelt thanks go to Ann Gleig, who first suggested to me that I take on this challenging, but ultimately profoundly rewarding, project. Lalle Pursglove, Lucy Carroll, Camilla Erskine, and Lily McMahon, at Bloomsbury, have been tremendously supportive and admirably patient with my many delays in submitting the manuscript. The rest of life does not slow down when one is writing a book! Their commitment to this project has helped to make it a reality. I would also like to thank the scholarly reviewers who gave my proposal encouragement and support at the outset and the reviewers of the first and second drafts of the manuscript, whose tremendously helpful comments have certainly improved the final product. I hope it meets, or even exceeds, the expectations they expressed for it. Any flaws it nevertheless possesses are, of course, entirely my responsibility.

Special thanks go to my informal research assistant, Loretto Taylor. Loretto painstakingly, and on an entirely voluntary basis, compiled a massive database of the websites of Hindu temples in the United States, which I hope can become part of an online resource connected with this book. This database is the foundation of the appendix at the end of this book, which lists Hindu temples and organizations in the United States as comprehensively as the two of us were able.

I would also like to thank the Taylor and Francis Group for permission to reprint portions of my essay, "Diasporic and Indigenous Hinduism in North America," which was originally published in P. Pratap Kumar, ed., *Contemporary Hinduism* (Acumen, 2013), pp. 17-31. The firsthand descriptions of HARI Temple and the Washington Kali Temple that appear in Chapter 5 are drawn from this essay. I also thank Matthew Brake for permission to include my portions of my two-part essay, "Hindu Themes in Western Popular Culture: A Tale of Two Georges," from the online journal *Theology and Popular Culture*, posted April 2, 2018 and April 9, 2018.

Last, but most certainly not least, I thank my best friend and partner in life—my wife, Mahua Bhattacharya—and my Gurudeva, both of whom have not only been constant sources of love and support, but also indispensable guides to the lived practice of Hinduism. The insights they both have shared with me are more than can possibly be contained in a single book.

Pronunciation Guide

Many terms in this book are from Sanskrit and other Indic languages. The scripts ("alphabets") of these languages are phonetic—that is, each character stands for exactly one sound, and there is a character for each sound. As a result, the Indic scripts have far more characters than the twenty-six letters of the Roman alphabet used in English and many other European languages. To render words from Indic languages in the Roman script in an exact way, scholars have developed a system of diacritical marks to distinguish between, for example, the short *a* of Sanskrit (pronounced like the "u" in "bud") and the Sanskrit long "*ā*" (which is pronounced like the "a" in the English word "father"). The correct pronunciation of Indic sounds, as depicted using this system, is as follows:

a: "uh," as in "bud"
ā: "ah," as in "father"
i: like the "i" in "bit"
ī: like "ee" in "beet"
u: like the "oo" in "book"
ū: like the "oo" in "boot"
ṛ: like the "ri" in "rig," with a slight roll of the tongue, though not as hard a roll as in Spanish
e: like "ay" in "say."
ai: like "aye" or "eye."
o: "oh," as in "Ohio."
au: like "ow" in "cow."

Consonants are mostly pronounced as in English, but consonants with a dot under them (e.g., "ṭ") are pronounced with the tongue touching the roof of the mouth. Consonants immediately followed by an "h" (e.g., "th," "dh") include an exhalation. So, the "h" is pronounced, producing somewhat of a softening of the consonant. The "h" is *not* a separate syllable. So "dha," for example, will be pronounced as "dha," and not "daha." Also, the letter "c" is not pronounced like a "k," as it typically is in English, but is pronounced "ch." So *Yogācāra* is *not* pronounced *Yogākāra*, but *Yogāchāra*.

The "ś" and "ṣ" sounds are almost indistinguishable and are sometimes confused even by native speakers. The "ṣ" sound is pronounced with the tongue at the roof of the mouth, but "ś" is not. Both sound somewhat like the "sh" in "she." So *Śiva* is *not* pronounced *Siva*, but *Shiva*.

The sound "ḥ," is always preceded by a vowel and produces a slight echoing of that vowel. So "aḥ" is pronounced "aha." The sound "ṃ" is slightly nasalized, sounding almost like an "n."

I have used this system for most terms, except proper names that have a popular modern spelling (e.g., Ramakrishna, not Rāmakṛṣṇa; Swami Vivekananda, not Svāmī Vivekānanda; and so on).

Prologue: A Personal Journey

My first encounter with Hinduism did not occur in India, nor did it even involve meeting any actual, practicing Hindus. It was an encounter, rather, with a song by a popular British artist: George Harrison's "My Sweet Lord." This song was Harrison's first hit after he left the world's most enduringly popular rock and roll band: the Beatles. Unabashedly devotional, "My Sweet Lord" could easily be taken—at least for the first three minutes of its four-minute and forty-second length—to be a Christian rock song. Harrison sings of his longing to see and to be with the Lord. Meanwhile, a chorus sings "Alleluia, Alleluia" in the background. (This "chorus" is actually Harrison's own multi-tracked voice, credited jokingly to the "George O'Hara Smith Singers.") Three minutes into the song, though, the chorus begins to intersperse its alleluias with a new chant, "Hare Krishna Hare Krishna, Krishna Krishna Hare Hare, Hare Rama Hare Rama, Rama Rama Hare Hare." The song culminates with "Gurur Brahma Gurur Vishnu, Gurur Devo Maheśvara, Guruḥ sākṣāt Paraṃbrahma, tasmai śri gurave namaḥ." The Hare Krishna, Hare Rama chant, I would later learn, is a very sacred mantra, or prayer, of the Vaiṣṇava tradition of Hinduism. The last verse, starting with Gurur Brahma, Gurur Vishnu, is a prayer to the guru, the divine teacher who guides one's progress on the spiritual path.

The first time I listened to this song closely, I was twelve years old, although it had played in the background for much of my life. (I was born in 1969. My parents both enjoyed the Beatles' music, although I would not call either of them hard-core fans.) I had been a Beatles fan since seeing the film *Help!* on television when I was ten and staying home from school due to an illness. After having amassed a rather large collection of Beatles albums, I began to explore their varied solo careers. Intrigued by "My Sweet Lord," and finding its chant to be hauntingly beautiful, I began to research Harrison and his music more deeply.

I soon realized that there was more going on in Harrison's music than simple fun. In some of his songs with the Beatles, and even more so in his solo work, one could find Indian themes, as well as lyrics suggestive of his philosophical bent of mind: songs like "Within You, Without You," from the 1967 album *Sgt. Pepper's Lonely Hearts Club Band*, and "The Inner Light," a relatively obscure B-side from 1968, recorded in Bombay, with Indian musicians.

My early exploration of Harrison's music was happening simultaneously with some of the most traumatic events of my childhood. When I was twelve years old, my father took his own life. He had been in a horrible accident the year before, which had left him badly injured. He was never able to cope with the permanent debilitation which resulted from these injuries. Living through these experiences, seeing my father suffer so much, and seeing my mother suffer with him as she devoted herself to his care, and then experiencing the additional trauma of his loss, I became preoccupied, perhaps even obsessed, with questions like, "What happens to us after we die?" and "Why is there so much suffering in our lives?" The philosophy that I discerned in Harrison's lyrics was attractive to me. I saw the film *Gandhi* when it came out in 1982—when I was thirteen—which further deepened my interest in India and its religions and philosophies.

The lyrics, interviews, and album cover art of George Harrison, as well as the writings of Gandhi and Fritjof Capra's book, *The Tao of Physics* (which intrigued me with its discussions of the intersections of science and Asian religions) all shared a common thread: their references to a text called the *Bhagavad Gītā*. It struck me that this must be a very wise and ancient book, which might hold some of the answers I was seeking. The *Bhagavad Gītā*, however, was not easy to find in the small Missouri town where I lived. I ended up coming across it in the most unlikely place.

My first encounter with the *Bhagavad Gītā* was in the parking lot of the local Methodist church. I was not a Methodist, but I was in the church parking lot because a flea market was being held there. I had gone with my grandmother, who was there to sell her handmade arts and crafts. My mission, beyond helping Grandma, was to buy old science fiction paperbacks and comic books, which could often be found at such markets. This was a spring day in 1983, when I was fourteen years old: the day I found the book that would change the course of my life.

On a table at the flea market that looked like a promising place to find interesting books, I saw the *Bhagavad Gītā*. It was sitting on top of a pile of old magazines. It was the richly illustrated *Bhagavad Gītā: As It Is*, the *Gītā* as translated by A. C. Bhaktivedanta Swami Prabhupada, founder of the International Society for Krishna Consciousness, and friend and teacher of George Harrison.

I opened the text, seemingly at random, to one of the illustrated plates—a portrait of a man who had died and who was surrounded by his grieving family. The picture hit me like a lightning bolt, as it seemed to sum up perfectly the experiences of my family over the past few years. Standing at some distance from this grieving family was a wise sage, gazing upon them with serene, compassionate detachment, and gifted with the ability to see the divinity in each family member (illustrated by a small image of Lord Krishna floating over each person's heart). Beneath this picture was a caption that read, "The wise lament neither for the living nor the dead," with a page number given.

I looked up the page reference indicated next to the caption and came to the eleventh verse of the second chapter of the text:

> Those who are wise lament neither for the living nor the dead. Never was there a time when I did not exist, nor you, nor all these kings; nor in the future shall any of us cease to be. As the embodied soul continually passes, in this body, from

boyhood to youth, and then to old age, the soul similarly passes into another body at death. The self-realised soul is not bewildered by such a change.[1]

I cannot begin to describe the power these words had for me that day, a power that resonates to the present. It seemed to me as if I was hearing the voice of God speaking directly to me in this Methodist church parking lot. Transfixed, I could not put the book down. Here was the wisdom which I had been seeking. Here were answers that actually made sense to me, both logically and intuitively. I bought the book for a quarter. I always say that this was the best quarter I ever spent!

The *Bhagavad Gītā* is actually a fairly small portion—eighteen concise chapters—of a much longer text—the *Mahābhārata*—which is roughly four times the length of the Bible. Composed, in its current form, about 2,000 years ago, in the Sanskrit language of ancient India, the *Mahābhārata* tells the story of a war between two branches of a royal family—the Kurus (or Kauravas) and the Pāṇḍavas, although it also includes many other stories and discourses on ethics and spirituality.

The *Bhagavad Gītā*, or "Song of the Blessed Lord," is simply called "the *Gītā*" by many Hindus, although many profound and beautiful *gītās*, or songs, have been composed through the centuries, such as the twelfth-century *Gīta Govinda* of Jayadeva, narrating the love story of Rādhā and Krishna, and the *Guru Gītā*, or hymn to one's teacher (from which comes the chant *Gurur Brahma, Gurur Vishnu*, and so on, found in "My Sweet Lord").

The *Bhagavad Gītā* recounts a dialogue at one of the most dramatic points in the plot of the *Mahābhārata*, just as the climactic battle of the Kaurava-Pāṇḍava war is about to begin. The Pāṇḍava hero, Arjuna, is about to lead his forces into battle by blowing the *śaṅkha*, or conch shell horn that will signal the charge. He asks his charioteer, Krishna (who is not only his cousin and best friend, but also, it turns out, God incarnate), to drive him to the center of the battlefield, between the two assembled armies. Arjuna then observes the brave, heroic, and noble men in both armies. His own teacher, Droṇa, and the grandfatherly Bhīṣma, adhering to their oaths of loyalty, have ended up on the other side of the battle against Arjuna and his brothers, although the mutual affection between the Pāṇḍavas and these two elders remains undiminished.

It is, in short, a classic civil war situation, with family members fighting family members. Arjuna, despondent at the thought of the slaughter to come, and the fact that he is duty bound to take up arms against the very men whose feet he has previously touched in respect—men whom he still looks up to with profound reverence, wishes that he was anywhere but on this field of battle. He turns to Krishna for advice.

Krishna—who, again, is no ordinary friend, but *Bhagavān*, or the Blessed Lord—proceeds to advise Arjuna. His advice may be shocking to someone who associates Hinduism with Gandhian nonviolence and who grew up during or in the wake of the great peace movements of the second half of the twentieth century, such as the movement against the Vietnam War in the 1960s.

Krishna does not tell Arjuna to become a pacifist and to embrace his enemies. He advises Arjuna, rather, to fight the battle before him as duty demands. But as Gandhi and others who adore this text attest—Gandhi famously called the *Gita* his "dictionary of daily reference" —the point here is not to endorse violence, but to inspire all of us to face the challenges of life with courage.[2]

From a literary perspective, the battlefield situation functions to give Krishna the occasion to launch into an extended discourse on the meaning of existence and the way to our ultimate goal: the supreme peace of Brahman (*brahma-nirvāṇa*). Beginning with the doctrines of the immortality of the Self and the process of birth, death, and rebirth (which were deeply reassuring in my youth and continue to be today), Krishna takes Arjuna on a comprehensive, detailed journey through the various spiritual paths, or *yogas*, that lead to ultimate bliss: the paths of action, wisdom, devotion, and meditation—karma yoga, jñāna yoga, bhakti yoga, and rāja yoga, respectively.[3]

It is not by avoiding the things we fear, the *Gītā* teaches us, that we become free. It is by facing them head-on, with the courage of a warrior, and offering each action and experience as an offering to the divinity who dwells in us all, that we can at last reach the state of transcendence. In this state, we will perceive God in everyone and everything we meet. And if God is everywhere, in everyone and everything, what is there to fear? This is a deeply encouraging message indeed: for a fourteen-year-old who has lost his father, and for people everywhere who are struggling to find a way to true and lasting inner peace.[4]

FIGURE 1 *Jalaram Prarthana Hindu temple, Leicester, UK. Fresco. Krishna the charioteer guiding Arjuna in the battlefield of Kurukshetra photo by Godong/Universal Images Group via Getty Images).*

Having encountered the *Bhagavad Gītā*, I plunged headlong into an ever-deepening study of the spiritual life, voraciously absorbing every book I could find on this topic. Many of the books I read during this period—my teenage years, prior to going to college—were, I would later discover, books that had inspired many Americans to delve more deeply into Hinduism. I read works like Paramahansa Yogananda's *Autobiography of a Yogi*, Aldous Huxley's *The Perennial Philosophy*, Swami Rama's *Living with the Himalayan Masters*, Huston Smith's *The Religions of Man*, Swami Prabhavananda's translations of classic Hindu texts like the *Upaniṣads*, the *Yoga Sūtra*, and the *Bhagavad Gītā*, as well as his *Sermon on the Mount According to Vedanta*, and numerous other books relating not only to Hinduism, but to spirituality in general, including works on Buddhism, Daoism, and Islam, as well as classics from the Roman Catholic tradition in which I was raised, and from other Christian traditions as well. I came to believe that profound and helpful truths can be found in all the world's religions and philosophies, a belief that continues to be foundational not only to my personal worldview, but to my career as a scholar of religion and philosophy.

A couple of years after coming across the *Bhagavad Gītā*, I finally had the opportunity to meet the one Indian family living in my small community when I volunteered to tutor one of the family's children in mathematics after they had sent a request for such a volunteer to the local high school. This family—the Patels—were Gujarati and ran the only motel in our small Missouri town.[5] The family found my fascination with Hinduism and Indian culture endearing and welcomed me warmly into their home. I became a regular fixture there on Monday evenings. This was when they performed their weekly *pūjā*, or worship—which I at first observed, and in which I eventually participated. *Pūjā* was always followed by a vegetarian Indian dinner.

My journey did not end when I left my hometown to go to college, and after that, graduate school. It continues to the present day, evolving into an intertwining set of commitments, both to gaining personal insight for myself as I continue to study and learn about the world's many wisdom traditions as a seeker, and also to sharing these insights with others through my professional career of teaching courses, writing books like this one, and serving—I would like to hope—as a bridge between the American, predominantly Christian world in which I was born and raised, and the Indian, predominantly Hindu world in which I have found my primary spiritual home. These are the worlds that continue to converge in the phenomenon of Hinduism in America: the cultural worlds of, on the one hand, inheritors of Hinduism, largely of Indian origin, who seek to preserve their traditions and pass them on to future generations in the country they have made their home, and on the other, people like myself, who were neither born nor raised Hindu, but who have found something deeply meaningful, sustaining, and transformative in Hindu traditions, and who seek to integrate the wisdom of these traditions, in various ways and to varying degrees, into our lives.

As time has passed, and as generations of Hindus have grown up in America, the story of Hinduism in America has also become the story of Hindus who were raised as American Hindus, whose lives have been informed, from the beginning, by their experiences of both the Hindu world which they have received from their families and of the American world in which they have lived and been formed: worlds which, for them, are one world, the world of American Hinduism. This book is the story of the coming together of all these worlds—worlds which increasingly interweave to form the complex phenomenon that is Hinduism in America.

Introduction: A Convergence of Worlds

Introduction Summary and Outline

This introduction gives an overview of global Hinduism and Hindu influence in North America. It focuses on demographic statistics, introduces the concept of the Hindu diaspora, gives a chapter-by-chapter overview of the book, and explains the author's methodology and approach.

Hinduism and Hindus: A World Religion, a Global Community

With roughly 1.11 billion adherents, as of 2019, Hinduism has the third largest following among the world's religions. Christianity has the largest, with 2.33 billion adherents, and Islam the second largest, with 1.72 billion adherents.[1] Buddhism has the fourth largest following, with 750.4 million adherents. Adherents of these four religions make up about 77 percent of humanity; 16.4 percent of people are estimated to have no religious affiliation, but this is difficult to verify;[2] 6.6 percent practice religions other than Christianity, Islam, Hinduism, or Buddhism.

The vast majority of the world's Hindus (93.2 percent) live in India, making up about 79.8 percent of the population, according to the 2011 census of India. The other 20.2 percent of Indians are Muslim (14.2 percent), Christian (2.3 percent), Sikh (1.7 percent), and Buddhist (0.8 percent), with the remaining 1.2 percent of the Indian population being divided among adherents of Jainism, Judaism, Zoroastrianism, the Baha'i Faith, and other religions, as well as people with no religious affiliation.[3]

The strong concentration of Hindus in India is an indicator of the close association between Hinduism and this country. Even the words *Hinduism* and *Hindu*—used to denote a religion and a practitioner of that religion, respectively—refer, in their origins, to India. *Hindu* is originally the Persian pronunciation of *Sindhu*, the Sanskrit name of the river which flows through what is today Pakistan, in the northwestern part of South Asia, the region that is traditionally known as the Indian subcontinent.[4] This river was called, by the Greeks, the Indus, and it is from *Indus* that the name *India* was originally derived as the name for the entire region.[5]

Similarly, in Persian, *Hindustan* became the name of the land on the other side (from Persia, or Iran) of the "Hindu" river, whose people gradually came to be known as Hindus, particularly as Persian-speaking powers began to rule parts of India. When the British, centuries later, came to India, they took up this terminology, and further coined the word *Hinduism* (by adding the English suffix–*ism* to the word *Hindu*) to denote the religion, or the family of religions, native to India.

The history of this term does not mean, as it is sometimes taken to suggest, that the British "invented" Hinduism. Although the word *Hinduism* is of British coinage, being derived from the older Persian term *Hindu*, the collection of religious traditions to which it points is considerably older, sometimes being described as the oldest religion in the world.[6] The historical development of Hinduism as a cohesive tradition, though, is often seen as being distinctive among the world's religions. While most religions are usually seen as having developed from the teachings of a single founding figure and from an original community imagined as a relatively cohesive unit which then divided, in time, into various branches or sects, one can see the history of Hinduism as something akin to the reverse of this process, in which many diverse traditions, originally distinct from one another, have gradually coalesced into or been re-imagined as a single, discrete tradition.[7]

How different does this make Hinduism from other religions? This is a debated topic; for some would argue that there is an artificiality to Hinduism not found in other religions which have grown out of a singular, cohesive center. Is this, though, how other world religions have, in fact, emerged? Conceptualizing the world's religions in this way tends to obscure the fact that most traditions have always been internally diverse, a point to which we shall return shortly. It suggests not so much that the "artificial" or "constructed" character of Hinduism has been overstated as that the "artificial" or "constructed" character of other religions, in comparison with Hinduism, has been understated. All religions have been "constructed," or abstracted from more basic elements, rather than having an "essence" that is unchanging and independent from the basic elements themselves. This is an emerging consensus among religion scholars, who have become increasingly critical of the "world religions paradigm."[8] Any tradition with over a billion adherents will not be perfectly unified, but will have many forms, with many interpretations of shared ideas, symbols, texts, and so on.

If one thinks, as many scholars do, of Hinduism as a tradition that has gradually coalesced from various sources, the question emerges, "At which point in this process is it proper to refer to this collection of traditions in the singular, as *Hinduism*?" When did Hinduism become Hinduism?

There are many ways to answer this question. For many Hindus, it is not even a question: Hinduism is an ancient tradition that dates back at least to the composition of its earliest attested source texts, the collection of sacred Sanskrit verses known as the *Vedas*. Talk of "coalescence," or of a time when there was no Hinduism, can be met with suspicion, as an attempt to undermine a traditional Hindu self-understanding or to divide the Hindu community.[9]

From another Hindu perspective, Hinduism is the eternal truth, or *Sanātana Dharma*. It has no beginning and no end, and underlies all the world's religions and philosophies. According to this understanding, Hinduism is "not a religion, but religion itself in its most universal and deepest significance."[10] The word *Hinduism* is simply a relatively recent label for this eternal truth (and one which some Hindus do not especially like, due to its geographical boundedness and its history of being a foreign imposition, although other Hindus wear this label with great pride).

The scholarly perspectives on this issue vary. Some will take a very strict line and argue that one cannot speak of Hinduism existing until the term actually came into usage: so, relatively recently—as late as the nineteenth century.[11] Others argue that Hinduism—the thing if not the word—was in place by the late medieval period, from roughly the fifteenth to sixteenth centuries of the Common Era; but that before this time, there were many disparate schools of thought which often disagreed on a variety of topics, and whose adherents did not see themselves as sharing a common religious identity.[12]

Still other scholars, respecting a Hindu sensibility, utilize the terms *Hindu* and *Hinduism* in a retroactive fashion to refer to all of that which today is seen by Hindus as making up Hinduism, up to and including the *Vedas*, at least.[13] The argument can also be made that this is not simply a matter of respecting Hindu sensibilities, but that a cohesive continuity of practice and thought can be discerned from the Vedic period to the present.[14]

Others still, as we have already suggested, will point out that it is not only Hinduism that is "constructed" from out of many diverse elements, but that this is true of all the world's religions. As scholar Julius Lipner writes of these traditions:

> We are familiar with the fact ... that each [religious tradition] comprises different denominations clustering under the same label. What does this mean? That each denomination is a species of an underlying, homogenizing essence or genus? ... It would be misguided to impose an essentialist understanding on these religious phenomena.[15]

In other words, the objections which are raised by some scholars to speaking of Hinduism as one, singular tradition can just as well be raised against speaking of a singular Christianity, a singular Judaism, a singular Islam, a singular Buddhism, and so on. Each tradition has many iterations.[16]

In terms of the question of the British "inventing" Hinduism through a colonial process of identifying particular texts and customs as "Hindu" and then imposing this on the people of India, it must be said that although British and other European scholars certainly played a role in the development of a Hindu identity and self-understanding in the modern period—including, not least, the coinage of the term *Hinduism*—the Hindu religion was not created out of whole cloth, nor can Hindu agency be denied in the development of modern Hinduism. As Brian Pennington explains:

> It would be a severe historical misrepresentation (albeit a faddish one, to be sure) to suggest, as many have, that Hinduism was the invention of the British. Adapting to the colonial milieu, Hindus themselves entered a dialectic space in which they endorsed and promoted the British publication of ancient texts and translations, resisted missionary polemics, and experimented with modifications, alternations, and innovations in Hindu religious forms.[17]

As Pennington further clarifies:

> "Adapting" perhaps implies more passivity than I intend, for many Hindus [such as the Hindu reformers discussed in Chapter 2] possessed considerable power to effect changes in social and religious arrangements under the conditions of the Raj.[18]

In addition to the fact that Hindus played a role in the definition of the term *Hinduism* in the modern period, and in developing a sense of what constitutes this tradition, Andrew Nicholson also argues that the process of the coalescence of a Hindu identity had been underway for centuries before the arrival of the British. It was a process that the British abetted, but in which they were far from being the sole actors, and which they certainly did not initiate:

> Between the twelfth and sixteenth centuries CE, certain thinkers began to treat as a single whole the diverse philosophical teachings of the Upaniṣads, epics, Pūrāṇas, and the schools known retrospectively as the "six systems" (*ṣaḍdarśana*) of mainstream Hindu philosophy. The Indian and European thinkers in the nineteenth century who developed the term "Hinduism" under the pressure of the new explanatory category of "world religions" were influenced by these earlier philosophers and doxographers ... Before the late medieval period, there was little or no systematic attempt by the thinkers we now describe as Hindu to put aside their differences in order to depict themselves as a single unified tradition. After this

> late medieval period, it became almost universally accepted that there was a fixed group of Indian philosophies in basic agreement with one another and standing together against Buddhism and Jainism.[19]

Before the British, then, a cohesive school of thought had emerged that could be called *Hinduism*.

As we have seen from its origins, however, although the word *Hindu* has come over time to refer to a specific set of beliefs and practices, albeit one drawn from a variety of earlier traditions, this term did not originally refer to a specific philosophy or system of practice distinct from others. *Hindu* basically meant *Indian*, in its origins, and *Hinduism* something like *Indianism*. It therefore encompassed all the traditions indigenous to India, including traditions such as Jainism, Buddhism, and Sikhism that are distinct from the Vedic traditions making up what is now called Hinduism. The original equation of the terms *Hindu* and *Indian* continues to haunt the discussion of Hindu traditions, despite the subsequent development of sophisticated understandings—both from within and from outside the Hindu community—of what it is to which these terms refer.

Why is the identification of *Hindu* with *Indian* an issue? First, as we have seen, roughly one in five Indians do not identify religiously as Hindu. The Muslim population of India, which consists of approximately 201 million people, as of 2019, is the second largest in the world, coming behind only the Muslim populations of Indonesia. Then there are also the Indian Christians, Jews, and Zoroastrians, plus adherents of other traditions native to India that are distinct from Hinduism: Buddhism and Jainism (traditions which Nicholson mentions as having long been an "other" to Hinduism) and Sikhism, which emerged after it. In short, not all Indians are Hindu.

Conversely—and this is a major theme of this book—a growing number of people who self-identify religiously as Hindu are not Indian, and some are not even of Indian descent. This is due to a combination of immigration to Western countries by Indian Hindus and the activities of Hindu teachers who have gathered global followings that include many non-Indian adherents.[20] So, just as not all Indians are Hindu, not all Hindus are Indian, either. *Hindu* cannot simply be equated with *Indian* without excluding non-Hindu Indians or non-Indian Hindus.

This is not only a terminological issue. The conflation of *Hindu* and *Indian* has real-world destructive effects upon those whose identities are erased in the process. As Khyati Joshi notes:

> Today Indian Americans are assumed to be of a certain faith (Hindu) ... Although the mere assumption of religious identity may seem an innocuous error to the casual reader, repeated experiences of religious misidentification is experienced by many Christian, Muslim, and Sikh Indian Americans as a negation of their religious identity ... The conflation of race and religion, when religion is racialized, results in a one-dimensional identity that is as likely to be inaccurate as accurate. With race and religion as proxies for each other, Indianness in the cultural,

> geographic, or linguistic sense—which is shared by Indian Christians, Jews, and atheists as well as by Hindus, Sikhs, Muslims, and others—becomes part of an indistinguishable mix colored by an assumed association with Hinduism. Distinction, like nuance, is lost.[21]

While Hinduism cannot be conflated with Indianness, because of the way this excludes any person who does not fit both categories—*Indian* and *Hindu*—and while Hinduism has philosophical systems which claim universal relevance—thus giving impetus to those teachers who have taken their traditions abroad and spread them around the world, to Indians and non-Indians alike—it is also true that a great deal of Hindu practice is closely centered upon India and its sacred geography. To make a pilgrimage to a holy river or to a temple associated with a major event in Hindu sacred literature is an important practice, greatly valued by Hindus to the present day: even by those who have made their homes in, or who hail originally from, parts of the world other than India. As Diana Eck has pointed out:

> The practice of pilgrimage, or *tīrthayātrā*, has long been an important part of ... [Hindu] religious life. As early as the epic *Mahābhārata* in the first two centuries C.E., *tīrthayātrā* was compared to Vedic sacrifice in its benefits.[22]

To be Hindu, then, does involve some level of connection with India, though what this means in an individual case can vary greatly: from living in India, to having lived in India, to having Indian parents, to simply feeling that one has an intangible "spiritual" tie to India as a sacred space.

In short, the terms *Hindu* and *Indian*, although they are closely intertwined, are nonetheless distinct. Most Indians are Hindu, and most Hindus are Indian, and many Hindu practices presume a deep connection between the practitioner and India, conceived as a sacred space. But at the same time, again, not all Indians are Hindu, and not all Hindus are Indian; and many Hindu philosophies are addressed not only to the human condition in general, but to the conditions of all living beings. As a result of this dynamic—the dialectic between the particular and the universal that any in-depth consideration of Hinduism involves—the reader will find that this book covers issues that pertain specifically to Indian Hindus, some relating to non-Indian Hindus, some relating to other non-Indians who have been influenced by Hinduism, and some relating to Indians, both Hindu and non-Hindu, living in America. Studying Hinduism in America involves casting a very wide net, conceptually speaking. It requires one to consider the immigrant community which has brought Hinduism, as a concrete, lived practice, to America; but it also involves consideration of the Indian American experience in general, of which Hinduism is an important, but not an all-encompassing, part. It further involves examining Hindu philosophies and practices which have been adopted by Americans, not of Indian origin, some of whom self-identify as Hindu, but many of whom do not. Finally, it involves discussing the pervasiveness of Hindu concepts in American popular culture, where most Americans do not even realize Hindu influence is present; but whether we are talking about openness to the idea that there is truth in many religions, or the ideas of karma and reincarnation, or the idea that God is not so much an omnipotent person as a spiritual presence like "the Force" in the *Star Wars* films, we are talking about Hindu concepts. In the words of Vasudha Narayanan, "Americans may not know it, but they've long been embracing Hindu philosophy."[23]

The Hindu Diaspora

If the overwhelming majority—93.2 percent—of Hindus live in India, where do the other 6.8 percent reside? Hindus live in countries which span the globe. Many, however—approximately 40 percent of Hindus living outside India—are concentrated in South or Southeast Asia. Nepal is home to 2 percent of the world's Hindus (roughly 23 million), while 0.6 percent of Hindus live in Bangladesh (roughly 13.5 million), 0.1 percent live in Indonesia (or roughly 4 million), and 0.03 percent and 0.02 percent (3.6 and 2.6 million) live in Pakistan and Sri Lanka, respectively. In all of these countries except for Nepal, which is 81.3 percent Hindu (a slightly higher percentage than India itself) Hindus are a minority. Most Bangladeshis, Indonesians, and Pakistanis practice Islam, while the majority of the population of Sri Lanka practices Theravāda Buddhism.[24] The Hindu populations of all these countries—India, Nepal, Bangladesh, Indonesia, Pakistan, and Sri Lanka—are longstanding. That is, Hindus have lived in these countries for many centuries—indeed, for a period long predating the existence of these countries themselves, as modern nation-states. Nepal, Bangladesh, and Pakistan are, of course, all contiguous with India, sharing borders with it, and Sri Lanka is a large island just off the southern Indian coast.

The case of Indonesia is particularly interesting because it is home to the world's oldest Hindu community outside of South Asia. This is significant due to the widespread misconception that Hindus historically never strayed far beyond India until the modern period. This idea arose in the minds of many Western scholars of Hinduism because of injunctions in some of the *Dharma Śāstras*, or Hindu legal texts, that forbid Brahmins, or members of the Hindu priestly community, from traveling beyond certain regions. Given that some of the places Brahmins are forbidden to travel are within India itself, and that Brahmins have lived in them for many centuries, it is an odd misconception, clearly based on a simplistic assumption that what is enjoined in ancient texts is always followed in actual practice. The existence of longstanding Hindu communities in such countries as Indonesia—as well as, in ancient times, Cambodia, Vietnam, Malaysia, and Thailand—further belies this odd misconception. Most Hindus in Indonesia are concentrated on the island of Bali. This distinctive Balinese community makes up the largest remnant of what was at one time a widespread Hindu presence in Southeast Asia.

FIGURE 2 *Balinese mask dancers perform a show at a sacred ceremony to celebrate the construction of Merajan (a Balinese-Hindu temple) in Jimbaran, June 2, 2019. Besides being entertaining, this dance also has strong religious values (Photo by Keyza Widiatmika/NurPhoto via Getty Images).*

It is also worth noting that, even in those countries whose majority population is Buddhist, or where Buddhism is a major part of the traditional religious heritage (as is the case for much of Asia), the imprint of Hinduism can be seen: images of deities revered in Hinduism and assimilated to Buddhist practice, often as guardian deities; the use of mantras—or prayers—that are also used in Hinduism; the recitation of traditional Hindu stories, such as the *Rāmāyaṇa*, the *Mahābhārata*, and the *Pūrāṇas*; and so on. Elements of Hinduism persist in the beliefs and practices of Muslims in Southeast Asia as well, so pervasive has the influence of Hinduism been in this region.[25] Even beyond Southeast Asia, as far away as Japan, Hindu influence can be discerned, most likely having been transmitted via Buddhism, which is not as sharply different from Hinduism as it is sometimes taken to be. For instance, the famous image of one thousand and one forms of the bodhisattva Kannon, or Avalokiteśvara, in Sanjusangendo temple in Kyoto is guarded by images of Hindu deities. Monks of the Shingon school of Japanese Tāntric Buddhism perform a fire ritual called *goma* that is essentially the Vedic *homa* ritual of Hinduism.

In Asia, the boundaries between religions are more fluid and porous than in religions as traditionally conceived in the West—though arguably, this is beginning to change in the West, as it becomes more popular to adopt a stance of being "spiritual but not religious," and to draw on many traditions in a pluralistic fashion, and also in Asia, as Western concepts of a fixed religious identity and corresponding ideologies of religious nationalism spread. Indeed, because of the non-mutually exclusive nature of these religions, as traditionally practiced, and for other reasons as well, there are many

Hindus and Buddhists who prefer not to refer to their traditions as "religions," but in more traditional terms, as forms of *dharma*, a term with a wide array of meanings including, but not limited to, the kinds of practices and beliefs typically associated with the term *religion* in the West.[26] As Pankaj Jain notes:

> [T]he general understanding of the term "religion" is largely based on ... Western theological connotations with [a] definite scripture, founder, historic events, and specific theologies and practices ... Transcending the boundaries of "religion," some Indian thinkers ... have included Jesus Christ and Muhammad as the eleventh and twelfth incarnations of Viṣṇu, thus incorporating Christianity and Islam into Indic traditions ... ["D]harma" is a better representation of Indic spiritual phenomena than "religion."[27]

Looking beyond Asia, roughly 4 percent of Hindus—about 60 percent of those living outside of India—do not live in India or in any of the countries of either South or Southeast Asia that have had Hindu populations for centuries. These remaining Hindus—those who are scattered around the world—are often referred to as the *Hindu diaspora* (though this term is sometimes used to refer to *all* Hindus residing outside modern India, including those in South Asia). The term *diaspora* has its origins in the history of Judaism, where it originally referred to the scattering of the Jewish people beyond their ancestral homeland. *Diaspora* has since come to refer more broadly, in the words of Steven Vertovec, to "a generalized context outside of a place of origin."[28] Like the term *Hindu*, though, aspects of this term's origins continue to shape how it is used in practice. As Vertovec further elaborates:

> "The Diaspora" was at one time a concept referring almost exclusively to the experiences of Jews, invoking their traumatic exile from a historical homeland and dispersal through many lands. With this experience as reference, connotations of a "diaspora" situation were usually rather negative as they were associated with forced displacement, victimisation, alienation, loss. Along with this archetype went a dream of return [to the homeland].[29]

These negative connotations of *diaspora*, as we shall see, both do and do not apply to the Hindu diaspora. Portions of the Hindu diaspora, such as the Hindus who were sent by the British to the Caribbean region as indentured labourers in the nineteenth century, have experienced a "traumatic exile" from India that is indeed comparable to the Jewish experience. Other portions of the Hindu diaspora, though, have had quite a different experience, such as those Hindus who have left India voluntarily in recent decades in order to pursue educational and economic opportunities.

Vertovec differentiates three meanings of the term *diaspora*. He lists these meanings as "'diaspora' as *social form*, 'diaspora' as *type of consciousness*, and 'diaspora' as *mode of cultural production*."[30] Diaspora as social form refers to diaspora as a set of relationships, specifically between members of the community who are in the diaspora and those in the "home" country. He mentions, regarding the Hindu diaspora, economic and political links between these two groups.[31] By diaspora as type of consciousness, Vertovec refers to an "awareness of multi-locality," a sense of one's identity being divided between several spaces at once. "Yet instead of being represented as a kind of schizophrenic deficit, such *multiplicity* is being redefined by diasporic individuals as a source of adaptive strength."[32] Haresh, one of my interviewees for this book, who settled in the United States in his college years and has since become a US citizen, refers to this sense of multi-locality as "having the best of both worlds." "I get the benefit of both cultures," he says, "Of being an Indian and an American." Finally, by "diaspora" as a mode of cultural production, Vertovec refers to the ways in which the exchange of goods through international trade and information through global media serves to reinforce both a diasporic social form and a diasporic consciousness.[33] Social media, in particular, has increasingly become an important tool for cultivating, negotiating, and contesting an emergent sense of global Hindu identity.[34]

Among diasporic Hindus, the vast majority—between 90 and 95 percent—live in countries with large English-speaking populations which were once part of the British Empire—as were India, Bangladesh, Pakistan, and Sri Lanka. The dispersal of Hindus across the globe is part of the legacy of colonialism. As such, consideration of the Hindu diaspora is inseparable from consideration of colonialism and its many impacts upon colonized peoples.

Under British rule, many Indians were forced to labor in various regions of the Empire. Their descendants can be found mainly in Caribbean countries, as well as in parts of Africa (mainly South Africa). Others emigrated to other nations of the Commonwealth that was formed after the Empire was formally dissolved.[35]

The United States, however, has the largest Hindu population of any single country outside of South or Southeast Asia: larger even than that of the UK, although Hindus make up a slightly larger *percentage* of the UK's population: 1.3 percent, compared with the 0.7 percent of the US population. The Hindu population of the UK is roughly 0.85 million.[36]

The United States became independent from the British Empire in the late eighteenth century—1776—almost two hundred years before the Empire dissolved in the mid-twentieth century, following the Second World War. The United States was thus never part of the Commonwealth, established in 1931, and made up of now-former British colonies which are home to much of the global Hindu diaspora.

Numbering at roughly 2.23 million, though, American Hindus make up the seventh largest Hindu population in the world (behind, in descending order, India, Nepal, Bangladesh, Indonesia, Pakistan, and Sri Lanka). Hindus make up, again, 0.7 percent of the US population, and roughly 70 percent of the Indian American population.[37]

Elsewhere in North America, there are approximately half a million Canadian Hindus, who make up 1.6 percent of the Canadian population. The Caribbean region has a Hindu population of roughly 280 thousand—over a quarter of a million—making up just over 1 percent of the population of this region.[38] The Hindu population of Mexico, on the other hand, is quite small, numbering not much more than one thousand, and making up less than 1 percent of Mexico's total population. The Hindus of Mexico consist of a mix of immigrants from India and members of the International Society for Krishna Consciousness (ISKCON). The membership of ISKCON in Mexico is largely made up of Mexican converts. There are eight ISKCON centers in Mexico, as well as a growing number of centers devoted to the teaching of the sage Sai Baba of Shirdi, who commands a large following in the United States as well.[39]

While the term *Hindu diaspora*, given the provenance of the word *diaspora*, may seem to refer exclusively to Hindus of Indian, or more broadly South and Southeast Asian, descent living "abroad"—that is, elsewhere in the world than South or Southeast Asia—given the distinctions which Vertovec makes between diaspora as a social form, a type of consciousness, and a mode of cultural production, one could say that all Hindus residing outside of South or Southeast Asia, regardless of ethnic origin, participate, in varying ways, in the Hindu diaspora. A recent Hindu immigrant to the United States from India who maintains close ties with her family in Mumbai and participates in her local temple community in Pennsylvania might be experiencing all three of the aspects of diaspora that Vertovec describes. A white convert to Hinduism who knows the tradition mostly through books and the internet and who is active on Hindu social media might only be experiencing diaspora as a mode of cultural production, or perhaps as a type of consciousness that involves the contrast between the environment of his upbringing and what he imagines India to be, through his reading and interactions with other Hindus online. Vertovec's multivalent conception of diaspora allows for varied types and degrees of participation.

The emergent phenomenon of persons who self-identify religiously as Hindu, but who do not hail from, or whose families do not hail from, traditionally Hindu parts of the world, is not one that is limited to the United States. Multi-ethnic Hindu organizations like the Vedanta Society and ISKCON have global followings. But it has developed into a distinctive feature of Hinduism in America. Because of the nation's largely Protestant Christian religious heritage (a heritage which emphasizes the importance of individual conscience in matters of religion, and which also emphasizes belief, or faith, over external observances), its widespread culture of individualism, and what could be called its largely consumerist outlook on many matters in life, religion is typically viewed by Americans as more of a matter of personal choice than as a matter of heritage or communal identity. Indeed, the right to make this choice for oneself, without external interference, is enshrined in the First Amendment to the US Constitution, in the words, "Congress shall make no law respecting an establishment of religion, or prohibiting the free exercise thereof ..."[40]

In America, then, Hinduism has increasingly come to be seen less as forming the identity of a particular ethnic community—though it still has this connotation—and more as an option in the marketplace of ideas available for Americans to choose from in their search for a meaningful and happy life. Partially, though, because the label *Hindu* does continue to retain its original sense as referring not only to a belief system, but also to an ethnic identity, many non-Indian Americans who draw from Hindu beliefs and practices do not identify themselves as Hindu. This has given rise to a vigorous debate regarding cultural appropriation (in which non-Hindu Americans have been accused by some Hindus of engaging) and Hindu nationalism (a political ideology to which Hindus who make such accusations have been accused of adhering).

At the same time, there have also been Americans who have taken up a Hindu identity and who identify Hinduism as their religion of choice. This has also given rise to controversy, as some Hindus are uncomfortable with Westerners "intruding," as it is sometimes seen, into Hindu sacred space, while other Hindus express happiness to welcome those whom they see as sincere spiritual seekers, and as allies in the process of assimilating into mainstream American society.

The American Hindu community largely remains an ethnically based one, made up of immigrants and descendants of immigrants, although, as is frequently pointed out, the vast majority of Americans—all but the Native Americans—are descendants of immigrants. The Indian Hindu community, though, is a fairly recent arrival from the perspective of many Americans (though, as we shall see, Hindus have been in the United States longer than most Americans realize). Hindus who self-identify ethnically as Asian make up roughly 91 percent of the 2.23 million Hindus in the United States.[41]

But while this is clearly a majority, it is not 100 percent; 2 percent of American Hindus identify themselves ethnically as being of a mixed heritage. (It is probably safe to assume that most, though not all, of these persons have a South Asian parent.[42]) But 7 percent of American Hindus do not self-identify as either Asian or mixed—4 percent of American Hindus self-identify as "white" (or European American), 2 percent as African American, and 1 percent as Hispanic.[43] This means there are roughly 89,000 white American Hindus, 45,000 African American Hindus, and 22,000 Hispanic American Hindus.[44]

These are not massive numbers, in demographic terms. The roughly 200 thousand Hindus in the United States who are not of Asian descent make up about 2 percent of 1 percent of the global Hindu population. It is therefore unsurprising that many persons—Hindu and non-Hindu—still identify the Hindu tradition with an ethnicity and a nationality. Hinduism continues to be seen by many as a way of life into which one must be born, which one inherits from and to which one is acculturated by one's family, and not as a religion, like Christianity, to which one might choose to convert.

This, however, is not only a question of numbers. First, the fact that there are roughly 200 thousand American Hindus who are not of Asian origin represents a conceptual shift in the way scholars of Hinduism, and many Hindus, think about the nature of this tradition. Again, it is not at all uncommon to hear Hindus describe Hinduism as a way of life into which one is born, and this is, far more often than not, actually the case. But this is actually true of most religions, even those to which conversion has traditionally been encouraged, such as Christianity and Islam. Philosopher of religion John Hick points out:

> The evident fact that in perhaps 99 percent of cases the religion to which one adheres (or against which one reacts) is selected by the accident of birth. Someone

> born to devout Muslim parents in Iran or Indonesia is very likely to be a Muslim; someone born to devout Buddhist parents in Thailand or Sri Lanka is very likely to be a Buddhist; someone born to devout Christian parents in Italy or Mexico is very likely to be a Catholic Christian; and so on.[45]

If most Hindus are born to their tradition, then, there is nothing about this fact that is particularly unusual or unique to Hinduism, to set it apart from proselytizing religions, whose adherents also consist overwhelmingly of people born to them.

There is some resistance to seeing Hinduism as a religion into which one might convert. Some of this resistance—though this seems to be less the case than it was twenty years ago—comes from scholars. Because there are scholars who, quite understandably, are drawn to study Hinduism from a personal, spiritual attraction, there is a worry that some will "go native" and lose scholarly objectivity. Some of the resistance comes from within the Hindu community itself. Reasons for this resistance include fear of cultural appropriation and loss of autonomy (of being overwhelmed by outsiders in a continuation of the colonial experience) and a deep-seated objection to the very idea of proselytizing or evangelizing (that Hindus should try to "convert" others, which many see as a form of violence to which Hindus have themselves often been subject historically).[46] Both of these concerns can be seen as having roots in the experience of colonization: the community does not wish to be re-colonized by outsiders seeking to make Hindu traditions their own—to appropriate them—and also does not wish to engage in the kind of behavior—evangelization—that was historically used to justify the colonization of India. At the same time, though, many non-Asian Hindus report being warmly accepted in their local Hindu communities (although some also report experiencing varying degrees of resistance or rejection), and rituals for conversion have developed.[47]

Moreover, religion scholars have documented a growing number of cases in which non-Asian Hindus have risen to positions of leadership in Hindu movements and communities.[48] Non-Asian leaders in American Hindu organizations include not only European-descended, or "white" Americans, but also African Americans and Hispanic Americans. Prominent white Hindu leaders have included figures like Satguru Sivaya Subramuniyaswami (who was born as Robert Hansen, 1927–2001). Subramuniyaswami started a magazine, *Hinduism Today*, which has emerged as an important voice in the global Hindu community.[49] There are also many monastic members of both Hindu and Hindu-based organizations—like the Ramakrishna Order, ISKCON, and Siddha Yoga, among others—who are white Americans. African American Hindu leaders have included Bhakti Tirtha Swami (who was born as John E. Favors, 1950–2005). Bhakti Tirtha Swami took a leading role in ISKCON. The most prominent Hispanic American Hindu leader in recent years has been Sri Dharma Pravartaka Acharya (who was born as Frank Morales).[50]

This means that non-Asian American Hindus have not simply self-defined their way into the tradition, but have been accepted by, and even placed in prestigious roles in, the community.

In my research for this book, I picked up a strong sense that many in the American Hindu community are deeply uncomfortable discussing matters of race and ethnicity, and show a decided preference for *not* seeing the Hindu tradition in these terms and for not speaking of Asian Hindus and non-Asian Hindus as distinct categories. This discomfort can be explained in several ways. One might be as an effect of a desire to assimilate with the majority population, which is not Indian, and so not to draw unwanted attention to one's difference, particularly given the history, and the current realities, of racism in America. It can also be seen, though, as arising from certain Hindu beliefs about the nature of the self. Hindus with whom I have discussed this issue have said such things as "It is the soul that matters, not the body. The soul is not white or black or brown." "It is your bhakti [religious devotion] that matters, not how you look or who your parents are." "Being a real Hindu is a matter of spiritual commitment. It's not race or nationality." "I have seen white Hindus who were better Hindus than many Indians." "There are not Indian Hindus or American Hindus, only Hindus." "If you think you are a Hindu, you are a Hindu."

In order to respect this sensibility, while at the same time being able to talk about the very real differences in the ways in which Hinduism is experienced by people who are related to it in different ways, and also to acknowledge the reality that human beings cannot easily be placed into compartments with neat labels like "Asian" or "non-Asian," or "brown" or "black" or "white," it is necessary to use another terminology when speaking of those who were born to the tradition and those who have come to it from outside.

Hinduism scholar Amanda Lucia has coined the extremely helpful, respectful, and precise terms *inheritors* and *adopters* to refer, respectively, to those who have been born to Hinduism and those who have been drawn to a Hindu practice and system of belief. She also notes important differences in the ways in which inheritors and adopters approach their Hindu practice. As we will see, these differences lead to a variety of other differences in the styles of practice and the general attitudes of these two types of Hindu practitioner:

> Inheritors and adopters have different sites of communal continuity; one seeks opportunities to reinforce inherited traditions [the inheritors], while the other seeks opportunities to develop self-styled interpretations of tradition [the adopters]. Thus groups of inheritors and adopters often find difficulties in establishing multi-ethnic congregations that can sustain this process of self-identification and the practical mapping of tradition ... Inheritors participate in congregations in order to reinforce their connections to Indian culture while simultaneously participating in the multi-cultural American religious landscape. Adopters are generally much less attached to the idea of congregation, but when they do participate, they do so to affirm their bricolage spiritualities [spiritualities composed of many sources] in the company of other like-minded individuals. Both groups aim to reaffirm their faith by participating in communal religiosity. However, inheritors do so by enacting rituals that emphasize their roots in the Hindu tradition and India. Contrarily, adopters must adapt to Hindu

ritual action in satsangs [spiritual gatherings], but they also find solace in gathering with other devotees who have similarly created their own unique spiritualities from an amalgam of practices and beliefs from a variety of religious traditions.[51]

Inheritors are, on the whole, seeking to preserve a tradition of practice that is ancient and that they have received from their families, and that they are trying to keep alive in the new environment they inhabit. Adopters are, on the whole, people who have found their inherited tradition to be, on some level, unsatisfactory, leading them to adopt a new tradition: finding something in the Hindu tradition that was missing in their experience of the tradition to which they were born. The adoption of Hinduism by non-Hindus is thus also a moment of self-critique within other traditions.

This dissatisfaction can be deep and intense—as in the case of Sam, a white Southerner who became alienated from the church of his upbringing as a result of a sexual abuse scandal involving his pastor, combined with poor relations with his family and with other church members—or it can be mild, as in the case of Melissa, also white, but a New Englander, who continues to identify with and attend the church of her upbringing, but supplements it with a Hindu practice which consists of daily meditation, reading books, and listening to podcasts by her guru, and occasionally taking part in congregational worship at a center run by the organization which her guru established.

While most adopters of Hinduism in America come from Christian backgrounds, a large, and probably disproportionate, number are Jewish. Based on my interviews and observations, the Jewish experience of adopting either Hinduism or Buddhism—of becoming a "Hinjew" or "Jubu," as the terminology goes—is far less about dissatisfaction with the tradition of one's upbringing than seems to be the case with Christian adopters. For Jewish adopters, it seems far more often to be a matter of supplementing a Jewish heritage that continues, in many cases, to be loving maintained alongside a Hindu or Buddhist commitment. More often than not, Jewish adoption of Hinduism or Buddhism seems to involve a dual or multiple religious belonging rather than a "conversion." This is of course the case with many Christian adopters as well, although there seems more often to be a tension between the exclusive commitment that is demanded by most Christian traditions and the kind of sensibility that is accepting of dual or multiple belonging.

Hinduism in America: A Source of Inspiration and Influence

In addition to those inheritors and adopters of Hinduism who identify themselves as Hindu, or as having, especially in the case of adopters, a hybrid or dual identity, like "Catholic Hindu" or "Jewish Hindu," there are also traditions with a Hindu origin or source of inspiration, having been founded by Hindu spiritual teachers, but whose adherents do not necessarily self-identify as Hindu.

Many members of Hindu or Hindu-inspired organizations—organizations like the Vedanta Society, Self-Realization Fellowship, ISKCON, Transcendental Meditation, and Siddha Yoga—fit into this category. In addition to not identifying themselves as Hindu, many would also not identify their Hindu-inspired practices and beliefs as a religion. Some continue to adhere to their earlier religious identities, prior to joining these Hindu-based traditions. Some engage in what scholars have come to call "multiple religious belonging." The same is of course the case, as just mentioned, of many adopters of Hinduism who *do* self-identify as Hindu while still maintaining their earlier religious commitment.

Respecting both the fact that Hindu-inspired organizations like these are distinct from more traditional forms of Hinduism, as well as the fact that not all their adherents define themselves as Hindu, scholar Lola Williamson has coined the term *Hindu-inspired meditation movements* (HIMMs) as a way to refer to these traditions and their adherents. As Williamson explains:

> There is a qualitative difference between people who have been raised in a tradition in which the rituals, the foods, the prayers, and the ethics are second nature, and people who have incorporated only parts of a tradition into their religious style ... While the religion of Hindu-inspired meditation movements certainly wears some of the garb of Hinduism, Western traditions of individualism and rationalism also influence the style and ethos of these movements.[52]

If we add those Americans who identify themselves as Hindu (inheritors and adopters) to the many organizations and movements in America that are rooted in Hinduism but distinct from it—HIMMs—we can deduce that the number of Americans whose spiritual lives are shaped, to some conscious extent, by Hinduism is actually larger than the 2.23 million who self-identify as Hindu. This larger number, made up of self-identified Hindus plus the adherents of HIMMs, is probably close to 3 million, although it should be noted that this number is a *very* rough estimate, and not scientifically derived, due to the great difficulty of counting how many people are members of HIMMs. Not all HIMMs keep a precise count of membership. Membership itself is also hard to quantify. For example, is a self-identified Presbyterian who attends a weekly *Bhagavad Gītā* study circle at her local Vedanta Society a "member" of the Vedanta Society? The numbers of people with varying degrees of affiliation to these organizations are fluid and inexact. Plus, there are some members of HIMMs who *do* self-identify as Hindu. So the membership of HIMMs and the community of self-identified Hindus overlap. Three million, though, is a number which one frequently hears in Hindu circles to refer to those with some kind of Hindu affiliation in the United States.

If one goes even beyond the 3 million-ish Americans who identify themselves as Hindu or adhere to Hindu-inspired beliefs and practices, one will find that the Hindu influence on American attitudes and religiosity is considerable. In a 2009 *Newsweek* editorial bearing the provocative title "We Are All Hindus Now," journalist Lisa Miller cites polling data indicating that a majority of Americans—an impressive 65 percent—believe that "many religions can lead to eternal life."[53] This includes a surprisingly high 37 percent of white evangelical Christians.

As Miller points out, this religiously pluralistic sentiment echoes an ancient, deeply revered Hindu scripture, the *Ṛg Veda*, according to which, "Though the Real is one, the wise speak of It in many ways."[54] This open attitude is also consistent with other Hindu scriptures, like the *Bhagavad Gītā*, in which the Supreme Being, in the form of the deity Krishna, proclaims, "In whatever way living beings approach me, thus do I receive them. All paths lead to me."[55] This accepting attitude was strongly advocated by one of the first Hindu teachers to visit the United States: Swami Vivekananda, who attended and spoke at the first World Parliament of Religions, held in Chicago in 1893.

The survey Miller cites also indicates that 24 percent of Americans—roughly one in four—believe in reincarnation. Reincarnation, or rebirth—the idea that the soul or the spiritual essence of a living being does not cease to exist upon the death of the body, but rather is transferred to a new body as that body begins its life—is the standard view about the afterlife in Hindu traditions. Many Americans are fascinated by this idea. There have even been scientific studies of children who at least appear to carry memories of past lives—information about periods of history and details about the lives of deceased persons that are difficult to explain in any other way.[56] There is a similar fascination with "past life regression," undertaken via hypnosis.[57]

Finally, the survey also indicates that 30 percent—almost one in three—of Americans identify themselves as "spiritual but not religious," thus choosing not to identify themselves too narrowly with any single culture or tradition. We shall see that this is also a typical Hindu attitude, leading to some ambiguity in the question of who should or should not be regarded as a Hindu; for, as we have just seen, there are persons whose beliefs and way of life appear, in many ways, to be Hindu, but who choose not to identify with this label (or often, with any label at all). Even many inheritors of Hinduism choose, for a variety of reasons, not to use this word to identify their beliefs. This is often due to the geographic and ethnic limitations the term *Hindu* places on a universal philosophy, or to a desire not to identify with conservative political groups in India that have laid claim to the term *Hindu*, much as the Christian right in America has laid claim to the term *Christian*.

The poll which Miller cites is not an outlier, for other reputable polls have yielded roughly comparable numbers in response to similar questions. Americans, in greater numbers than ever before, are religiously pluralistic, believe in reincarnation, and do not wish to limit themselves to any particular religious label. Growing numbers also practice yoga and vegetarianism. Although not all people who have adopted these ideas, attitudes, and practices identify themselves as Hindu, and although these ideas, attitudes, and practices can be found in other traditions as well (such as Jainism, Buddhism, and Sikhism), they all do have *some* historical or philosophical connection or resonance with Hinduism.

"Hinduism in America" then—the phenomenon explored in this book—touches on not only the beliefs and practices of Hindus—both inheritors and adopters of this religious tradition—but the total Hindu presence in American culture, from ahiṃsā (or nonviolence) to yoga.[58]

What This Book Will Explore

In short, this book will tell a story of two worlds that converge: one of Hindu immigrants to America who want to preserve their traditions and pass them on to their children in a new and foreign land, and one of American spiritual seekers who find that the traditions of India fulfill their most deeply held aspirations. Another perspective—that of the children and grandchildren of Hindu immigrants who have grown up in a Hindu American environment—who are Hindu *and* American by birth—will be included as well, as it is in many ways distinct from the perspectives both of their parents and of the non-Indian seekers who have adopted the tradition.

The first chapter will provide an overview of Hinduism as a whole. What is this tradition, or family of traditions, that has increasingly come to find a home in America, and that has had a profound influence on American culture without most Americans even realizing this is the case? The basic teachings and forms of Hinduism will be explored as these have unfolded over the course of a long history, from the Indus Valley Civilization to the early modern period, with particular attention to those elements which are especially relevant for understanding Hinduism in America.

The second chapter will take up this historical thread in the early nineteenth century, with the emergence of Hindu reformers like Ram Mohan Roy and Swami Dayananda Saraswati. The rise of modern Hinduism in India will be traced in tandem with simultaneous developments in the Western world which led to an intensified interest in Hindu thought and practice among a growing number of Westerners in the nineteenth century, like the Transcendentalists and the Theosophists. This chapter will essentially explore the historical developments in India which culminated in the departure of Swami Vivekananda for the West at the end of the nineteenth century and the changes in America that led to its being a relatively welcoming and receptive environment for him.

The third chapter will begin with Swami Vivekananda's journey to America and the effects that resulted from it: the establishment of Vedanta Societies in various urban centers, managed by Vivekananda's fellow monks and their successors. The influence of these societies on intellectuals in particular—figures like Christopher Isherwood, Aldous Huxley, and Joseph Campbell, whose work played a major role in the propagation of Hindu thought into the wider American culture—will then be explored.

This chapter will also discuss Paramahansa Yogananda and his establishment of the Self-Realization Fellowship, and the teachings of Jiddu Krishnamurti. Other pioneers of yoga in the West will also be examined, including two figures—Sri Aurobindo and Sri Ramana Maharshi—who, although they never personally set foot in America, nevertheless have large American followings, and have made a major imprint on how Hinduism in general—and yoga in particular—is perceived. This chapter will then turn from famous gurus and their early Western disciples to the wider Hindu and Indian diasporas in America during the same period and their struggles with fierce racism and rejection in the United States, culminating with the passage of the Asian Exclusion Act of 1924.

The fourth chapter will explore the next wave of American interest in Hinduism. The rise of the counter-culture of the 1960s, in tandem with the lifting of the Asian Exclusion Act, created conditions for the arrival of new Hindu teachers with a ready audience of ardent spiritual seekers. Maharishi Mahesh Yogi, A.C. Bhaktivedanta Swami Prabhupada, Swami Satchidananda, Swami Muktananda, Sri Chinmoy, and many more gurus will be examined, as well as influential Western devotees, such as George Harrison of the Beatles, who helped bring aspects of Hindu thought and practice into the American mainstream.

With the lifting of the Asian Exclusion Act, in 1965, Indian immigration to the United States and the number of practicing Hindu immigrants increased. Hindu communities began to emerge across the United States with sufficient membership to fund the building of temples. The main focus of the fifth chapter will be the inheritor Hindu communities of America. Temple communities will be examined—their emergence, the challenges they have faced, their organizational structures, and the ways in which Hindu temples in America differ from Hindu temples in South Asia.

This chapter will also discuss the inclusion of practitioners of other Indic traditions—Jain practitioners in particular—in American Hindu temple communities. It will be noted that certain Hindu traditions and organizations have especially strong presences in the American environment. These include the Vedanta Society, ISKCON, and the Swaminarayan movement, as well as the movement of devotees of the late nineteenth- and early twentieth-century Indian holy man, Sai Baba of Shirdi (1838–1918), whose following extends to both Hindus and Muslims.

In addition to the histories of the Hindu community in the United States, the distinctive history and practices of Hinduism in Canada and in the Caribbean region will also be explored briefly in this chapter. The Caribbean region, in particular, was a destination for Indian indentured laborers in the nineteenth century. These laborers were mainly sent to work on plantations. Separated from the rest of the Hindu community, Caribbean Hindus developed a distinctive self-understanding which differentiates them both from Indian Hindus and from the later Hindu community that arose in the United States after the lifting of the Asian Exclusion Act in 1965.

The sixth chapter will turn to Hindu influence in American culture, starting with adopters of Hinduism—Hindus not by birth, but by choice—and move on to HIMMs. The relationship of adoptive Hindus and Hindu-inspired movements to the inheritor community will be explored, along with the issue of race and its role in the question of Hindu identity. Is the adoption of Hindu belief, practice, and identity an exercise in "white privilege," or does it represent the genuine dissemination of a global religious tradition? Given the relatively small number of white practitioners, their impact on how Hinduism is perceived in the wider population—and even among many Hindus—is clearly disproportionate. The power dynamics of race and white privilege shape Hinduism in America, even when this is not intended to be so.

This chapter will also include discussion of yoga, vegetarianism, and religious pluralism. The relationship of these phenomena to Hinduism as a whole will be explored, as well as the self-understandings of those who adopt these practices or views without self-identifying as Hindu. In what sense are yoga, vegetarianism, and religious pluralism "Hindu," and in what sense are they practices and ideas available to anyone, of any worldview, who wants to adopt them? We will see that Hinduism is one of several factors that have influenced the adoption of practices and views of this kind, and the particular shape they have taken in the American environment.

Yoga in particular has been the subject of controversy between Hindus and persons in the yoga community over what many Hindus see as erasure of Hindu dimensions of yoga, and what many non-Hindu yoga practitioners see as heavy-handed attempts by Hindus to regulate their yoga practices. This chapter includes an extended interview with a white American yoga practitioner.

The seventh chapter will look into the impact of Hinduism upon American popular culture—in particular, via the Beatles and the *Star Wars* films—as well as representations of both Hinduism and India more generally in the popular media. The unique cultural role of the Beatles—and George Harrison especially—will be explored in relation to the dissemination of Hindu and Hindu-inspired ideas and practices to the wider American society. Stereotypes of Indian Americans in popular media will also be discussed, such as the character of Apu in *The Simpsons* and of Raj Koothrappali in *The Big Bang Theory*. These stereotypes will be contrasted with the increasing prominence of Indian Americans as experts in the popular media on various fields, such as the roles of Sanjay Gupta and Fareed Zakaria as experts on CNN.

The eighth chapter will look at the emergence, as the twentieth century has ended and the twenty-first begun, of an increasingly assertive, socially, and politically active American Hinduism, with a special focus on the Hindu American Foundation, a prominent Hindu advocacy group.

The book will end with concluding reflections upon the material it has explored. Having looked at its past and present, what might the future hold for Hinduism in America? What issues are Hindus in America likely to continue to face? And what contributions will they make to the consciousness of American society at large?

Each chapter will begin with a summary of its contents (like the one found at the start of this introduction). The chapters will end with a set of study questions, as well as suggestions for further reading. After the concluding chapter, there will be an appendix consisting of a list of Hindu temples and organizations in the United States, organized by state, followed by a glossary of Hindu terms mentioned in the book.

A Note on Methodology

A considerable—and growing—body of excellent scholarly literature has emerged on Hindu traditions in North America, examining both diasporic Hindu communities and the phenomenon of HIMMs, organizations, and teachers, as well as on yoga, broadly conceived. In the course of writing and researching this book, I have drawn upon this scholarship extensively, although, being a constantly growing field, I cannot claim to have read everything in it.

At the same time, I have myself been both a participant and observer in Hindu and Hindu-inspired environments in North America throughout my adult life. Even long before I knew I was going to be writing this book, I was making observations, having discussions, and conducting both formal and informal interviews with Hindus, yoga practitioners, and spiritual seekers from a wide array of perspectives and backgrounds, simply out of interest in the topics explored here. Persons whose words I have cited in this book come from a wide range of age groups. For those drawn from the Indian American community, they range from seniors who were part of the wave of Indian immigration into the United States that began in the late 1960s and early 1970s to teenagers whose parents—and in a few cases, grandparents—were part of that same wave of immigrants. For those not drawn from the Indian American community, they similarly range from seekers whose interest in Hinduism began with the counterculture of the 1960s to young professionals drawn to yoga for peace of mind and professional productivity. They also include monastic practitioners of Hindu or Hindu-inspired traditions, scholars, political activists, and business leaders. Interviews occurred both in person (mainly one-on-one) and online (mainly through email or Facebook Messenger).

In this book, I have followed the standard anthropological practice of protecting the identity and confidentiality of each person I have interviewed. I have used pseudonyms for this purpose, which is also a standard anthropological practice. Actual names of persons have been used only when I have cited public statements that they have made. In such cases, the persons involved were clearly not concerned about confidentiality and were indeed happy to be associated with whatever statements they made. Such public statements include published works and social media postings, as well as published or online interviews with scholars or journalists.

Protecting the confidentiality of one's conversation partners is especially important when the topics under discussion are controversial, or of a political nature, as is the case with some of the topics covered in this book. It is also essential for safeguarding privacy, such as when people are talking about personal rituals or beliefs which would not generally be shared with the public. Whenever making alterations to protect confidentiality, I have striven to ensure that the resulting alterations have had no impact on the accuracy of the information presented on the topic at hand.

Regarding terminology, I am following Amanda Lucia's lead in using the term *inheritors* to refer to people who were born Hindu. To refer to people who identify themselves religiously as Hindu but who were not born or raised in the tradition I use the term *adopters*. Although people in the first group will typically be of Indian or South Asian descent and people in the second group will not, there are exceptions both ways (like those people whose grandparents joined ISKCON in the 1960s and were thus born to a Hindu tradition, even if they are not South Asian, or people from non-observant South Asian Hindu families who have subsequently been drawn to the practice of Hinduism, possibly via a HIMM, such as the Vedanta Society, Self-Realization Fellowship, or ISKCON).

When using traditional Sanskrit terminology, I have typically used the system of diacritical marks deployed by scholars globally when transliterating Indic scripts to the Roman alphabet. I have provided a guide to this system.[59] In many cases, however—particularly considering that this book's topic is Hinduism in America—there are words which have become recognizable in forms which do not follow this standardized system of transliteration, and which will likely be far more accessible to readers in these non-standardized forms. I therefore refer to *Krishna*, for example, instead of *Kṛṣṇa*, and *Shiva* instead of *Śiva*, and *Vedanta* instead of *Vedānta* when talking about the Vedanta Society. Similarly, with the proper names of human teachers, such as Sri Ramakrishna and Swami Vivekananda, I have used these forms rather than the more technically correct but less familiar *Śrī Rāmakṛṣṇa* and *Svāmī Vivekānanda*.

Indeed, it could be argued that, for most of his American devotees *Vivekananda*, with the stress on the second-to-last syllable—Vivekanánda—is a more recognizable name than the original and "correct" pronunciation, Vivekānanda, with the stress on the long "ā" (pronounced "ah"). Like all religious traditions that have been carried from one cultural environment to another, Hinduism in America is becoming, in many ways, "Americanized" (just as Buddhism became Sinicized when it was taken to China, and Japanized when it was taken to Japan). The fact that a growing number of Sanskrit terms of Hindu origin are becoming part of the American English lexicon—such as the ubiquitous words *karma* and *yoga*—is just one more facet of this transformation. At the same time, it can produce dismay for those concerned with retaining cultural authenticity.

Finally, being fully aware that the term *America* denotes, in its fullest sense, the continents of both North and South America, and that even the continent of North America includes not only the United States, but also Canada, the Caribbean region and a substantial part of Latin America, and also being fully aware of how irritating it is to people in the rest of the Americas when people from the United States use the word *America* simply to refer to the United States, I will note that this book is focused primarily upon Hinduism in the United States (and the related phenomena which I have mentioned). While there will be some brief discussion of Hinduism in Canada and the Caribbean region, I freely admit that this book's title should likely have been *Hinduism in the United States*, which is its real focus. This restriction of my focus is due to the limits of my time and expertise, and not to any nationalistic sense that the United States is any more important than any other country in the world. For better or worse, the term *Religion in America* has come to denote the subfield of the study of religion devoted to examining religion in the United States. The title of this book is but a reflection of this convention, and nothing more.

So, what is Hinduism? And what do most Hindus believe and do? This is the topic of our next chapter.

Study Questions

1. Why is it problematic to use the word *Hindu* to denote a national or ethnic identity? Why is it nevertheless common to do so? How is Hinduism related to India?
2. What is a *diaspora*? What are the various dimensions of this phenomenon?
3. What is the difference between inheritors and adopters of Hinduism? How are their styles of approaching Hinduism different? How can this lead to conflict? How do they converge?
4. How do Hindu-inspired meditation movements differ from Hinduism? And how are they related to it?

Suggestions for Further Reading

Murali Balaji, ed., *Digital Hinduism: Dharma and Discourse in the Age of New Media* (Lanham, MD: Lexington Books, 2018).

Tim Cooke, ed., *National Geographic Concise History of World Religions: An Illustrated Time Line* (Washington, DC: National Geographic, 2011).

Christopher R. Cotter and David G. Robertson, eds., *After World Religions: Reconstructing Religious Studies* (New York: Routledge, 2016).

Diana Eck, *Darśan: Seeing the Divine Image in India* (Delhi: Motilal Banarsidass, 2007).

Juli L. Gittinger, *Hinduism and Hindu Nationalism Online* (New York: Routledge, 2019).

Pankaj Jain, *Dharma and Ecology of Hindu Communities: Sustenance and Sustainability* (New York: Routledge, 2016).

J.E. Llewellyn, ed., *Defining Hinduism: A Reader* (London: Equinox, 2005).

Amanda J. Lucia, *Reflections of Amma: Devotees in a Global Embrace* (Berkeley: University of California Press, 2014).

Lisa Miller, "We Are All Hindus Now," *Newsweek* (August 15, 2009).

Andrew Nicholson, *Unifying Hinduism: Philosophy and Identity in Indian Intellectual History* (New York: Columbia University Press, 2010).

Brian Pennington, *Was Hinduism Invented? Britons, Indians, and the Colonial Construction of Religion* (Oxford: Oxford University Press, 2005).

Vijay Prashad, *The Karma of Brown Folk* (Minneapolis: University of Minnesota Press, 2000).

Vijay Prashad, *Uncle Swami: South Asians in America Today* (New York: The New Press 2012).

Sarvepalli Radhakrishnan, *The Hindu View of Life* (New York: Macmillan, 1973).
Jim Tucker, *Return to Life* (New York: St. Martin's Griffin, 2015).
Steven Vertovec, *The Hindu Diaspora: Comparative Patterns* (London: Routledge, 2000).
Lola Williamson, *Transcendent in America: Hindu-Inspired Meditation Movements as New Religion* (New York: New York University Press, 2010).
Lola Williamson and Ann Gleig, *Homegrown Gurus: From Hinduism in America to American Hinduism* (Albany: State University of New York Press, 2013).
Robert L. Winzeler, *Popular Religion in Southeast Asia* (Lanham, MD: Rowman and Littlefield, 2016).

1

What Is Hinduism? A Brief Overview

Chapter 1 Summary and Outline

This chapter gives an overview of Hindu beliefs and practices and a summary of Hindu history, with a particular emphasis on aspects of Hinduism that are especially relevant to Hinduism in America.

Defining Hinduism

John Cort, a prominent scholar of Jain traditions, has rightly observed, "Anyone who has ever taught about India knows that for every true statement about India there is an opposite, contradictory, yet equally true statement."[1] This observation is as relevant to the study of Hindu traditions as it is to the study of India as a whole. Any attempt to summarize the entirety of Hindu belief and practice is bound to involve statements with which someone, somewhere, will disagree. Hinduism is such an internally diverse tradition, or family of traditions, that, as we shall see, there are scholars who argue that even to refer to it as an "it"—to use the term *Hinduism* in the singular at all—is to engage in an act of deception, or to refer to a concept with no corresponding reality. This is certainly not the view of many Hindus and is, as we shall see, problematic if it is taken to an extreme. It does, however, point to just how incredibly varied Hinduism is. One textbook on Hinduism, in fact, makes this point in its title: *Living Hinduisms.*[2]

As we saw in the last chapter, the very terms *Hindu* and *Hinduism* have some controversy attached to them. For most of history, the people who adhere to what is now called *Hinduism* did not use the term *Hindu* at all to speak of a singular religious tradition. They referred, rather, to what would now be regarded as Hindu "sects": traditions with names like Vaiṣṇava, Śaiva, Śākta, Sāṃkhya, Yoga, and so on.

With that being said, most (though by no means all) Hindus today have embraced the term *Hindu* as a designation for their religious identity—and often, as we have seen, as a national and an ethnic designation as well. *Hinduism*, though, as a term, is less well received, with many preferring to use the terms *Hindu Dharma* or *Sanātana Dharma*. Many Hindus also express discomfort with the idea that the Hindu tradition is a "religion," preferring to see it as *dharma* or a "way of life."

For any serious religious person of any tradition, of course, a religion *is* a way of life. The frequently expressed discomfort one finds among many Hindus, and among practitioners of non-Western traditions worldwide, with the word *religion* is specifically with the idea of religion as a private orientation, largely removed from the rest of one's existence: a distinctly modern notion of religion, which is rooted in the constitutional separation of church and state in Western democratic polities, and ultimately in Protestant Christian conceptions of religious faith and the belief through which this faith is expressed as a matter between the individual believer and God. The religious warfare of Europe, too, which emerged after the Protestant Reformation, and the desire to avoid violence of this kind have also played a role in the modern privatization of religious belief.

This modern approach to religion is often contrasted with the more holistic ideal of *dharma*, which encompasses one's beliefs and spiritual practices, but also one's day-to-day responsibilities as a member of society.[3] Again, *religion* can have this meaning as well, but the idea of separating religiosity from the secular sphere—a largely Western preoccupation—is seen by many Hindus as a foreign concept, and not reflective of a traditional Hindu sensibility. This is one of the reasons the idea of secularism enshrined in the constitution of the Republic of India does not resonate with all Hindus. From the perspective, especially of those Hindus who are drawn to the political movement of Hindu nationalism—which sees India as a Hindu nation, in much the same way that the Christian right in the United States sees the United States as a Christian nation—the separation of religion from the state is not only unnecessary to ensure the protection of minority religious communities, but rather it is precisely the breadth and pluralism of Hindu traditions that can best provide such protection. This is, of course, a hotly contested view in India, particularly in light of modern history, in which there has been violence between Hindus and others, especially during the partition of India and Pakistan, which led to the deaths of more than a million people, and the displacement of over 15 million more.[4]

It is often pointed out by critics of the terms *Hindu* and *Hinduism* that these terms are not of Hindu origin but are distorting foreign impositions on what is really, again, a great variety of diverse traditions. Indeed, the first attested use of the term *Hindu* can be traced to the Persian king, Darius the Great. As Indologist Asko Parpola notes:

> The etymology of "Hindu" goes back to about 515 BCE, when the Persian king Darius the Great annexed the Indus Valley to his empire. *Sindhu*, the Sanskrit name of the Indus River and its southern province—the area now known as Sindh—became *Hindu* in the Persian language.[5]

As noted in the previous chapter, the Persian pronunciation of *Sindhu* is the historical and linguistic source of the word *Hindu*. This fact is noted by scholars who aim to critique the idea of a singular Hindu tradition as a construct of colonialism, as well as by Hindus with a preference for indigenous terms, such as *Sanātana Dharma*, to denote the traditions by which Hindus live and practice.

In later centuries, *Hindu* came simply to mean *Indian*—an inhabitant of *Hindustan*, or India.

The original use of this term to refer to an ethnicity and a nationality continues to shade its meaning today. The Hindu nationalist political movement, which identifies Hinduness—or *Hindutva*—with Indianness, works with this understanding. For Hindu nationalist thought, as codified by one of its founding figures, Vinayak Damodar Savarkar (1883–1966), a Hindu is a person who is Indian by ethnicity, by nationality, and by religion.[6]

The term *Sanātana Dharma*, by way of contrast, has the connotation of an eternal *dharma*: an eternal order or way of life, with no beginning or final end point in time. It also has connotations of universality. For Hindu universalists, *Sanātana Dharma* conveys the idea of a religion with no boundaries, or of a deeper philosophy undergirding and encompassing all religions. Adherents of Vedānta in the modern period—a central system of Hindu thought—see this philosophy in universal terms. *Hindu*, with its ethnic and geographic implications, is seen as too limiting to convey eternal truth. In the words of Pravrajika Vrajaprana, one of its contemporary exponents:

> Vedanta is the philosophical foundation of Hinduism; but while Hinduism includes aspects of Indian culture, Vedanta is universal in its application and is equally relevant to all countries, all cultures, and all religious backgrounds.[7]

Such a universalist understanding of a central Hindu system of thought is, of course, conducive to the extension of adherence to Hinduism beyond India, and into environments like North America. If the philosophical foundation of Hinduism is universal, it can be adopted by anyone.

The localized geographic and ethnic connotations of *Hindu* and *Hinduism* have, of course, been complicated by the rise of the Hindu diaspora and conversions to Hinduism among the non-Indian majority populations of countries to which Hindus have emigrated, as well as, within India, by the fact that many Indians do not identify, religiously, as Hindu, but rather as Muslim, Christian, Sikh, Jain, and so on. Some members of traditions indigenous to India, but distinct from Hinduism, describe themselves as "culturally" Hindu but not religiously.[8] These persons use the term *Hindu* much as its etymology suggests, to refer to something native to India, and in this case, to refer to the larger religious culture of India and the many elements it includes that are shared by adherents of many distinct traditions. It is not uncommon, for example, for Jains to worship the goddesses Lakṣmī and Saraswatī, and even to frequent Hindu temples on certain occasions. This is for events and observances that are seen as part of the shared Indian—*Hindu* in this sense—cultural heritage. But Jains look to their distinctive Jain authorities and practices for the pursuit of *mokṣa*, the highest spiritual goal. It is in this sense that Jainism is their *religion*.

Hinduism, as a word that refers to an ideology, a belief system, or a way of life, is a term of relatively recent coinage. It is an English word, originally used to refer to the worldviews and lifeways of the whole variety of people found in India (a term which itself traditionally referred to the entire region now known as South Asia). It excluded those religions with an Indian following that were already known to the Europeans: Islam, Christianity, Judaism, and Zoroastrianism. And though it originally included other traditions of Indian origin of which Europeans had, at that point, only limited awareness—Sikhism, Buddhism, and Jainism—it has come to refer, specifically, to the Indic traditions which adhere, in some sense, to the idea of the authority of an ancient set of texts known as the *Vedas*—a Sanskrit term which literally means "wisdom."

FIGURE 3 *Hindu Goddesses Lakṣmī and Saraswatī, on left and right, respectively, flanking the Jain Goddess Cakreśwarī, from a Jain temple in Michigan (Photo by Jeffery D. Long).*

Just as the geographic and the ethnic connotations of the term *Hindu* continue to resonate, in spite of the fact that not all Hindus are (nationally or ethnically) Indian and not all Indians are (religiously) Hindu, the extension of this term to encompass all religions of Indian origin is also a usage which continues to appear in various contexts—including the constitution of India, in which Sikhs, Buddhists, and Jains are treated as Hindus.[9]

The reactions of Sikhs, Buddhists, and Jains to being incorporated into some definitions of Hinduism vary enormously. It is also an issue on which feelings can be very strong and can run very deep. Some, particularly in rural areas, where religious identities are often fluid in practice, with multiple religious participation being a common phenomenon, do not mind seeing themselves as participants in a wider religious culture designated as *Hindu* while at the same time emphasizing the distinctiveness of their own spiritual heritage and lineage.

Others, however, sharply reject this designation and view it as an imperialistic attempt to incorporate them into another religion: in short, as an attempt at Hindu domination by definition. In light of widespread violence against Sikhs in the 1980s, as well as the fact that many Indian Buddhists are converts or descendants of converts who left the Hindu tradition in order to avoid caste prejudice, one finds this suspicion to be especially strong in these communities, although it is not entirely absent among Jains either.

The further back one looks into history, the more this issue is complicated by the traditional Indian attitudes toward religious labels and identities, which are not in the direction of singular or mutually exclusive definitions but of fluid, flexible, porous boundaries. The hardening of these boundaries has been a relatively modern development. The point here is not that everyone was once Hindu, but rather, that Indians simply did not concern themselves with this issue traditionally, as what the West calls *religion* was not a matter of exclusive allegiance and singular identity.[10]

Hindu Texts and Basic Beliefs

As already mentioned, Hinduism encompasses a range of systems of belief and practice. This is why, to paraphrase John Cort, for every true statement about Hinduism, there is an opposite, contradictory, yet equally true statement. Generalizing, therefore, about what Hindus believe and do is a difficult proposition, because one is bound to exclude someone or other even in the course of an expansive and detailed account of Hinduism. If the reader bears in mind, though, that there are exceptions to every general principle that will be stated, one can draw attention to common themes shared by most forms of Hinduism.

Although British scholars initially defined *Hinduism* as encompassing all religiosity native to India apart from Judaism, Christianity, Islam, and Zoroastrianism (with Sikhism, Buddhism, and Jainism later differentiated as well), this term has come to refer to a system of religiosity based on the *Vedas*.

The *Vedas* are an ancient collection of writings regarded as sacred by Hindus, and to regard the *Vedas* as sacred and authoritative is definitive of Hindu identity as it has come to be understood by scholars. The composition of these texts encompassed a period of over a thousand years. The compilation of the oldest of the *Vedas*, the *Ṛg Veda*, is typically placed by scholars around the year 1500 BCE. It is certainly possible, given that they were handed down orally for generations, that at least portions of this text are more ancient than this dating suggests, and that 1500 BCE marks the period when these already ancient texts were compiled in their current form.[11] The *Ṛg Veda* is followed by the *Yajur Veda* and *Sāma Veda*, possibly composed between 1500 and 1000 BCE, which are, in turn, followed by the *Atharva Veda*, which was possibly compiled in its current form around 1000 BCE.

FIGURE 4 *Indian boy reciting Vedas, Hindu Scripture, Kumbakonam, Tamil Nadu, India (Photo by Education Images/Universal Images Group via Getty Images).*

These original or primary Vedic texts are followed by collections of commentary which elaborate upon and unpack the meanings of the often-obscure and difficult-to-understand verses of the original texts. These collections of commentary are, themselves, also regarded as forming part of the *Vedas* as a whole. The most ancient of these commentarial collections on the original Vedic texts is called the *Brāhmaṇas*, or "Priestly Texts." They elaborate on the rituals prescribed in the original Vedic texts. The *Brāhmaṇas* are followed by the *Āraṇyakas*, or "Forest Texts," which are in turn followed by the *Upaniṣads*, or "Secret Doctrine."

Given their location at the end of the Vedic literary corpus, as well as the belief that they represent the culmination of Vedic thought, the *Upaniṣads* are also known as the *Vedānta*, or the "End of the *Veda*." "End" (*anta*) in Sanskrit has the same range of connotations as "end" in English. *Vedānta* thus means, literally, the "End of the *Vedas*"—the final portion of Vedic literature to have been composed—but also the "End of the *Vedas*," meaning that these texts express the ultimate aim or purpose of the entire Vedic tradition. *Veda* itself means "wisdom," so *Vedānta* also means the ultimate aim or purpose of all knowledge. In subsequent centuries, *Vedānta* came to refer to a set of doctrines taught in the *Upaniṣads*. These doctrines eventually developed into a distinct set of systems of philosophical reflection, which itself gave rise to numerous branches and sub-varieties. Vedānta, as we shall see, has had a massive influence on Hindu thought in America, as well as on modern articulations of Hinduism in India.

What it means to adhere to the authority of the *Vedas* varies greatly across Hindu traditions. It is fair to say that a close study of the original Vedic texts just described—whose compilation and composition range from roughly 1500 BCE (in the case of the *Ṛg Veda*) to the period between 800 and 200 BCE (in the case of the *Upaniṣads*)—is not a pursuit in which the average Hindu typically engages. There is a widespread sense that these texts are sacred—that their utterances were received or "heard" by ancient sages known as the *ṛṣis* (meaning sages, or seers), and that these ṛṣis were able to perceive the true nature of reality and express it in the form of the Vedic texts. Because they were received or "heard," rather than composed from the imaginations of the ṛṣis, the Vedic texts are known, collectively, as *śrūti* (which literally means "heard"). For most Hindus, these texts are also encountered by being "heard" in the very concrete sense of the term, for Vedic verses are chanted by priests in the course of such major life rituals as weddings, funerals, and ceremonies to celebrate the naming of a newborn child and a baby's first eating of solid food. This does not mean that these texts are understood particularly well by all who are in attendance when they are chanted in this way. They are recited in their original Sanskrit form, and Sanskrit has not been a language spoken by most Indians for thousands of years.

In some Hindu traditions, the perceiving or "hearing" of the true nature of reality by the ṛṣis is understood as more or less an impersonal process—as the culmination of the practice of a spiritual science, which anyone might, in principle, pursue, through learning the correct meditative forms and dedicating oneself to their practice. In other Hindu traditions, this process is seen as more akin to divine revelation: that the Supreme Being—called *Īśvara* or *Bhagavān*, the Lord or Blessed One—revealed the

Vedas to the ṛṣis once they had opened their minds in the manner required to receive the divine word.

What the *Vedas* actually teach, however, is mediated to most Hindus through a later body of literature—the *smṛti*, or "remembered" texts, whose authority is derivative from that of the *Vedas*. The smṛti includes two massive epics—the *Rāmāyaṇa* and *Mahābhārata*—likely composed, in their current forms, during the period between 200 BCE and 200 CE, although the events they describe are believed to have occurred much earlier than this.[12] Smṛti also includes a collection of texts known as the *Pūrāṇas*, or "ancient lore." There are eighteen major *Pūrāṇas* and numerous minor ones.

The *Pūrāṇas* describe the deeds of the major Hindu deities: Vishnu, Shiva, and Shakti, or Devī (the Mother Goddess). Six of the eighteen major *Pūrāṇas* are dedicated primarily to Vishnu, six to Shiva, and six to Devī (also known as Mahādevī, or Shakti, the Mother Goddess), who is typically presented as the wife of Shiva. These three deities are also the chief focus of worship, respectively, in the three main branches of Hinduism: the Vaiṣṇava, Śaiva, and Śākta traditions. A fourth branch, the Smarta tradition, is focused not on a specific deity but on the smṛti tradition as a whole (hence its name). While adherents of the three main theistic traditions tend to see their respective supreme deities as *the* Supreme Being, the Smarta tradition teaches that each deity is a form or manifestation of the impersonal ultimate reality of Brahman. Beyond these four traditions, there are numerous other branches of Hinduism. Some, like the Gaṇapatya tradition, are centered, like the Vaiṣṇava, Śaiva, and Śākta traditions, on the worship of a particular deity. As its name indicates, the Gaṇapatya tradition is focused on Gaṇapati, or Ganesha, as the supreme being. Other Hindu traditions are localized to particular regions or groupings within Hindu society, while others are centered on devotion to a human teacher who is regarded either as an enlightened being or as an *avatar*, or divine incarnation. Some HIMMs, mentioned in the previous chapter, are of this last kind.

In addition to the two major epics and the literatures of the three main theistic traditions, the smṛti literature also includes texts on a great variety of subjects, both "religious" and "secular," including philosophy (*Darśana*), medicine (*Ayur Veda*), political science (*Artha Śāstra*), drama (*Nātya Śāstra*), architecture (*Vastu Śāstra*), and aesthetics (*Kāma Śāstra*).

The smṛti texts—and their local variants, which are often communicated not in Sanskrit, but in vernacular languages, and are often circulated orally more than in writing—are the chief vehicle by which Hindu beliefs and values are transmitted from one generation to the next. While the *Vedas* are largely the preserve of scholars and ardent spiritual seekers, even young Hindu children can narrate the basic plots of the *Rāmāyaṇa* and the *Mahābhārata*, going on to tell one who their favorite characters are and why, which episodes of these massive narratives they like best, and so on. These texts have inspired, throughout the centuries, popular plays and songs—and, in the modern period, comic books, television shows, films, and novels.[13]

FIGURE 5 *Lord Shiva, Hindu American Religious Institute, New Cumberland, Pennsylvania (Photo by Jeffery D. Long).*

The same is true of the *Pūrāṇas*, stories from which are mediated to the Hindu community in the form of ritual re-enactments. The ten-day festival of Durgā Pūjā, for example, which is especially popular among Bengali Hindus, is a re-enactment of the Pūrāṇic account of the descent of the goddess Durgā to the earth on her mission to destroy the wicked Mahīṣāsura, or Buffalo Demon, who had conquered it.

The basic belief system expressed—again, with a number of important variations—in the vast literature of Hinduism and the local practices of Hindus across the globe is one which centers on a Supreme Being. This Supreme Being is conceptualized in various ways. In the Advaita, or non-dualistic, system of Vedānta, the supreme reality is an impersonal ground of being which is known as *Brahman*. (Perhaps more accurately, Brahman is seen in this tradition as beyond concepts such as "personal" and "impersonal.") Most importantly, according to the *Upaniṣads*, Brahman, as the basis of all that exists, is also the basis of the personal existence of each of us. In other words, our essential Self—or *ātman*—is finally identical to Brahman. Realizing this identity

FIGURE 6 *Durgā Pūjā being celebrated in Harrisburg, Pennsylvania (Photo by Jeffery D. Long).*

is the ultimate aim of our existence. Brahman, in its essential nature, is *anantaram sat-chit-ānandam*: infinite being, consciousness, and bliss. To realize Brahman is to be released from all suffering and all limitation.

In most systems of Hinduism, the supreme Brahman is conceived in personal terms, either as the deity Vishnu or Shiva or Shakti, or as one of a variety of other deities. Hinduism eludes an easy categorization as either monotheistic (having one supreme God) or polytheistic (having many gods and goddesses) because dimensions of both monotheism and polytheism are present in it. It affirms a singular supreme reality, but also many manifestations of that reality. It is also pantheist, in the sense that Brahman literally becomes all of existence, and panentheistic, inasmuch as the supreme *personification* of Brahman—the Supreme Being—dwells within all beings as the Self.

From a Vaiṣṇava perspective, Vishnu is the one Supreme Being and all other deities can be seen either as Vishnu's servants or His forms, manifestations, or projections. A particular trait of Vishnu's is that He manifests periodically in time and space as an *avatar*—which literally means "descent," or incarnation. Some of the most popular Hindu deities are avatars of Vishnu. Two in particular, Rāma (or Rām, in most modern Indian languages) and Krishna, are especially popular.

Rām is the main protagonist of the *Rāmāyaṇa* (the title of which means "The Life of Rāma") and Krishna is a major character in the *Mahābhārata*. In fact, one of the most popular Hindu texts of the modern period (and a major foundation for Vedānta philosophy, along with the *Upaniṣads* and a text known as the *Brahmā Sūtra*) is the section of dialogue from the *Mahābhārata* known as the *Bhagavad Gītā*, or "Song of the Blessed One."

FIGURE 7 *Sri Vadapathira Kaliamman Hindu temple. Avatar of Vishnu. Lord Rama, the seventh incarnation. Singapore (Photo by Godong/Universal Images Group via Getty Images).*

From a Śaiva perspective, though, it is Shiva who is the one Supreme Being and all other deities are either His servants or manifestations. Śākta theology similarly sees the Supreme Being as the Mother Goddess. Both Śaiva and Śākta theology, however, affirm a non-dualism in which literally everything is ultimately Shiva or Shakti.

There is also a teaching, held in most Śaiva and Śākta schools of thought, that Shiva and Shakti are, themselves, ultimately one being. This unified deity is represented as *Ardhanarīśvara*, a deity visualized as Shiva on one side and Shakti on the other. This is in contrast with Vaiṣṇava theologies, which tend to emphasize the importance of the distinction between the Supreme Being, on the one hand, and His devotees, on the other.

FIGURE 8 *The first "Transgender" Durga image (Ardhanarīśvara) of the country at the studio of artist China Pal, at Kumartuli on October 16, 2015, in Kolkata, India. Udyami Yubak Brinda Durga Puja Committee, a paara (community) organization, in partnership with transgender rights activist group Pratyay Gender Trust, is all set to make history with its idol that has been modelled on the Ardhanarishwar or the composite androgynous form of Lord Shiva and his consort Parvati (Photo by Subhendu Ghosh/Hindustan Times via Getty Images).*

Historically, one of the first systems to branch out of the original, non-sectarian Vedānta of the *Upaniṣads*, *Brahmā Sūtra*, and *Gītā* was Advaita Vedānta, which teaches the non-duality of Brahman and all beings. Advaita Vedānta is rooted in the teachings of Śaṅkara (Shankara), who likely lived from 788 to 820 CE. Śaṅkara interprets the original Vedāntic texts as teaching that Brahman alone is real and that the rest of the cosmos is an "appearance," or *māyā*, which is neither fully real nor fully unreal. Realization comes when one fully comprehends that one is Brahman. Māyā is often likened in Advaita Vedānta to a rope which one has mistaken for a snake. If one comes across a rope lying on the floor in a poorly lit room, it is possible that one will take it to be a snake. Once the room is lit, one can see that what one had thought to be a snake was, in fact, only a rope. Similarly, when the light of true awareness dawns in one's mind, one sees that what one has taken to be a world of discrete entities is truly Brahman. Like the snake, the world is "real" as long as one is perceiving it. When true awareness dawns, it disappears.

Because Advaita Vedānta relegates the personal Supreme Being to the realm of māyā—as the Supreme Being, *Bhagavān* or *Īśvara*, in the realm of appearance whose existence is necessary to the maintenance and upholding of that realm—it is seen by Vaiṣṇava Vedāntic thinkers as unduly downplaying the important practice of *bhakti*, or devotion, which is a cornerstone of much of Hindu spirituality. Vaiṣṇava teachers after Śaṅkara developed alternative systems of Vedānta in order to interpret the scriptures in a way that would give a more robust role to devotion and the distinction between the Supreme Being and His devotees—which bhakti, or devotion, as a relational experience, presupposes. For Śaṅkara, bhakti is an important part of the spiritual path, but it is a preliminary practice, which serves to purify the mind and prepare it for true knowledge, or *jñāna*. For Śaṅkara, jñāna essentially constitutes mokṣa—or liberation from the cycle of rebirth. For the Vaiṣṇava systems of Vedānta, though, bhakti is not merely a preliminary practice. Rather, it is bhakti—the blissful, loving relationship of complete devotion with the divine reality, the Supreme Person—that constitutes mokṣa.

According to the Vaiṣṇava schools of thought, like the Viśiṣṭādvaita Vedānta of the scholar Rāmāṇuja (who lived from the eleventh to the twelfth centuries CE) and the Dvaita Vedānta of Madhva (1238–1317), māyā is not ultimately a false appearance, but is the creative power of the Supreme Being to manifest new phenomena.

Viśiṣṭādvaita Vedānta, developed by Rāmānuja, affirms the identity of Brahman with all existence, but does not see the distinctions between self, world, and Īśvara as a mere appearance, or *māyā*, but as reflecting real differences *within* Brahman. Brahman constitutes an organic unity rather than an undifferentiated one. Dvaita Vedānta, established by Madhva, affirms very strong distinctions among Īśvara, living beings (*jīvas*, or souls), and the rest of the universe. "Union with Brahman," for Madhva, represents a loving union, a union of wills, not an ontological identity. For Rāmānuja, there is oneness in the sense of organic relationality, but not of complete identity.

The Śaiva and Śākta traditions, often characterized as *Tāntric* traditions, are non-dualist, but in a somewhat different sense from that of Śaṅkara. In Tāntric thought, as in Advaita Vedānta, the supreme reality—taken as either Śiva or Śakti—has literally become all things. However, as we have seen, in Advaita Vedānta, the cosmos of entities distinct from the supreme reality *appears* to have come into being. This appearance, or māyā, is not fully real and obscures the truth of the undifferentiated Brahman at the basis of all existence. In Tāntric thought, however, much like in Vaiṣṇava theology, māyā is the creative power of the divine reality, and the cosmos a celebration of divine bliss. The divine play of creation is often depicted in terms of the loving relationship of Śiva and Śakti, who represent divine consciousness and divine creative power or māyā, respectively. Śakti is māyā, and māyā is Śakti. Rather than seeing beyond māyā to the supreme reality beyond, in Tāntric non-dualism, one aims to experience the supreme reality both within and *as* the world of the senses. This celebration of the senses is one reason why Tāntric practice is seen with some suspicion in other Hindu traditions, as a potential rationalization for sensory indulgence.

Whatever their conceptions of the precise nature of the Supreme Being and its relationship with the rest of existence, and whatever the varied representations of the Supreme Being they use in worship, Hindu traditions all affirm that the physical body and the events of its lifetime do not exhaust who and what we really are. Hinduism teaches that the true nature of the Self, as we have seen, is ultimately that of an infinite consciousness, unlimited by time, space, or causation. Even Hindu traditions that affirm a distinction between the individual Self or soul and the Supreme Being affirm that the Supreme Being dwells *within* all beings as the Supreme Self, or *Paramātman*.

The individual, living Self—the *jīvātman*, or *jīva*—is not identical to the physical body. It, rather, resides within—or better, identifies itself with—the body in order to learn the lessons it needs to learn in order to make spiritual progress. The cosmos follows an orderly pattern. The order of existence is known as *dharma*. *Dharma* also refers to our duties within the world—pre-eminently our social duties. One can see dharma, ultimately, as the cosmic order, which manifests at the level of our day-to-day existence in the form of the duties we must perform to maintain that order as a function of our place within it.

One of the principles by which the universal order is maintained is the principle of action, or *karma*. Karma refers to a principle according to which any intentional action one commits—whether in thought, word, or deed—results in a corresponding effect returning to the doer of that action. In short, if one does good, one will receive good effects, and if one does harm, one will receive harmful effects. We receive back from the universe what we give to it. This is not precisely divine reward and punishment, although most Hindu schools of thought see the Supreme Being as playing a role in the process by which karma plays out. But the process itself is seen as impartial and inexorable. It is up to us to determine the nature of our future with our freely made choices in the present, and our present conditions have similarly been shaped by our own past choices.

A logical corollary of this concept of karma is the idea of rebirth, or reincarnation. It is not the case, as anyone can observe, that all of the good that a person does is rewarded in this lifetime, and that not all of the harm a person does is punished. Similarly, we do not all begin life on a level playing field. All of our various advantages and disadvantages are understood, from a Hindu point of view, as results of our varied karma, based on actions we performed in past lives. And the not yet experienced karmic results of our current actions will lead us to be reborn in a form and at a time and place appropriate for bringing these results to fruition.

The ultimate aim of existence, according to Hinduism, is to learn the lessons we are being taught, on a soul level, by this cosmic process of trial and error, and achieve liberation from the cycle of rebirth, with all the suffering and limitation that life within this cycle involves.

This state of liberation—or *mokṣa*—can be seen as the Hindu analogue of the Christian idea of salvation. Both are eternal states, free from suffering, death, and the alienation from our own deepest divine Self that characterizes life in the realm of rebirth. There is no eternal damnation in Hinduism, though; for if one has not yet achieved Self-realization, one simply comes back until one does so. Indeed, according to some Hindu thinkers, all beings will eventually achieve moksha. Given infinite time, it is inevitable that one will eventually be drawn to take up the spiritual path and achieve the highest realization.[14]

There are "heavens" and "hells," according to Hindu theology—realms known respectively as *Svārga* and *Naraka*. These are, however, temporary abodes in which one experiences the results of either very good or very bad karma before returning to a more or less neutral realm, like that of human beings.[15]

It is important to note that, as a being of pure consciousness, the soul, or jīva, is not human. It can take many forms, including those of a plant, an animal, or a celestial being. Hinduism is not an anthropocentric tradition, although most Hindu systems of thought typically view the human form as particularly conducive to spiritual progress. In the words of Hinduism scholar Arvind Sharma, "We are not human beings having a spiritual experience; we are spiritual beings having a human experience."[16]

What happens after liberation? Hindu traditions are united in affirming that it is a state of infinite bliss, free from suffering and death, and ultimately incapable of being described adequately in words. Specific conceptions of liberation, however, vary, as one might expect, across the Hindu traditions. More non-dualistic systems of thought conceive of an awakening from the illusion of personal identity and a kind of absorption into the consciousness of the infinite: realizing that the "snake" of the world is really the "rope" of Brahman. Systems that have a more dualistic emphasis, though, envision a blissful heavenly existence with the Supreme Being, not unlike the concepts of salvation found in Western religions. In the Vaiṣṇava tradition, this realm of ultimate salvation is known as *Vaikuṇṭha*. Those who are utterly devoted to Lord Krishna enjoy his presence, singing his divine names eternally in Vaikuṇṭha.

Although liberation is the ultimate aim of existence, many Hindus view it as a more or less remote goal, which one will attain someday, most likely in a future lifetime. Much of Hindu ritual activity is focused upon the more immediate goal of attaining a state of relative happiness in one's next lifetime and, of course, within this lifetime itself. These more immediate goals are defined in Hindu texts as *dharma* (goodness, a life lived in harmony with the cosmos), *artha* (material power and wealth in order to secure happiness for oneself and one's family, as well as to support the good of society), and *kāma* (sensory enjoyment).

Hinduism in Practice

It is often stated that Hinduism places greater emphasis on right practice (*orthopraxy*) than on right belief (*orthodoxy*). As we have already seen, there is considerable latitude regarding the specific beliefs that Hindus might hold within the broad parameters of the worldview that we have described. And even this broad description, due to the limitations of space, has excluded a variety of systems of thought that fall under the umbrella of Hinduism. The variety of philosophical and theological positions available to Hindus is indeed vast—and mind-boggling to those who adhere to religions with a stronger emphasis on doctrinal orthodoxy as a measure of fidelity to tradition. It is, of course, typically the case that Hindus adhere to the system of thought and practice which has been passed on to them by their families. The children of Vaiṣṇavas thus typically grow up to be Vaiṣṇavas and so on. But it is also the case that, even within a single family, varieties of Hindu thought can co-exist. There is even a tradition of intermarriage, not only across Hindu traditions, but even between Hindus and non-Hindus, so long as essential practices are shared. In the western Indian region of Gujarat, it is not uncommon for Vaiṣṇavas and Jains to intermarry, despite the differences between Vaiṣṇava Hindu and Jain beliefs. The Vaiṣṇava-Jain couples I have had the occasion to query about this phenomenon have consistently pointed to one fact that makes their union work from a religious perspective: the fact that both Vaiṣṇavism and Jainism strongly enjoin vegetarianism. Practice matters far more in these unions than questions about whether the ultimate reality is personal or impersonal, one or many, and so on. It is remarkable, though, from a Western perspective—shaped by a religious history in which differences of opinion on such matters have, at times, been literally a matter of life and death—that such theological variety within families can not only exist, but can be relatively common in an Indian context.

This is not to say that conflict has never arisen among Hindus regarding matters of belief, or that such conflict has never led to actual, physical violence. But such occasions have been far less common in the history of Hinduism than in the histories of Western religions, where belief is more central. As long as their adherents have followed certain behavioral norms—in Hindu terms, as long as they have followed dharma—varied systems of belief have been free to flourish among Hindus.[17]

What are these norms? Hindu moral and social ethics, of course, center around the concept of dharma: the commitment to an essential ordering of existence according to basic principles of unity and harmony. "Unity" does not mean "uniformity." We shall see that Hinduism possesses a frank awareness that not all beings, nor even all human beings, are the same. We are each located differently within the spiritual universe, defined by proximity to the ultimate goal of liberation. It is not unity in the sense of uniformity that is valued in Hindu traditions. The ideal, rather, is of an *organic* unity, in which each part plays its role for the good of the whole.

Dharma, in terms of human duty, is of two basic kinds: *sādhāraṇā dharma* and *svadharma*. Sādhāraṇā dharma is universal duty, or universal morality: the basic principles which are binding upon all human beings. Svadharma is one's own duty: the duty particular to oneself, depending on one's specific life circumstances.

Sādhāraṇā dharma is often presented in terms of the *yamas* and *niyamas*, found in the *Yoga Sūtra* of Patañjali, an early guide to the practice of meditation. As we shall see later, the question of the relationship of yoga to Hinduism is one of the issues that are contested in contemporary Hindu discourse in America. The *Yoga Sūtra* and the Yoga tradition reflected in it of course date from a time before the coalescence of various *darśanas*, or systems Indian philosophy, to form what came eventually to be regarded as Hindu philosophy. Yoga was thus distinct, originally, from Vedānta. As Nicholson, however, has shown, later Vedāntic thinkers engaged with and commented on the *Yoga Sūtra* and incorporated it into the emergent worldview of Hinduism.[18] From a contemporary point of view, this source is certainly seen as an authoritative document for Hindus, and the *yamas* and *niyamas* are widely viewed as constituting universal Hindu morality.[19]

The *yamas*, taken collectively, constitute an ethical code of restraint based on the avoidance of actions regarded as unethical, or *adharmic*. *Niyamas* are injunctions to perform or cultivate actions or virtues which one ought to perform or cultivate. Yamas, in other words, tell one what *not* to do, and niyamas tell one what to do (and how to be).

There are five ethical principles listed under each of these categories. The *yamas* are the following:

1. *Ahiṃsā*: non-injury; freedom from even the desire to harm any living being; non-violence in thought, word, and deed.
2. *Satya*: truth; refraining from lying, breaking promises, or any form of dishonesty.
3. *Asteya*: non-stealing.
4. *Brahmacarya*: self-control in regard to one's sensory impulses, especially in the area of sexuality; celibacy, for one who is not married, and fidelity for one who is married.
5. *Aparigraha*: non-attachment; freedom from materialistic or covetous feelings.

The *niyamas* are the following:

1. *Śauca*: purity—inner and outer.
2. *Santośa*: contentment—material and spiritual.
3. *Tapas*: ascetic practice—disciplines that help control the body and mind.
4. *Svadhyāya*: self-study, including both the examination of one's conscience and the study of sacred texts and spiritual philosophies.
5. *Īśvara-praṇidhāna*: Contemplation of God; loving reflection on the divine reality; the cultivation of bhakti, or devotion.

Again, the yamas and niyamas collectively delineate a universal morality: a general set of principles all human beings ought to strive to uphold as best as possible. It is acknowledged in the Hindu legal literature, or *Dharma Śāstras*, that duties can sometimes conflict. There are situations in which one may need to engage in moral reasoning, to weigh different duties against one another. As one engages in such reflection, according to these texts, it is proper to take account not only of the general principles of Hindu morality, but also one's local customs, the words of wise persons, and one's own particular needs and desires.

In addition to universal morality, there is svadharma, which is particular to certain persons at certain times. Traditional Hindu thought divides human society vertically into four main groups, or *varṇas*, each of which has particular duties. It also divides human life horizontally into a series of stages, or *āśramas*. The performance of the duties specific to one's varṇa and āśrama constitutes one's svadharma. The four varṇas are further subdivided into *jātis*, or birth-based occupational groups, with specific duties attached to each. The varṇas and jātis together make up what is today called *caste*, or the *caste system*.

The *Brāhmaṇa* or "Brahmin" varṇa has duties that are connected primarily with intellectual and religious life. The *Kṣatriya* varṇa has duties which involve maintaining social order, such as military service, law enforcement, and administration. The *Vaiśya* varṇa has duties connected with economic production. Finally, the *Śūdra* varṇa has duties involving service and physical labor, as well as in areas such as medicine, that ensure physical health. Again, each varṇa is further divided into jātis, or hereditary sub-groups. Therefore, the Kṣatriya varṇa, for example, includes jātis that specialize in particular skills, such as archery, swordsmanship, wrestling, and so on.

It is not clear that the varṇas were always hereditary, but their conflation with jātis—which are birth-based groups akin, conceptually, to Western ideas of race or ethnicity—led to their being largely hereditary in practice by the time of the Buddha (roughly the fifth century BCE). There are some indications that, during the period of the composition of the *Ṛg Veda*, members of different occupational groups could be part of the same family.[20] In the teaching of the Buddha, as well as in the *Upaniṣads*, one finds an alternative doctrine of varṇa articulated, in which the basis for one's being a member of a particular varṇa is not one's birth (*jāti*), but one's personal qualities (*guṇa*).[21]

If the varṇas and their jātis make up a vertical division of society, the *āśramas*, or stages of life, can be seen to divide an individual lifetime horizontally, over the course of time. The first āśrama is *brahmacarya*, which one might note is also the yama which enjoins sensory restraint. In terms of the āśramas, it refers to the student stage of adolescence. Its name signifies an emphasis on sexual discipline during this stage. This stage commences with a ritual rebirth, or *upanayana*. This does not have anything to do with rebirth, in the sense of reincarnation. In the course of this ritual, a young person is invested with a sacred thread and is thus initiated into adulthood. This ritual is traditionally confined to Brahmins, who are for this reason also called "twice-born." The next stage is *garhasthya*—the stage of the householder—which begins with marriage and continues until one's children are married and one's household duties are fulfilled. The third stage, called *vanaprastha*—or literally, "forest dwelling"—is the stage of life in which one begins to withdraw from one's earlier responsibilities. In this stage, one is traditionally cared for by one's children, often sharing a home with an adult child and that child's spouse, and with one's grandchildren.

The fourth stage is *sannyāsa*—or renunciation—in which one completely renounces worldly ties in order to pursue the spiritual goals of life. Although it is listed as the fourth stage of life, this ascetic path, focused wholly upon spiritual pursuits, can be chosen at any time in life. Rather than the fourth stage out of four, it is better to see sannyāsa as an alternative to the first three, which can all be seen to make up what could be called the worldly life. The fourth stage, though, is for those who are intent upon liberation from the cycle of rebirth. These two streams of life—worldly and renunciatory—are traditionally called *pravṛtti* and *nivṛtti* in Hindu traditions. Most Hindus are in the pravṛtti stream, which involves pursuing a career, raising a family, and eventually retiring. Those who take up the nivṛtti path, though comparatively few in number, are highly regarded due to the sacrifice which they are seen as making for the sake of spiritual realization. In many Hindu traditions, this sacrifice is represented by the wearing of an orange robe, the color of which evokes a sacrificial flame. Whenever one refers to Hindu *monks* or *nuns*, one is referring to men or women who have undertaken the life of sannyāsa. Sannyāsīs and sannyāsinīs—monks and nuns—belong to traditions of renunciation, or orders, and follow a *guru*, or teacher, in a spiritual lineage.

The Issue of Caste

The system of varṇas and jātis—today known collectively as *caste*—has often been depicted in scholarly literature and textbooks on Hinduism as a rigid, inflexible, oppressive social system that essentially determines for life which occupation one may hold, whom one may marry, where one may live, and with whom one may associate. It has been depicted as particularly cruel to those who are regarded as being at its bottom—not so much the Śūdras, or servants, as the fifth, *asparśa*, or "untouchable" castes, whose occupations, like cremating corpses and disposing of human waste, render them impure in the eyes of mainstream Hindu society, placing them even below the Śūdras.

While this depiction of caste is not inaccurate, it is also not the complete truth. Depending on how it is presented, it can involve a number of distortions and assumptions that lend themselves to a gross mischaracterization of Hinduism as a religious tradition. This stratified social system is often presented as something that is intrinsic to and essentially identical with Hinduism as a whole. There are numerous systems of Hindu thought and practice, though, to which this system is either irrelevant, or which specifically reject caste prejudice—or *casteism*—as a significant moral defect, especially for one who is intent upon the spiritual path and strives to see the divine in all beings. Hinduism, as a whole, is not simply equal to caste. It even includes significant currents that oppose caste-based prejudice.

There have been Hindu movements for many centuries which have resisted caste prejudice, and resistance to caste structures by Hindus has long been part of Hinduism. Many Hindu teachers and movements—from ancient times to the present—have rejected notions of caste as involving the superiority of some persons over others. Examples of individuals and groups which have opposed caste-based prejudice include the fourteenth- to fifteenth-century figure Swami Ramananda, the founder of the largest monastic order in India, Kabir (1440–1518), Ravidas (fifteenth to sixteenth century), and many more. Groups like the Śaiva Lingayats of the southern state of Karnataka, the Vaiṣṇava Vairagi ascetics, and more recently the Rāmnāmis of Chhattisgarh have been sharply critical of caste.[22] It could be said that resistance to caste-based discrimination has been at least as much of a feature of Hindu society as has reinforcement of the caste system as essential to the social order.

The Hindu movements of resistance to caste-based discrimination have, for the most part, been inspired by the teachings of the equality and inherent divinity of all beings that can be found throughout authoritative Hindu texts. In the *Bhagavad Gītā*, for example, it is explicitly said that it is possible, through devotion to Krishna, for any person, regardless of caste or gender, to attain liberation.[23] The fourth chapter of the *Chāndogya Upaniṣad*, too, famously recounts the story of Satyakāma Jabala, who is accepted by his teacher, Haridrumata Gautama, as a Brahmin—regarded traditionally as the "highest" Hindu caste—on the basis of his honesty, despite the fact that, in terms of jāti, or birth-caste, his mother is a servant woman and his father is of an unknown caste. This is in a text that is at the heart of Hindu orthodoxy, regarded as part of the *Vedas* themselves.

In regard to Hinduism in America, in particular, scholar Joyce Burkhalter Flueckiger notes that many diasporic Hindus, as well as middle-class Hindus in India, find the topic of caste to be a source of embarrassment.[24] It is less and less the case, as the economy of India develops and more egalitarian ways of thinking become predominant, that Hindus actually practice those occupations traditionally associated with their varṇa or jāti. What is the jāti for a computer engineer? Or for an astrophysicist? These occupations did not exist when this system of social organization began to emerge centuries ago. Many Hindus see casteism as an unfortunate holdover from the past and not as intrinsic to the practice of Hinduism.

While caste prejudice is widely criticized—and, it should be noted, is still widely practiced, especially in Indian villages—caste, as such, as a form of social organization, is quite deeply rooted in Indian society. As Flueckiger notes, jāti does not refer only to one's traditional occupation. In practice, caste can be seen as akin to an ethnic identity. In her words:

> This *jati* identity is assumed to permeate one's everyday action, from hygiene to food, from dress to ritual and festivals. In a discussion about caste with some university professors in Hyderabad a few years ago, several of them insisted that caste was no longer relevant on a day-to-day basis in their lives. However, when the discussion shifted to an upcoming dinner celebration, a comment was made about the delicious shrimp dish Mudaliars (a South Indian *jati*) made. Here, *jati* was an ethnic designation rather than one of hierarchical difference.[25]

It is also unclear that the complete elimination of caste, as Flueckiger characterizes it, is entirely to be desired. It could be that elimination of caste, as a marker of community membership, is as wrongheaded as attempts to turn the United States into a "colorblind" society, if this means that the only way to overcome prejudices against persons different from oneself is not to learn to appreciate those differences, but to pretend that they do not exist. Another dimension of caste that is not often mentioned in textbook accounts of Hinduism is the role it plays in providing a certain measure of security and social cohesion. Arvind, an elderly man with whom I discussed this issue, pointed to the fact that, in his youth, the elders in his local caste ensured that all of the families of that caste were cared for when they ran into financial difficulties or other personal problems. And in earlier eras, when caste was much more closely tied to occupation, it provided job security by assuring that one had a trade to pursue that would not be taken away by someone else.

On the other hand, persons who have been victimized by casteism—particularly from castes traditionally regarded as "low," who now identify themselves as *Dālits*, meaning, "the oppressed"—often argue that caste itself is the problem: that this way of dividing humanity is itself inherently violent and oppressive. The mid-twentieth-century Dālit leader, B.R. Ambedkar (1891–1958), who authored the Constitution of

India, saw caste as a form of violence, and also saw it as having been so thoroughly tied up with Hinduism as a whole that it was impossible to remain within the Hindu tradition and become free from caste prejudice. He therefore led other members of his community in a mass conversion to Buddhism. "Ambedkarite Buddhists" remain a major force to the present day. Ambedkar's work is continued in America by Dālit activists like Thenmozhi Soundararajan, an artist and journalist who uses her work to express resistance to casteism and draw attention to the ongoing casteism that occurs even in the Hindu American context.[26]

Hindus of "higher" castes who have not experienced the kind of oppression experienced by Dālits, but who are nevertheless sensitive to the suffering casteism has produced, are more often inclined to see caste not as intrinsic to Hinduism, but as something that is distinct and separable from Hindu religiosity, and as an outdated social system that may have worked in ancient times, but no longer applies to the contemporary world. This view is anticipated by Swami Vivekananda when he describes

FIGURE 9 *Bhimrao Ramji Ambedkar served as India's law minister from 1947–1951, where he championed the low-caste Hindus called Harijans, also known as the "untouchables" (Photo by Bettmann via Getty Images).*

caste as "simply a crystallized social institution, which after doing its service is now filling the atmosphere of India with its stench, and it can only be removed by giving back to the people their lost social individuality."[27] Many Hindus view caste as deeply rooted in Indian society, but as something that can and should be discarded by Hindus in America, where inter-caste, inter-ethnic, and inter-religious, marriages, for example, are not at all uncommon. At the same time, as the experiences of Soundararajan and others serve to demonstrate, even in America, the "baggage" of casteism has not been completely left behind and remains an issue in the Hindu and wider Indian American community.

The Yogas

Beyond the universal moral norms of sādhāraṇā dharma and the more localized constraints of svadharma (whether conceived in terms of caste or in more personal terms, as pertaining to the particular life situations of an individual), another important dimension of Hindu practice is *yoga*.

The term *yoga*, in this context, does not refer—or at least it does not refer exclusively, nor even primarily—to the system of physical postures and stretches that is the first thing most people in the West think about when they come across this term. A yoga is a spiritual discipline, intended, typically, to advance one toward the goal of moksha—of liberation from the cycle of rebirth through the attainment of Self-realization. Traditionally, there have been a great variety of yogas developed over the course of the history of the Hindu traditions. They have often been grouped into a set of four categories. This categorization was systematized in the modern era by Swami Vivekananda. These four yogas can be practiced individually or in tandem.

The philosophy which underlies this fourfold categorization of spiritual practice is that the variety of human psychological types lends itself to variety in the spiritual life as well. No single path is required for all to follow. Each of us reaches liberation in the way that is appropriate to us individually. This system of four yogas is also a way to conceptualize the great variety of spiritual practice that one finds not only in Hindu traditions but indeed in all of the religions of the world. Each tradition can be categorized in terms of the yoga that is predominant within it.

Karma yoga, the spiritual discipline of action, consists of performing one's duties—one's dharma—without attachment to the results. One, in other words, does good, not out of hope for the karmic reward which typically comes from such actions, but in a spirit of renunciation. One offers one's good works, as it were, as a sacrifice. While this practice originally refers to the performance of the ritual actions enjoined in the early Vedic literature, in the modern period, it has come to refer to *seva*, or service rendered to help suffering beings—again, with no thought of recognition or reward. This emphasis on karma yoga as service rendered to suffering beings is especially strong in the teaching of Swami Vivekananda, whose Ramakrishna Order shocked many Hindus in India when its monks, departing from the traditional role of renouncers as people focused exclusively on study and meditation, began to provide concrete social services to people of all backgrounds.

Jñāna yoga, the spiritual discipline of knowledge, consists of using one's intellect in order to differentiate what is real from what is unreal—to perceive Brahman in one's experience, and to differentiate it from *māyā*, or appearance. This is a practice traditionally associated with monastic life, although, in the modern period, it has come to appeal to intellectuals from all walks of life. It has been seen by many Hindu teachers who have come to America as a path particularly appealing to people of a rationalistic or scientific bent, given that it does not focus so much on the personal concept of a deity as on an impersonal process of transforming consciousness.

Bhakti yoga, the spiritual discipline of devotion, is by far the most popular of the yogas. It is a pervasive feature of Hindu religiosity. Most of what a Westerner would recognize as Hindu religious activity falls under the heading of bhakti. In bhakti yoga, one cultivates a relationship of intense loving devotion toward the Supreme Being in the form of a specific deity. The deity which one chooses to make the object of one's devotion is one's *iṣṭa-devatā* (a term that literally means "chosen deity," or "preferred deity"). In terms of Hinduism, broadly speaking, it is possible for any of the deities to be one's chosen deity, for Brahman is infinite, and cannot be confined to any one form. Specific bhakti traditions, though, focus upon a particular deity as identical to the Supreme Being. The most popular of these are the already mentioned Vaiṣṇava, Śaiva, and Śākta forms of Hindu practice, focused, respectively, on Vishnu, Shiva, and Shakti.

The practice of bhakti yoga involves the cultivation and expression of devotion. One way to do this is through singing devotional songs to one's chosen deity. Devotional songs are called *bhajans*, and group singing of bhajans is known as *kīrtan*. One also cultivates and expresses bhakti through *pūjā*, or worship, typically utilizing a *mūrti*, or image of one's chosen deity.

The images of the many deities of Hinduism are one of the characteristics of this tradition that often come to mind whenever it is mentioned in a Western context. It has also been a frequent source of conflict between Hindus and non-Hindus, particularly Muslims and Christians, through history and in the contemporary period as well. The Abrahamic religions—Judaism, Christianity, and Islam—are strictly monotheistic and aniconic; that is, they teach that there is one and only one God and that God is not to be represented in a physical form (or "graven image," as the biblical injunction states, though some Christian traditions, such as Roman Catholicism, do make extensive use of religious imagery). The use of images in the practice of bhakti yoga is thus widely seen by adherents of these traditions as "idolatry" or "idol worship," and as polytheistic, given the great variety of the Hindu deities. The appearance of the Hindu deities is also something that some find alarming, due to the fact that these deities are often represented as human beings, but with multiple pairs of arms, as well as multiple faces or heads, and sometimes with non-human heads, like Ganesha's elephant head.

FIGURE 10 *Lord Ganesha, Washington Kali Temple, Burtonsville, Maryland (Photo by Jeffery D. Long).*

Some Hindus in the modern period have sought to mitigate and defuse the potential of the Hindu deities to offend the religious sensibilities of non-Hindus by emphasizing the Vedantic idea of the ultimate unity of Brahman. It is even sometimes argued that Hinduism is monotheistic, but the Hindu doctrine of the unity of Brahman is distinct from Abrahamic monotheism. As Flueckiger explains:

> With all this diversity [of deities], there also coexists for some Hindus the concept of the singular *brahman*, ultimate reality that has no shape, form, or mythology, that exists beyond the created world. And it is to this concept that Hindus are referring when they say, for example, "God is one," or "There are many forms and names of god, but there is only one." But "god" here is not the theistic [concept] that the term implies in English; rather, it is an Upanishadic concept developed by Vedantic philosophers who argue that reality is singular: the created and non-created worlds [or the manifest and the unmanifest]—and *brahman* is that singular identity that cannot be known except by yogis who follow strict discipline and practice. Thus, when a Hindu says, "God is one," this is very different from a Muslim, Christian, or Jew who may say, "There is only one god."[28]

Brahman, in other words, is not a type of entity of which more than one could conceivably exist. It is being itself. In the milieu in which the Abrahamic religions arose, there were societies in which having many deities was the religious norm. What differentiated Judaism, Christianity, and Islam, as forms of monotheism, from these other religions, was precisely their affirmation that it is proper to worship only one deity. In early Christianity, and in some forms of Christianity even today, the belief about the many gods of other traditions was not that these gods were mythological or did not exist, while the one God did, but that these other gods were actual beings of a demonic nature who were competing with the one true deity for human worship and allegiance. This way of thinking is utterly foreign to Hinduism.

From a Hindu perspective, Brahman is not one being among others in a group among whom there can be competition for loyalty. Rather, Brahman is the underlying unifying reality, not only behind the many deities, but of all existence. All beings are manifestations of Brahman, at least in the non-dualistic, or Advaita tradition of Vedānta, as well as, in a somewhat different sense, in the qualified non-dualism that underlies much of Vaiṣṇava practice. The many deities are simply different ways of accessing, in a personal form, the supreme reality of Brahman, in order to enter into the saving relationship of devotion, of bhakti, with that supreme reality.

Brahman, as an abstract concept, is difficult to comprehend, much less relate to in a loving fashion. This is the function served by the deities: to be concrete manifestations, with a personal character, to which bhakti can be directed and from engagement with whom it can be evoked.

The use of images in pūjā is an extension of this same basic philosophy. It is much easier to visualize a personal deity if one has a concrete image in front of oneself, with which one is able to interact in concrete, tangible ways. Most pūjā rituals are enactments of the idea that the deity has come into one's home as an honored guest. First, the deity is installed in the image through a ritual of breathing life into it—*prāṇapratiṣṭhā*. The image is thus becoming, for the purposes of the ritual, a real person. The image is then bathed, clothed, offered food and drink, and entertained with song. At the end, the deity departs back to the heavenly realm and the physical food and drink that have been offered are consumed by the worshipers as *prasād*, or divine grace.

Given just how different, aesthetically and theologically, the practice of bhakti yoga is from most Western religiosity, one might expect this style of Hindu practice—the most popular style in India—to be the least appealing to Westerners. We shall see, though, that in the history of Hinduism in America, bhakti-based traditions have had a considerable appeal. One of the largest and most recognizable of the global Hindu movements is the Hare Krishna movement, identified most with ISKCON. Arising out of Gauḍīya, Bengali Vaishnava tradition, this movement, with its emphasis on ecstatic chanting and cultivation of love for Krishna, has been viewed by many Americans as particularly exotic. But it has also attracted many who have come from devotional Christian backgrounds (as well as a fair number of Jewish devotees) who have become alienated, for various reasons, from the tradition of their upbringing, but for whom devotion to a personal divinity is an absolutely essential element of spiritual life and practice.

FIGURE 11 *Prasad for Śivarātrī, Hindu American Religious Institute, New Cumberland, Pennsylvania (Photo by Jeffery D. Long).*

Rāja yoga, the royal spiritual discipline, also known as *dhyāna yoga*, the spiritual discipline of meditation, is the yoga most closely associated with yoga as this has come to be known in the Western world. Typically, the chief textual guide to the practice of dhyāna yoga is taken to be the *Yoga Sūtra* of Patañjali, a text composed, in its current form, in the early centuries of the Common Era. Patañjali defines the practice of yoga as *citta-vṛtti-nirodhaḥ*: "calming the modifications of the mind."[29] This essentially means controlling one's thought processes: quieting one's internal mental "chatter" and reining in one's thoughts and emotions. The idea is that mental and emotional activity obscures one's perception of the inmost Self. By stilling this activity, one enables the Self to shine forth, thus accelerating the process of realization.

As we shall see, in the modern period, and particularly as it has been transmitted into the Western world by a variety of Hindu teachers, Rāja yoga, with its accompanying system of *āsanas*, or physical postures (designed to help calm the body and keep it from being a distraction), takes on a life of its own as a system of total mental, physical, and spiritual well-being. This system can be seen as a synthesis of Patañjali's system of mental cultivation and the Haṭha Yoga tradition of the Śaiva Nāth Yogis, which places a strong emphasis on physical postures and practices.

Hindu History

Hinduism is the oldest of the world's major religions. Its roots can be traced to the Indus Valley Civilization—a civilization contemporary with those of ancient Egypt and Mesopotamia. In fact, the people of the Indus Valley traded with the Sumerians of Mesopotamia, whose civilization is the oldest known to human history. The precise legacy of the Indus Valley Civilization in regard to Hinduism is difficult to discern because its writing system has yet to be deciphered. Certainly, a number of physical artifacts from this civilization are evocative of specific dimensions of what we now know as Hindu practice. Some scholars have suggested that the Śaiva and Śākta traditions have roots in this civilization, along with the practice (and therefore, perhaps, the philosophy) of yoga.[30]

Hinduism has no single founder or institutional location. Unlike most world religions, its history cannot be traced to a single person, who established a community which then subsequently branched out into various sub-sects. For Hinduism, the process has been almost the opposite, with a variety of traditions gradually coalescing under the concept of Vedic authority—a concept which itself allows for considerable variety, as we have seen.

FIGURE 12 *Mohenjo-Daro, or "Mound of the Dead," is an ancient Indus Valley Civilization city. Mohenjo-Daro was abandoned in the nineteenth century BCE as the Indus Valley Civilization declined, and the site was not rediscovered until the 1920s. Built around 2500 BCE, it was one of the largest settlements of the ancient Indus Valley Civilization, and one of the world's earliest major urban settlements, contemporaneous with the civilizations of ancient Egypt, Mesopotamia, Minoan Crete, and Norte Chico (Photo by SM Rafiq Photography via Getty Images).*

More certain knowledge of Hindu history begins with the *Vedas*, which, unlike the writings of the Indus Valley Civilization, are in a known language—Sanskrit—and which have, in fact, been studied in great depth for many centuries by Hindu scholars, and for roughly the last two centuries by scholars in the Western world as well.

It was once theorized that the Indus Valley Civilization was destroyed by invaders from Central Asia who spoke an Indo-European language and called themselves the *Arya*, meaning "noble" or "civilized." Unfortunately, there were Westerners in the nineteenth and early twentieth centuries who romanticized the idea of the ancient marauding Aryan warriors. Thus was born the highly destructive myth of the "pure Aryan race," which became the basis for ideologies such as Nazism. More recent, up-to-date archaeological evidence has revealed that the civilization of the Indus Valley, which was at its technological height from 2600 to 1900 BCE, declined due to natural causes, including a two-hundred-year-long drought and declining trade with the Sumerians.

The idea of an "Aryan invasion" of ancient India has been superseded, in the work of most scholars, by the idea that there was a gradual, more peaceful migration on the part of a relatively small number of persons from Central Asia who brought Indo-European language and culture into India some time either during or after the gradual decline of the Indus Valley civilization from its technological height. The intent of this theory, which has recently been confirmed by new genetic studies, is to explain the fact that Sanskrit bears close resemblances to ancient European languages, such as Greek, Latin, and Celtic and Germanic languages.[31]

On the other hand, some have argued for an Indian point of origin for the Indo-European family of languages, although the weight of scholarship tends to lean against this. This remains a contested issue in some circles. It has been a politically charged debate from the beginning, when the "Aryan Invaders" were taken by groups like the Nazis as forebears of a "superior white race."

In any case, the decline of the Indus Valley Civilization seems to have been followed by a more nomadic phase among the peoples of northern India. The center of gravity of Indian culture gradually shifted eastward, toward the Gaṅga, or Ganges river valley. Beginning around 900 BCE, a second wave of urbanization began in India, this time in the Ganges valley. The Ganges region remains a major center of Indian cultural life to the present day.

Simultaneously with the rise of cities in the Ganges river valley, civilization also thrived in the southern portion of the Indian subcontinent. The culture of the Tamil-speaking peoples, from the southernmost tip of India, is at least as ancient as that in the north. Hinduism as a whole has drawn from cultural sources throughout the subcontinent, interacting, integrating, and exchanging ideas and practices.

The period of the second urbanization of India—roughly the first millennium BCE—is also the period of the composition of the *Upaniṣads* and the first articulations of Vedanta, which would eventually become the dominant philosophical system of Hinduism. This was an extremely rich period, in terms of the development of philosophy and religion. While the earlier Vedic texts are focused primarily on the performance of rituals intended to maintain the cosmic order, the thought of the later Vedic texts—the *Upaniṣads*—is focused more upon a process of inward transformation, and of the realization of the identity of the Self (ātman) and the supreme reality known as Brahman.

This inward emphasis corresponds with the emergence of the institution of renunciation—or *sannyāsa*—which, as we have seen, eventually comes to be enshrined as the fourth āśrama, or stage of life. This ideal of renunciation is also pursued, in this period, in the Jain and Buddhist traditions. More will be said momentarily about these two traditions, as well as Sikhism, as their histories have been intertwined closely with that of Hinduism in America.

The latter half of the first millennium BCE marks a period of Buddhist and Jain ascendancy in India, particularly with the conversion to Buddhism of the Emperor Aśoka. Aśoka was the third ruler of the Maurya Dynasty, and reigned over most of South Asia during the third century BCE.

In response to this rise of Buddhism, the Brahmin priesthood tasked with upholding Vedic traditions began to compile their thought into texts. This process included the organization of the Vedic literature itself, as well as the compilation of much of the smṛti literature, mentioned earlier, such as the *Rāmāyaṇa*, the *Mahābhārata*, the *Pūrāṇas*, the *Dharma Śāstras*, and the root texts, or *sūtras*, of the Vedic systems of philosophy.

The Vedic systems of philosophy are traditionally listed as Sāṃkhya (which is a system of metaphysical psychology), Yoga (the root text, or sūtra, of which is the *Yoga Sūtra* of Patañjali, mentioned earlier), Nyāya (a system of logic), Vaiśeṣika (a system of cosmology), Mīmāṃsā (the philosophy of the Vedic ritualists), and Vedanta. These originally independent schools of thought have gradually become assimilated to Vedanta, which now draws upon all of them.[32]

While the emphasis of the *Upaniṣads* is on the attainment of liberation—mokṣa—through a process of achieving transformative knowledge—jñāna yoga—the emphasis of much of the smṛti literature is on bhakti. It is in the early centuries of the Common Era that theistic systems of Hinduism—the Vaishnava, Shaiva, and Shakta systems, as well as others—become more prominent. A bhakti movement—beginning, significantly, among members of the so-called "lower" castes—transforms Hinduism during this period into something closer to the Hindu traditions of today, with a strong emphasis on devotional worship, songs, and poetry, and visual representations in temples of Hindu deities. The poetry of the Vaiṣṇava Aḷvars of southern India, among others, takes on a status among regular Hindu devotees comparable to that of the *Vedas* themselves. In fact, the collected poetry of the Aḷvars is considered in the Śri Vaiṣṇava tradition, established by Rāmānuja, to be the "fifth Veda."

The coming of Islam, starting around the end of the first millennium CE, and continuing in the first half of the second millennium, had a major impact on Hinduism. Temples and centers of religious learning were destroyed in northern India, while Indian Buddhism essentially ceased to exist in this period.[33] This dimension of Indian history is often emphasized in communal discourse in the contemporary period, when an effort is made to instill suspicion and fear of Islam in Hindus.

The other part of the story, though, is that, gradually, as Islam settled into the religious life of the subcontinent, a great deal of mutual borrowing and creative transformation occurred which brought Hindus and Muslims together, particularly between adherents of the bhakti movement of Hinduism and the mystical Sufi movement of Islam. Sufism emphasizes, much like Yoga and Vedānta, the direct experience of divinity through spiritual practice, and has often been viewed with suspicion by upholders of Islamic orthodoxy. A third, distinct new tradition—Sikhism—also emerged in the middle of the second millennium, drawing much of its inspiration from both Hindu and Islamic traditions. The Sikh faith is a powerful embodiment of the ideal long taught in Hindu texts that, while truth is one, the ways to its realization are many. God accepts people of all faiths.

In the late fifteenth and the early sixteenth centuries, European merchants and missionaries began to come to India in ever larger numbers. There had been some limited contact between the West and India since antiquity. Although they cannot be confirmed and are believed by many to be legendary, there are stories of Pythagoras and Plato—and even Jesus Christ—traveling to India and being inspired by its philosophies and spiritual practices.

Alexander of Macedon's invasion of India and his establishment of Hellenistic kingdoms in the north-western part of the subcontinent in the fourth century BCE led to more extensive trade, and Indian texts after Alexander's time display awareness of Westerners. In these Indian texts, Westerners are typically referred to as "Yavanas" (a term that refers specifically to Greeks—literally "Ionians"), "Romakas" (Romans), and "Mlecchas" (a more general term meaning "barbarians"). The renowned Italian traveler, Marco Polo, chronicled his stay in India in the early fourteenth century. But it was with the coming of the Portuguese—who were soon followed by the Dutch, the French, and of course, the British—that the Indian encounter with the West began in earnest.

India, for most of its history, was a land of fabled wealth. European powers were keen to establish trading centers along its coasts. Portuguese centers such as Goa, Daman, and Diu, the French port at Pondicherry, and the British port at Kolkata (then spelled Calcutta) were among the first European settlements in India in the colonial period. During the early phase of colonization, the Mughal Empire held sway over most of the subcontinent, and the ability of the Europeans to project power into India was quite limited. In the eighteenth century, though, the Mughal Empire entered a period of decline. More than any other power, it was the British who stepped into the vacuum which was thus created. Taking advantage of divisions among various smaller kingdoms, and often pulled into local conflicts by the need to make alliances to secure their trading posts, the British—under the auspices of the British East India Company—had become a major power in India by the end of the eighteenth century.

The British and other Europeans brought with them new ideas, new philosophies, and new forms of social organization. As they became the dominant power in the subcontinent, the Hindu traditions found themselves challenged by many aspects of Western thought. The creative ways in which Hindu leaders addressed this challenge led to the rise of modern Hinduism.

As Hindu intellectuals in India engaged with Western thought, many Western intellectuals simultaneously found themselves both challenged and inspired by Indian thought, particularly as knowledge of India began to trickle back to the West in the form of translations of Sanskrit texts into European languages.

Ironically, even as certain Western intellectuals became quite deeply impressed by ancient Indian thought—such as the Romantics of Europe and the Unitarians of America—other Westerners went about essentially enslaving the Indians of their own time.

This is a paradox that overshadows the history of Hinduism in America to the present day. While some Westerners are fascinated by, and even deeply respectful toward, Hinduism and Indian culture, the West continues to exert dominance over much of the rest of the world, including India, and racism and attitudes of religious and cultural superiority continue to pervade the atmosphere of relations between India and the West.

This is one major reason why the "convergence of worlds" to which the subtitle of this book refers has not always been an easy or pleasant process. The points of contact between the Western world and Hinduism have often been sites of conflict and contention.

In our next chapter, we shall begin to explore and unfold the complex history of this convergence. But first, it will be worthwhile to spend time familiarizing ourselves with the other traditions that have come from India that form part of the history of Hinduism and that continue to shape, in a variety of ways, the experience of Hinduism in America. Again, religious boundaries have often been far more open and porous in India than one might expect if one thinks of religions as mutually exclusive. Jainism, Buddhism, and Sikhism, as well as Islam, Christianity, and Zoroastrianism, have all shaped and been shaped by what we now call Hinduism, and Indian American adherents of these traditions share certain experiences in common that fall within the purview of this book.

Jainism

Jainism is a tradition with a claim to antiquity that rivals that of Hinduism itself. Similarly to Hindu traditions, Jainism teaches that the cosmos has always existed and that it runs based on certain eternal laws or principles. Much as in Hinduism, the cosmos is seen as passing through a series of cycles. Over the course of each of these cycles, twenty-four beings are born on the earth who discover the path to liberation from the cycle of rebirth, the *mokṣa mārga*. These beings are known as *Tīrthaṅkaras*: those who have created a "ford" or a crossing to take those who follow it across the river of death and rebirth to the further shore of liberation. In our cosmic epoch, the twenty-fourth Tīrthaṅkara has already come: an historical figure named Mahāvīra, whom Jain texts claim lived from roughly 599 to 527 BCE, and who is believed to have been a contemporary of the Buddha.

Jainism emphasizes a very strict practice of *ahiṃsā*, or nonviolence in thought, word, and deed. The Jain community is divided into ascetics, both female and male, who practice ahiṃsā to the highest degree humanly possible, and householders, also both female and male, who materially support the ascetics. Jains are strict vegetarians, avoiding even some vegetables—those which must be pulled up by the root in order to be eaten, thus doing violence to the entire plant.

Jain relations with the larger Hindu community have historically ranged from hostility, such as when Śaiva kings in southern India exiled many Jains from the region, to close friendship, such as in the western state of Gujarat, where it has not been uncommon for Jains and Vaiṣṇavas to intermarry. Jainism exerted a considerable impact on the thought of Mohandas K. Gandhi.

In America, Jains have frequently partnered with Hindus in the building and maintenance of temple facilities. In such temples, a portion of the building is dedicated to the housing of images of Jain Tīrthaṅkaras. In some temples, such as the Hindu-Jain Temple of Pittsburgh, the Jain and Hindu images are in distinct sections of the building (though it is very easy to move from one to the other, so the distinction is not intended to create an impenetrable barrier of separation between the two). In other temples, like HARI in New Cumberland, Pennsylvania, and the Lehigh Valley Temple Society in Allentown, the Jain images are fully integrated with the Hindu images.

While Jainism in America is distinct from Hinduism, the two are closely interwoven and sometimes even integrated in practice.

Buddhism

Buddhism had largely died out in India by the medieval period. It has only been revived in modern India by the Ambedkarite Dālit tradition and by Tibetan refugees who fled to India after Tibet was invaded by Communist China in the 1950s. In America, Buddhism is more often associated, in the popular imagination, with China, Korea, Japan, and Southeast Asia than it is with India.

Buddhism bears a number of resemblances to Jainism, which Buddhism scholar Richard Gombrich argues exerted a strong influence upon the Buddha.[34] Like Jainism, Buddhism teaches that the cosmos passes through a beginningless and endless series of cycles, during which great enlightened beings—*Buddhas*, or "awakened ones"—appear to show living beings the way to become free from the cycle of rebirth and the inevitable suffering that accompanies it.

Buddhism is distinguished by what could be called a highly pragmatic and metaphysically minimalist approach to spirituality. Rather than positing a self that becomes free from suffering, the Buddha teaches that the concept of "self" is itself at the root of our problems. We tend to reify our experiences into abstract concepts and then mistakenly place importance on those concepts.

Buddhism does traditionally teach the doctrine of rebirth, so its teaching of "no self" does not amount to a materialist denial of the existence of the soul—a concept that the Buddha explicitly rejected. It is a communication, rather, of the insight that what we conventionally think of as "self" is a *process* rather than a *thing*. The "self" can thus be changed. We are capable of transforming ourselves, through diligent practice, gradually getting insight and awakening to the true nature of reality: our true, awakened, "Buddha Nature."

It is generally agreed that the Theravāda Buddhist tradition, predominant in Sri Lanka and Southeast Asia, is the older thread of Buddhist teaching. The more prominent form of Buddhism in East Asia is called Mahāyāna. It emphasizes compassion and the ideal of the *bodhisattva*. In Mahāyāna thought, a bodhisattva, or "awakening being," is still in the process of becoming a fully "awakened being," or Buddha, but being a bodhisattva is a praiseworthy goal in its own right, for bodhisattvas, although they are so near to awakening that they could easily choose to "cut the cord" of attachment to the material world and free themselves from the cycle of rebirth, they choose, out of their great compassion, to remain in the cycle and assist other beings on the path to freedom. In the Gelugpa school of Tibetan Buddhism, the Dalai Lama and other heads of Tibetan monastic orders are believed to be living, incarnate bodhisattvas.

America's fascination with Buddhism has closely paralleled its fascination with Hinduism. Meditative practices such as those prominent in the Zen traditions of Mahāyāna Buddhism and the mindfulness and insight meditation practices of Theravāda Buddhism have also been particularly attractive to Americans. This can be seen as paralleling the popularity of Yoga and meditatively focused movements like Vedanta and Transcendental Meditation. At the same time, it has, to some extent, led to an assumption by many Americans that Buddhism simply is meditation, abstracted from the kind of lived practice that one finds in traditional Buddhist societies—practice which is in many ways akin to Hindu practice. Multiple deities, rituals, and so on have been as much a part of Buddhism as of Hinduism, traditionally, but have been less prominent in American Buddhism. Zen, interestingly, is the Japanese pronunciation of the Chinese character for *Chan*, which is itself the Chinese pronunciation of *dhyāna*, the Sanskrit term for meditation. Indian Buddhist monks carried this practice to China.

Sikhism

The Sikh faith arose with the teaching Guru Nanak (1469–1539), the first in a series of ten gurus, or teachers, the last of whom was Guru Gobind Singh (1666–1708). By the proclamation of Guru Gobind Singh, after his death, the guru of the community became its scripture, the *Adi Granth*, known thenceforeward as the *Guru Granth Sahib*. This sacred text is a compilation of the writings of both Hindu and Muslim saints, as well as writings by the Sikh gurus themselves. A copy of this text is kept in the place of highest honor in a place of Sikh worship, called a *gurdwara*.

The Sikh tradition shares many features of Hinduism and Islam. Much of its terminology is shared with Hinduism, as well as its basic cosmology of karma and rebirth, and its soteriology of liberation from the rebirth process. The figure of the guru, the living teacher, is of particular importance to both Sikhs and Hindus. Many of the Hindu traditions which have come to America have been centered on particular gurus, and have emphasized the personal connection between an individual spiritual aspirant and his or her guru.

Like Islam, though, Sikhism is aniconic. It does not deploy images in worship. It is also monotheistic in a sense closer to that which one finds in monotheistic religions, emphasizing the unity of God. It also does not emphasize asceticism to the degree that the Hindu, Buddhist, or Jain traditions do, having a strong focus on serving the human community and doing good in the world.

One of the distinctive elements for which Sikhs are known in America is the practice by many Sikh men of wearing a turban and growing a beard. These practices trace to Guru Gobind Singh, who established a group of spiritual warriors known as the *khalsa*, or "pure ones." Members of the *khalsa* are consecrated to God, so they do not shave or cut their hare. The turban is a way to keep the hair clean and out of the way in day-to-day life.

Relations between Sikhs and Hindus in America vary greatly. At least two temples in the United States include shared facilities, akin to those shared by Jains and Hindus. In these temples, the *Guru Granth Sahib* is kept in a special location where Sikhs can gather for its reading as they would do in a gurdwara. It is more often the case in the United States, though, that gurdwaras are separate facilities from Hindu temples.

Zoroastrianism

A little known religion in the Western world, Zoroastrianism originated in ancient Iran. It has a community of practitioners in India, though, primarily in the region of the city of Bombay-Mumbai. A Zoroastrian guru, though, Meher Baba (1894–1969), found a following in the 1960s in the Western world, drawing from the same countercultural milieu that was attracted to a variety of Hindu teachers during the same period. His most famous disciple was Pete Townshend, the lead guitarist from the popular British rock band, The Who. However, the world's most famous Zoroastrian is undoubtedly Farrokh Bulsara (1946–91), better known as Freddie Mercury, the lead singer of another popular British rock band, Queen.

Zoroastrianism is genealogically related to Hinduism—specifically, to the ancient tradition whose beliefs and practices are recorded in the *Vedas*. The centerpiece of worship in this ancient religion is the sacred fire—the embodiment, in Vedic teaching, of the deity Agni. The sacred fire is central to Hindu life rituals to the present day, such as weddings and funerals, which do not seem to have changed considerably for thousands of years. Zarathustra, an ancient priest of the Iranian iteration of this tradition, was a theological reformer, giving a monotheistic interpretation to this tradition, in which Ahura Mazda, the Wise Lord is the Supreme Being. Zoroastrianism influenced the Abrahamic religions through having been the state religion of the Persian Empire for hundreds of years, shaping Abrahamic concepts such as an "enemy," or Satan figure who is opposed to God, the idea of linear time, and the idea of a resurrection of the dead at the end of time. Its Vedic roots are still evident as well, though, in its ritual practice, which is centered upon the sacred fire, as the manifest form of Ahura Mazda. Just as Hinduism, Buddhism, and Jainism teach the importance of nonviolence "in thought, word, and deed," Zoroastrianism similarly enjoins its adherents to practice "good thoughts, good words, and good deeds."[35]

Indian Islam, Christianity, and Judaism

These traditions all have considerable followings in the Western world, but they do in India as well: especially Islam, whose Indian following is the third largest in the Islamic world.

Islam, Christianity, and Judaism in India have all, to varying degrees and in varying ways, adapted themselves to the broader Indian religious and cultural environment. Contrary to popular belief in the West, for example, Jewish, Islamic, and Christian castes exist.[36]

Elements of pan-Indian practice such as multiple religious participation and an emphasis on the mystical can be found in all three traditions, particularly Indian Islam, whose Sufi tradition, as we have already seen, has provided a particularly rich space in which synthesis and inclusion of certain elements of Hindu practice could occur.

Communal tensions do exist, though, especially in the contemporary period. The relations between Hindus and Muslims are particularly fraught, due to the increasing rise of ideologies of religious nationalism among the adherents of both traditions. Interviews with Indian Americans from both traditions are strongly suggestive of a desire to avoid religious conflict in the American environment. Yet this reassuring trend is also often coupled with some amount of suspicion of the other community. In the words of Aminah, a Muslim interfaith activist, "There's reason for hope, but we have a long way to go."

Study Questions

1. Why is Hinduism more difficult to define and describe than most other religious traditions?
2. What is moksha and how is it achieved? Is there only one way to moksha? What are the views of various Hindu schools of thought on this topic?
3. What are some of the complexities involved in the issue of caste?
4. How is Hinduism both similar to and different from Buddhism? Jainism? Sikhism? Islam?

Suggestions for Further Reading

P.M. Bakshi, *Constitution of India: Selective Comments* (New Delhi: Universal Law Publishing Company, 2006).

Edwin Bryant, *The Quest for the Origins of Vedic Culture: The Indo-Aryan Migration Debate* (New York: Oxford University Press, 2004).

John Cort, ed., *Open Boundaries: Jain Communities and Cultures in Indian History* (Albany: State University of New York Press, 1998).

Wendy Doniger, *The Hindus: An Alternative History* (Oxford: Oxford University Press, 2009).

Nancy Auer Falk, *Living Hinduisms: An Explorer's Guide* (Belmont, CA: Thomson Wadsworth, 2006).

Gavin Flood, *An Introduction to Hinduism* (Cambridge: Cambridge University Press, 1996).

Joyce Burkhalter Flueckiger, *Everyday Hinduism* (Oxford: Wiley Blackwell, 2015).

Eileen Gardiner, *Hindu Hell: Visions, Tours, and Descriptions of the Infernal Underworld* (New York: Italica Press, 2013).

Nicholas F. Gier, *The Origins of Religious Violence: An Asian Perspective* (Lanham, MD: Lexington Books, 2016).

Peter Gottschalk, *Beyond Hindu and Muslim: Multiple Identity in Narratives of Village India* (Oxford: Oxford University Press, 2000).

S. Hay, ed., *Sources of Indian Tradition, Volume Two* (New York: Columbia University Press, 1988).

Veena Howard, ed., *Dharma: The Hindu, Jain, Buddhist, and Sikh Traditions of India* (London: I.B. Tauris, 2017).

Tony Joseph, *Early Indians: The Story of Our Ancestors and Where We Came From* (New Delhi: Juggernaut, 2018).

Jonathan Mark Kenoyer, *Ancient Cities of the Indus Valley Civilization* (Oxford: Oxford University Press, 1998).

Ramdas Lamb, *Rapt in the Name: The Ramnamis, Ramnam, and Untouchable Religion in Central India* (Albany: State University of New York Press, 2002).

Jeffery D. Long, *Jainism: An Introduction* (London: I.B. Tauris, 2009).

Jeffery D. Long, *Historical Dictionary of Hinduism* (Lanham, MD: Scarecrow Press, 2011).

Jane McIntosh, *A Peaceful Realm: The Rise and Fall of the Indus Civilization* (Boulder, CO: Westview Press, 2002).

Patrick Olivelle, trans., *Upaniṣads* (London: Oxford University Press, 2008).

Asko Parpola, *The Roots of Hinduism: The Early Aryans and the Indus Civilization* (New York: Oxford University Press, 2015).

Gregory L. Possehl, *The Indus Civilization: A Contemporary Perspective* (Lanham, Maryland: Rowman and Littlefield, 2002).

Hillary P. Rodrigues, *Introducing Hinduism* (Second Edition) (New York: Routledge, 2016).

George Thompson, trans., *Bhagavad Gītā: A New Translation* (New York: North Point Press, 2008).

Pravrajika Vrajaprana, *Vedanta: A Simple Introduction* (Hollywood, CA: Vedanta Press, 1999).

2

Hindu Reform and Western Fascination: The Nineteenth Century

Chapter 2 Summary and Outline

This chapter describes the Hindu reform movements of the nineteenth century, which developed in response to the British presence in India, and the simultaneous fascination with Hinduism among intellectuals, particularly in America, during the same period. The chapter culminates with Swami Vivekananda's departure for America in 1893.

The Colonial Context, Its Contradictions, and Hindu Responses

The nineteenth century marks the beginning of extensive engagement between Hindus and the Western world—and with America, in particular. On the one hand, by the end of the eighteenth century, India had become, for all intents and purposes, a colony of the British Empire. Although much of the subcontinent remained under the nominal rule of Indian kings—Hindu and Muslim—it was more often than not the case that these kings were allied or indebted to the British East India Company. The British crown would not directly control India until 1858—in response to the mutiny of 1857, known in India as the First War of Independence.

For most of the nineteenth century, it was the British East India Company that controlled much of India, exerting dominance over political and economic affairs and essentially turning the country into a massive mercantile operation in the service of the British economy. This, at its most basic, is how colonialism works: the colonizing nation undermines the indigenous industries of the places it colonizes. It then turns these regions into sources of raw materials from which products can be manufactured in the colonizing country, or in factories that it controls, and sold back to the colonies.[1]

In fact, much of the crushing poverty for which India has come to be known today can be traced, at least in part, to the systematic removal of its wealth by Europeans in the colonial period. Utsa Patnaik, an Indian economist, has recently made the staggering calculation that the British Empire removed the equivalent of $45 trillion, in terms of today's currency, from India during the course of its roughly two-hundred-year rule of the Indian subcontinent.[2] Indian politician and essayist Shashi Tharoor has argued that the UK owes reparations to India for centuries of colonial exploitation and rule—a view which has been contested by British historian John MacKenzie.[3]

Colonialism, however, is a complex phenomenon. Although its central purpose is economic exploitation in the service of increasing the power of the colonizing nation and advancing its varied political and economic interests, in order to enlist large numbers of citizens in the colonial project, other incentives—ideological incentives—also need to be present. The colonial projects of all the various European powers were seen by many of those who participated in them as part of a great civilizing mission, justified by the mandate of Christianity to "go forth and make disciples of all the nations."[4] For many Europeans, the colonial project was not merely a way to make money (although there were fortune seekers aplenty who went to the colonies for this very reason). For many, it was a sacred duty: a moral obligation. It could thus be justified and win the support even of those who would otherwise be uncomfortable with a project of naked economic exploitation.

This duty had many dimensions. It was, of course, religious, for those devout Christians who believed it was their calling to become missionaries and spread their gospel in foreign lands. But it also had strong nationalistic and ethnic dimensions. Christianity was not, for those Christians who were in support of the colonial project, separable from European civilization. This is why, as Gandhi recounts in his autobiography, many Indians who converted to Christianity took on not only faith in Christ, but also European habits and customs—such as consuming alcohol and beef—and, in many cases, European (or "Christian") names.[5]

Simultaneously, many Europeans were convinced at this time of their racial superiority to people of other ethnicities, and that this superiority—reflected in a superior religion and culture—also placed an obligation upon them to "uplift" the "inferior races." This obligation was famously named by the poet Rudyard Kipling as the "white man's burden."[6]

This is one of the many contradictions inherent to colonialism. It involves, simultaneously, the exploitation of a people to whom one feels superior—who are seen as less human than oneself—combined with the feeling of a certain moral obligation toward those same people. The logical trajectory of the "upliftment" of "inferior" peoples would, presumably, point in the direction of their eventual equality to oneself, although the racist dimension of this thinking militates against full equality ever being realized. As we shall see, this contradiction was obvious to many Indians in the nineteenth century, and would eventually be used to make the case for Indian independence.

The British colonial establishment in India required large numbers of Indians to cooperate with it. The Indian subcontinent is much larger than Britain, and has always had a vastly larger population. As has already been discussed, the ability of the British to dominate India was due, in part, to the fact that there was not a unified political unit known as "India" which the British had to conquer in order to exert control. India, like Europe, had, for most of its history, been made up of numerous polities. The British were able to exploit the divisions and rivalries among these polities successfully. This policy of exploiting divisions is typically called the "divide and rule" policy, and it was used at various stages of the British occupation of India.[7]

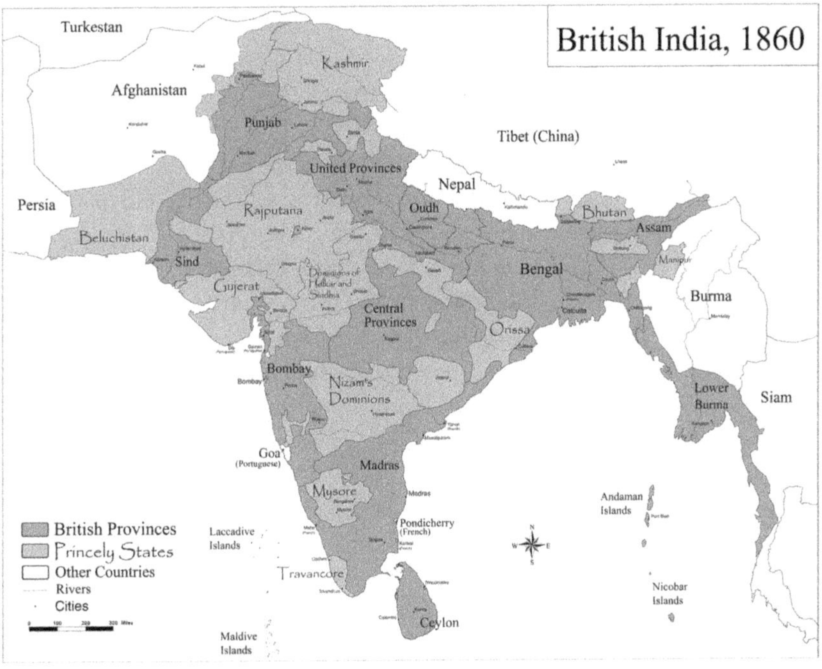

FIGURE 13 *Map of British India (Photo by Kmusser via Wikimedia Commons).*

Once established, however, the maintenance of the British administration in India required the cooperation of large numbers of Indians in order to maintain it. Securing Indian cooperation in the colonial venture required—as securing support for it in Britain itself did—a larger incentive than the promise of employment and advancement in the new social and political order. It required Indians to buy into the ideology of British colonialism, with its varied religious, nationalist, and racialist dimensions. It required Indians to believe that their own civilization was inferior to that of the British and that they needed the British to "uplift" them.

This, in turn, required Indians to be educated and acculturated with British, Christian values and a British, Christian worldview. This educational venture also fit well with the sense of many Europeans who participated in the colonial project that part of their duty was to uplift the Indians by sharing with them the gifts of European religion and culture. Many therefore went to India as missionaries, but also as teachers, establishing schools in which teaching occurred in the medium of English and where the curriculum established European views and values.

The "Europeanization" of subject peoples that colonialism entailed had devastating effects upon the subjectivity of those peoples: effects which have continued long past the end of actual, formal colonial rule. According to Ashis Nandy, colonialism is successful "not only because the ruling country subjugates through superior technical and economic resources, but also because the rulers propagate cultural subservience of the subject people."[8] As we shall see, the absorption by many Indians of a "colonial mentality" is an issue that persists today, and is relevant to various aspects of the phenomenon of Hinduism in America.

The fact that British rule in India required considerable Indian cooperation in order to be successful was the weak spot eventually exploited by Mohandas K. Gandhi (1869–1948), known to his admirers as "Mahatma," or "Great Soul." If British rule in India required Indian cooperation, what, Gandhi thought, would happen if such cooperation were withdrawn? What if Indians could be persuaded that British rule was not in their best interests, but was, in fact, destructive, exploitive, and ultimately, evil? Non-cooperation with British rule thus became the cornerstone of Gandhi's resistance movement, known for its nonviolent—though firm—stance of opposition. Gandhi himself was a product of the nineteenth-century dialogue between India and the West.

How did Hindus initially respond to the colonial presence? As it relates to the spread of Hinduism to America, two responses are particularly relevant. First, there were many Hindus who were forcibly taken to the Americas to serve as plantation laborers, particularly in the Caribbean islands. We shall return to their story in the fourth chapter of this book. Then, there were Hindu intellectuals—leaders within Hindu communities—whose response to the British and their religious and educational system varied. Some did, indeed, buy into the ideology of colonization, adopting British manners and customs, taking jobs in the colonial administration of the country, and, in at least a few cases, converting to Christianity—although this last move was not very common, as it typically involved suffering social sanctions from the Hindu community. Hindus who converted were seen as having lost their identity, which could involve a severing of family and other social relations. One group in Bengal, who called themselves "Derozians," after a European freethinker living in India, Henry Derozio (1809–31), who was their chief inspiration, adopted the styles of Western dress and tried to free themselves from the strictures of traditional Indian society, despite the disapproval of their more traditional family members.[9]

Many Hindus—particularly leaders of traditional Hindu institutions and teaching lineages—simply ignored the British presence. While the consequences of British rule for India were, indeed, massive, it did not, everywhere and in every place, affect daily life. The numbers of actual British people in India during the colonial era was always relatively small, compared to the number of Indians, and it was possible to be an Indian in this period and, depending on where one lived, never even see a British person (though one would certainly see fellow Indians uniformed as soldiers or police, and one's local administrators, even if ethnically Indian, would likely be English-educated). Many Hindus continued in their traditional beliefs and practices, with their leaders regarding the British as ultimately, from a religious point of view, uninteresting "mlecchas," or barbarians.

Other Hindus, however, took a different approach, which was to lead to the development of new ways of conceptualizing Hinduism, and of being Hindu. Rather than embracing Western values, sometimes even to the extent of converting to Christianity, or ignoring the West altogether, carrying on with the practice of Hinduism as though the British did not exist, this third group of Hindus took what could be called a "middle path" (to borrow a term from Buddhism), seeing the value in certain aspects of Western thought, and the validity of criticisms of Hinduism, while yet remaining committed to the core worldview and principles of the Hindu traditions. This was the path of the Hindu reformers. It was the "reformed Hinduism" of these figures that was often the first point of contact between the world of American culture and the world of Hinduism, and their work played a major role in shaping how Hinduism would be perceived in America.

Ram Mohan Roy and the Brahmo Samāj

The first of the Hindu reformers, often called the "father of modern Hinduism," was Ram Mohan Roy, who lived from 1772 to 1833. A highly educated Brahmin landowner, Roy found an affinity between what he viewed as the true message of Christianity and the true teaching of the Vedas. He saw both as teaching an original monotheism—a belief in a single Supreme Being who underlies all of existence. He believed that both traditions had become corrupted—Christianity, by belief in the literal divinity of Christ, and Hinduism by the incorporation of the many deities and rituals of the Pūrāṇas into what he saw as the pure monotheism of the Upaniṣads. "His enthusiasm for reform may be traced in part to Hindu and Islamic thought, including Vedāntic philosophy and Muslim theology, and partly to Western ideas, including Unitarian doctrines and … deism."[10]

A number of Hindu customs were criticized in Roy's time by Christian missionaries, such as casteism and patriarchy (the subordination of women to men—although Christians themselves were, in many respects, deeply patriarchal). These same customs were also rejected by Roy as being untrue to Vedāntic egalitarianism, which enjoins its adherents to see divinity in all beings. Roy was deeply critical of all aspects of both Hinduism and Christianity that he regarded as non-rational.

In this respect, Roy's thought is close to that of Unitarianism. Traditionally, Unitarianism "has been defined theologically as a Christian heresy that denies the doctrine of the Trinity and affirms instead God's unity."[11] Unitarianism, as a movement, has focused primarily not upon theological issues so much as on the way human beings ought to live together and treat one another. Seeing Jesus Christ more as a great moral teacher and exemplar than as a divine being, Unitarians have often been in the forefront of movements for social reform and applying reason to religious teachings.

FIGURE 14 *Raja Ram Mohan Roy (Wikimedia Commons).*

Roy was, for all intents and purposes, a Unitarian, albeit one who had drawn most deeply from the Vedic scriptures in articulating his worldview. Like Unitarians in the West, Roy believed the original message of all religions was one of unity: the unity of the Godhead, but also the unity of all of humanity. Unitarians in the West would prove to find Roy's vision most compelling.

Outspoken and articulate, Roy was a thorn in the side of both Christian missionaries and the conservative Brahmin priesthood of Hinduism. He outraged many Hindus by rejecting the use of images in worship—*mūrtipūjā*—which he labeled "idolatry," using the same language as Christian missionaries. He also militated against the practice of *satī* (or "suttee"), in which widows of high-caste men were expected to immolate themselves on their husbands' funeral pyres as a symbol of marital devotion. Roy successfully petitioned the British government to ban this practice, which it did in 1829. He also translated the principle *Upaniṣads* into vernacular languages—Bengali and English—and disseminated them widely. He also published a version of the Christian gospels under the title *The Precepts of Jesus: The Guide to Peace and Happiness*, a book which outraged many Christians by omitting all references to Jesus' divinity and any miracles performed by him. In this sense, Roy's gospel was very much like that of his American contemporary, Thomas Jefferson, titled *The Jefferson Bible*, published during the same period, and similarly omitting all elements that Jefferson regarded as irrational.

In order to advance his vision of a rational, unitarian Hinduism, Roy established a reform organization in 1828 called the *Brahmo Sabhā*, or "Assembly of Brahman." Much better known by its later name, the Brahmo Samāj (or "Community of Brahman") was most popular among those middle-class Bengali intellectuals who had received major exposure to European culture, due to the work of Christian missionaries and the British educational establishment in India. While these intellectuals, mostly Hindus, were, in many ways, deeply Westernized (as was Roy himself), they also had a strong sense of identification with and pride in Hinduism and Indian culture. The effort of these intellectuals was to reform Hinduism, opposing practices like casteism, patriarchy, and the use of images in worship, which they perceived as later additions to an originally monotheistic Hinduism taught in the *Vedas*. Brahmo Samāj worship was modelled upon Protestant Christian worship services, but with hymns and sermons drawing upon the *Upaniṣads*, rather than the Bible.

As already mentioned, the teachings of the Brahmo Samāj have strong theological affinities with Unitarianism. This was so much the case that a number of Brahmo Samāj members traveled to England in the nineteenth century in order to study theology at the Unitarian seminary which was established at Manchester College (now Harris-Manchester College) in Oxford.

Many prominent Bengali Hindu thinkers of the nineteenth and twentieth centuries had ties to the Brahmo Samāj. These include Roy's successors in leading this organization, Debendranath Tagore (1817–1905) and Keshub Chunder Sen (1838–84). They also include Tagore's son, the renowned poet, playwright, composer, and Nobel laureate, Rabindranath Tagore (1861–1941), and Narendranath Datta (1863–1902)—

better known by his monastic name, Swami Vivekananda—who was a member of the Brahmo Samāj until he became an ardent disciple of Sri Ramakrishna.

Although highly influential in the nineteenth century, the Brahmo Samāj has a fairly small, but quite devoted following today, largely confined to the Bengal region of India.

With its emphasis on an original, "pure" Vedic monotheism, believed to have later been "corrupted" into popular Hindu polytheism, Brahmo Samāj teaching in many ways anticipates that of another major Hindu reform organization established in the nineteenth century, this one in the northwestern Punjab region of India: the Ārya Samāj of Swami Dayananda Saraswati.

Swami Dayananda Saraswati and the Ārya Samāj

Swami Dayananda Saraswati, who lived from 1824 to 1883, was, like Ram Mohan Roy, a critic of Purāṇa-based Hinduism, with its mūrtis, its pūjās, and its polytheism. Born in Gujarat, in western India, to a Shaiva family, it is said that he began to question the use of images in worship when, as a child, he kept a night vigil in a Shiva temple and witnessed mice eating the food offered to the deity. He left home to undertake renunciation (sannyāsa) at the age of twenty-two, when his parents wanted to arrange a marriage for him. Wandering eventually to Mathura, a northern Indian city believed to be the birthplace of Krishna, Dayananda studied the Vedas under his guru, or spiritual teacher, Swami Virjananda, who was known as the "Blind Sage of Mathura."

In 1875, Dayananda established the *Ārya Samāj*, a Hindu reform organization which could be considered northern India's answer to the Brahmo Samāj. Rather than the *Upaniṣads*, though, Dayananda focused upon the early Vedic hymns as the wellspring of authentic Hindu practice. He both revived and popularized the practice of worship centered on the sacred fire, as opposed to the use of images, which he viewed as a later accretion upon "pure" Vedic worship.

Dayananda interpreted the *Vedas* as teaching a monotheistic doctrine and, much like Ram Mohan Roy, he did not find any Vedic warrant for later Hindu practices, found in texts such as the *Purāṇas* and sought to eliminate these practices. He intended for the Ārya Samāj to revive and promote a "purified" Vedic Hinduism, with no use of images in worship and no caste prejudice. He was also highly critical of Christianity and Islam, especially for the proselytizing activities of the missionaries of these two traditions in India. Indeed, another purpose of the Ārya Samāj, in addition to reforming Hinduism, was to neutralize Christian and Islamic missionary activities by preaching Hindu values and enabling Indian Christians and Muslims whose ancestors had been Hindu to "return" to the Hindu tradition. He established a ritual of conversion to enable those who wished to become Hindu to do so. A century later, as we shall see, as non-Indians have come to be drawn to Hindu belief and practice, even to the extent of taking on a Hindu religious identity, the conversion ceremony of the Ārya Samāj has become a means to take on this identity in a way that confers legitimacy to such converts in the eyes of many in the Hindu community.

Keshub Chunder Sen's "New Dispensation"

Unlike Swami Dayananda Saraswati, the Brahmo Samāj leader, Keshub Chunder Sen, who lived from 1838 to 1884, was known for his open admiration of Christianity and his concept of a "New Dispensation." He envisioned this new mode of religiosity as a synthesis of both Christian and Hindu elements, and ultimately, a unification of all religions. In Sen's own words:

> Such is the New Dispensation. It is the harmony of all scriptures and prophets and dispensations. It is not an isolated creed, but the science which binds and explains and harmonises all religions. It gives to history a meaning, to the action of Providence a consistency, to quarrelling churches a common bond, and to successive dispensations a continuity. It shows marvellous synthesis how the different rainbow colors are one in the light of heaven.[12]

Sen's ideas led him to split with the Brahmo Samāj, starting a new organization called the Brahmo Samāj of India in 1866.

As Sen's ideas continued to evolve, he began to take his organization in a more traditionally Hindu direction—very likely under the influence of Sri Ramakrishna, whom he met in 1876. On the topic of the use of images in worship, in particular, Sen's stance softened. He once commented that if the system of image worship could produce a being as saintly as Ramakrishna, then it could not be entirely wrong. A number of his followers, unhappy with his perceived deviations from the original ideals of the Brahmo Samāj, split from the Brahmo Samāj of India to form the Sādhāraṇ Brahmo Samāj ("Universal Community of Brahman") in 1878. Sen played an important role in bringing Ramakrishna to the attention of a wider audience of Bengali intellectuals—including the young Narendranath Datta, later Swami Vivekananda, whose first encounter with Sri Ramakrishna was in Sen's home, during a gathering to sing devotional songs. Although it would be Ramakrishna to whom Vivekananda would ultimately turn as his guru and spiritual master, the imprint of Sen's thought on Vivekananda's can clearly be discerned, particularly in regard to the idea of a deep core of truth running through the world's religions and a harmony of religions, despite their differences.

Sen and Dayananda Saraswati can each be seen to embody different poles which have come to identify Hindu approaches to other religions in the modern era: one universalist and open, seeing the common ground in all religions, the other more concerned to preserve and protect the uniqueness of Hinduism. Both tendencies can be seen to co-exist within the individual subjectivities of many Hindus, while some tend more toward universalism and others toward a defensive nationalism.

Sri Ramakrishna and Swami Vivekananda

It is probably not an exaggeration to say that Ramakrishna, who lived from 1836 to 1886 is one of the most remarkable figures of not only Indian but world's religious history. Barely literate, Ramakrishna was not a philosopher in the sense of having specialized training in the study and elucidation of Sanskrit texts. He was born into a poor Brahmin family in the Bengali village of Kamarpukur. When he was nineteen years old, he and his elder brother were hired as priests at a temple of the Goddess Kali in Dakshineshwar, on the outskirts of Calcutta. Before this time, Ramakrishna was known locally for his ecstatic trances, or samādhīs, in which he would lose consciousness of the outer world and become immersed in a state of divine bliss. Both during and after his lifetime, skeptics expressed the view that he likely suffered from a neurological disorder. He came out of these experiences, though, believing he had been absorbed in God-consciousness, and he appeared to have a deep knowledge of many topics discussed in the Hindu scriptures, even without the benefit of having studied them. The belief of the community of devotees that gradually developed around him was that his knowledge came from his direct experiences of the realities the scriptures describe. His experiences were often induced by devotional activity, like the singing of songs on sacred themes. The Kali temple at which he served was on a popular pilgrimage route, and holy persons from diverse traditions frequently stopped there and engaged him in discussion of spiritual topics. Some believed him to be an avatar, or divine incarnation.

FIGURE 15 *Sri Ramakrishna (Wikimedia Commons).*

Ramakrishna, according to accounts of his life, performed *sādhana*, or spiritual practice, following a variety of traditions. His aim was to realize God in as many ways as possible. He thus followed various Hindu traditions—Śākta, Śaiva, and Vaiṣṇava—as well as Christianity and Islam, until he would enter a state of samādhi through their respective practices. According to the beliefs of the community that developed on the basis of his life and teachings, he achieved God-realization in all of them, thus establishing an experiential basis for the ancient Hindu teaching of religious pluralism.[13] In his own words: "God can be realised through all paths. All religions are true. The important thing is to reach the roof. You can reach it by stone stairs or by wooden stairs or by bamboo steps or by a rope. You can also climb up by a bamboo pole."[14]

The young Narendranath Datta was an adherent of the Brahmo Samāj, but he also had quite a skeptical mind, having absorbed the thinking of many modern European philosophers over the course of his English education. He was encouraged by one of his teachers, a Scottish theologian named William Hastie (1842–1903), to seek out Ramakrishna, whom Hastie had heard was a "man of God." Datta had already met Ramakrishna briefly at the home of Keshub Chunder Sen, as we have seen. On his teacher's advice, he dutifully paid a visit to Sri Ramakrishna at Dakshineshwar. Initially thinking Ramakrishna to be insane, Datta nevertheless found himself mysteriously drawn to this holy man, who seemed more a product of ancient India than the modern world in which he found himself immersed—the world presented to him by his English education. A number of young men of Calcutta, finding themselves caught between traditional India and the modern world of their education—and between traditional Hinduism and the modernized version presented to them by the Brahmo Samāj—felt similarly drawn to Ramakrishna. After Ramakrishna's death from throat cancer in 1886, some of these disciples became renouncers—or sannyāsis—and formed a new group of Hindu monks called the Ramakrishna Order. Their leader, Datta, took the monastic name Swami Vivekananda.

The vision of the Ramakrishna Order represents, in many ways, an adjustment of the path of reform initially paved by the Brahmo Samāj. While it continues the progressive vision of Roy, Sen, and others in many respects—such as in regard to casteism and openness to other religions—it does not reject the use of images in worship. Arguably, it was this rejection by the Brahmo Samāj which prevented it from ever being embraced more widely by the larger Hindu populace. It also did much to advance the ideal of karma yoga as selfless service to the poor, becoming the leading Hindu relief organization in India in the modern period.

Regarding Hinduism in America, Swami Vivekananda and the Ramakrishna Order play a very central role, as Vivekananda became the first monastic teacher in a Hindu tradition to travel to America—in 1893—to teach Hindu thought and practice to Westerners, and even initiating some as monks and nuns of his order. (Swami Vivekananda was preceded by a Brahmo Samāj teacher, Pratap Chandra Majumdar, but Majumdar was not a sannyāsi and did not gather a large following.)

Hinduism in America

Connections between Hinduism and America, however, did not begin with Vivekananda's famous voyage. The first connections between Hindus and America were forged in the early days of the United States as a former colony of Britain. Even before the United States became independent from the British Empire, in 1776, ships bringing goods to America from India—also a British colony at the time, and remaining so until 1947—were arriving in American ports. Indeed, the tea dumped into the Boston Harbor during the renowned "Boston Tea Party" protest of 1773, leading up to the American Revolution, was tea from India which had been shipped to the Americas by the British East India Company. In 1784, a ship called the United States, originating in Salem, Massachusetts, arrived in the French colony of Pondicherry.[15] In the decades that followed Indian goods became available in Salem, Boston, and Providence, and it was in the New England region of the United States that interest in Hinduism first took root. A reference to "Hindoos," for example (as "Hindus" was often spelled at this time), can be found in an 1801 dictionary of religions authored by Hannah Adams (1755–1831), an early scholar of comparative religions based in Massachusetts.[16] Even the founding fathers of the new country took a keen interest in Hindu thought. John Adams, for example, wrote in a letter to Thomas Jefferson in 1813 that he had "been looking into Oriental History and Hindoo religion. I have read voyages and travels and everything I could collect."[17]

According to scholar Michael J. Altman, the first extant textual reference to Hinduism by an American author predates even this early period. Altman dates the first American reference to Hinduism at 1721, in a work by the renowned Puritan minister, Cotton Mather (1663–1728). This work, a book titled *India Christiana*,

> reflected the connections [Mather] saw between the East and West Indies on the boundary of Christendom. It contained a sermon Mather gave to the Commissioners for the Propagation of the Gospel Among the American Indians ... followed by two letters, one from Mather to the Dutch Lutheran mission in South India and a response from the Dutch missionary John Ernest Grundler. *India Christiana* highlighted the ways Mather saw the work among the Indian "heathens" as the same whether it was in America or India ... Whether in Martha's Vineyard or on the west coast of India, Indians were Indians, heathens were heathens, and they all needed the Gospel.[18]

For Mather, Hinduism held no inherent fascination. Hindus were only heathens to be converted.

As Altman notes, American writings about Hindus and Hinduism in the eighteenth and the nineteenth centuries were at least as much attempts to define America and American religiosity as they were accounts of Hinduism itself. For some, like Mather, Hinduism was an "other" in a highly negative sense: a contrast to what he saw as the true religion, Christianity. For others, though, as we shall see, Hinduism was an "other" in a more positive sense: a key to deeper truths which had become obscured over the course of time in the West. As Altman explains:

> Americans deployed representations of religion in India in their arguments about religion in America. In some cases "the religion of the Hindoos" was the "heathenism" or "superstition" that marked the boundary of "true religion." In other cases, "Brahmanism" provided the contemplative side of religion necessary to form a Universal Religion. For some Americans, India was the land of esoteric religious power. For others, India provided an example of brown heathen despotism, in contrast to white Christian democracy in America. Throughout the nineteenth century, India provided a useful foil for Americans as they debated the contours of religion ... When Americans talked about religion in India, they were not really talking about religion in India. They were talking about themselves ... [R]epresentations of religion in India functioned as arguments about what it means to be "American." ... Each of these representations, then, revealed more about the Americans involved than it did anything about people in India. One way to argue about being American was to argue about heathens, Hindoos, and Hindus.[19]

This dynamic, as we shall see, is not confined only to the period from 1721 to 1893, which Altman considers and which is our topic in this chapter as well. To the present, American discourse about Hindus and Hinduism can be seen as primarily reflecting American anxieties and aspirations.

As mentioned previously, there were numerous affinities between the religious thought of Ram Mohan Roy and the Unitarian movement in the West, which affirmed a simple monotheism and expressed skepticism about ideas such as divine incarnation. Unitarians were non-conformists in the context of orthodox Christianity, with its affirmations of a divine trinity and the incarnation of God the Son as Jesus Christ. American Unitarians were intensely interested in the work of Ram Mohan Roy, whom they regarded as a kindred spirit. The universalist philosophy of the Brahmo Samāj, which did not see truth as confined to a single religion, but was willing to view both Jesus Christ and the seers of the *Vedas* as inspired teachers, attracted positive attention from Unitarians, starting in the period from roughly 1810 to 1820. It especially attracted the attention of a Unitarian minister who would later be known as the "Sage of Concord": Ralph Waldo Emerson.

The Transcendentalists

Ralph Waldo Emerson lived from 1803 to 1882, most of which he spent in his native New England. Emerson was a philosopher, author, and Unitarian minister, and is widely regarded as a founding figure of the Transcendentalist movement—a movement which represents the first wave of deep interest in Hindu thought in North America.

FIGURE 16 *Portrait of Ralph Waldo Emerson (1803–82). Vintage etching circa late nineteenth century (Photo by Power of Forever via Getty Images).*

Emerson attended Harvard University from 1817 to 1821, which is where he first became aware of Hindu thought. Knowledge of Hinduism in the form of the writings of the first generation of Western Indologists—or scholars of Indian culture—had begun making their way into America at this point, as evidenced by Adams' 1813 letter to Jefferson. This was also, of course, the period of Unitarian interest in the work of Ram Mohan Roy. By the 1830s, Emerson had acquired English translations of the *Ṛg Veda*, the principle *Upaniṣads*, the *Laws of Manu*—which is a translation of the *Manusmṛti* the first of the *Dharma Śāstras* to be rendered into English—the *Bhāgavata Pūrāṇa* (a foundational Vaishnava text, viewed by some Vaishnavas as the "fifth *Veda*"), and, a copy of a text that was apparently Emerson's favorite, the *Bhagavad Gītā*.[20]

Emerson was quite taken with the philosophy he discovered in these Hindu texts. Likely reading them through the lens of Roy's and his own Unitarian outlook, Emerson found a spiritual approach that he felt was perfectly suited to the young American nation: a philosophy rooted in a personal quest for truth within oneself and within nature, a philosophy rooted in freedom, rather than in obedience to any limited creed or institution. This philosophy of self-reliance was central to Emerson's thought and, as we shall see, was translated into action by his student Henry David Thoreau.

Emerson scholar Robert Gordon says that Emerson drew four main ideas from the Hindu sources that were available to him:

1 An appreciation of India "as a country of deep spiritual wellsprings,"
2 The idea that the material universe is an emanation of a divine power [Brahman] and that the purpose of human life is to realize its inherent unity with its source [Brahmanirvāṇa—God-realization, or Self-realization, leading to moksha, or liberation from the cycle of rebirth],
3 The concept of *maya*, which sees the multiplicity of material forms as a kind of illusion that obscures the knowledge of oneness, and
4 The transmigration of souls from body to body through successive lifetimes [rebirth, or reincarnation].[21]

The impact of the *Bhagavad Gītā*, in particular, on Emerson's thought can be discerned in his 1856 poem, *Brahma*, which is worth repeating here in its entirety:

If the red slayer think he slays,
Or if the slain think he is slain,
They know not well the subtle ways
I keep, and pass, and turn again.

Far or forgot to me is near;
Shadow and sunlight are the same;
The vanished gods to me appear;
And one to me are shame and fame.

They reckon ill who leave me out;
When me they fly, I am the wings;
I am the doubter and the doubt,
I am the hymn the Brahmin sings.

The strong gods pine for my abode,
And pine in vain the sacred Seven;
But thou, meek lover of the good!
Find me, and turn thy back on heaven.

The first stanza of this poem is, essentially, a translation of *Bhagavad Gītā* 2:19-20:

> One who thinks he is a slayer, or one who thinks he has been slain, are both wrong. He [the Self] does not slay, nor is he ever slain.
>
> He is not born, nor does he die at all. One who exists cannot cease to exist. Unborn, eternal, permanent, primordial—one is not slain when the body is slain.[22]

In the original verses, Krishna is explaining to his friend—the warrior, Arjuna, a major character of the *Mahābhārata* of which the *Bhagavad Gītā* forms a portion—that the spiritual essence of a being, the Self or ātman, does not perish with the death of the physical body. From the perspective of the Self, then, death is unreal. "One who exists cannot cease to exist."

The second stanza conveys the *Gītā*'s philosophy of remaining "alike in joy and sorrow." "One to me are shame and fame." Through such detachment, according to the *Gītā*, one can be free from the cycle of rebirth. Investing action with desire is what causes action to lead to reaction: the process of karma. If one can free oneself from attachment, remaining "alike in joy and sorrow," one can act in a way that does not bind karmic effects to oneself. One must act selflessly, for the good of all beings, and not out of selfish desire. This is a major theme of Buddhism as well.

The third stanza evokes the tenth chapter of the *Gītā*, in which Krishna proclaims himself to be all things, and the foremost of each category of being. This stanza would fit quite well into this chapter of the *Gītā*.

The fourth stanza mentions the gods and the "sacred Seven," pining for Krishna's abode: the abode of moksha, or liberation, beyond even the heavens (beautiful, but temporary, realms), the Vaikuṇṭha of the Vaishnava tradition of Hinduism, where the liberated dwell joyfully forever.

The "sacred Seven" refer to the *saptarṣi*, or Seven Seers to whom the *Vedas* were revealed. "Find me, and turn thy back on heaven" refers, again, to the idea that Krishna's realm of liberation is beyond even the heavens to which one aspires to be reborn through good karma. This stanza is evocative of a verse in the climactic eighteenth chapter of the *Gītā*, in which Krishna tells Arjuna to "Give up all other dharmas and take refuge only in me."[23] "Turn thy back on heaven" would certainly be an unusual sentiment in the religious environment of nineteenth-century America.

Among his fellow New Englanders, Emerson was not isolated in his enthusiasm for Hindu ideas. In the 1840s, Transcendentalism, as the Hindu-inspired philosophy of Emerson came to be known, became a movement, including a variety of philosophers, Unitarian ministers, and poets. Authors who were members of this movement included philosopher Amos Bronson Alcott (1799–1888) and Unitarian reformer Theodore Parker (1810–60). "They took Hindu thought seriously, and viewed the many historic religions as local variants of a universal religious impulse toward the Transcendent."[24] Unitarian theologian James Freeman Clarke (1810–88) and independent preacher Samuel Johnson (1822–82)—both of whom were also abolitionists, a common stance in the Transcendentalist movement—disseminated Hindu religious thought in their books: Clarke's *Ten Great Religions* and Johnson's *The Religions of Asia.*

The Transcendentalist interest, not only in Hinduism, but in Asian thought more generally, helped to fuel the scholarly study of "Eastern" religions. In 1842, the American Oriental Society was established in Massachusetts—home to the Transcendentalist movement, in order "to advance scholarship on Asian topics. Its publication, the *Journal of the American Oriental Society*, which still exists today, was instrumental in establishing scholarly work on Asian thought in America."[25]

Possibly the best known of the Transcendentalists, apart from Emerson, was Henry David Thoreau (1817–62). Thoreau, even more than Emerson, sought to translate the Transcendentalist philosophy into action, both in his lifestyle and his political activism. In 1838 to 1839, he famously retreated to a small cabin at Walden Pond, near Concord, Massachusetts. This "experiment with truth"—to paraphrase Gandhi—consisted of Thoreau becoming, in a sense, an American sannyāsi, setting aside social life in favor of solitude and contemplation of the divinity within both nature and himself.

By Thoreau's account, the *Bhagavad Gītā* accompanied him in this retreat. He read the text regularly, drawing inspiration from it, and comparing his reading of the *Gītā* on the banks of Walden Pond to a Brahmin *paṇḍit* studying the *Vedas* on the banks of the Ganges. He famously wrote, "In the morning I bathe my intellect in the stupendous and cosmogonal philosophy of the *Bhagavad Gita* in comparison with which our modern world and its literature seem puny and trivial."[26]

Both an abolitionist and a pacifist, Thoreau was briefly jailed in 1846 for his opposition to the Mexican-American War and slavery, which he expressed by refusing to pay taxes. His essay, *Civil Disobedience*, had a tremendous influence on Mohandas K. Gandhi, who assimilated the idea that one could resist evil non-violently, through acts of disobedience and non-cooperation. In this way, one can thus see the two-way nature of the exchange between Hinduism and America in this period, with Thoreau and other Transcendentalists being influenced by the *Gītā*, and then, in effect, returning the favor by influencing Gandhi—who would, himself, later return the favor yet again through his influence on Martin Luther King, Jr., and the American Civil Rights movement.

Yet another renowned Transcendentalist, New Yorker Walt Whitman (1819–92), shows Hindu inspiration in his poetry. Whitman's "Song of Myself" can be puzzling if one is unfamiliar with the Hindu concept of the ātman, the universal Self which binds all beings. Far from being a hymn to narcissism, "Song of Myself" celebrates the unity of all:

> I celebrate myself, and sing myself,
> And what I assume you shall assume,
> For every atom belonging to me as good belongs to you.[27]

Religiously speaking, the chief legacy of the Transcendentalists in America has been to open the Unitarian tradition to non-Christians. In 1867, the Free Religious Association split from the more conservative Unitarian church, giving greater emphasis to Hindu and Buddhist thought. Nearly a century later, in 1961, the conservative and more universalist branches of this movement came together to form the Unitarian-Universalist Association.

In this association, some members today identify themselves as Christians, but others self-identify as Buddhists, Hindus, Wiccans, and Neo-pagans, with a strong emphasis on the idea that all religions are paths to the same goal. This is also, of course, a central teaching of modern Hindu figures such as Keshub Chunder Sen, Sri Ramakrishna, and Swami Vivekananda. Unitarianism is a good example of convergence between a Western tradition and certain forms of Hinduism.

FIGURE 17 *Walt Whitman (Photo by George C. Cox via Wikimedia Commons).*

The Theosophical Society

America in the nineteenth century was (and remains) overwhelmingly Christian, in terms of the religious affiliations of the vast majority of the population. It was also, in many ways, quite a conservative nation—which, in many quarters, it continues to be today.

At the same time, though, particularly given its ethos of religious freedom (as enshrined in the First Amendment of the US constitution), America has also been a place of experimentation in the area of religion. The rise of the Mormon faith—the Church of Jesus Christ of Latter Day Saints, which was established in 1830—is an example of American religious innovation. As the example of the Transcendentalists demonstrates, it was also possible in the nineteenth century, at least in some parts of the country, for Americans to embrace ideas from beyond the bounds of Christianity.

Transcendentalism constituted a broad and loosely organized movement, without a central institutional authority—not unlike Hinduism itself. As we have seen, though, it was largely situated within the Unitarian tradition. Although its adherents' enthusiasm for Hinduism led to a split with the mainstream Unitarian church—a split later healed in the early 1960s, and in a resolution largely favoring the more open branch of the tradition—it can be characterized as, primarily, a Unitarian phenomenon, with Unitarianism itself being a highly progressive outlier relative to the mainstream of American Christianity.

The next major movement in nineteenth-century America to embrace Hindu influence—and also to "return the favor" in much the same way that Thoreau "returned the favor" to Gandhi and helped to inspire his movement of nonviolent non-cooperation with British rule, exerting influence on events in India—was the Theosophical Society.

Unlike the loose Transcendentalist movement, the Theosophical Society was, as its name suggests, institutionally situated. It was a Society: an organization which was developed to achieve a specific set of aims and purposes. These were:

- To form a nucleus of the universal brotherhood of humanity, without distinction of race, creed, sex, caste, or color.
- To encourage the comparative study of religion, philosophy, and science.
- To investigate unexplained laws of nature and the powers latent in humanity.[28]

Theosophy also took a more confrontational stance toward mainstream Christianity than did the Unitarian Transcendentalists, helping to foster, as we shall see, the Indian independence movement and making alliances with both Hindus in India and Buddhists in Sri Lanka who wanted to counter the influence of Christian missionaries.

The Theosophical Society was established in New York City in 1875, by Helena Petrovna Blavatsky and Henry Steel Olcott. Blavatsky (1831–91) was born in Ukraine. She was the first Russian to take up US citizenship. Deeply interested in philosophy and the mysteries of existence, she is said to have traveled extensively before settling in America. She claimed to have traveled in, among other places, Tibet, where she said that she had studied with Tibetan Buddhist masters. Doubts about these claims have been raised by many, but there is no doubt that they served the purpose of creating and perpetuating an aura of mystery and of "Asiatic exoticism" around her.

In the 1870s, she became deeply involved in the Spiritualist movement in the United States. Spiritualism, another nineteenth-century American religious innovation (though with roots not so much India as in Europe), teaches that it is possible to contact the spirits of the deceased and receive information from them. Spiritualists would typically gather in one another's homes. Gatherings would be led by a *medium*, a person believed to have a special bond with the spirit world.

Images of séances found in popular culture, with a group of people holding hands around a table in a dimly lit room while their medium contacts the spirits of the dead, have their origins in this movement, as do practices such as the use of the Ouija Board, or planchette. An outspoken, colorful, controversial figure, Blavatsky was, among other things, a spirit medium. It was through their shared interest in Spiritualism that Blavatsky first became acquainted with Henry Steel Olcott (1832–1907).

Serving the US army in the American Civil War, Olcott reached the rank of Colonel. He and Blavatsky jointly started the Theosophical Society in order to advance the ideal of a universal religion based on the scriptures of many ancient civilizations. Initially displaying a strong interest in ancient Egyptian religion, Blavatsky's first published work on theosophy (which literally means "divine wisdom" or "knowledge of the divine") was the monumental *Isis Unveiled*. It was issued in 1877, just two years after the founding of the Theosophical Society, and provides a good guide to Blavatsky's early thought processes. With a deepening interest in Asian thought, Blavatsky and Olcott moved in 1880 to India. In 1882, the pair purchased land in Adyar, a neighborhood of the southern Indian city of Madras, today known as Chennai. Adyar remains today the location of the global headquarters of the Theosophical Society.

Viewing Hinduism and Buddhism as the most complete remnants of the ancient universal wisdom tradition which they believed could be discerned in the ancient scriptures of many cultures, members of the Theosophical Society saw one of their tasks to be to combat the dogmatism of the Christian missionaries in India—becoming, in effect, "reverse missionaries," seeking to arouse in the people of India a pride in their own ancient traditions. Blavatsky and Olcott were thus viewed with suspicion by the British government in India. Blavatsky's Russian origins, in particular, were a source of suspicion, and it was believed in some quarters that she might be a Russian spy.

While it is unlikely that Blavatsky was a Russian spy—an outspoken critic of the European presence in India seems an unusual cover for a spy, given that spies typically wish to blend in with the environments in which they operate—her vocal criticisms of Christianity and aim of advancing the cause of Hinduism certainly drew the attention of Hindu leaders.

The most well-known of these Hindu leaders was Swami Dayananda Saraswati—who, as one might recall, established the Ārya Samāj in 1875 in India, the same year that the Theosophical Society was started in America. Dayananda, also desiring to counter the influence of the Christian missionaries in India, and to establish a means for Indian Christians and Muslims to "reconvert" to Hinduism, saw Blavatsky and Olcott as his natural allies. Blavatsky and Olcott even briefly gave their society a new name: the "Theosophical Society of the Ārya Samāj of India," and listed Swami Dayananda Saraswati as its official head.[29]

This alliance, however, would prove to be short-lived. Olcott was even more fascinated with Buddhism than he was with Hinduism, and Blavatsky did not view the differences between the two traditions to be of any great significance. When the two formally converted to Theravāda Buddhism during a visit to Sri Lanka, Dayananda, who was a proponent of what he regarded as a pure Vedic philosophy, objected deeply and ended his association with them.

Olcott went on to spend considerable time in Sri Lanka, even authoring a text in 1881 called *A Buddhist Catechism*—a text which came to be used by Theravāda Buddhists in Sri Lanka to teach Buddhism to their children. This is another case of Westerners "returning the favor" to an Asian tradition which has come to influence them enormously. Olcott's interpretation of Buddhism has helped to shape Sri Lankan Buddhism to the present day.[30]

Blavatsky and Olcott's travels in India, as well as the activities of many other Theosophists in the United States and Europe, led the theosophical movement to grow considerably, in India and the West.

Despite the falling out between Swami Dayananda Saraswati and Blavatsky and Olcott, the Society continued to draw a Hindu following, and Western theosophists continued to travel to India with the aim of promoting the cause of Hinduism. Allan Octavian Hume

(1829–1912), a Theosophist, was a founding member of the Indian National Congress. Established in 1885, the Indian National Congress was the party that would eventually—with the guidance of Mohandas K. Gandhi—lead the movement for Indian independence. Hume, a Scotsman, was a botanist and ornithologist working in the British civil service in India. In addition to his scientific interests, Hume was a keen student and promoter of theosophical ideas, and contributed to theosophical publications.

Hume was far from being the last Western Theosophist to take a leading role in the Indian National Congress. Probably the most famous of Theosophists, apart from Blavatsky and Olcott, Annie Besant (1847–1933) was elected to the office of president of the Indian National Congress in 1917. A socialist who was active in struggles for social justice in England, Besant met Blavatsky in 1890. Seeing the struggle for social justice and search for spiritual enlightenment as components of the same process—in very much the same way that Gandhi did—Besant joined the Theosophical Society and took up the cause of Indian political independence. A number of Europeans, in fact, were quite sympathetic to the Indian cause and allied themselves with it publicly.

In 1911, Besant met a Hindu teacher, Madan Mohan Malaviya, and the two of them agreed to work toward the development of a Hindu university in India. Their efforts

FIGURE 18 *Annie Besant, 1847–1933. British Theosophist, women's rights activist, writer, orator, and supporter of Irish and Indian self-rule. From* Bibby's Annual *published 1910 (Photo by Universal History Archive/Universal Images Group via Getty Images).*

bore fruit with the establishment of Banaras Hindu University in 1916, which remains a major Indian university to the present day. BHU, as it is widely known today, is probably best known for its programs in medicine and engineering.

In terms of the history of Hinduism in America, the role of the Theosophical Society is a pivotal one. The Transcendentalists had taken inspiration from Hindu texts, but it is unlikely that any of them ever met an actual Hindu, nor did Emerson, Thoreau, or Whitman travel to India. The Theosophists, however, took an active role in the struggle for Indian independence—on the side of India. These were Westerners who identified with Hinduism (and Buddhism) and took up the task of working for the cause of Asian traditions, in quite explicit opposition to the Christian missionary project which was one of the pillars of European colonialism—and, as we have seen, of an American self-perception as well. Theirs was not an "armchair" interest in India, but one for which they were willing to make sacrifices and take risks.

While Thoreau's essay on civil disobedience was a major influence on Gandhi, it was an influence that occurred posthumously, after Thoreau's death. (Thoreau died seven years before Gandhi was born.) But when Gandhi traveled to London to study law, in 1888, he encountered a number of English Theosophists, two of whom gave him a copy *The Song Celestial*, Sir Edwin Arnold's translation of the *Bhagavad Gītā*.

FIGURE 19 *Indian nationalist leader Mohandas Karamchand Gandhi (1869–1948), popularly known as Mahatma Gandhi, whose policy of peaceful demonstration led India from British rule to independence (Photo by Elliott & Fry via Getty Images).*

This was the first time that Gandhi read the entire text of this important Hindu scripture. It soon became his favorite book. He referred to it fondly as his "dictionary of daily reference."[31] It proved to be a major influence upon his thought. It is not only that the Theosophists, like the Transcendentalists, took an interest in India and let themselves be influenced by it. They went further and took an active role in Indian affairs.

Combined with their roles in helping to establish and lead the Indian National Congress—as well as Besant's role in the establishment of Banaras Hindu University and Olcott's writing of his *Buddhist Catechism*—the Theosophists certainly "returned the favor" to India (and Sri Lanka), not only being influenced by, but in turn helping to shape, Indian religious traditions.

The Theosophists raise important critical questions as well, which will continue to arise as we examine later waves of Western interest in Hinduism. Even though the Theosophists actively worked against both the ideology and the concrete reality of colonialism, in the form of British rule of India and Christian missionary activity, they nevertheless, as Westerners, held a privileged position in relation to the Hindus whose traditions they held in such high regard. To what extent does their "returning the favor" of influence on Hinduism—and Buddhism in Sri Lanka—constitute an innocent cultural exchange and to what extent is it, itself, an exercise in power, shaping the traditions of Asia according to Western perceptions and preoccupations, and possibly distorting the natural course of the development of these traditions? In other words, does the Theosophical Society represent a moment of resistance against colonialism, or is it itself, rather, an example of colonialism, even if a well-intentioned one, motivated, again, by the specific preoccupations of the Westerners who took part in it rather than a genuine understanding of Hindu or Buddhist traditions, which could perhaps be gained by a longer, more patient, and deeper study of those traditions than what the earliest Theosophists actually pursued (including mastering the Indic languages, such as Sanskrit and Pali, in which the thought of these traditions is expressed)? Variations of these same questions persist to the present, as Westerners adopt, for example, the practice of yoga, and in some cases re-export it to India—and to younger generations of Hindus living in America—in new forms.

Is what we are describing here a genuinely creative exchange across cultural boundaries, between equal partners, or are non-Western traditions being remolded after a Western pattern that is based on the assumptions, interests, and agendas of the Westerners who engage with them?

While these questions are certainly worthy of reflection, though, they themselves emerge from assumptions which are also worthy of interrogation. Questions such as these arguably arise from a conception of traditions like Hinduism and Buddhism as fragile exotic plants which need to be handled with care, if at all, rather than as the ancient and resilient traditions—upheld by living human agents with the ability to make their own choices—that they are. These are *living* traditions, not historical relics to be kept in a museum. Persons have been engaging with and transforming them for centuries. Why should this process end? Is there a responsible middle ground between being completely inattentive to the power dynamics between

Western and non-Western cultures and being so sensitive to these that one does not venture forth to explore diverse ideas and practices from which one might receive practical benefit?

The agency of Hindus and Buddhists themselves should also not be downplayed. It is not, in other words, that Gandhi was helpless to resist the allure of Thoreau's *Civil Disobedience* or Arnold's *Song Celestial*, or that generations of Sri Lankan Theravāda Buddhists were somehow forced to use Olcott's *Buddhist Catechism* to impart Buddhist teaching to their children. Gandhi and the Theravāda Buddhists made use of these books because they found something useful in them. And when Swami Dayananda Saraswati disagreed with the approach taken by Blavatsky and Olcott—with its conflation of Hindu and Buddhist traditions—he chose to end his association with them. When we say that Westerners have been influenced by Hinduism and that Hindus have also, in turn, been influenced by resulting Western interpretations of it, in neither case did such "influence" occur magically, without involving the conscious choices and the cooperation of those so influenced. People are drawn to traditions, texts, and ideas, for their own reasons, and to serve their own purposes. The point is valid, though, that the relative power and prestige of the West make its role in such an exchange disproportionate. Cross-cultural conversation requires respect for the sensibilities of all involved, but especially those who may be at a disadvantage in it.

Although there is certainly validity in the claim that the theosophical imprint on both modern Hinduism and modern India is bound up in many complex ways with the legacy of colonialism, it is also true that genuine human bonds were forged across cultural boundaries during the nineteenth century, and into the twentieth, as the Indian independence movement unfolded. Far from seeing themselves as agents of the empire, Western anti-colonialists were often, themselves, marginalized persons in Western society: religious or political non-conformists, as we have seen in the case of at least some Theosophists, as well as ethnic minorities, people with differing sexual orientations, and so on. Many identified not with the imperial activities of their governments, but strongly and sincerely with the colonized peoples whom those governments were subjugating. As Nandy points out, Gandhi and other leaders of the Indian independence movement "resisted their rulers in British India by building on the lifestyle, values, and psychology of ordinary Indians *and by heeding dissenting voices from the West*."[32]

In an important study of this period, *Affective Communities: Anticolonial Thought, Fin-de-Siécle Radicalism, and the Politics of Friendship*, scholar Leela Gandhi (who is also, incidentally a great-granddaughter of Mohandas K. Gandhi) has examined "individuals and groups that have renounced the privileges of imperialism and elected affinity with victims of their own expansionist cultures." Gandhi inquires into what she describes most evocatively as "the onerous politics of 'betrayal,' 'departure,' 'flight,' [and] 'treason' exemplified by metropolitan anti-imperialists"—that is, anti-imperialists who grew up in the heart of the empire.

> What ethical imperatives ... rendered some Europeans immune to the ubiquitous temptations of an empire described ... as a machine or factory "for making

> imperialist-minded citizens"? Which were the intolerable domestic pressures exercised by empire upon its own citizenry, such that some among it chose to betray the claims of possessive nationalism in favor of solidarity with foreigners, outsiders, alleged inferiors?[33]

As we shall see, similar questions can be asked of Americans in the twentieth and twenty-first centuries who are drawn to Hinduism. A certain measure of discontentment with traditional Western culture, religion, and philosophy typically accompanies a fascination with traditions such as Hinduism and Buddhism. Those who do not feel they "fit in" within a more normative Western context turn to other contexts for a sense of meaning and belonging. As one informant has said—a Westerner who has become a monastic practitioner in a Hindu-Inspired Meditation Movement—"I'm too scientific for most religious people and too religious for most scientific people."

And yet, one is also not able wholly to escape one's context. Particularly in an American setting, the very idea that one has the right and the ability to "choose" one's religious identity, for example, emerges from a specific historical situation quite different from that which has shaped the consciousness of most Hindus: the Protestant Christian heritage of the United States as well as the enshrinement of the ideal of religious freedom in the First Amendment of the US Constitution. The differing cultural starting points of Indian Hindus and of most Americans render a certain measure of mutual miscommunication and misunderstanding inevitable.

Again, though, in the contemporary American situation, as in the colonial situation of the nineteenth and early twentieth centuries, the relative power and prestige of the West make its role in such exchange disproportionate. Americans who are in a position to draw upon diverse religious traditions much as they would draw upon consumer products in a shopping mall are in an uneven power relationship with those upon whose traditions they are drawing. The point made earlier bears repeating: *cross-cultural conversation requires respect for the sensibilities of all involved, but especially those who may be at a disadvantage in it.*

New Thought

In addition to the Transcendentalist movement and the Theosophical Society, still another American spiritual movement of the nineteenth century that bears strong affinities with Hinduism is the New Thought Movement. Arguably more contemplatively oriented than Transcendentalism, and not possessing the political dimensions of Theosophy, New Thought is a distinctive branch of American religiosity that incorporates Hindu concepts into a vocabulary that is largely shaped by Christianity. Even conceptually, aspects of New Thought were already present in experientially based currents of Christianity, such as Pietism, during the period of its emergence.

New Thought is very much like Transcendentalism in being a decentralized movement, with no core institution or formal creed; and there are differences among its various strands and in the writings of its various charismatic teachers. However, as characterized by Philip Goldberg, "New Thought's various constituencies have held in common certain premises that could not be more Vedantic." These premises are that:

- There is one infinite, all-inclusive, creative, living Intelligence beyond and within the universe. *Whether we call it God, Brahman, Allah, Spirit, or some other name, It is the Great All in which all things exist and of which all things have been made.*
- Our essential nature is spiritual. *We are spiritual beings having a human experience, and as spiritual beings, we share in God's essential nature.*
- We have a creative relationship with our experience of life. *The spiritual universe operates according to spiritual laws, which allows us to co-create our life experience consciously. Through right alignment with spiritual law and conscious contact with the Creative Intelligence within, we can achieve happiness and fulfillment.*
- Life is a spiritual journey toward an awareness of the true source of our being. *The ultimate destiny of every individual soul is to awaken to the true source of its being—God Itself.*[34]

Although it certainly bears affinities to Hinduism, New Thought is also rooted in strains of Christian thought that became particularly attractive to many Americans in the nineteenth century. The pioneering American psychologist and pragmatist philosopher, William James (1842–1910) traces the roots of New Thought, which was quite popular in his time, to such diverse sources as Christianity, Transcendentalism, Berkeleyan idealism (a philosophy that holds, not unlike Advaita Vedānta, that reality is essentially consciousness, with the material world being an appearance or form in which consciousness manifests to itself), Spiritualism, variations of late nineteenth-century evolutionary thought (which took the process of biological evolution not to be the result of a series of accidents, but as evidence of a guiding intelligence inherent in the very fabric of being), and, of course, Hinduism.[35]

One major source for New Thought included the visionary writings of the Swedish mystic, Emanuel Swedenborg (1688–1772). Although he lived before Indian religions were well known in the Western world, dimensions of Swedenborg's thought have strong resemblances to Hinduism and Buddhism, making a synthesis of his thought with elements of Vedanta a fairly easy process. Among other things, Swedenborg describes a process of spiritual growth through a variety of levels in the afterlife that parallel Hindu and Buddhist accounts of the heavenly realms.

Although organizations emerging in the late nineteenth and early twentieth centuries based on New Thought continue to thrive today—organizations such as the Unity Church, established in Kansas City, Missouri, in 1889 by Charles and Myrtle Fillmore, and Christian Science, established in New England by Mary Baker

Eddy (1821–1910)—the imprint of New Thought can be felt largely in the New Age movement, with its teaching that one's thoughts eventually manifest in the material world. Ideas with considerable popularity in America—such as the power of positive thinking, as pioneered by Norman Vincent Peale (1898–1993)—are drawn from New Thought, and have made their way into mainstream American culture, and even American Christianity.

The deeper ontology, or conception of reality, in which such thought is based is essentially that of Advaita Vedānta, as well as the Yogācāra philosophy of Mahāyāna Buddhism: that reality ultimately has the nature of consciousness. Thus, the reality that one experiences is a reflection or a manifestation of the state of one's consciousness. The American twist on this is that one can therefore change one's material reality by changing one's consciousness: attracting health, wealth, and so on by thinking positively and visualizing what one desires. While it is rooted in Vedāntic and Buddhist ontology, the American variant on this philosophy diverges from traditional Indian thought, in which the realization that reality is of the nature of consciousness leads to detachment from physical desires, which are revealed as merely ephemeral sensations, not giving ultimate joy. In other words, in traditional Hindu and Buddhist thought, the realization that life is like a dream leads to a desire for awakening. In its American variant, it leads to a desire to make the dream a pleasant one.

Swami Vivekananda Leaves for America

Thus far, we have explored Hindu reform movements of the nineteenth century—Hindus in India responding to a Western culture which has come to them in the form of a colonizing power. We then looked at Westerners—specifically, Americans—who felt drawn to Hindu thought by Hindu texts, which were becoming available in English translation through the efforts of scholars in the emergent field of Indology. We examined the Transcendentalists, whose encounter with Hinduism was entirely with books: translations of the Upaniṣads, the Bhagavad Gītā, and so on.

We then saw, as the nineteenth century unfolded, that there were also Westerners—such as Theosophists—who were drawn not only to study Hindu thought and experiment with incorporating it into their own lives, but to go to India themselves and work for the advancement of Hinduism and Buddhism, defend these traditions from the criticisms of Christian missionaries—their fellow Westerners—and to work for the cause of India's independence from British rule.

What, though, of Hindus in America? When does Hinduism actually come to America, not in the form of books, but of living, practicing Hindus?

Although he was preceded, as we shall see, by a number of other Hindu practitioners and teachers—including a prominent member of the Brahmo Samāj—Swami Vivekananda is widely credited with being the first Hindu spiritual teacher to have a lasting impact on America's religious landscape: to travel to America in person and sow the seeds of Hinduism in America. He is thus the precursor for the many Hindu teachers who subsequently brought their traditions to the United States.

It is sometimes suggested that Vivekananda's role in bringing Hinduism to America has been overstated.[36] Certainly he was not alone in his efforts, nor was his Vedanta Society the only Hindu tradition to be brought to America during the late nineteenth and early twentieth centuries. We shall see that other teachers as well played a role in this process, as did ordinary Hindus and other Indians, whose struggles helped pave the way for future generations of Indians to find a home in America, and for future Americans of all ethnicities to find inspiration in Hinduism.

Vivekananda's role, though, was pivotal. A larger-than-life figure, for many Hindus today, in America and globally, he is regarded as a hero, whose career marked a turning point in Hindu and in world history.[37]

After the death of his master, Sri Ramakrishna, in 1886, Vivekananda wandered the length and breadth of India. He studied under a variety of teachers, and also, himself, taught all who were interested in hearing what he had to say. In 1893, under the encouragement of the Raja of Ramnad, the ruler of a small princely state in southern India who was impressed by his teachings, he agreed to be a delegate to the first World Parliament of Religions, to be held in Chicago, and to carry the message of Vedanta to the Western world.

Ultimately, Vivekananda did become a delegate to this assembly and made the long journey to America to deliver a famous speech that, for many, marks the true emergence of Hinduism onto the global stage as a tradition not only for India, but for the entire world. As we shall see in our next chapter, he inspired other teachers to travel to America as well, and to continue the process of infusing elements of Hindu thought and practice into the American consciousness.

Study Questions

1. What is meant by the "contradictions" of colonialism?
2. What are some similarities and differences between the Brahmo Samāj and the Ārya Samāj?
3. Why does the Vedanta movement based on the teachings of Ramakrishna and Vivekananda seem to have had a wider appeal than the Brahmo Samāj?
4. What are some similarities and differences between the Transcendentalists and the Theosophical Society?
5. What are some of the issues raised by the phenomenon of Westerners "returning the favor" to Hindus by influencing Hinduism, after themselves being influenced by it?
6. Should New Thought be described as a Hindu movement? As a Christian movement? As both?

Suggestions for Further Reading

Michael J. Altman, *Heathen, Hindoo, Hindu: American Representations of India, 1721–1893* (Oxford: Oxford University Press, 2017).
Helena Petrovna Blavatsky, *The Key to Theosophy: A Simple Exposition Based on the Wisdom-Religion of All Ages* (Pasadena: Theosophical University Press, 1889).
Bipan Chandra et al., *India's Struggle for Independence* (New York: Penguin Books, 2012).
Ralph Waldo Emerson, *Essential Writings* (New York: Modern Library Classics, 2000).
Leela Gandhi, *Affective Communities* (Durham, NC: Duke University Press, 2006).
Mohandas K. Gandhi, *The Story of My Experiments with Truth* (Mineola, NY: Dover, 1983).
Brian Hatcher, *Bourgeois Hinduism, or Faith of the Modern Vedantists* (Oxford: Oxford University Press, 2007).
Christopher Isherwood, *Ramakrishna and His Disciples* (Mayavati: Advaita Ashrama, 1969).
Carl T. Jackson, *The Oriental Religions and American Thought* (Westport, CT: Greenwood Publishing Group, 1982).
Richard King, *Orientalism and Religion: Postcolonial Theory and the "Mystic East"* (London: Routledge, 1999).
Jeffrey D. Lavoie, *The Theosophical Society* (Irvine, CA: Brown Walker Press, 2012).
Ashis Nandy, *Intimate Enemy: The Loss and Recovery of Self Under Colonialism* (London: Oxford University Press, 2009).
Swami Nikhilananda, trans., *The Gospel of Sri Ramakrishna* (New York: Ramakrishna-Vivekananda Center, 1942).
Barbara L. Packer, *The Transcendentalists* (Atlanta: University of Georgia Press, 2007).
Glyn Richards, *Sourcebook of Modern Hinduism* (Surrey, UK: Curzon Press, 1985).
Edward Said, *Orientalism* (New York: Vintage Books, 1979).
Arvind Sharma, *Gandhi: A Spiritual Biography* (New Haven: Yale University Press, 2013).
David Smith, *Hinduism and Modernity* (London: Wiley-Blackwell, 2003).
Leonard Smith, *The Unitarians: A Short History* (Ashland, OR: Blackstone Editions, 2008).
Anne Taylor, *Annie Besant: A Biography* (Oxford: Oxford University Press, 1992).
Shashi Tharoor, *An Era of Darkness: The British Empire in India* (New Delhi: Aleph Book Company, 2016).
Henry David Thoreau, *Walden and Civil Disobedience* (New York: Signet Classics, 2012).
Thomas A. Tweed and Stephen Prothero, *Asian Religions in America* (New York: Oxford University Press, 1999).
Peter van der Veer, *Imperial Encounters: Religion and Modernity in India and Britain* (Princeton: Princeton University Press, 2001).
Walt Whitman, *Song of Myself and Other Poems by Walt Whitman* (Berkeley: Counterpoint, 2010).

3

"Hinduism Invades America": The Early Twentieth Century

Chapter 3 Summary and Outline

This chapter will begin with Swami Vivekananda's journey to America and its effects: the rise of Vedanta Societies in various urban centers, established by Vivekananda's fellow monks and their successors. The influence of these societies on intellectuals—figures like Christopher Isherwood, Aldous Huxley, and Joseph Campbell—will be explored, as well as Paramahansa Yogananda and his establishment of the Self-Realization Fellowship, the teachings of Jiddu Krishnamurti, other Hindu pioneers in America, and two figures—Sri Aurobindo and Sri Ramana Maharshi—who never set foot in America, but nevertheless have considerable American followings, and have made a major imprint on how yoga and Hinduism are perceived. Varied American reactions to Hindus and Hinduism will also be discussed, up to the Asian Exclusion Act, with a particular focus on the intense racism faced by Indians in America at this time. The violence directed at ordinary Indians (Hindu and Sikh) is a jarring contrast with the welcome accorded to figures like Vivekananda and Yogananda—though even these celebrity teachers had painful experiences with racism in America.

Swami Vivekananda in America

In 1893, Swami Vivekananda arrived in an America that was still, in many ways, a deeply conservative nation. Slavery had been formally abolished by President Abraham Lincoln a mere thirty years prior to his coming, but the Civil War required to put an end to it had continued to rage for another two years after that. The freed African American slaves and their descendants would not be, in every sense, equal under the law for many decades to come. Even today, racism lingers in America, and even seems to be on the rise. And, of course, India was still, during Vivekananda's time, firmly in the grip of British rule. Indians were viewed through the lens of racism. To many Europeans—and Americans—Indians were an "inferior race," in need of the civilizing influence of the West; and the Hindu religion was "heathen," and in need of replacement by Christianity.

Religiously, even those progressive Christians who had launched the World Parliament of Religions at which Vivekananda spoke—a gathering of representatives from an array of religious traditions—saw this event as a venue for demonstrating the superiority of Christianity over all other religions, and "preparing the way for the reunion of all the world's religions in their true center—Jesus Christ."[1] The intent was *not* to celebrate the religious diversity of the world.

The groundwork for a paradigm shift had been established, however, by those Americans who were attracted to the wisdom they found in those Hindu sacred texts that had been translated into English, some of which were available to American readers as early as the eighteenth century: texts such as the *Bhagavad Gītā* and some of the major *Upaniṣads*. Similarly, the Theosophical Society, established in 1875 in New York City—which was also the location of the first Vedanta Society, established by Swami Vivekananda in 1894—was made up of Westerners whose thought was profoundly shaped by Indian philosophies like Vedanta, Yoga, and Buddhism. As we saw in our last chapter, some of these persons—persons such as A.O. Hume and Annie Besant—participated actively in the movement for Indian independence. Besant also helped to establish Banaras Hindu University, and was a mentor to another major Indian thinker who found a home in America: Jiddu Krishnamurti. So, while there was certainly resistance to Swami Vivekananda and his message by many Americans, there were also those Americans who were ready and eager to learn from him.

At the Chicago World Parliament of Religions, Hindus, for the first time, presented their teachings to American audiences. Vivekananda was not, in fact, the very first Hindu teacher to visit North America. A Brahmo Samāj representative, Pratap Majumdar, had been in America a few months prior to Vivekananda, and he also attended and spoke at the 1893 Parliament, along with B.B. Nagarkar, another member of the Brahmo Samāj. Other Hindu representatives at the Parliament were Narasimha Chari and S. Parthasarathy Ayyangar (both representing Vaishnava traditions), Mohan Dev, Manilal N. Dvivedi, and, of course, Swami Vivekananda. In addition, there were a Jain

FIGURE 20 *From left to right: Virchand Gandhi, Anagarika Dharmapala, Swami Vivekananda, and (possibly) G. Bonet Maury (Wikimedia Commons).*

representative—Virchand R. Gandhi—and a Buddhist representative from Sri Lanka who had previously been a student of Henry Steel Olcott—Anagarika Dharmapala.[2] There were also Buddhist representatives from East Asian countries, such as Japan.

While Swami Vivekananda was not the first or the only representative of an Asian religion, or even of Hinduism, to come to the United States during this time, he was easily the best received, becoming a celebrity figure whose travels and teachings were followed by the major newspapers of the day. He was the first celebrity Hindu monk, and a forerunner of many more to follow.

Swami Vivekananda's first address to the Parliament, delivered on September 11, 1893, set the tone for the rest of his lectures, and presented Hinduism as a pluralistic religion, not only of tolerance, but of universal acceptance. It is worth quoting in its entirety:

Sisters and Brothers of America,

> It fills my heart with joy unspeakable to rise in response to the warm and cordial welcome which you have given us. I thank you in the name of the most ancient order of monks in the world; I thank you in the name of the mother of religions; and I thank you in the name of millions and millions of Hindu people of all classes and sects.
>
> My thanks, also, to some of the speakers on this platform who, referring to the delegates from the Orient, have told you that these men from far-off nations may well claim the honor of bearing to different lands the idea of toleration. I am proud to belong to a religion which has taught the world both tolerance and universal

acceptance. We believe not only in universal toleration, but we accept all religions as true. I am proud to belong to a nation which has sheltered the persecuted and the refugees of all religions and all nations of the earth. I am proud to tell you that we have gathered in our bosom the purest remnant of the Israelites, who came to Southern India and took refuge with us in the very year in which their holy temple was shattered to pieces by Roman tyranny. I am proud to belong to the religion which has sheltered and is still fostering the remnant of the grand Zoroastrian nation. I will quote to you, brethren, a few lines from a hymn which I remember to have repeated from my earliest boyhood, which is every day repeated by millions of human beings: "*As the different streams having their sources in different places all mingle their water in the sea, so, O Lord, the different paths which men take through different tendencies, various though they appear, crooked or straight, all lead to Thee.*"

The present convention, which is one of the most august assemblies ever held, is in itself a vindication, a declaration to the world of the wonderful doctrine preached in the Gītā: "*Whosoever comes to Me, through whatsoever form, I reach him; all men are struggling through paths which in the end lead to me.*" Sectarianism, bigotry, and its horrible descendant, fanaticism, have long possessed this beautiful earth. They have filled the earth with violence, drenched it often and often with human blood, destroyed civilization and sent whole nations to despair. Had it not been for these horrible demons, human society would be far more advanced than it is now. But their time is come; and I fervently hope that the bell that tolled this morning in honor of this convention may be the death-knell of all fanaticism, of all persecutions with the sword or with the pen, and of all uncharitable feelings between persons wending their way to the same goal.[3]

"Sisters and Brothers of America" were bold words with which to begin a speech by an Indian monk in America in 1893. Racism, again, was still rampant, and India remained under the heel of British imperial rule. Many Americans of European descent still did not regard people of other ethnic groups as equal to themselves. Placing the word "sisters" before "brothers" was also not insignificant. This was twenty-seven years before women in America were granted the right to vote, through the passage of the Nineteenth Amendment to the US constitution. Many of Swami Vivekananda's most generous benefactors and some of his closest disciples in America were, in fact, women, such as Josephine MacLeod (1858–1949) and Christine Greenstidel (1866–1930), the latter of whom took monastic vows and subsequently went by the name of Sister Christine. Indeed, Vivekananda's most renowned Western disciple—and possibly his most famous disciple of all—was an Irish woman, Margaret E. Noble, who is better known to the world by her monastic name: Sister Nivedita.

Sister Nivedita writes movingly, in a letter to a fellow devotee, Josephine MacLeod, dated July 26, 1904, of her relationship with Swami Vivekananda and its effects on her life:

> Suppose He had not come to London that time! [Nivedita met Vivekananda when he visited London in 1895, on his way back to India from his first visit to America.] Life would have been like a headless torso—for I always knew that I was waiting for something. I always said that a call would come. And it did. But if I had known more of life, I should perhaps have doubted whether when the time came I should certainly recognise. Fortunately, I knew little, and was spared that torture ... always I had this burning voice within, but nothing to utter. How often and often I sat down, pen in hand, to speak, and there was no speech. And now, there is no end to it! As surely I am fitted to my world—so surely is my world in need of me, waiting, ready. The arrow has found its own place in the bow. But *if* He had not come! If He had meditated on the Himalayan peaks.[4]

Many in India today view Swami Vivekananda primarily as an Indian cultural hero, and as a revitalizer and a reformer of the ancient Hindu traditions. In the context of America, he was in the vanguard of progressive social thought, treating people of all races, and men and women alike, as equals—albeit viewing men and women as having distinct natures and roles, so not altogether feminist in the contemporary sense of the term. Vivekananda based his progressivism upon the Vedantic teaching he learned from his master that God dwells in all beings. The significance of his opening words—Sisters and Brothers of America—was not lost upon his audience, who roared their approval, forcing him to pause to let their applause die down before proceeding with the main body of his speech.

The major theme of Swami Vivekananda's address would be a central one of his teaching—and, as we saw in our introduction, an idea to which 65 percent of Americans surveyed in 2009 would give their assent—the idea of "toleration and universal acceptance." Speaking as a Hindu, he says, "We believe not only in universal toleration, but we accept all religions as true."[5]

The opposites of toleration and acceptance are, of course, bigotry and fanaticism, which Vivekananda denounces in the second half of his speech. In his closing lines, he says, "I fervently hope that the bell that tolled this morning in honor of this convention may be the death-knell of all fanaticism, of all persecutions with the sword or with the pen, and of all uncharitable feelings between persons wending their way to the same goal."[6] These lines are especially poignant if one bears in mind that this address was delivered on September 11, 1893—or precisely 108 years to the day before the infamous attacks on America on the same date in 2001.

Immediately following the Parliament, Swami Vivekananda's speaking tour took him to such American cities as Madison, Wisconsin; Minneapolis, Minnesota; Des Moines, Iowa; Detroit, Michigan; and Memphis, Tennessee.[7] The Vivekananda phenomenon, however, was not without resistance. Racism, as mentioned, remained rampant, and the United States was still a very deeply Christian nation. There were those who sought to counter his influence. But there was also a deep vein of religious progressivism into which he successfully tapped. This dual American reaction is well exemplified by the fact that, while the halls where he spoke would frequently be packed with eager listeners, there would also be picketers outside, frequently led by conservative Christian preachers, to protest these events. The venues where he spoke were often Unitarian churches—a fact that should not be at all surprising, given the legacy of the Transcendentalists.

Vivekananda remained in America until 1897, at which time he returned to India. In 1894, he established the first Vedanta Society, in New York. The Vedanta Society is the oldest Hindu-based organization in America. Vivekananda did not, however, through initiating Westerners into the practice of Vedanta, see himself as converting them to Hinduism. He presented Vedanta as a universal philosophy underlying all religions, and was, in fact, very averse to the notion of religious conversion, preferring, rather, that persons of different religions draw inspiration from one another:

> Do I wish that the Christian would become Hindu? God forbid. Do I wish that the Hindu or Buddhist would become Christian? God forbid ... The Christian is not to become a Hindu or a Buddhist, nor a Hindu or a Buddhist to become a Christian. But each must assimilate the spirit of the others and yet preserve his individuality and grow according to his own law of growth.[8]

As we shall later see, today, some Western adherents of Vedanta view themselves as Hindu and some do not. On the one hand, there are those who identify Vedanta, as Vivekananda did, not as a religion, distinct from the religions in which they were raised, but as, in the words of Sarvepalli Radhakrishnan, "not a religion, but religion itself in its most universal and deepest significance."[9] On the other hand, there are those who feel the need for an easy label and find *Hindu* works well.

After returning to India, Swami Vivekananda established the Ramakrishna Mission—which is essentially the Indian equivalent of the Vedanta Society—and organized the remaining monastic disciples of Sri Ramakrishna into the Ramakrishna Order. Most Vedanta Societies in America are affiliated to the Ramakrishna Order, although some are independent. Most are also run by monks of the Ramakrishna Order, some of whom are Americans and some of whom come from India for the purpose of serving the cause of Vedanta in the West.

The Vedanta Societies and Their Many Ripple Effects

In 1899, after two years in India, Swami Vivekananda returned to America and established a Vedanta Society in San Francisco. He brought with him two of his fellow monks who had also been, like himself, disciples of Ramakrishna: Swami Trigunatitananda and Swami Abhedananda. Vivekananda appointed Trigunatitananda to preside over the Vedanta Society of San Francisco and Abhedananda to preside over the first Vedanta Society, in New York. In the coming years, the number of Vedanta Societies would continue to expand. Today, there are roughly twenty such centers. Most are full-fledged centers, with their own buildings and with swamis appointed to run them. Others are smaller, meeting in the homes of members and bringing swamis from the other centers as guest speakers. Some, such as the Ramakrishna Vedanta Ashrama of Pittsburgh, have a building, but not a swami in residence. The Vedanta Society of Kansas City has recently acquired a swami in residence. For most of its history, though, it was a satellite of the Vedanta Society of St. Louis, whose swami visited regularly to give talks and provide instruction to the members.

The typical Vedanta Society in America does not have a temple, but rather, a chapel. These spaces for meditation and worship are closely modelled on Protestant Christian churches, having either benches or rows of chairs set on either side of a central aisle that leads to an altar and pulpit. The altar typically includes a large photograph of Sri Ramakrishna—usually the most famous of the three photographs taken of him during his lifetime, in which he is sitting in an ecstatic state of spiritual absorption, or samādhi. To the left of this photograph (or to the right side, from a viewer's perspective) is a photograph of Ramakrishna's wife, Sarada Devi, who is known to devotees in this tradition as the Holy Mother. To Ramakrishna's right (or left, from the viewer's perspective) is a photograph of Swami Vivekananda. Often, photographs of the other fifteen original monastic disciples of Sri Ramakrishna line the chapel walls.

Some of the larger Vedanta centers, though, have a full-fledged temple on their premises. The first of these temples—one of several claimants to the title of oldest Hindu temple in America—is that of the Vedanta Society of San Francisco. It was built in 1906. Eclectic in its architecture, it reflects the philosophy behind it, including Hindu, Christian, and Islamic elements.[10]

Early in the twentieth century, the fledgling Vedanta Societies, though they grew steadily, also experienced some setbacks. The first was the death, on July 4, 1902, of Vivekananda, at the young age of thirty-nine. He passed away in India, at Belur Math, the monastic headquarters of the Ramakrishna Order, near Kolkata. Interestingly, a young Mohandas K. Gandhi—thirty-two years old at the time—sought an audience with Swami Vivekananda while traveling to Kolkata for a meeting of the Indian National Congress. The swami, however, was far too ill to receive visitors, and what would have been a great historical meeting never occurred.[11]

The second was a split within the Vedanta Society of New York, which occurred in 1910. To the present, there are two different Vedanta centers in New York—the original Vedanta Society of New York and the Ramakrishna-Vivekananda Center. Both of the centers are affiliated with Belur Math, with swamis of the Ramakrishna Order serving as minister-in-charge.[12] The division between the two seems to have arisen based on what could be called differing stylistic issues within the Vedanta community: divisions over how "Western" or "Indian" the Societies should be.

The Vedanta Society of New York follows procedures which are more akin to those found in a Hindu temple—such as the removal of one's shoes upon entering the building. Shoes are worn, though, within the Ramakrishna-Vivekananda Center—even in the chapel. Also, the swamis at the Ramakrishna-Vivekananda Center—with the noteworthy exception of the minister-in-charge, who wears a monk's traditional saffron robes—wear Western-style suits and ties. Although the relations between the two centers are good—with members of each center participating in events sponsored by the other—they clearly have taken distinct approaches to the question of how much a Hindu-inspired organization needs to adapt to the American context versus how much it needs to preserve from its original Hindu source. We shall see that this issue and the various responses that it evokes continue to be an ongoing source of questioning and debate among Hindus and the adherents of Hindu-inspired meditation movements in America. It is relevant to note that for a few years in the early twentieth century, Vedanta monks wore black robes and Roman collars like those of Jesuits.

Subsequent to the New York split, a number of Vedanta Societies in America have become independent of the Ramakrishna Order. Some of these, while institutionally distinct from Belur Math, nevertheless have swamis of the Ramakrishna Order serving in them. Unlike the Roman Catholic Church, the organization of Vedanta Societies is relatively loose. Degrees of affiliation to the central institution vary. Societies that disagree with the central organization simply separate.

One particularly prominent example of such a separation occurred on the basis of gender. Swami Paramananda (1884–1940), an Indian disciple of Vivekananda who was deeply dedicated to Vivekananda's vision of gender equality established two Vedanta communities specifically for women who wanted to take up the path of sannyāsa as part of the Ramakrishna Order. One was based in Boston and the other, called the Ananda Ashram, was in La Crescenta, California. These centers, which were established in 1923, were supervised by Swami Paramananda's first American disciple, Sister Devamata (1867–1942), who was also the author of several books on Vedanta. Not confined to American women, the first Indian woman to join this community was named Gayatri Devi (1906–95), who first came to America to be an assistant to Swami Paramananda and ended up heading one of the ashrams which he established.

These centers for women, unfortunately, split from the Ramakrishna Order in 1941, after the passing away of Swami Paramananda. The Order insisted that the heads of all of its affiliated Vedanta Societies be monks trained at Belur Math—essentially preventing the women from running their own organizations. These centers took the name of the Order of Ramakrishna Brahmavadin.

Despite divisions and controversies like these, the Vedanta Society experienced a growth spurt in the 1930s that continued into the 1940s (during the Second World War). Vedanta Societies opened in Portland, Oregon; Hollywood, California; Providence, Rhode Island; Chicago, Illinois; St. Louis, Missouri; and Seattle, Washington. Membership in the Vedanta Societies as a whole "tripled in the 1930s and grew steadily until the 1950s, when it levelled off again."[13]

Vedanta Societies during this period became magnets for important intellectual and literary figures who played a major role in disseminating Vedantic teachings throughout American culture. Christopher Isherwood (1904–86)—famed novelist and associate of such literary figures as W.H. Auden, E.M. Forster, and Somerset Maugham—assisted his guru, Swami Prabhavananda, founder of the Vedanta Society of Southern California, in his translations of such important works as the *Bhagavad Gita*, the *Yoga Sutras* of Patañjali, and the *Viveka Chudamani* of Shankara. Finally, drawing upon his considerable

FIGURE 21 *Christopher Isherwood in Los Angeles (Photo by Allan Warren via Wikimedia Commons).*

literary talents, Isherwood wrote what is probably the most popular biography of Ramakrishna in the English language: *Ramakrishna and His Disciples.*[14]

Aldous Huxley (1894–1963), also affiliated to the California center and also a disciple of Swami Prabhavananda, was an essayist and novelist who wove many Vedantic themes throughout his fictional and non-fictional works. His well-known essay, *The Perennial Philosophy*, outlines Swami Vivekananda's ideal of a universal religion that underlies all religions through a common core of direct mystical realization—an echo of the idea of a universal wisdom religion taught by the Theosophists. Huxley defines this universal religion as follows:

> The metaphysic that recognises a divine Reality substantial to the world of things and lives and minds; the psychology that finds in the soul something similar to, or even identical with, divine Reality; the ethic that places man's final end in the knowledge of the immanent and transcendent Ground of all being.[15]

A major theme of Huxley's novels is the expansion of consciousness, and one of his most provocative works, *The Doors of Perception*—an exploration of the use of psychedelic drugs to expand consciousness—is the source from which the popular California-based band of the 1960s, the Doors, took its name.

Another prominent literary figure—and a fellow British expatriate settled in California who took Swami Prabhavananda as his guru—was Gerald Heard (1889–1971). Heard, in turn, served as a mentor to Bill Wilson, a founding figure of Alcoholics Anonymous, which is based on the ideal of a "higher power" within all people, to which we all have access through our consciousness.

Shifting from the West Coast to the East Coast, author J.D. Salinger was associated with the Ramakrishna-Vivekananda Center. Salinger was a disciple of Swami Nikhilananda, translator of *The Gospel of Sri Ramakrishna*, and is best known in America as the author of *The Catcher in the Rye*, a novel of youthful alienation and protest against the norms of conventional Western society. His later works, like *Frannie and Zooey*, are replete with Vedantic themes and references. Salinger abruptly withdrew from society at the height of his fame—a retreat that was the source of much speculation until after his death, in 2010, when it came to light that he spent the last five decades of his life practicing meditation and studying the *Bhagavad Gītā* under the guidance of the swamis at the Ramakrishna-Vivekananda Center.

Two major American scholars of religion of the mid-twentieth century, Huston Smith and Joseph Campbell, were deeply influenced by Indian values and philosophies—and particularly by Vedanta. Smith transformed the study of the world's religions into a popular discipline, in demand on nearly every college campus in the United States, particularly with his television series *The Religions of Man*.

Campbell assisted Nikhilananda both in his translation of *The Gospel of Sri Ramakrishna* and in his four-volume translation of the principle *Upaniṣads*. Like Smith, he also popularized the comparative study of religion and mythology, partially through his own scholarly work, such as the celebrated book, *The Hero with a Thousand Faces*, on the theme of the mythic archetypes, but also indirectly, through his collaboration with filmmaker George Lucas.

Lucas, inspired by the work of Campbell, dreamed of developing a distinctively American mythology drawing upon Indic and other world spiritual traditions. This vision took the form of the wildly popular *Star Wars* films. Especially in the teaching of the Jedi Master Yoda, one can hear echoes of Vedanta in the *Star Wars* universe. "Luminous beings are we," Master Yoda tells his disciple, Luke Skywalker, "not this crude matter." This reflects the teaching of the *Bhagavad Gītā* that the true Self is beyond the realm of the body and the senses. "Just as the embodied one experiences childhood, and youth, and old age, in this body, in the same way he enters other bodies. A wise person is not disturbed by these changes. O Arjuna, contact with the material world induces sensations of cold and heat and pleasure and pain. They come and go. They are impermanent."[16]

Even the relationship between the initially doubting and scornful Luke Skywalker and his eccentric, seemingly mad master, as depicted in *The Empire Strikes Back*, reflects the relationship of the young Naren, who would one day emerge as Swami Vivekananda, and the divine madman, Sri Ramakrishna. This is a topic to which we shall return.

The Vedanta Societies that were established by Swami Vivekananda and his fellow monks of the Ramakrishna Order and subsequent generations of disciples were a major source of direct infusion of Hindu thought and practice into American society, but they were not the only such source. As we have seen, prior to the coming of Vivekananda, the Transcendentalists and the Theosophical Society had already helped to popularize ideas such as the reality of an all-pervasive divine force in the universe, integral both to the human person and to the cosmos as a whole, practices of yoga or meditation aimed at connecting with and manifesting that latent divine potential within one's own life, karma and rebirth, and the idea that wisdom is universal—to be found in many religions rather than in only one. In the Vedanta Societies, though, one could encounter actual Hindu monks, conveying these concepts as they had learned them from their masters in India. Certainly, there was an air of exoticism about taking up a spiritual practice such as Vedanta, which could well have been part of its initial appeal for some. It can also be argued, though, that this practice spoke to a genuine spiritual hunger—a truly felt need—on the part of many Americans for a spirituality which was not dogmatic, but yet spoke with the authority of "an old intelligence."[17]

Paramahansa Yogananda and the Self-Realization Fellowship

After the coming of Swami Vivekananda, other Hindu teachers, from other lineages, soon followed, and continued the work of popularizing many aspects of Hindu thought and practice in America. The most influential of these early post-Vivekananda teachers, particularly in the first half of the twentieth century, was certainly Paramahansa Yogananda.

With a career that in some ways parallels that of Swami Vivekananda, Yogananda (1893–1952), a Bengali Hindu spiritual teacher, first came to America in 1920 to attend the International Congress of Religious Liberals, which was sponsored by the Unitarian Church and held in Boston. He remained in the country and, also in 1920, established the Self-Realization Fellowship in order to disseminate the practice of *Kriya Yoga*, a form of spiritual practice into which he had himself been initiated by his guru, Sri Yukteśwar Giri (1855–1936), and into which Giri had been initiated by his guru, Lahiri Mahasaya (1828–95). The founder of the lineage, known as Babaji, is said in the tradition to be an ageless being, centuries old. In 1917, prior to leaving India, Yogananda established the Yogoda-Satsang, of which the Self-Realization Fellowship is the American branch (much as the Vedanta Societies are the American branch of the Ramakrishna Mission in India).

Rather than returning to India, Yogananda remained in America. In the course of ten years, he established twelve centers across the United States. These centers boasted a total membership, by 1930, of twenty-five thousand, outpacing even the highly popular Vedanta Societies. Among the distinctive aspects of the Self-Realization Fellowship is a strong emphasis on devotion to Jesus as an enlightened master and avatar. It is likely that, for many Americans, this emphasis facilitated their ability to adopt what might otherwise seem like a new and foreign spiritual practice. It could be seen more easily as something akin to a "church," rather than as something exotic. "Until 1965 when significant numbers of immigrants from India began to arrive, this movement was the largest and most extensive Hindu organization in the U.S."[18]

Among the wider public, Yogananda is probably best known as the author of the classic *Autobiography of a Yogi*, a work that continues to be popular today among many Americans who feel drawn to Indian traditions. Through this book, this teacher's influence continues to resonate.

In 1952, after Yogananda's death, one of his closest disciples, an American monk with the name Swami Janakananda (formerly James Lynn), took over the leadership of the organization. He was succeeded in 1955 by Sri Daya Mata, who continued to head the organization until her own departure in the year 2010.

The death of Swami Yogananda attracted considerable media attention due to the attested incorruptibility of his physical body for twenty days after his passing. As had been the case with the Vedanta Society, the Self Realization Fellowship saw division after the death of its founder. Several of Yogananda's followers established new organizations, including the Self-Revelation Church of Absolute Monism in Washington, DC, the Prema Dharmasala in Virginia, the Temple of Kriya Yoga in Chicago, and the Ananda Church of God-Realization.[19]

Jiddu Krishnamurti: "Truth Is a Pathless Land"

Yet another prominent Indian spiritual teacher to develop a following in America was Jiddu Krishnamurti (1895–1986). In the year 1909, when he was only fourteen years old, Krishnamurti was identified by prominent members of the Theosophical Society as a special being whom they believed would later grow up to be the "World Teacher"—the next Buddha, Maitreya, the next avatar of Hinduism, and the second coming of Christ all in one. Annie Besant herself came to believe this very deeply and essentially adopted him as her own child, taking charge of his education and upbringing, and grooming him for his future role. A new branch of the Theosophical Society, the Order of the Star in the East, was developed with the specific purpose of preparing the way for this messianic figure.

In the early 1920s, the theosophists moved Krishnamurti to Ojai, California—a place which Krishnamurti enjoyed so much; he spent a great deal of the rest of his life there. In 1922, he had a series of intense spiritual experiences which resulted in a transformation of his personality. Some of these experiences continued to recur throughout his life. He had a powerful sense of a spiritual presence accompanying him, and also of a deep truth, beyond the ability of words to capture.

These experiences led him to a radical new realization. In 1929, at a meeting of the Order of the Star in the East, he abruptly dissolved the organization with the following statement:

> I maintain that truth is a pathless land, and you cannot approach it by any path whatsoever, by any religion, by any sect. That is my point of view, and I adhere to that absolutely and unconditionally. Truth, being limitless, unconditioned, unapproachable by any path whatsoever, cannot be organised; nor should any organisation be formed to lead or coerce people along a particular path ... This is no magnificent deed, because I do not want followers, and I mean this. The moment you follow someone you cease to follow Truth. I am not concerned whether you pay attention to what I say or not. I want to do a certain thing in the world and I am going to do it with unwavering concentration. I am concerning myself with only one essential thing: to set man free. I desire to free him from all cages, from all fears, and not to found religions, new sects, nor to establish new theories and new philosophies.[20]

Krishnamurti continued to write and teach throughout the rest of his life. His basic thesis remained ever the same as in his statement dissolving the Order of the Star in the East: that truth is not something that can be captured or contained in any religion, philosophy, or organization, but can only be perceived directly by the individual, inquiring freely.

One could question whether it is even appropriate to discuss Krishnamurti in the context of a discussion of Hinduism in America, given his rejection of all limiting identifications. Yet this very rejection is so much of a piece with much of the Hindu thought that has been brought into the Western world, and his own background so interwoven with the larger narrative of this book—given his birth into a Hindu family and his close interactions with the theosophists in some of the most formative years of his life—that it would seem to be more problematic to exclude this important voice. Certainly, the wider counterculture that would eventually emerge in America in the 1960s, and which was also intertwined with Hindu concepts, bears the imprint of Krishnamurti's deeply anti-authoritarian approach to truth. His speech dissolving the Order of the Star in the East could almost be the creed of the "spiritual but not religious" movement that has drawn deeply from Hindu thought and practice—were creeds not antithetical to that movement. The idea that truth is beyond the words—that it is "not this, not that," or *neti, neti*—can be found as early as the *Bṛhadāraṇyaka Upaniṣad*.

Of course, no formal organization—no Vedanta Society or Self-Realization Fellowship—has emerged from Krishnamurti's teachings—opposed as they are to attempts at institutionalization. There is the Krishnamurti Foundation, which disseminates his writings, but that is its sole purpose.

Other Early Hindu Teachers in America

A number of important Hindu teachers came to America in the early years of the twentieth century, apart from Vivekananda, Yogananda, and Krishnamurti. Another adherent of Vedanta, Swami Rama Tirtha (1873–1906) came to America in 1902, touring and lecturing until 1904. He did not establish an organization, but helped disseminate Vedanta philosophy with his talks in the San Francisco area. Although no organization grew up around his teachings during his lifetime, his American followers held him in very high esteem. In 1917, one of his Indian followers, Swami Omkar, founded Shanti Ashrama—the "Spiritual Retreat of Peace"—in Madras in his memory. In 1923, he established an American branch of this same organization in Philadelphia, known as the Sri Nariya Ashrama.[21]

While Vivekananda, Yogananda, and, to some extent, Krishnamurti could all be seen as having a focus primarily on the jñāna yoga and rāja yoga approaches to spirituality—more focused either on the intellect or on the transformation of consciousness through the practice of meditation—another style of spirituality, one more reflective of the religiosity of most Hindus in India, has also been brought to America. This is the form of practice associated with *bhakti*, or deep devotion to a personal Supreme Being. The Vaishnava traditions being the most widespread among Hindus in India, it is not surprising that devotion, specifically, to Krishna has been a particularly prominent religious export. In the latter half of the twentieth century, Krishna devotion has been primarily associated with ISKCON, established by A.C. Bhaktivedanta Swami Prabhupada in 1966.

In 1902, however, a Bengali devotee in the same Gauḍīya Vaishnava tradition which would later give rise to Prabhupada—Baba Premanand Bharati—came to America. Rooted in the teachings of the medieval Vaishnava scholar and saint, Sri Chaitanya Mahaprabhu (who lived from 1486 to 1534), Baba Premanand Bharati lectured in New York, Boston, and Los Angeles, where he is said to have built a Hindu temple. He established the Krishna Samāj, or "Community of Krishna." The Krishna Samāj "was the first bhakti-oriented form of Hinduism to reach American soil, a precursor to the Hare Krishnas of the 1960s. Bharati returned to India in 1907."[22]

In 1903, Akhay Kumar Mozumdar, an Indian teacher of New Thought, came to America. Mozumdar, in a series of short publications titled *The Life and Way Series*, presented his ideas as "an eclectic blend of Hinduism and Christianity."[23] In 1911, Mozumdar became the first Indian to take up American citizenship. In 1923, however, in a tragic turn of events that was emblematic of America's fickle relationship with Hinduism, he became the first naturalized citizen from India to be stripped of his citizenship, for reasons we shall explore shortly.

Two very prominent Indians spent short amounts of time in the United States during this period as well. The renowned Bengali songwriter, poet, essayist, and playwright, Rabindranath Tagore, the grandson of Brahmo Samāj leader Debendranath Tagore, visited the United States in 1912 and again in 1917. B.R. Ambedkar, who would later become a major leader of the Dalit community in India, as well as the author of the Indian constitution, studied from 1913 to 1915 at Columbia University.

Three more Indian spiritual teachers who spent time in America during this period include a teacher of yoga, a teacher who was not born Hindu but whose teaching partakes strongly of the worldview and sensibility of Hinduism (particularly as presented to Westerners at this time), and the founder of a Hindu lineage that has given particular importance to women.

FIGURE 22 *Rabindranath Tagore. This is the most striking photo ever taken of the great poet and philosopher of India, Sir Rabindranath Tagore. He has won the Nobel Prize for his works. He has also established at Shantinketan, India, a university which promises to become one of the leading centers of Oriental culture (Photo by Bettmann via Getty Images).*

Manibhai Haribhai Desai, "who as a guru adopted the title Shri Yogendra," was one of the first yoga teachers to visit America who emphasized the physical dimensions of yoga practice—that is, *āsana*, or posture—and the health benefits of such practice.[24] This would prove to have massive repercussions in the West. To the extent that yoga could be differentiated from its religious context of a quest for spiritual realization, it could be more readily assimilated into the lives of Westerners who were suspicious either of "heathen" religions or of religion as such. Desai traveled in the United States from 1919 to 1922, speaking on the benefits of yoga and performing demonstrations of āsanas.

Meher Baba (1894–1969) was not a Hindu, but a Zoroastrian He "later became a mystic who transcended the confines of any tradition. He was seen by his followers … to be an avatar."[25] His later followers, in the 1960s, included Pete Townshend, the lead guitarist and main songwriter for the British rock band, The Who. A number of the songs on Townshend's first solo album, *Who Came First*, released in 1970, are rooted in Meher Baba's teachings.

Meher Baba first visited America in 1932. In 1952, his American devotees established the Meher Spiritual Center, at Myrtle Beach, South Carolina. Meher Baba visited this center in 1952, 1956, and 1958.[26]

Dada Lekhraj, also known as Prajapitar Brahma, came to America in 1937, establishing the World Spiritual University in New York, and a movement of female followers known as the Brahma Kumaris. "Brahma Kumari" means Daughter of Brahma. The movement is now based at the Brahma Kumari Spiritual University on Mount Abu, in the Indian state of Rajasthan. Lekhraj passed the leadership of the organization to his female followers, with whom it has remained. The Brahma Kumaris teach a path of asceticism with a special emphasis on abstention from alcohol. They also hold a belief in the imminent end of the current world order and the coming of a new Golden Age. This is an unusual belief for a Hindu-inspired organization to hold, although there is a widespread belief among Hindus that humanity is currently living through the *Kali Yuga*—the final, degenerate part of the current cosmic epoch, after which the universe will be regenerated.

Sri Aurobindo

Two important Hindu teachers of the early twentieth century with considerable followings in America who have both made a considerable impact on how Hindu thought is understood in the West never actually traveled to America—although one did spend a portion of his growing up years in the West and developed a powerful synthesis of Western and Indian thought. These two teachers are Sri Aurobindo and Sri Ramana Maharshi.

Aurobindo Ghose (1872–1950), better known as Sri Aurobindo, was a freedom fighter for Indian independence and later a major philosopher, Hindu reformer, and advocate of a system of thought and practice known as *Integral Yoga*. Trained in Western philosophy, Sri Aurobindo's writings seek to unite and integrate both Western and Indian metaphysical themes.

Born into a wealthy Bengali Brahmin family, Sri Aurobindo was sent to England for his education in 1879, where he studied in Cambridge University. In 1893, he returned to India where he served as a minister for the Maharaja of Baroda in Gujarat. Wanting to strengthen his ties to his Bengali heritage, he moved to Kolkata (then spelled *Calcutta*) in 1906.

Both during his service in Baroda and subsequently in Calcutta, Aurobindo was drawn to the cause of Indian independence. Aligning himself with the militant branch of the independence movement, Aurobindo advocated violent revolution against the British government in India.

As a result of his political activities, the British government arrested Aurobindo in 1908 on the suspicion that he was connected with an anti-government bombing. Although he was acquitted in this bombing case, he was nevertheless imprisoned for a year for sedition, because of the radical content of his writings. During the period of his imprisonment, he practiced yoga extensively and wrote of experiencing a number of powerful spiritual visions at this time. These included visions of Krishna and of Swami Vivekananda, who had died just a few years earlier (in 1902), and whose spiritual heir Aurobindo felt himself to be.

In 1910, after his release from prison, he announced his retirement from politics. Moving to the French colony of Pondicherry, he dedicated himself to spiritual practice and philosophical writing, developing his system of Integral Yoga.

A prolific author, Aurobindo's writings include *Integral Yoga*, *The Synthesis of Yoga*, *The Secret of the Veda*, *The Upanishads*, *Essays on the Gita*, *Rebirth and Karma*, the epic spiritual poem *Savitri*, and the monumental *The Life Divine*.

One of the major themes of Aurobindo's writing is the integration of Western thought, with its emphasis on the material world and the evolution of mind from matter, and Indian thought, with its emphasis on pure consciousness and what Aurobindo calls the "involution" of mind into matter. These two complementary processes are really one process viewed from different perspectives, according to Aurobindo's account. The term *involution* is drawn from the writings of Swami Vivekananda, and Aurobindo says several times that he sees himself as building on and continuing the work that was begun by Vivekananda and his master, Ramakrishna, both of whom sought the reconcile the concepts of the absolute realm of spirit and the relative realm of time, space, matter, and change.

In *Rebirth and Karma*, Aurobindo also articulates the idea—now common among many Americans who believe in the Hindu idea of rebirth—that reincarnation is a learning process for the soul: that our karma consists of "work" that we need to accomplish in order to advance spiritually.

Aurobindo dedicated his life to bringing divine awareness, or "supermind," into the realm of concrete, physical expression through the practice of yoga. Before his death, he claimed to have achieved this manifestation within himself.

Aurobindo also popularized an approach to the *Vedas* that was a striking contrast with the dominant Indological paradigm of his time. Rather than seeing the early Vedic literature as the relatively primitive nature poetry of a nomadic society which only later developed into the more sophisticated Vedanta philosophy of the *Upaniṣads*, Sri Aurobindo suggests that the early Vedic poems already presuppose the fully developed philosophy, presenting it in a symbolic form. It is only as the key to this ancient symbolic code is slowly forgotten that Vedic philosophy needs to be articulated more explicitly in the *Upaniṣads*, which are thus seen as an unpacking of what was already present in the early Vedic texts, rather than as an evolutionary development from them.

Aurobindo attracted many followers, including Westerners. The most famous of these was a French woman named Mira Richard, to whom Sri Aurobindo and his followers referred to as "the Mother." Aurobindo saw Richard as an incarnation of Shakti, the Mother Goddess and feminine energy of creation. Richard took over Aurobindo's community and spiritual work after his death in 1950, emerging as a charismatic leader in her own right.

Sri Ramana Maharshi

Sri Ramana Maharshi (1879–1950) was born Venkataraman Iyer, near the sacred temple city of Madurai, in the southernmost region of India. He is believed by his followers to have been *jivanmukta*—that is, liberated while still alive. Not unlike Sri Ramakrishna, he was born a Brahmin in a small village. He is said to have had an incredibly good memory, and it is also said that, rather like Sri Ramakrishna, he experienced states of deep spiritual absorption in his childhood. When he visited temples, he would feel a deep bliss. He found himself particularly drawn to the sacred mountain of Arunachala. He received an English education and became familiar with Christianity; however, not unlike Sri Ramakrishna before him, he was largely indifferent to studies, being more interested in exploring spiritual states and having an experience of God. He spent a good deal of time in the elaborate and beautiful temples of southern India, but Arunachala continued to beckon him.

From 1899 to 1922, Sri Ramana spent most of his time meditating in caves on Arunachala. It was during this time that he began to develop a following among Indians, who were drawn to this sage whose every word seemed to convey profound wisdom.

FIGURE 23 *Sri Ramana Maharshi (Photo by Eliot Elisofon/The LIFE Picture Collection via Getty Images).*

In 1922, he relocated to Sri Ramanashramam, the spiritual institution that grew up around him, and which eventually included a library and a hospital.[27] In the 1930s, Westerners began taking an interest in Sri Ramana. Visitors to his ashram included the author Somerset Maugham, also an associate of Isherwood, Huxley, Heard, and Prabhavananda. One of the central characters in Maugham's novel, *The Razor's Edge*—though he appears only near the novel's end—is an Indian sage named Shri Ganesha who is modelled on Sri Ramana Maharshi:

> When I got down to Travancore I found I needn't have asked for information about Shri Ganesha. Everyone knew of him. For many years he'd lived in a cave in the hills, but finally he'd been persuaded to move down to the plain where some charitable person had given him a plot of land and had built a little adobe house for him. It was a long way from Trivandrum, the capital, and it took me all day, first by train and then by bullock cart, to get to the Ashrama. I found a young man at the entrance of the compound and asked him if I could see the Yogi. I'd brought with me the basket of fruit which is the customary gift to offer. In a few minutes the young man came back and led me into a long hall with windows all around it. In one corner Shri Ganesha sat in the attitude of meditation on a raised dais covered with a tiger skin. "I've been expecting you," he said. I was surprised, but supposed my friend of Madura had told him something about me. But he shook his head when I mentioned his name. I presented my fruit and he told the young man to take it away. We were left alone and he looked at me without speaking. I don't know how long the silence lasted. It might have been for half an hour. I've told you what he looked like; what I haven't told you is the serenity that he irradiated, the goodness, the peace, the selflessness. I was hot and tired after my journey, but gradually I began to feel wonderfully rested. Before he said another word, I knew that this was the man I'd been seeking.[28]

While Sri Ramana, not unlike Krishnamurti, did not identify explicitly or exclusively with any particular system or school of thought, his teaching is most often identified with non-dualistic, or Advaita, Vedanta, according to which the only reality is the infinite Brahman. Sri Ramana's teaching method, however, is quite distinct from that of classical Advaita. Rather than the study of the *Upaniṣads*, Sri Ramana always encouraged his students to look within—pursuing self-inquiry and asking the question, "Who am I?" (Or, in his native Tamil, "Nan yar?")

American teachers inspired by Ramana Maharshi are sometimes said to advocate a "Neo-Advaita," distinct from traditional Advaita and focused on the self-inquiry taught by Sri Ramana.[29]

Thinkers who are inspired by Aurobindo, on the other hand, tend to emphasize an "integral" approach to spirituality, synthesizing the material and spiritual realms.[30] Aurobindo's perspective and that of the movement of "integral studies" based upon his thought are akin to that of Tāntric Hinduism. This particular understanding of non-duality is characterized not by a devaluation of the material, sensory realm as a realm of potential objects of attachment, but by a valuing of the material as the field of manifestation and actualization of the spiritual.

American Reactions to Hinduism

Earlier in this chapter, I described America's relationship with Hinduism as "fickle." This is not an entirely fair generalization, as it suggests that the same group of people are having varied and unpredictable responses to this tradition. The reality, rather, is that America, like Hinduism itself, is internally varied, and no single generalization can ever be adequate to the task of capturing American reactions to anything. Some Americans have embraced Hindu ideas and practices with genuine and enduring enthusiasm, in some cases even risking ridicule and the loss of standing in their native society. Every Hindu teacher who has been mentioned in this chapter who succeeded in starting an institution—and there have been many—attracted at least enough of a following among the American public to sustain that institution (at least the ones which have endured, such as the Vedanta Society, the Self-Realization Fellowship, and the Brahma Kumaris). Even those who did not establish institutions in America, like Krishnamurti, Sri Aurobindo, and Sri Ramana Maharshi, have had enduring legacies in terms of their influence upon American thought—Sri Aurobindo and Sri Ramana Maharshi without even setting foot in the country.

At the same time, however, as we saw in our demographic analysis in the introduction to this book, the number of actual Hindus and members of Hindu-inspired meditation movements is slightly less than 1 percent of the total population of the United States. While it is true, as Lisa Miller observes, that certain Hindu ideas, such as religious pluralism and reincarnation, have a far larger following than this, many Americans who adhere to these ideas do not self-identify as Hindu and are largely unaware, or are only dimly aware, of the Hindu provenance of these beliefs. There has thus been influence, but there has also been, at some level, erasure as well.

Just as many Americans flocked to Hindu teachers in the first half of the twentieth century, many others reacted to these teachers and their popularity with deep alarm. As the timeline of Hinduism in America developed by the Pluralism Project at Harvard University notes:

> In 1911, a sensational article by Mabel Potter Daggett, "The Heathen Invasion" was published. Shortly thereafter, in 1912, a Mrs. Gross Alexander published her "American Women Going after Heathen Gods." These articles expressed concern about the large percentage of women in Vedanta centres, presenting them as duped by the charms of Asian teachers.[31]

The Project also notes that in 1927:

> Hinduism was viciously attacked by [Katherine] Mayo's best-seller *Mother India*, a book which sharply critiqued the most sensational practices—"idol worship," animal sacrifices, child marriage, and widow burning. Left entirely untouched were the higher ideals of the tradition expressed by the Hindu reformers of the day. The book set off considerable controversy. Swami Omkar [founder of Shanti Ashrama], among others, responded vehemently to the book.[32]

Another publication from this period, Wendell Thomas's cleverly titled *Hinduism Invades America*, released in 1930, "chronicles the early history of Hinduism in America and the varied responses of Americans to this religious tradition."[33] It is clear from reading the Thomas book that its title is tongue-in-cheek. His book is far from an attack on Hinduism—quite unlike Daggett's, Alexander's, and Mayo's efforts. It is a reasonably even-handed overview of the arrival of Hindu ideas and practices in America and the reactions, both positive and negative, to it.

Behind much of the negative reaction to Hinduism, clearly, was genuine religious anxiety. Many Americans in the nineteenth and early twentieth centuries saw their country as, essentially, a "Christian nation"—as many still do. For every Transcendentalist, Theosophist, Yogi, Vedantin, or adherent of New Thought, there were many more devout and conservative Christians, many of whom saw humanity as, in the famous words of the eighteenth-century Puritan preacher, Jonathan Edwards, "sinners in the hands of an angry God," whose only hope lay in recognizing their sinful nature and humbly accepting the saving grace offered through the atoning sacrifice of Jesus Christ. What were they to make of the words of Swami Vivekananda?

> Children of immortal bliss—what a sweet, what a hopeful name! Allow me to call you, brethren, by that sweet name—heirs of immortal bliss—yea, the Hindu refuses to call you sinners. We are the Children of God, the sharers of immortal bliss, holy and perfect beings. Divinities on earth—sinners! It is a sin to call a man so.[34]

To cultural misfits—dissenters and nonconformists, the people described by Leela Gandhi in her work on anti-colonialism in the West—these powerful words of Swami Vivekananda sound like a declaration of spiritual independence, of liberty from dogmatic and oppressive concepts like sinfulness, judgment, and damnation. To others, though, they are satanic blasphemy, representing the height of humanity's sinful pride in actually daring to claim divinity for itself.

Religious disagreements alone, however, are an insufficient explanation for the vehemence with which Hindu teachers were attacked during this period. How do they explain the anxieties, for example, about American women, in particular, being "duped by the charms of Asian teachers?" Something else is lurking behind the negative American reactions to Hinduism: racism. Even the very positive contemporary accounts of Hindu teachers, like Swami Vivekananda, place a highly sexualized emphasis on their physical appearance and their appeal to (white) American women. From a Hindu point of view, thinking of spiritual teachers in this way is highly inappropriate. As one Hindu informant named Mahadevi points out, "It's not religious to think anything like that of a swami." As Altman describes the early newspaper accounts of Swami Vivekananda: "Observers described him as 'a large, well-built man, with [the] superb carriage of the Hindustanis.' … 'Scores of women' walked over their benches to get near the young swami" after his speech was over.[35] Paramahansa Yogananda faced great difficulties in this regard, being subjected to allegations and insinuations about:

"the overwhelmingly female constitution of [his] audience. Yogananda's organisation was repeatedly referred to as a 'love cult' and presented as part of a sort of rising epidemic." It was also alleged that "a love-cult [was] being conducted under the cloak of the Vedantic religion of India," and that Yogananda was "the writer of various books and pamphlets in which an unusual philosophy of love and sex control are declared to be unfolded."[36]

A number of court decisions early in the twentieth century bear out the conclusion that not only religious anxiety but also racism underlay negative American reactions to Hindus and Hinduism. One such case led to A.K. Mozumdar's loss of his American citizenship in 1923, and eventually, to the Asian Exclusion Act. If anything, Mozumdar was at least as Christian as he was Hindu in his worldview and the language in which he expressed his views. As Thomas elaborates:

> What happens [in Mozumdar's thought] is an identification of the Hindu conception of a divine universal Self with the Hebrew conception of a divine creative Power ... Mozumdar makes this synthesis on the basis of his faith in Jesus Christ. Mozumdar worships Jesus as the supreme religious genius ... Says he [now citing Mozumdar], "Jesus's teaching is the greatest and simplest revelation of God, and is different from other teachings of Truth ... He came to teach us that the human expression is not an illusion ... but ... a vital reality ... Instead of following a specific path to realise God, you let God direct your life ... It need not take you millions of years to dispel millions of years" accumulated darkness [that is, accumulated karma from past lives]. It will take but a flash of light from God to light your entire mental life.[37]

The author of such words did not lose his citizenship because of the ideas these words express, but because he was Indian, and not deemed by the court to be worthy of American citizenship under the laws of that time.

Court cases such as these continued to mount until, in 1924, the Asian Exclusion Act was passed. This Act of Congress reduced immigration from India (as well as from China and Japan) to almost nothing. Only a small handful of students and persons with exceptionally strong letters of support from American persons and institutions were admitted into the country until the Act was lifted in 1965. Although the Vedanta Societies and Self-Realization Fellowship continued to exist, and even to thrive, the flow of new Hindu teachers from India was reduced to the merest trickle. These Hindu-inspired meditation movements, during this period, were almost entirely dependent upon the goodwill of their American adherents.

As we shall see in the next chapter, when the Asian Exclusion Act was finally lifted, a new generation of Hindu teachers began to arrive. They arrived in a very different America, though, from the one which was visited by their forerunners in the late nineteenth and the early twentieth centuries. The next generation of Hindu teachers would arrive in an America in the throes of a major cultural transformation.

The Trials and Tribulations of the Early Indian Diaspora in the United States

During the same period that we have been exploring in this chapter—when some Americans were taking a great interest in Hinduism, and famous gurus came to America to discover a ready audience of Western disciples (and no small amount of opposition as well)—what was the situation of the wider Hindu diaspora in America? How did ordinary Hindus fare during the period when Hinduism "invaded" America?

The early Hindu diaspora in North America as a whole consisted not of renowned spiritual teachers, but ordinary people, many of whom were forced to come to the Americas as indentured laborers, under the pressures of the British Empire. The Caribbean region, in particular, was a destination for Indian indentured laborers, sent primarily to work on plantations. Separated from the wider Hindu community in India, Hindus in this region developed a self-understanding which differentiates them both from Hindus in South Asia and from the later Hindu diaspora which arose in the United States after the lifting of the Asian Exclusion Act in 1965, and which consisted largely of relatively well-off professionals seeking to better their lives and those of their families by improving their financial status.

It is also important to note that the experiences of Hindus in America during this period are inseparable from the experiences of the wider Indian community in America. Indeed, one can well argue that this is the case in every historical period, up to and including the present. The reality of racism that the Indian diaspora as a whole has faced in each period cuts across religious boundaries. We shall therefore speak now not specifically of a Hindu diaspora, but of a wider Indian diaspora: a diaspora, ironically, often referred to by Americans as "Hindoo."

As Vinay Lal points out, the circumstances under which the early Indian diaspora came to the Americas—pre-1924—in contrast with the circumstances under which the later Indian diaspora came to the Americas—post-1965—are so different that it seems to stretch the capacity of a single word—*diaspora*—to cover them both:

> Perhaps the word "diaspora" flattens too much and fails to distinguish between … diasporas that have arisen under circumstances of extreme repression and diasporas that suggest more benign histories of ambition, self-improvement, economic advancement, or sheer adventure.[38]

Prior to the Asian Exclusion Act of 1924, small communities of Indian immigrants could be found in various regions of the United States. On the East Coast, there were Indians studying in elite universities. On the West Coast, the Indian immigrants were primarily working class. The latter group, in particular, frequently found themselves to be on the receiving end of racist attacks, the most notorious being the Bellingham Riots of 1907.

American Anti-Asian sentiment—a sentiment which was directed at Chinese and Japanese people, as well as at Indians, or "Hindoos"—culminated in the passing of the Asian Exclusion Act, which stopped the flow of Indian immigration (including that of Hindu monks and other spiritual teachers) until this Act was overturned by another act of Congress in 1965. An exploration of the treatment of Indians in America prior to 1924 serves as an opportunity to explore the contradiction between the American fascination with Indian traditions during this period and the racism and the violence which were simultaneously perpetrated against actual Indians in America. One can almost speak of two Americas: one open to Indian ideas and Indian people, the other decidedly closed.

Why were Indians during this period so often referred to as *Hindoos*, despite the fact that they included members of other religious communities as well, particularly Sikhs and Muslims? One can of course point out the fact that the differences among Indian religions were very poorly understood in the Western world at this time, certainly among mainstream Americans who were not scholars of Asian traditions. But this lack of understanding was not entirely innocent. It was often an expression of contempt—that the distinctions among these "heathen," "Hindoo" religions were not important enough to learn. This of course hearkens back to the rhetoric of Cotton Mather, which Altman has described, in which distinctions among "heathen" religions were not especially important. All were seen as being in need of conversion to Christianity. All that really needed to be known about these religions was that they were false and led their practitioners to damnation. Religious bigotry thus went hand-in-hand with racism. Much racist violence against people designated, at this time, as "Hindoo," such as the violence of the Bellingham Riots, was directed against Sikh immigrants. The erasure of these Sikhs' identities was just one more facet of the violence that they faced.

In their in-depth study, *The Other One Percent: Indians in America*, Sanjoy Chakravorty, Devesh Kapur, and Nirvikar Singh have made the following important observations about the early Indian diaspora in America:

> There are three notable features of the Indian-American presence prior to 1965; first, it was miniscule; second, despite their tiny numbers, the immigrants encountered virulent animosity; and third, there was a high degree of ignorance and confusion among Americans about people from the Indian subcontinent.[39]

In regard to the first feature, the number of Indians in America was, indeed, miniscule in the period prior to 1965—even more miniscule than at present, when the Indian population makes up 0.9 percent of the US population. In regard to the second point, the hostility and the resistance Indians experienced in America in this early period were, indeed, virulent: not to mention that the circumstances under which many came to the country were often quite difficult as well. The high degree of ignorance and confusion mentioned is well illustrated by the fact that historical records do not differentiate clearly between Hindus and Sikhs, Hindus and Jains, Hindus and Muslims, and so on.

This contemptuous failure to differentiate among the various religions represented by Indians in America has echoes in the contemporary period, when Hindus and Sikhs, along with South Asian Muslims, have become targets of Islamophobia. Most racist violence against Hindus and Sikhs today is, in fact, aimed at Muslims, which Hindus and Sikhs are mistakenly taken to be. This is also despite the fact that Islam is a global religion with a highly ethnically diverse following.

In regard to the United States, specifically, as Chakravorty, Kapur, and Singh point out:

> The few Indians who arrived in the United States in the nineteenth century often came as sailors on ships plying waters between Indian and American ports. According to one source, the first recorded mention of Indians visiting America was "six or seven Indian sailors" brought to New England seminaries in the 1820s.[40]

Regarding Indian sailors, there was an East India Marine Society, which was established in Salem, Massachusetts, in 1799 and consisted of sailors who had traveled one of the routes—Atlantic or Pacific—to India. There is an account of, again, "a half dozen" Indians from this society who marched in the Salem Fourth of July parade in 1851.[41] It is not clear if many, or any, of these Indian sailors actually chose to settle in the United States, or if they eventually returned to India. The census figures for Indian Americans are quite small during the nineteenth century: 586 in 1870 and 2,031 in 1900.[42] These numbers are a far cry from the roughly 3 million Asian Indian Americans of the present day.

The Indian sailors of New England were, presumably, entirely male. The first records of Indian women traveling to America are of two students:

> Anandibai Joshee [*sic*], who graduated from the Women's Medical College of Pennsylvania in 1886 (and apparently "startled her American student counterparts by appearing in a sari in her first anatomy class"), and Pandita Ramabai, a social reformer.[43]

Both Joshi (1865–87) and Ramabai (1858–1922) returned to India. Neither of them immigrated to the United States on a permanent basis, to make it their home. Both, in fact, took up the cause of social reform upon their return to India. Joshi is described as holding views close to those of the Brahmo Samāj.[44] She holds the distinction of being India's first female physician. A proud Hindu, her life was tragically cut short by tuberculosis. Pandita Ramabai attended Joshi's medical school graduation in 1886. A widow—and therefore, according to the Hindu customs of the time, a marginal person in traditional Hindu society, despite her status as a Sanskrit scholar—Ramabai converted to Christianity. As Deborah Logan recounts, contrasting Ramabai with Joshi:

> The Christian conversion of this revered Sanskrit scholar polarized both her admirers and detractors; but, whereas Joshi resisted Christianity's perceived threat to Hindu cultural mores, Ramabai embraced its capacity to recuperate social outcasts like herself whose singular "crime" was, simply, widowhood.[45]

In the early twentieth century, three distinct groups of Indians began to immigrate to both the United States and Canada. The first group consisted of "former soldiers and policemen who had served the British colonial forces in China and the Far East. Instead of returning to India, they sailed east and decided to seek their fortunes in Canada and the United States." These immigrants were entirely male, mostly from the Punjab region, in northern India, and mostly Sikh, with a few Muslims. They were, however, classified as Hindus by the American immigration officials, thus reflecting the early identification, mentioned previously, of the terms *Hindu* and *Indian*.[46]

The second group, also overwhelmingly male, Punjabi, and Sikh, were originally farmers in India. This group of immigrants settled on the West Coast of the United States, from Vancouver to Northern California. "Initially recruited by the Western Pacific Railroad to construct railway lines in the Pacific Northwest, they gradually branched out to working in lumber and construction, and as they moved farther south, they worked as agricultural laborers."[47] Finally, the third group of Indian immigrants consisted of university students, who were mostly Hindu, but also included a few Sikhs and Muslims.

The animosity against these Indian immigrants was, again, quite virulent. Its most dramatic expression occurred in 1907, taking the form of a riot in the town of Bellingham, Washington:

> On a September night … a mob of six hundred lumber-mill workers, incited by the AEL [Asiatic Exclusion League], attacked the compounds of immigrant workers from India. A news report on the riots at the time commented that the rioters struck with excessive violence to "impress upon employers the resentment of the laboring men against the import of Hindu workmen." A hysterical article … warned that America faced an inundation of "Hindus," since the Vedas obliged them to "cover the earth." The AEL held the Indians responsible for the riots, claiming [that] their willingness to work for low wages and … their "filthy and immodest habits" invited reprisals.[48]

As Lal further recounts, after this riot:

> The local newspaper, the *Morning Reveille*, noted that the "small police force was overpowered" and in the fracas many Indians were hurt. They were given notice that they must leave Bellingham; the next day, about 300 Indian laborers quit town. Meeting in San Francisco in February 1908, the Asiatic Exclusion League declared that from everywhere in coastal California complaints "are made of the undesirability of the Hindoos, their lack of cleanliness, disregard of sanitary laws, petty pilfering, especially of chickens, and insolence to women."[49]

One cannot help but note the continuity between the language deployed by the xenophobic Asiatic Expulsion League and contemporary anti-immigrant language in America which focuses upon immigrants' "willingness to work for low wages." The recipe for anti-immigrant violence is not simply racism but racism combined with economic insecurity.

In the years following the violence at Bellingham, anti-Indian sentiment was expressed in a series of court decisions and Congressional hearings which culminated with the passage of the Asian Exclusion Act of 1924. In 1914, the US Congress held "Hindu Immigration Hearings" that featured testimony by Representative Denver S. Church, who was supported by the AEL.[50]

The absolute ignorance even of members of Congress regarding the religious beliefs of the Indian immigrants is well illustrated by an exchange from these hearings, involving Representative Church:

Mr. Church:	They have their religion; in fact, it seems to be about all there is to a Hindu, his religion.
The Chairman:	Is that the Mohammedan [*sic*][51] religion?
Mr. Church:	As I understand.[52]

In February 1917, an act was passed which prohibited most Indians from migrating to the United States. This was followed by the notorious "Hindu German conspiracy trials."[53] These trials were of eight Indian immigrants, at least some of whom were members of the Gadar Party—meaning "Revolutionary Party." This was an early twentieth-century organization among Indian immigrants in North America to support the violent overthrow of the British government in India. It sought to foment rebellion among Indians serving in the British army and to gain support from the United States in the cause of Indian independence.

This movement, led by Har Dayal (1884–1939), suffered a major setback when the United States entered the First World War as an ally of Britain. Dayal was arrested and eventually fled to Germany. Some Indian immigrants in the United States and Canada returned to India to help with the revolution, but the British government was aware of their plans and arrested them.

At the end of the First World War, Dayal returned to India. He then renounced violence and joined Gandhi's nonviolent independence movement. The Gadar Party ceased to be a major force at this point, and dissolved when independence was achieved in 1947. Interestingly, although the United States jailed the Gadarites, "American authorities staved off British pressure to extradite them to India, bowing to domestic public pressures that were still instinctively anticolonial."[54]

The setbacks faced by this movement in the United States should be seen in the context of anti-Indian racism during this period. One might expect—as the Gadarites themselves did—that the United States would be a natural ally of the Indian independence movement, given that the United States itself had once been a British colony. Rather than identify with the Indians as a fellow colonized people seeking freedom from British rule, though, the US government saw them as foreigners and, once Britain had become an American ally in the First World War, as enemy agents. Indeed, the US government went to rather dramatic lengths to show its support for Britain in this war, not only opposing the Gadar movement, but also jailing the movie producer Robert Goldstein for ten years under the Espionage Act because he made a film about the American Revolution that depicted the British (understandably, given that the film was about the American Revolution) in a bad light.[55] It was easier for most white Americans to identify with the British than with colonized Indians.

While the 1917 Act prohibited Indian immigration to the United States, a 1923 decision by the US Supreme Court further prohibited naturalization of Indians already residing in the United States. An Indian immigrant named Bhagat Singh Thind "was granted citizenship twice, in 1918 and 1920, only to have the Immigration and Naturalization Service (INS) cancel his naturalization each time."[56]

Thind appealed his case to the Supreme Court, which ruled against him on the basis of a 1790 act which stated that a "free white person" residing in the United States for two years or more could become a US citizen.

> In a decision written by Justice George Sutherland, the Supreme Court examined Thind's claim that as "an ethnic north Indian Aryan" he was Caucasian and therefore eligible for naturalization as a "free white person." ... Sutherland now wrote that Thind, though of Caucasian ethnicity, could not be naturalized because he was not "white" in the "popular" meaning of the term.[57]

It was on the basis of the Thind decision that Indian New Thought teacher A.K. Mozumdar, the first naturalized US citizen to come from India, mentioned earlier, lost his American citizenship in 1923. Thind's claim was an interesting one. Rather than challenging the racist law that limited immigration to "free white persons"—a challenge that would certainly have had no hope of receiving a sympathetic hearing during that period—it operated within the framework of the law as it stood and tapped into the Indological knowledge of the time. Thind's claim to be "an ethnic north Indian Aryan" of Caucasian descent was rooted in the concept of Aryan invasion or migration that remains a topic of heated discussion for many in regard to the origins of Hinduism.

The Asian Exclusion Act, passed the following year, effectively closed the door to Indian immigration to the United States, with the exception of a small handful of students and a few other individuals who had American citizens to vouch for them.

This situation would not change until 1965, due to massive cultural and political shifts in American society. These shifts—arising largely not only from the Civil Rights Movement but also from the emergent youth counterculture—would lead to a rekindling of American interest in Hinduism, and to far more positive attitudes toward actual, practicing Hindus from India than those which had prevailed in the late nineteenth and early twentieth centuries. This new cultural situation and its implications for Hinduism and its reception in America are the topic of our next chapter.

Study Questions

1. What is the central thesis of Swami Vivekananda's first address at the Chicago World Parliament of Religions in 1893?
2. What aspect of the teaching of the Self-Realization Fellowship may possibly have made it an especially easy Hindu-based organization for Americans to join?
3. How have Sri Ramana Maharshi and Sri Aurobindo influenced American perceptions of Hinduism?
4. What two factors have contributed to American opposition to Hinduism?

Suggestions for Further Reading

Sri Aurobindo, *The Life Divine* (Pondicherry, India: Sri Aurobindo Ashram, 2010).
Gwylim Beckerlegge, *The Ramakrishna Mission* (Oxford: Oxford University Press, 2001).
Sanjoy Chakravorty, Devesh Kapur, and Nirvikar Singh, *The Other One Percent: Indians in America* (New York: Oxford University Press, 2017).
Thomas Forsthoefel, ed., *Gurus in America* (Albany: State University of New York Press, 2005).
Anya P. Foxen, *Biography of a Yogi: Paramahansa Yogananda and the Origins of Modern Yoga* (Oxford: Oxford University Press, 2017).
David Godman, *The Power of the Presence (Part One)* (Lithia Springs, GA: New Leaf Distributing Company, 2000).
Aldous Huxley, *The Perennial Philosophy* (New York: Harper and Row, 1944).
Christopher Isherwood, *Ramakrishna and His Disciples* (Hollywood: Vedanta Press, 1965).
Carl T. Jackson, *Vedanta for the West: The History of the Ramakrishna Movement* (Bloomington: Indiana University Press, 1994).
Vinay Lal, *The Other Indians: A Political and Cultural History of South Asians in America* (New Delhi: HarperCollins, 2008).
Joseph Lelyveld, *Great Soul: Mahatma Gandhi and His Struggle with India* (New York: Vintage Books, 2012).
Lisa Lowe, *Immigrant Acts: On Asian American Cultural Politics* (Durham, NC: Duke University Press, 1996).
Ramana Maharshi, *The Spiritual Teaching of Ramana Maharshi* (Boulder, CO: Shambhala Publications, 2004).
Gurinder Singh Mann, *Buddhists, Hindus, and Sikhs in America* (Oxford: Oxford University Press, 2007).
Somerset Maugham, *The Razor's Edge* (New York: Vintage Books, 1943).
Swami Shuddhidananda, ed., *Vivekananda as the Turning Point: The Rise of a New Spiritual Wave* (Mayawati: Advaita Ashrama, 2018).
Mark Singleton and Ellen Goldberg, eds., *Gurus of Modern Yoga* (Oxford: Oxford University Press, 2014).
Eleanor Stark, *The Gift Unopened: A New American Revolution* (Portsmouth, NH: Peter E. Randall, 1988).
Wendell Thomas, *Hinduism Invades America* (Whitefish, MT: Kessinger Publishing, 2003).
Thomas Tweed and Stephen Prothero, *Asian Religions in America: A Documentary History* (New York: Oxford University Press, 1999).
Swami Vivekananda, *Complete Works* (Mayavati: Advaita Ashrama, 1979).

4

The Rise of a Counterculture: A New Wave of Western Fascination

Chapter 4 Summary and Outline

This chapter will explore the next wave of American interest in Hinduism: that which was centered in the 1960s. The rise of the counterculture of the 1960s, in tandem with the lifting of the Asian Exclusion Act in 1965, created conditions for the arrival of a new wave of Hindu teachers with a ready audience of ardent spiritual seekers: Maharishi Mahesh Yogi, A.C. Bhaktivedanta Swami Prabhupada, Swami Satchidananda, Swami Muktananda, Sri Chinmoy, and more. Intellectuals, such as those drawn to the Esalen Institute, and figures from Western popular culture, such as the Beatles, helped to disseminate Hindu thought, as they understood it, to the wider culture, helping to prepare the way for a renewal of Hindu immigration into the United States. A number of themes of the 1960s counterculture drew upon or correlate with various dimensions of Hinduism.

The Rise of a Counterculture

The two world wars, followed by the withdrawal of the European powers from their various colonies—including, prominently, the British withdrawal from India on August 15, 1947—marked a period of crisis in the Western world. Gone was the nineteenth-century confidence in the inevitable progress of civilization. The colonial faith in Western cultural superiority had been severely battered by the Holocaust and the realization that even members of an "advanced" society could perpetrate the most barbaric crimes imaginable upon their fellow human beings. The atomic bombing of the civilian populations of Hiroshima and Nagasaki—as well as the no less devastating conventional bombings of Dresden and Tokyo—revealed that even the Allied Powers—or the "good guys," to use a popular American phrase—even while seeing themselves as fighting for the values of democracy against totalitarian oppression, were capable of wreaking horrific destruction.

Indians, of course, with their experiences of British colonial violence in India and of racism directed against them in America, were already aware that Western powers were capable of great evil. After the Second World War, though, this reality began to dawn upon many Westerners as well.

In America, the 1950s saw an economic boom and the rise of an affluent middle class. For perhaps the first time in human history, the average person began to have access to social resources such as excellent medical care and a college education which were beyond even the wildest dreams of previous generations. As with ancient societies, in which an increase in standards of living led to the rise of sophisticated systems of philosophical and religious thought, similarly, the increase in leisure time to which the prosperity of 1950s America gave rise to serious reflection on the part of many in the new middle class—particularly among the youth—about the meaning and purpose of their existence. While many Americans enjoyed unprecedented material abundance, their lives were overshadowed by the threat of nuclear annihilation. With the Cold War, and the development of nuclear weapons not only by the United States but by its Soviet opponents, the fear that all life could end at any moment in a flash of atomic fire produced a pervasive undercurrent of anxiety. Much of this anxiety can be seen reflected in the science fiction genre, which became increasingly popular in this period.

It also started to become increasingly clear to many young white people that many of their fellow citizens were largely excluded from the prosperous society that they enjoyed, and for which their parents had fought. African Americans, treated as second-class citizens in the southern states by Jim Crow laws, and experiencing prejudice in the north which was no less vicious for not being enshrined in legislation, had begun to speak out and protest for their rights as equal citizens under the US constitution. The dignity of Martin Luther King, Jr.'s nonviolent movement for civil rights, which was both inspired and informed by Gandhi's nonviolent movement for Indian independence, contrasted starkly with the hatred and the violence expressed by white bigots and policemen who unleashed dogs and turned water cannons on peaceful protesters. King's "I Have a Dream" speech, delivered on August 28, 1963, served as a call of awakening to the conscience of Americans—a call to which many among the youth responded with enthusiasm.

Finally, the escalating war in Vietnam, in which the military might of America looked to be pitted against a people fighting tenaciously for their independence, made many Americans start to question whether their nation really was on the right side: the side of peace and freedom. By the mid-1960s, King's protest methods came to be applied by anti-war activists to the movement to end this war. The iconic photograph of anti-war protester sticking a flower into the barrel of a gun, pointed at him by a military policeman, expresses well the spirit behind this movement.

It was in this context of discontentment with the racism, militarism, and materialism which many youth found to dominate the culture of their parents that a counterculture began to emerge, which questioned the dominant values of American society and the seemingly insatiable quest for ever greater material prosperity that defined it.

What is a *counterculture*? As it is defined by Paul Oliver:

> The term counter-culture tends to be used where a sub-culture evolves which is significantly different from conventional society in terms of values and patterns of behavior. Such a counter-culture exhibits and antipathy towards the established institutions of society. It could be argued that counter-cultures have existed since society has existed, since only through periodic challenges to the prevalent power structures, can society change ... Indeed one might further argue that it is part of the concept of a counter-culture that it seeks to subvert the existing society.[1]

As Oliver further points out, the conditions were ripe in the 1950s and 1960s for the emergence of a counterculture in the United States—and indeed, globally:

> There was ... at the beginning of the 1960s an increasing demand for freedom, equality, and autonomy in many areas of life. Where inequalities were deeply embedded within the existing social structure, as for example with race and gender inequalities, the coming decade would see a concerted challenge to these existing cultural norms.[2]

It could well be argued that those Americans of the nineteenth and early twentieth centuries who took a profound interest in Hinduism—even to the point of participating in the movement for Indian independence, taking up monastic vows, or both—were also creating and participating in a counterculture, in Oliver's sense of the term. The Transcendentalists overwhelmingly supported the abolition of slavery, and many worked actively toward this goal. Similarly, the Theosophists rejected claims of Western and Christian superiority by working for the preservation of Hinduism and for Indian independence. And Theosophy and the Vedanta Society both had women leaders.

This early version of a counterculture is what Leela Gandhi has also described in her work on the anti-imperialist Westerners of this period—people like the Theosophists and Sister Nivedita. The main difference between the countercultural movement of the earlier period—the late nineteenth and early twentieth centuries—and that of the 1960s seems largely to be one of scale. Westerners drawn to, for example, the Vedanta Society or the Self-Realization Fellowship, in the early decades of these organizations, numbered in the thousands or tens of thousands, at the most. Westerners drawn to the counterculture of the 1960s, though, numbered in the millions.

To be sure, not all of these participants in the counterculture embraced Hinduism or joined Hindu-inspired organizations. Hinduism was part of a much larger mix of elements that were part of this complex movement. The Hindu elements are significant, though, on several levels. First, of course, they simply represent the openness to diverse cultures—the rejection of Western cultural superiority—that characterized the movement as a whole. But specific Hindu ideas, as well, came to inform the counterculture as a totality, even if the degree to which individual participants in this culture explicitly identified with these ideas—or were even aware of their Hindu provenance—varied greatly. This continues to be the case today; for the Hindu-infused attitudes that are described by Lisa Miller in her 2009 article, "We're All Hindus Now," have come to hold the sway they have, in large part, as an after-effect of the countercultural movement of the sixties. Because this was a mass movement, on such a large scale, the diffusion of ideas within it and their eventual infusion into the larger American cultural milieu have been far from uniform. The degree of specific Hindu influence, then, on any given individual either within the sixties counterculture or in the American culture shaped by it, ranges from an explicit embrace of Hinduism to a broad attitude of acceptance.

As with the earlier counterculture, the first rumblings of the counterculture of the 1960s—in the work of the beat poets of the 1950s—were characterized by a fascination with Asian religions. Jack Kerouac (1922–69), author of *The Dharma Bums*, and poet, Allen Ginsberg (1926–97), both had deep interests in Buddhism. Ginsberg actually traveled to India as well. Similarly, from within the bastion of Western conservatism—the Roman Catholic Church—came the Trappist monk, Thomas Merton (1915–68), who studied yoga and Zen and included them in his spiritual life.

The Popularization of Yoga

In the 1950s, postural yoga—traditionally known as *Haṭha Yoga*—which focuses upon breath control and the physical positions which are known in Patañjali's *Yoga Sūtra* as *āsanas*—became increasingly popular. According to the Harvard Pluralism Project,

"Yoga teachers demonstrated postures on television and bookstores carried books on yoga techniques. They were taken up by many people who had little interest or knowledge about their religious underpinnings."[3]

The differentiation of the physical practice of yoga from its "religious underpinnings" is a phenomenon that would become a major source of contention later on in the history of Hinduism in America—contention which is as yet unresolved today.

The term *Haṭha Yoga* literally means "the yoga of force." In its classical Indian form, this system of physical postures, stretches, and breathing exercises is typically attributed to a twelfth-century ascetic of the Shaiva Nāth Yogī tradition named Gorakhnāth. When most Westerners use or hear the term *yoga*, they usually have this system in mind. The original purpose of this system is not, however, the pursuit of physical health as an end in itself, but to prepare the physical body for higher yogic disciplines, such as meditation and the Tāntric practice of raising the Kuṇḍalinī energy that, according to this tradition, resides at the base of the spine.

Starting in the early twentieth century and continuing to the present day, many innovations have been made in Haṭha Yoga. A number of the stretches and āsanas used in contemporary Haṭha Yoga are not part of Gorakhnāth's original system. Indeed, some of these innovations have even come from the West; for while early modern yoga teachers influenced Westerners to take up this practice, they were also not hesitant to incorporate new knowledge into their system.[4]

As is evident from his book, *Rāja Yoga*, Swami Vivekananda did not have particularly high regard for Haṭha Yoga. Often undertaken by its practitioners for the sake of developing paranormal abilities—literally, "perfections," or *siddhis*—Vivekananda saw such aims as dangerous distractions from the goal of moksha. His focus was on inculcating a system of meditation, to which any kind of physical practice would be seen as subservient. On Vivekananda's understanding, one practices āsana, if one does so at all, in order to prevent the body from becoming a distraction in meditation.

Paramahansa Yogananda, too, was focused chiefly upon spiritual liberation, but his system of Kriya Yoga also integrated a physical dimension with the meditative practice, with elements of posture (āsana) and breath control (prāṇayama) being understood by practitioners in this tradition to be essential to the cultivation of the meditative state.

Many of the subsequent teachers of yoga, though, focused on the physical dimensions of the practice primarily, or even exclusively, while others integrated both aspects. In any case, yoga came to be seen less and less, at least in the Western world, as a component of a spiritual practice and more and more as a practice pursued for the sake of physical health. Indeed, many teachers of yoga presented it as something more akin to a medical practice than a spiritual path.

The reasons for this approach were complex. Many of the early teachers of yoga, it seems, saw the physical practice of yoga as lending itself—perhaps even inevitably leading—to experiences which would evoke in their practitioners a desire to go more deeply, and pursue the higher spiritual meaning behind yoga. Some of these teachers were happy to take their students to this point, once they proved ready to do so. At the same time, it seems that there was always a strong concern not to give offense to the religious sensibilities of Western yoga students—whether these were Christian sensibilities or a more rationalistic skepticism about anything that sounded like a religion. Finally, when yoga teachers like Krishna Pattabhi Jois (1915–2009) and B.K.S. Iyengar (1918–2014)—both students of the famous yoga master, Tirumalai Krishnamacharya (1888–1989)—sought to develop certification programs in their respective yoga practices, it was important that they be able to meet the Western legal requirements related to the teaching of health-related therapies. Their claims, in other words, had to pass scientific muster, and so needed to focus on observable phenomena, like the effects of the practice upon the body. They also needed to be able to ensure that the practice, if done in the correct way, would not be injurious. This placed any kind of strong emphasis on the spiritual dimensions of yoga in the realm of religion—and so outside of the bounds of governmental regulation and the validity a certification might confer. One cannot legally "certify" that a spiritual practitioner has reached moksha. One can certify, though, that a student has passed, for example, a required course in anatomy and other subjects needed to teach and practice yoga responsibly.

An especially prominent yoga lineage that was brought to the West in the fifties and sixties was that of Swami Sivananda Saraswati (1887–1963). A monk of the Daśanāmi lineage established by the founding teacher—or *acharya*—of the Advaita Vedānta tradition, Śaṅkara, Swami Sivananda himself never visited the United States. His career preceded the lifting of the Asian Exclusion Act. He did, however, establish a spiritual organization called the Divine Life Society in India in 1936.

FIGURE 24 *B. K. S Iyengar seen during his ninety-fourth birthday celebration in November 2012 in Belur, India (Photo by Dominik Ketz via Getty Images).*

A branch of the Divine Life Society was eventually established in the West—in Canada—by one of Swami Sivananda's disciples, Swami Vishnudevananda Saraswati (1927–93). This was the Sivananda Yoga Vedanta Centre of Montreal. It was established in 1959. It was established in Canada, and not the United States, in part because the Asian Exclusion Act still held sway, while Indian immigration to Canada—a British Commonwealth country—was not restricted at this point. Similarly, in the Caribbean, the Bahamas—also a Commonwealth country—provided the location for a second center—the Swami Sivananda Ashram—which Swami Vishnudevananda established in 1967. Two years before he formally established this ashram, Swami Vishnudevananda famously met the Beatles, who were in the Bahamas to film their second movie, *Help!* He gave each member of the band a copy of his book, *The Completed Illustrated Book of Yoga*. In 1971, with the Asian Exclusion Act lifted, he went on to start Sivananda ashrams in New York and California.

In 1966, another prominent disciple of Swami Sivananda, Swami Satchidananda, "attracted many seekers to the discipline of yoga."[5] Probably best known for speaking at the famous free rock festival in Woodstock, New York, in August 1969, Satchidananda later went on to found the headquarters of the Integral Yoga Institute in the United States, at Yogaville, in Virginia.[6]

Other yoga centers established in America in the sixties include the Ananda Meditation Retreat. It was started in 1968 by Swami Kriyananda (who was born J. Donald Walters), a disciple of Paramahansa Yogananda who left the Self-Realization Fellowship in 1962. There was also the Ananda Marga Yoga Society, in New York. This was the American branch of a movement begun in India by Prabhat Ranjan Sarkar

FIGURE 25 *Main meditation hall, Swami Sivananda Ashram, Bahamas (Photo by Jeffery D. Long).*

(1921–90), also known as Anandamurti. The word *Ananda*, or "bliss," appearing in the names of both of these yoga centers gives a sense of the aim of many Americans in pursuing the path of yoga: to find happiness and peace of mind in a stressful world.

Yoga and the Psychedelic Experience

The yoga movement predates the rise of the counterculture of the sixties; and while it does overlap with the counterculture, it is in many ways distinct from it. The overlap comes from the fact that, as the counterculture emerged, with its openness to alternative philosophies and ways of life, it was quite natural for it to attract many of the same people who were drawn to various aspects of the counterculture. One branch of the counterculture was focused, to a great extent, on physical health and on pursuing a way of life more natural or "organic" than the dominant American culture of manipulating nature—including the body—through technology. Yoga fits very well with the same sensibility that would promote organic farming, vegetarianism, and what could generally be seen as a more environmentally friendly lifestyle. Part of this same sensibility is a natural approach to health, and a corresponding suspicion of artificially produced medicines, or "chemicals." Yoga, as a holistic and non-invasive approach to physical health, again, fits with all of these ideas very well.

But yoga is also in tension with another dimension of the counterculture that is much more widely associated with this counterculture in the popular consciousness. This is the dimension of the counterculture represented by experimentation with hallucinogenic or "mind-expanding" (i.e., *psychedelic*) drugs, particularly LSD. Clearly, a holistic, organic, yoga-based approach to the health of the body which is suspicious of conventional medicine and its pharmaceuticals is at odds, arguably, with an approach the expansion of consciousness that gives a central role to artificially produced chemicals.

Experimentation with LSD as a means of expanding consciousness beyond its conventional boundaries can be traced to the LSD experiments of Aldous Huxley, mentioned earlier. Huxley was also, of course, a practitioner of Vedanta, and a disciple of Swami Prabhavananda, founder of the Vedanta Society of Southern California.

Many participants in the counterculture of the sixties experimented with drugs—especially LSD. It created a sense of cosmic consciousness and a sacred connectedness with all of existence akin to that described by advanced meditation practitioners. In the later sixties and seventies, many young people used yoga and meditation to give up drugs and have this experience in a natural way.

Continuation of Earlier Hindu Influences: Vivekananda, Yogananda, and Krishnamurti

Another source of inspiration for the counterculture of the sixties, and for its specifically Hindu components, was the ongoing influence of those Indian masters who had come to

America in the earlier period of the late nineteenth and early twentieth centuries, before the imposition of the Asian Exclusion Act of 1924. The Vedanta Societies established by Swami Vivekananda and his successors and the Self-Realization Fellowship established by Paramahansa Yogananda were still active and still attracting followers throughout the period of Asian exclusion. It was, in fact, during this period that many intellectuals who had been drawn to the Vedanta Society, as already discussed in the last chapter, were actively producing many of the works that would attract great interest by the youth of the sixties. Yogananda's *Autobiography of a Yogi*; Huxley's *The Perennial Philosophy*, *Brave New World*, and *The Doors of Perception*; Somerset Maugham's *The Razor's Edge*; Joseph Campbell's *The Hero with a Thousand Faces*; Christopher Isherwood's numerous collaborations with Swami Prabhavananda on translations of classic works of Vedanta such as the *Upaniṣads* and the *Bhagavad Gītā*, as well as his solely authored *Ramakrishna and His Disciples*; Huston Smith's *The Religions of Man*—most of these books were, in effect, "required reading" by members of the counterculture of the sixties. When George Harrison, of the Beatles, first went to India in the fall of 1966, after the band had completed its last concert tour, the two books that he took with him, and that he read voraciously while vacationing in a houseboat on a lake in Kashmir, were Swami Vivekananda's *Rāja Yoga* and Yogananda's *Autobiography of a Yogi*.

Jiddu Krishnamurti, too, with his message of radical freedom from all forms of dogmatism, truly came into his own during the period of the counterculture, when his message resonated most strongly with this movement's "increasing demand for freedom, equality, and autonomy in many areas of life."[7] Krishnamurti remained an active public speaker until his death in 1986, and his career continued unbroken from his dissolution of the Order of the Star in the East in 1929 until the end of his life. He did not see himself, though, as a standard-bearer of the counterculture, or of any ideology. He famously stated, "All ideologies are idiotic, whether religious or political, for it is conceptual thinking, the conceptual word, which has so unfortunately divided man."[8]

The Esalen Institute

As we have already seen, many intellectuals helped propagate Vedantic concepts into the wider American culture. These included philosophers like Huxley, literary figures like Isherwood, and scholars of religion and mythology like Smith and Campbell. It also included scientists, such as inventor Nikola Tesla (1856–1943), and physicists Niels Bohr (1885–1962), Erwin Schrödinger (1887–1961), J. Robert Oppenheimer (1904–67), and David Bohm (1917–92).

The Esalen Institute, located in Big Sur, California, and established by Stanford graduates Michael Murphy (1930–present) and Richard Price (1930–85), became an intellectual hub for the countercultural movement, particularly for those interested in the expansion of consciousness and of human potential. Price was influenced by an Aldous Huxley lecture he had heard in 1962, with the title "Human Potentialities."[9] Huxley had of course been influenced by the Vedantic teaching that "Each soul is potentially divine."[10] Murphy, for his part, had spent a period of several months in Sri Aurobindo's ashram in Pondicherry.[11] Together, the two established Esalen in 1962. The name of the institute is derived from the name of the Native American tribe—the Esselen—who were the original human inhabitants of the land on which the institute was built.[12] Esalen soon became a magnet for countercultural intellectuals interested in pushing the boundaries of consciousness, and of science. It came to be known for its experiential workshops, as well as the eclectic blend of philosophies on which it drew—including Hindu and Buddhist thought.

Renowned thinkers and writers of the 1960s, including Alan Watts (1915–73), Timothy Leary (1920–96), and Ram Dass (born Richard Alpert, 1930–present) all had connections with Esalen, as did psychologists such as Abraham Maslow (1908–70) and B.F. Skinner (1904–90). Watts is known primarily for his writings about East Asian traditions, like Buddhism and Daoism, Leary for his advocacy of psychedelic drugs, and Ram Dass for his embrace of Hinduism. (His Hindu name literally means "Servant of Rāma.") Ram Dass was the catalyst for making a large number of Americans aware of the teachings of his guru, Neem Karoli Baba (1900–73). Neem Karoli Baba was a deep devotee of Hanuman, the most famous servant of Rāma: the ape deity who is Rāma's assistant in the *Rāmāyaṇa*, and an embodiment of the power of devotion.

Maslow is known for his theory of a hierarchy of human needs, which brings to mind Hindu concepts, such as the *puruṣārthas*, or personal goals (*dharma*, or goodness; *artha*, wealth; *kāma*, sensory enjoyment; and *mokṣa/moksha*, or liberation). It is interesting that Maslow refers to the highest of the human needs as "self-actualization," which resonates with Vedantic concepts such as "Self-realization," or "God-realization."

Esalen also attracted figures whom we have already mentioned who had been influenced deeply by Vedanta, such as Huxley (one of the institute's inspirations) and Campbell.

Viewed by skeptics as promoting "fringe" science, it is nevertheless noteworthy that Esalen became a second home to a large number of renowned and respected scholars.

Return of the Gurus

In terms of direct Hindu influence on American culture, though, certainly the main sources for such inspiration were, as in the earlier period of Hindu influence, Indian spiritual teachers who came to America and developed large followings among those who felt deeply drawn to alternative spiritualities such as those presented by these Indian masters, as well as countercultural celebrities who also turned to these gurus for guidance and inspiration. The first guru of this period to gain a large following, as we shall see, was the Maharishi Mahesh Yogi, who began teaching in the West in 1958, although not in the United States, which was still closed to most Indians. Interest among the youth of America, though, combined with the lifting of the Asian Exclusion

Act in 1965, led to a veritable flood of such teachers. As we shall see, teachers from India became numerous in the sixties, with the trend continuing into the seventies, and even to the present day.

Maharishi Mahesh Yogi and Transcendental Meditation

The Maharishi Mahesh Yogi (1918–2008) was likely the most famous of the Indian gurus of the second wave of American interest in Hinduism that emerged as part of the counterculture of the sixties. This fame today is at least in part attributable to the Maharishi's brief association with the Beatles. Beyond this celebrity association, though, the Maharishi's meditation method became quite popular in the late sixties and into the seventies and eighties. It even gave rise, in the nineties, to a political party based on the ideal of improving society through meditation.

FIGURE 26 *Maharishi Mahesh Yogi—Huntsville, Alabama, January 1978 (Wikimedia Commons).*

The Maharishi referred to the meditative technique he taught as Transcendental Meditation, popularly known as TM. Transcendental Meditation represents, in some ways, a return to Swami Vivekananda's emphasis on meditative states over physical postures. It also includes some of the same elements as Vedantic meditation, such as the imparting of a secret mantra—a word or verse, typically in Sanskrit, to be recited silently while one is meditating. The mantra is used to focus the attention while one meditates. Most systems of meditation begin the practice with a focus on the breath. Meditating on the breath alone, though, is quite difficult, due to the tendency of the mind to wander. Repeating a mantra gives the mind something to focus on, in tandem with the breath, making it easier to maintain one's focus. Mantras are also believed to hold an inherent power. A secret mantra is a mantra that one does not disclose to anyone else, and is given directly by one's guru at the time that one takes *dīkṣa* (diksha), or initiation into the meditation lineage.

The Maharishi—or "great seer"—began to teach meditation in the West in 1958. His most famous students, again, were the Beatles, who visited his ashram in Rishikesh, India, in February of 1968. Born Mahesh Prasad Varma, the Maharishi earned a degree in physics from Allahabad University in 1942, following which he studied meditation under the tutelage of his guru, Swami Brahmananda Saraswati (1869–1953), who is known to the Maharishi's disciples as "Guru Dev," or "Divine Teacher."

Like the Hare Krishna Movement, Transcendental Meditation was a popular component of the counterculture of the 1960s and early 1970s. Unlike the Hare Krishna Movement, which (until fairly recently) reveled in its "Indianness," with followers dressed like medieval bhakti saints and chanting mantras in public places, Transcendental Meditation has presented itself, much like yoga has been presented, as a scientific and universal practice, promoted for health and peace of mind, rather than as a religious tradition with strong Hindu (specifically Shaiva) roots.

The Maharishi referred to his effort to promote Transcendental Meditation as the "Spiritual Regeneration Movement." It involved establishing branches of an organization called the Students International Meditation Society (SIMS) on hundreds of college campuses. (An unreleased song by the Beatles from 1968 includes the chorus, "Spiritual regeneration was my salvation.")

Starting in the 1970s, Transcendental Meditation began to focus on promoting itself as "a scientifically verifiable means to creativity and peace of mind attractive to professionals."[13] The members of the movement, in the name of promoting the practice, began to cultivate less of a "hippy," countercultural appearance and more of a conservative, professional look, involving suits and ties for the men and dresses for the women. As recounted by Joseph, a TM instructor who was active in the movement during this period, "The aim was not to deceive anyone. We just didn't want to scare people away. We really believed in the practice and that it could do a lot of good for the world and for society. That involved presenting ourselves in a way that would not put people off of the practice. It was all about the practice."[14]

In 1974, the movement established Maharishi International University in Fairfield, Iowa, on the grounds of what had been Parsons College. This university has served as the main center of the movement in the West and continues to thrive today, promoting

Transcendental Meditation as a cure for many problems which beset the modern world. Although contested by mainstream scientists, the movement claims to have carried out studies verifying the "Maharishi Effect," in which rates of crime and other incidents of violence diminish in a given geographic area when a large enough number of persons are practicing meditation in that area. In 1992, the organization even fielded a political party—the Natural Law Party—"founded on the principles of Transcendental Meditation, the laws of nature, and their application to all levels of government."[15]

The Beatles, Ravi Shankar, and Rock Star Yogis

The Beatles were, of course, a wildly successful popular music group and a major cultural phenomenon. It is difficult to exaggerate their fame and their cultural influence. But what do they have to do with Hinduism in America?

As will be discussed in more detail in a later chapter, after reaching the heights of worldly success, the Beatles—almost like a microcosm of their generation—found themselves dissatisfied with life in the material world. They were each filled with a yearning for a higher, transcendental reality and purpose in life, but none more so than George Harrison (1943–2001), who developed a deep and enduring interest in Hindu thought and practice.

Harrison was the member of the Beatles who encouraged the rest of the band to look into Transcendental Meditation. The Beatles' association with the Maharishi was relatively short-lived after the band became alienated from him upon hearing a rumor that he had made an inappropriate sexual advance toward one of his students during the Beatles' stay at his ashram in Rishikesh in the February of 1968. Near the end of the band's career, in 1969, Harrison developed a much more enduring relationship with A.C. Bhaktivedanta Swami Prabhupada, the founder and acharya of the International Society for Krishna Consciousness (ISKCON). Wherever the Beatles went, their fans tended to follow—both literally and metaphorically—and their interests in meditation and Harrison's role with the Hare Krishna movement led to a similar interest among fans in Europe and North America.

Harrison's interest in Hinduism was initially sparked by an interest in Indian music, which prompted him to befriend Ravi Shankar (1920–2012), from whom he learned how to play the sitar. Hindu themes were a prominent part of Harrison's song lyrics from 1967 until his death in 2001, his most famous Hindu-influenced song being his 1970 hit, "My Sweet Lord," "the most successful solo single by any of the former Beatles during the seventies."[16]

Shankar was an Indian classical musician who was instrumental in popularizing the musical traditions of India—especially the sitar—in the Western world. In his youth, he traveled frequently to North America and Europe as part of a dance troupe run by his brother, Uday Shankar. In 1938, he gave up dancing to learn the sitar, the instrument for which he is best known. Although Indian music had long been enjoyed by a small number of Western connoisseurs, Shankar's association with Harrison, starting in 1966,

FIGURE 27 *Ravi Shankar at Woodstock, August 1969 (Wikimedia Commons).*

brought him, and Indian classical music more generally, to a much wider audience. Shankar performed at the Monterey Pop Festival in 1967—a precursor of the much larger Woodstock festival of 1969—and, probably most famously, at the Concert for Bangladesh, in 1971. The Concert for Bangladesh was first conceived by Harrison when Shankar approached him about the devastation wrought by the civil war between West and East Pakistan (which became the independent country of Bangladesh as a result of this war). The Concert for Bangladesh was the first rock charity concert, and brought together a number of luminaries from the world of rock, including Harrison, Ringo Starr, Eric Clapton, and Bob Dylan.

Once the Beatles took a serious interest in Indian spirituality, numerous rock stars followed suit. Mick Jagger, of the Rolling Stones, also attended the Maharishi's meditation retreat in Wales in late 1967, which the Beatles attended. Mike Love of the Beach Boys and folk singer Donovan both attended the Rishikesh retreat in 1968, also attended by the Beatles. Love and Donovan still practice Transcendental Meditation today. Sixties rock artists who incorporated Indian sounds or Hindu themes into their music are too numerous to list. They include—besides the Beatles and the Stones—the Who (whose guitarist, Pete Townsend, is a disciple of Meher Baba), the Moody Blues, Procol Harum, and Traffic. Moving from the sixties to the seventies, there are bands such as Led Zeppelin and Yes (whose lead singer, Jon Anderson, is a disciple of Paramahansa Yogananda).

ISKCON: The International Society for Krishna Consciousness

ISKCON, the Hindu organization with which George Harrison had the longest and closest association, was first established in 1965 by Abhay Charan De, who is better known as A.C. Bhaktivedanta Swami Prabhupada.

Prabhupada (1896–1977) arrived in New York in 1965, making him one of the first of this new wave of Indian spiritual teachers to take advantage of the lifting of the Asian Exclusion Act. He was seventy years old when he arrived. His movement of devotion to Lord Krishna, rooted in the Gauḍīya Vaishnava tradition of his native Bengal, grew within a few years to include dozens of ISKCON centers. The central focus of the Gauḍīya Vaishnava tradition is bhakti, or devotion to the Supreme Being in a personal form. According to the theology of this tradition, Krishna is not merely an avatar, but the Supreme Personality of Godhead, to whom all devotion is due.

Upon his initial arrival in New York, Prabhupada soon found a home with a group of young people who were part of the countercultural movement of the period. It was largely from young people in this movement that the following of ISKCON was first drawn. Members of ISKCON, more widely known as the Hare Krishnas, were considered quite eccentric by many Americans in the 1960s and 1970s—even more so than the Transcendental Meditation movement, whose members took to wearing suits and ties in the seventies, and presenting themselves in a much more socially conservative manner.

The Hare Krishnas, on the other hand, dressed and wore their hair in the same manner as medieval Vaishnava devotees in Bengal. They danced on busy city street corners, showing their devotion by energetically chanting and singing the Hare Krishna mantra and soliciting donations from passersby. Their unconventional mannerisms soon brought the disapproval of mainstream society, and the group was one of the first Hindu-inspired organizations to be labeled a "cult."

Despite these disadvantages, ISKCON gathered a sufficient following to establish a rural ashram called New Vrindavan in the hills near Wheeling, West Virginia. Named after the popular childhood home of Krishna in India—Vrindavan—New Vrindavan gradually became a popular place of pilgrimage not only for Hare Krishnas, but for American Hindus in general. The site is known for its golden-domed temple and for the excellent vegetarian food that is served there. Harrison also famously gave the group one of his houses in England to serve as its London temple.

FIGURE 28 *Hare Krishna ceremony held in July 1979 at Château de Valencay, France (Photo by Gilbert UZAN/Gamma-Rapho via Getty Images).*

Since the seventies, ISKCON has become a more mainstream religious organization. It is less common to see Hare Krishnas engaged in public chanting, and one also finds more members of the organization dressed, like members of TM, in a conventional American manner. With the resumption of Indian immigration in 1965, more Indian families have joined the organization and it is now seen less in countercultural terms and more as an established religion. Today, it even has a multigenerational membership.

Swami Muktananda and Siddha Yoga

The teachers who came to the West from India during the period of the counterculture were representative of a variety of Hindu traditions. As we have already seen, Maharishi Mahesh Yogi taught a form of meditation derived from a Shaiva tradition, focused on jñāna yoga and the direct experience of the Self through concentration on a private mantra. Prabhupada, on the other hand, taught an ecstatic Vaishnava devotional practice, and the earlier yoga teachers emphasized postural āsana practice.

Swami Muktananda (1908–82) brought Tāntric practice into the West. First visiting the United States in 1970, his teaching was focused on the experience of the Kuṇḍalinī Shakti, or a latent energy believed in this tradition to be coiled at the base of the spine.

According to Tāntric teaching, this Shakti is the essential life force and power of creation. It is believed to inhabit the "subtle body," or body made of energy, which is said in this tradition to coexist with the physical, or "gross" body. If it can be elevated, rising up a nerve channel known as the *sushumna nadi*—which corresponds, physically, with the spinal cord—this Shakti, or creative energy, can activate the seven energy centers, or chakras, that are said to exist along the spinal cord. Each chakra is believed to have a certain quality of spiritual energy associated with it. The heart chakra, for example, is associated with compassion, while the "third eye" chakra, located between and just above the eyebrows, is associated with wisdom. The activation of the chakras is believed to accelerate spiritual evolution.

It is not coincidental that the term for the spiritual energy evoked in this tradition is called by the name *Shakti*—which, the reader may recall, is also the name of the Hindu Mother Goddess, the wife of Shiva. The deity Shakti is the personification of the power of creation that resides in all beings. In Tāntra, the idea of this indwelling Shakti is not a mere metaphor, but is seen as an energy that can be tapped using specific meditative techniques.

The Tāntric worldview and the techniques associated with it are not limited to Hinduism. Tantra is an area where Hinduism and Buddhism overlap a great deal. Tāntric Buddhism, which is also known as Vajrayāna, is the dominant Buddhist tradition of Tibet, Nepal, and Bhutan.

In Siddha Yoga, it is said that the Shakti can be made to rise up the spinal column to merge with the chakra, or energy center, in the crown of the head through the grace of the guru. This can be done through a thought, word, or gesture on the part of the guru—a process known as *shaktipat*. Muktananda received shaktipat from his guru, Swami Nityananda (1897–1961), a solitary monk who resided in a cave in Ganeshpuri, near Bombay (now called Mumbai).

In 1974, Swami Muktananda established Siddha Yoga centers in Oakland, California, and in the Catskill mountains of New York. "The South Fallsburg, New York center eventually became the international headquarters of the organization. By 1976, there were some eighty Siddha Yoga meditation groups and five ashrams, claiming 20,000 followers."[17]

Before his death in 1982, Swami Muktananda designated his translator—Malti Shetty—and her brother to be his successors. After a falling out between the brother and sister team in 1985, the sister, now known by her monastic name of Swami Chidvilasananda (and more widely known as Gurumayi) took over the lineage.

Interestingly, in 1957, several years prior to Muktananda's arrival in the United States, an American master in the same lineage as Muktananda's guru, Swami Nityananda, established an organization known as the Nityananda Institute. This American, known by his monastic name of Swami Chetanananda, was a direct disciple of Swami Rudrananda, who was himself a disciple of Nityananda and, like Chetanananda, an American, not of Indian descent. Chetanananda took his vows of sannyāsa under Swami Muktananda in 1978.[18] By the early seventies, the Nityananda Institute had grown, with "centers in Portland, Oregon; Cambridge, Massachusetts; Santa Monica, California; and Ann Arbor, Michigan providing yoga classes, study groups, retreats and a daily practice of chanting."[19] Rudrananda was known for his informal and unconventional style, for a Hindu monk. He did not typically wear monk's robes, but Western-style clothing, and preferred to be called "Rudi." As Helen Crovetto describes his teaching:

Rudi reinterpreted Kashmir Shaivism [a Shaiva philosophical tradition that developed in the area of Kashmir between the eighth and twelfth centuries] for a twentieth-century American audience. He taught the construction of a basic internal spiritual structure designed to transfigure its practitioners and effect union with the ultimate nature reality, nondual consciousness. At the time of his death in a plane crash in 1973, Rudi had thousands of students and had engendered a group of teachers with eclectic approaches to spiritual development.[20]

Other Important Gurus

In addition to the early teachers of yoga in the West, such as Swami Vishnudevananda, as well as Maharishi Mahesh Yogi, A.C. Bhaktivedanta Swami Prabhupada, and Swami Muktananda, a number of other important gurus came to America directly or developed American followings during the period of the counterculture. So many gurus, in fact, have come to America since the sixties that it is impossible to discuss them in a single book. I shall mention a few more, to give a sense of their variety and kinds of focus that each had. Not mentioning any particular guru, though, is not to suggest that that guru is unimportant. It should be seen only as a limitation of the author.

Satya Sai Baba (1926–2011) is believed by his disciples to be a reincarnation of Sai Baba of Shirdi (1835–1918), an Indian holy man with both Hindu and Muslim followers. He began to develop an American following in the seventies. "By 1984, the Satya Sai Baba Council of America listed seventy-six Satya Sai Baba Centres," the largest being those in New York, Los Angeles, and Chicago.[21]

As shall be discussed in the next chapter, a large number of Hindu temples in America are actually devoted to Shirdi Sai Baba, who continues to command a considerable following more than a century since his passing. He is comparable, in this respect, with Sri Ramakrishna. In my conversations with devotees of Shirdi Sai Baba, I found a variety of views regarding the claim that Satya Sai Baba is his reincarnation. Some accepted the claim, some rejected it quite strongly, and others were agnostic on the matter, saying it was possible, but not committing either way.

Sri Chinmoy (1931–2007), a disciple of Sri Aurobindo, and an athlete and artist as well as a spiritual teacher, began to lead meditations for world peace at the United Nations in the 1970s. Based in the borough of Queens, in New York, Sri Chinmoy came to be known in America and throughout the world for his many initiatives dedicated to world peace.[22] Interestingly—and rather unusually for a Hindu spiritual teacher—Sri Chinmoy was a weightlifter. The harmony of the mind and body is a major theme of his teaching, as is unconditional love for all beings.

Many of Sri Chinmoy's disciples have continued, after his death, to reside in the vicinity of the Sri Chinmoy Centre, in Queens, where a number of them run stores that specialize in books on spiritual topics and shops selling items for use in devotional activity, such as incense sticks and images of Hindu deities, as well as an excellent vegetarian restaurant.

Brij Kishore Kumar Dhasmana (1925–96), better known by his monastic name of Swami Rama, spent many years as a wandering sannyāsi, or Hindu monk, in the Himalayas: wanderings chronicled in his book, *Living with the Himalayan Masters*, a text which is in many ways akin to Yogananda's *Autobiography of a Yogi*. In 1971, Swami Rama founded the Himalayan Institute, in Blue Mountain, Pennsylvania. After Swami Rama's death, running of the institute passed to his successor, Pandit Rajmani Tigunait, who administers it to the present day.

Finally, one of the more unusual stories of Indian gurus coming to America is that of Prem Rawat (1957–present), also known as Guru Maharaj Ji. Rawat's father, Sri Hamsa Maharaj Ji, was the head of a Hindu organization known as the Divine Light Mission. Guru Maharaj Ji succeeded his father as the head of the organization in 1966, when he was only nine years old. In 1971, at the age of thirteen, he brought the Divine Light Mission to America, establishing its international headquarters in Denver, Colorado. In 1974, he married an American woman against his mother's wishes. This led to a rift in the Divine Light Mission, which was renamed *Elán Vital* in 1983.

Rawat continues to speak on spiritual topics but goes by his birth name rather than being called Guru Maharaj Ji, and dresses in conventional Western clothing (a suit and a tie), rather than in the traditional robes of a Hindu spiritual master.

The Guru Phenomenon: Critical Reflections

The role of the guru, or teacher, is an important one in most Hindu traditions. One's guru is one's guide on the spiritual path. By receiving initiation—*dīksha*—from a guru, one becomes part of that guru's teaching lineage, and inherits the spiritual power—or *guru shakti*—that flows through that lineage from its founder, a divine or enlightened being. Typically, it is believed one should follow one's guru blindly, with an absolute faith that whatever he or she instructs one to do is for one's benefit, even if it is unconventional and appears, at that moment, to have no reason.

Such absolute faith in many ways cuts against the emphasis on freedom and individualism that have been part of American culture from the early days of the Republic. The Transcendentalists were drawn to Hindu philosophy in large part because of its emphasis, as they understood it, upon self-reliance. The same spiritual reality that is at the heart of, and that ultimately is, oneself is the same reality that resides in all of nature. One therefore does not need to look outside oneself for truth. One is ultimately responsible for one's own spiritual practice and one's realization.

It is therefore ironic, in one sense, that members of a counterculture focused on "freedom, equality, and autonomy"[23] would be drawn in such large numbers to teachers demanding complete loyalty and obedience as a condition for receiving the full spiritual benefits of their teaching. This would seem to be the opposite of what those who embraced the counterculture were seeking.

This issue is not limited only to Hinduism in America. Buddhist traditions, particularly Zen, were at least as popular as Hindu or Hindu-based teachings in the fifties, sixties, and seventies. In Zen, as in the guru-based traditions, the teaching of one's *roshi*, or Zen master, is absolute.

Some of the Asian teachers who have come to America, both Hindu and Buddhist, have been alleged—sometimes quite credibly—to have committed sexual and other improprieties with the people who have come to them for spiritual guidance. This quite naturally raises the question as to why such scandals befall these teachers. Is there something in the guru-disciple relationship which lends itself to abuse?

As the televangelist scandals of the 1980s demonstrate, as well as the horrific revelations of extensive child abuse in the Roman Catholic Church dating back decades, abuse of power is not unique to Hinduism or Buddhism, or to Hindu- or Buddhist-based organizations. The argument could be made, though, that religious faith in holy persons and organizations needs to be tempered with an awareness that even the holiest person is susceptible to human imperfection, as well as an open-eyed realization that those organizations which confer power and authority over others upon their representatives might attract those with less-than-noble intentions to their ranks. One would hope that there would be checks built into the traditions to guard against abuse. Such checks do exist. Some traditions, for example, do not permit their monastic practitioners to be alone with members of the opposite gender, although this would of course not be a preventative measure should the monastic in question be homosexually or bisexually oriented.

It is also important to note that this is not simply a question of "bad apples" getting involved in a spiritual organization for nefarious purposes. Credible allegations have been made against some teachers who were known for having practiced years of spiritual discipline, and who had, prior to the allegations, impeccable reputations for moral rectitude.

Might it be, then, that the institution of guru, with the absolute obedience that it commands, lends itself to abuse? This is also disputable, however, because there are many gurus and many organizations about which there have been absolutely no allegations of impropriety, and others in which the few allegations that exist have been shown to be false.[24]

One could argue that, if the guru has integrity, and if the organization is also made up of persons sincerely committed to the views and values for which it stands, abuse is less likely occur. On the other hand, though, one could also argue that to give so much authority to any human being, even one of deep integrity and spiritual commitment, is a path fraught with peril. It is a test of the humility and self-discipline, even of a deeply spiritual person, to be placed in a position of absolute authority over others.

A number of psychological studies have been done on the effects of giving one person or group of people absolute power over others.[25] Even "normal," psychologically healthy people in situations where they are given control over other people have been demonstrated, under particular conditions, to be capable of cruel and sadistic behavior from which they would otherwise recoil. As Robert Jay Lifton has recounted, many Germans who participated in the Holocaust were people who were otherwise "normal."[26]

The #MeToo movement has recently shown, quite dramatically, that men in positions of power in a wide range of fields—education, entertainment, business, and politics, and many others as well—take advantage of this power and abuse those whom they see as powerless with a frequency that has, upon being exposed, greatly shaken the public's perceptions of and confidence in figures who would at one time been viewed with great respect. Why should the field of religion be different than any other in this regard? Indeed, given the pervasiveness of the abuse that #MeToo has revealed, one could well conclude that the question to ask is not "Why have so many gurus been accused of abuse?," but rather, "Why have more gurus *not* been accused of abuse?"

Swami M., a monastic practitioner in a Hindu lineage in America, when asked candidly to speak about this issue of abuse and the absolute power of the guru, said:

> We teach our students and must constantly remind ourselves that the true guru, the divine guru, the Gurudeva, is the one inside all of our hearts. The human teacher is merely an externalisation of the higher spiritual reality inside of oneself. The worship and honor we give to our human teacher is done out of gratitude, but it is also an expression of our devotion to the divine teacher within. We [teachers] are conduits for that higher reality. That is all. The moment ego comes in, we have failed in our mission. We must remind ourselves of that constantly. "I am but thy instrument." A teacher who forgets this will fall.

For many in the counterculture, following a guru was initially an act of rebellion: following an unconventional practice and an unconventional teacher. The idea of a teacher as a living conduit to higher knowledge, versus the idea of blind faith in an ancient text, was appealing to many from this period. The goal was to become like the teacher: to manifest within oneself the wisdom that one found in one's guru, to bring forth from within oneself the inner guru with the aid of the outer one. This was, however, easier said than done, as many of the deeply conservative and traditional conventions surrounding the guru-disciple relationship could also clash deeply with the American ethos of equality and freedom.

This is also not simply a question of "Eastern" absolutism and "Western" individualism. The teachings of Jiddu Krishnamurti, one might recall, were deeply opposed to dogmatism and finding the truth through any organizational structure or external teacher. Yet, paradoxically, people came to Krishnamurti for teaching. His unorthodox, unconventional, independent-minded approach is precisely what made him attractive to American seekers as a person whom they would trust and to whom they would be willing to give absolute authority. Krishnamurti, to his credit, always resisted attempts to put him on a pedestal or turn him into a guru.

Ironically, some American seekers themselves, through their pursuit of an independent-minded, countercultural approach to the spiritual life, themselves came to be seen as gurus by many of their contemporaries: as authoritative figures whose word was a guide to truth. Oliver gives us the example of Alan Watts, mentioned earlier in connection with the Esalen Institute:

> Watts was eclectic in his writing and philosophy, integrating ideas from Taoism, Buddhism, and Hinduism ... He did not concentratae on teaching the formal concepts of Buddhism or Vedanta, but tried to relate these ideas to people's everyday lives. He emphasizes the practical relevance of the teachings of Eastern religions such as the use of meditation to help people cope with periods of psychological stress ... His approach was almost inevitably a personal, subjective interpretation of the teachings of Buddhism and Hinduism, but this appeal to many young people of the counter-culture who wanted to find their own spiritual way. Whether or not Alan Watts sought it, he was, in effect, cast in the role of a spiritual guru for many thousands of people.[27]

In the wider culture, Bob Dylan, too, could be seen as another example of an independent-minded individual who said, "Don't follow leaders"[28]—and thereby became a leader for his generation.

As Oliver writes:

> The central purpose of the guru within Hinduism is to guide and assist the spiritual student in attaining ... religious union with God. The guru employs a variety of practical strategies to help students, including meditation, the analysis of scriptures, the repetition of mantras and the practice of yoga ... This approach of enabling the individual to attain a form of spiritual fulfilment was very attractive during the counter-culture. It was not an approach which depended upon submitting to a set of religious rules [though in particular lineages, such rules could and did come into play], but rather one which encouraged each individual to find their own unique pathway to God. This appealed to the autonomous, individualistic mood of the 1960s.[29]

Countercultural Themes and Their Hindu Inspirations

There was far more to the counterculture of the 1960s, and to the Hindu inspirations for it, than the guru phenomenon that we have been exploring in this chapter, though the various guru-based movements of this period are the most visible and obvious location of Hindu influence on the counterculture. Oliver draws attention to a variety of aspects of the counterculture that can be seen to have some measure of Hindu inspiration, or to correlate with various dimensions of Hindu traditions. He is also careful to point out that the Hindu provenance of many aspects of the 1960s counterculture should not lead to a view of India or of the Hindu community more broadly as akin to a giant Woodstock festival. India is, in many ways, a deeply conservative country, culturally speaking, and Hinduism a deeply conservative religion. "Conservative" and "progressive," though, mean different things in different contexts. To self-identify as Hindu and to proclaim oneself on a search to discover one's inner divinity are a fairly mainstream thing to do in India. To do the same thing in a deeply evangelical Christian community in the American south would be quite radical. The 1960s counterculture drew upon Hindu ideas, but also transformed and adapted these to a new environment, and to a culture in many ways quite different from that of India.

Countercultural themes and their Hindu correlates which Oliver notes include:

1 An experiential approach to spiritual life: Many threads of Hindu thought, particularly the Vedantic and Yoga traditions, emphasize the authority of direct experience over that of faith in an external text or institution. This appealed to American individualism in the1960s.
2 Nonviolence: Gandhi's Jain-inspired philosophy of ahiṃsā was attractive to both the Civil Rights Movement and the anti-Vietnam War movement.
3 Sexual liberation: Elements of Hindu thought such as the Tāntric emphasis on sensory experience as a means to spiritual awakening and the validation of sensory enjoyment in texts such as the *Kāma Sūtra* appealed to Americans who were interested in breaking away from the puritanical norms of 1950s American culture.
4 Communal living: The Hindu idea of the *āśrama* (ashram), or spiritual retreat became a model for a more communitarian, less consumerist mode of living, with which many in the 1960s experimented.
5 Natural medicine and environmentalism: Alternative medicine was another topic in which interest grew in the 1960s. The traditional Indian system of healing—*Ayurveda*, the "science of long life"—became a popular form of alternative medicine, along with traditional Chinese and Native American forms of healing. An ethos of environmentalism and promoting "the natural" can be seen to flow from the Transcendentalists' interpretation of Hinduism as teaching the all-pervasive existence of divinity in the natural world.[30]

Setting the Stage for a New Indian Diaspora

The passage of the Immigration Act of 1965, an outcome of the Civil Rights Movement, made it once again possible for Indians to come to America. The Act gave preference to those whose skills were needed in the United States and those with professional qualifications. Immigration from India rose dramatically and a highly educated and affluent Indian immigrant population began to grow in the United States. It is to the story of this new Indian diaspora that we turn in our next chapter.

Study Questions

1. What were the conditions that led to the rise of the American counterculture?
2. Which features of Hindu teaching were attractive to Western spiritual seekers?
3. How does the guru phenomenon both fit well and exist in tension with countercultural values?
4. In what ways is the Hindu-influenced American counterculture starkly different from traditional Hinduism, as practiced by Hindus?

Suggestions for Further Reading

Sarah Caldwell, "The Heart of the Secret: A Personal and Scholarly Encounter with Siddha Yoga," in *Nova Religio: The Journal of Alternative and Emergent Religions*, 5:1 (October 2001), 9–51.

Philip Goldberg, *American Veda: From Emerson and the Beatles to Yoga and Meditation—How Indian Spirituality Changed the West* (New York: Three Rivers Press, 2010).

Philip Goldberg, *The Life of Yogananda: The Story of the Yogi Who Became the First Modern Guru* (Carlsbad, CA: Hay House, 2018).

Jeffrey J. Kripal, *Esalen: America and the Religion of No Religion* (Chicago: University of Chicago Press, 2008).

Gita Mehta, *Karma Cola: Marketing the Mystic East* (New York: Fawcett Columbine, 1990).

Paul Oliver, *Hinduism and the 1960s: The Rise of a Counter-culture* (London: Bloomsbury, 2015).

Mark Singleton, *Yoga Body: The Origins of Modern Posture Practice* (New York: Oxford University Press, 2010).

5

America: Land of Temples

Chapter 5 Summary and Outline

With the lifting of the Asian Exclusion Act, in 1965, Indian immigration to the United States and the number of practicing Hindu immigrants greatly increased. Soon, Hindu communities emerged across the United States with sufficient membership to fund the building of temples. The main focus of this chapter will be these Hindu temple communities—their emergence, the challenges they have faced, their organizational structures, and the ways in which Hindu temples in America and Canada differ from traditional Hindu temples in South Asia. This chapter will also include brief discussion of the Hindu diaspora in Canada and the countries of the Caribbean region.

A New Indian Diaspora

With the overturning of the Asian Exclusion Act in 1965, Hindus began to migrate to the United States in ever-larger numbers. This steady flow of immigration, which continues up to the present, contrasts with the small trickle of immigrants prior to 1924, who were primarily poor and working class. The current wave of Indian immigrants consists for the most part of highly trained professionals in fields such as the sciences, engineering, business, and medicine (as well as, though to a lesser extent, scholars in the humanities). It is this largely Indian immigrant community that makes up the bulk of the Hindu diaspora in America today. Approximately 91 percent of American Hindus are of Asian descent, many from Nepal, Indonesia, Bangladesh, Pakistan, and Sri Lanka. Most—roughly 93 percent, so about 85 percent of the total US Hindu population—are from India.

This Indian immigrant community is well represented by Arvind Mehta:

> Arvind Mehta graduated with top scores in chemical engineering from the Indian Institute of Technology in Bombay, now called Mumbai, in the early 1970s. By that time, he had already received a job offer from a company in Houston, Texas. Mehta travelled by train to Bombay to apply at the U.S. consulate for a visa for permanent resident status in the United States and for the coveted "green card" that would permit him to live and work there legally. With official school records and the formal job letters in his briefcase, he entered the building nervously for his interview with the consular officer. He considered this the most important conversation of his life, because it would open or close the door to all the opportunities that America promises to immigrants.
>
> Mehta returned home to his home village to await the decision. In the meantime, his parents selected a girl from a neighboring village to be his wife. Just before the wedding, he received the good word from the consulate, and the family celebrated his future prospects by holding an elaborate wedding for more than a thousand guests. Shortly afterward, he left his bride with his parents to await her visa and flew to New York to register as an immigrant. From there he travelled on to Houston to settle in to his new job and make arrangements for his wife to follow him.
>
> Five years later, Mehta had achieved considerable success. His wife had joined him, and they had two children, who had automatically become Americans by being born in the United States. He had worked hard to earn significant salary raises and two promotions. He and a few other immigrants from India had organized a monthly meeting of other such families to watch films from home and enjoy meals together. Because he had already decided that he and his family would not return to India, Mehta took advantage of the option offered by the United States, and not by many other countries, for legal immigrants to apply for citizenship. He stood before a judge in the company of immigrants from many countries to be made a U.S. citizen and pledge allegiance to his new homeland.[1]

Mehta's experience is quite typical of male Indian professionals who immigrated to the United States in the late sixties and seventies. Gautam, an engineer who migrated to the United States in 1970 to work for a steel company, says, "America was the dream. A place where you could live a good life and be rewarded for all your hard work, where your children could get a good education and have all the opportunities that we did not have in India." When asked why opportunities were not available in India, Gautam responds, "Too many people! There were a lot more qualified people than jobs in those days. And too much red tape! The Indian economy was hyper-regulated that time. America at the time had a great economy and was the envy of the world. It still is, even now."

The move to America was not always easy, though. Like Mehta, Gautam brought his wife, Aruna, to the United States shortly after they had entered into an arranged marriage together. "It was very lonely in those days," Aruna says. "There was not yet much of an Indian community. Plus, I was far away from my family. It was hard. There was no one around to talk to when he [Gautam] was at work. There was nothing to do. It was better after the children came. [Gautam and Aruna have two children, now adults with children of their own.] But it was hard in the beginning to find the kind of food you were used to, movies, music, everything. It's very different now. There are lots of Indians and lots of Indian grocery stores. But back then? Nothing." Aruna subsequently made a number of good friends in the local, primarily white, community, but socializing was initially difficult, due to the lack of the kind of common cultural ground that she would have shared with other women from India. "I made some good friends. Very good friends. But it was hard in the beginning. They were all very nice, and curious about India, but it was different."

Gradually, over the course in the seventies, other Indians moved into the community where Gautam and Aruna lived. Most were Hindu. These families eventually pooled their resources and started a temple. Beginning as a series of gatherings in Indian families' homes, today, this temple has grown into a major community center, with hundreds of members.

Home Shrines

In terms of Hinduism as a whole, the Hindu diaspora represents the entire range of varied Hindu traditions that can be found in South Asia: Vaiṣṇavas, Śaivas, and Śāktas, with each of their many sub-varieties, as well as other traditional Hindu systems, plus more recent Hindu traditions that have grown up around the teachings of particular guru lineages.

Although a great variety of Hindu temples, representing all of these varied traditions, have been built in the United States, for most Hindus, the main site of religious activity is in the home. Hinduism is a highly decentralized tradition. There is no requirement for Hindus to attend any public, communal worship services. In fact, one sometimes hears it said that one could be a perfectly good Hindu and never set foot in a temple.

It would be extremely rare, though, for an observant Hindu not to have some kind of a space in the home dedicated to worship.

Ravindra Marri is a good example of this. When he left India to work in America, one of the first things his mother was concerned to ensure was that he would have what he would need in order to perform worship at home:

> As Dr. Ravindra Marri left his home in Bangalore, India, to enter a medical residency program at a hospital in New York City, his mother carefully handed him cloth-wrapped religious objects from their home shrine. They included a small image of Ganesh, a copy of the *Bhagavad Gītā*, images of Krishna and Radha, a picture of the family's *guru* in a silver frame, a small oil lamp, and an incense holder. In his New York apartment, Marri placed these objects on a shelf beside his bed. Later he went back to India to get married and returned to New York with his wife. She brought sacred objects from her home and set up a small shrine in the kitchen. They consolidated the objects in a home shrine in the family room of their first house.[2]

Flueckiger describes the home shrine of another Indian Hindu family settled in America: Ravi and Sasikala Penumarthi. The Penumarthis' shrine

> is located in the kitchen, in an east-facing cabinet with glass doors that was specifically constructed for this purpose when they built their house in the Atlanta suburbs. Sasikala explained that she wanted the shrine close to where she prepared the food offered to the deities (rather than in an upstairs bedroom dedicated to this purpose, which is quite common in American Hindu homes), so that [the food] didn't have to "pass over all kinds of floors and carpets to get to another room," which may result in the offerings coming in contact with impurities.[3]

As Flueckiger notes, having an upstairs bedroom dedicated to religious activity is very common in American Hindu homes. The particular deities enshrined in a "pūjā room," as these rooms tend to be called, vary with each family and the forms of Hindu devotion to which its members adhere:

> Sasikala identified the central deities of [her] shrine to be Venkateshvara [a form of Vishnu popular in southern India] and his two wives, Padmavati and Bhu Devi [the Earth Goddess]. She explained that these are family deities from both her husband's family and her own father's family. Before they moved to their newly constructed house, these deities had been represented by framed lithographs; but for the new house they purchased the metal images that are now installed. Other deities in the cabinet shrine, and the stated reasons they are present, include: Shiva and Parvati, her mother's side's family deities; the half-woman/half-man Ardhanarishvara form of Shiva, which, she explained, represents the centrality of the "couple"; Durga because her mother used to worship her; Rama, because her mother-in-law "liked him a lot"; Hanuman, because her father had

told her that Hanuman gives strength and courage; a small Lakshmi, which was a wedding gift given by her aunt; and an unusual Ganesha made from laminated grains and lentils given to Sasikala by her sister. Prominent on the *puja* shelf is the dancing Nataraja form of Shiva; as Sasikala explained, "Shiva is my main god because of dance. [She is a dancer.] He's my *ishtadevata*. I first pray to Shiva. Then [I think of] Venkateshvara." Her husband Ravi, on the other hand, said he thinks of Venkateshvara first.[4]

America: Land of Temples

One of the most striking aspects of the Hindu presence in America today is what could be called the "temple phenomenon." This does not only refer to the fact that Hindus, once immigrating to the United States in sufficient numbers to support such projects, started building temples. The "temple phenomenon" refers both to the role which temples play in the lives of American Hindus and the reception with which they have been met in American society.

Hindu temples in South Asia are traditionally centers of worship alone. As we have seen, Hindus typically have a family shrine at home where daily worship—pūjā—is performed. Temples, though, typically house images, or *mūrtis*, much larger than images of deities that can normally be kept in a home. The temple deity images have also been specially consecrated and cared for on a daily basis by priests. All of this, as well as the fact that these deities have served as focal points for devotion from the many devotees that have visited the temple, is believed to make deities in a temple more spiritually powerful than those in one's home altar. It is therefore seen as beneficial to visit temples periodically, for the experience of *darśan* (darshan)—that is, both seeing and being seen by the deity. Darshan is typically the main purpose for visiting a Hindu temple in India.

Hindu temples in America, however, also serve as community centers in much the same way that churches do. In America, Hindus are not the majority population, but a tiny minority. In order to connect with other people, not only of one's own religion, but also who speak one's mother tongue and who share the same culture, cuisine, and so on, one needs a community center. Social events, therefore, often take place in American temples that would not normally be held in a temple in India. In addition to pūjās and religious festivals, temples often host "cultural programs," featuring performances of Indian classical dance, musical performances, and also talks on spiritual topics. The performances that occur in many temple cultural programs—those that do not feature visiting professional artists—are carried out by children from the Hindu community. It is a common expectation of many young Hindu girls and women that they will receive some training in classical Indian dance forms, such as Bharatnatyam, which have a religious meaning, but which are also seen as celebrations of Indian culture. The community takes great pride in these performances.

After Hindus began migrating to the United States from India and other parts of the world, it was not long before they began building communities and then temples to house the activities of these communities. Before temples were built, it was not uncommon for Hindus to rent local halls for events—high school gymnasiums or fire station halls. This is still commonly the case in many Hindu communities, particularly in areas where there is no temple or where temple facilities are too small to accommodate the increasingly large numbers of people attracted to these events.

The first Hindu Temple Society incorporated in North America was established in the state of New York, in Flushing, Queens, in 1970. "It worked toward the building of a temple for Lord Ganesha in Queens, which was consecrated in 1977."[5] Also in 1977, a very large temple—the Sri Venkateswara Temple—was consecrated in Penn Hills, Pennsylvania, near Pittsburgh. The main deity in this temple, also mentioned in connection with the Penumarthis's home shrine, "is the form of Vishnu known as Venkateśvara, whose shrine at Tirupati in south India is a popular place of pilgrimage."[6]

From 1975 to the present, Hindu temples have continued to be built across the United States. The prominent Hindu temples incorporated during the period from 1975 to 1979 include:

> The Bharatiya Temple (Troy, Michigan), the Capital District Hindu Temple (Albany, New York), the Sri Meenakshi Temple (Houston), the Hindu Temple Society of Southern California (Calabasas), the Hindu Temple of Greater Chicago, the New England Hindu Temple Incorporated (Boston), and the Connecticut Valley Hindu Temple Society (Middletown).[7]

Not all of these temples were built during this same period. As the first example, the Hindu Temple Society of Flushing, suggests, it can take a number of years from the legal incorporation of a temple community to its building of a temple structure to the consecration of that structure for use as a place of Hindu worship. The Flushing temple was incorporated in 1970 and consecrated in 1977.

Hindu Temple Societies continued to be formed throughout the eighties and nineties. They include temples in Lanham, Maryland; Nashville, Tennessee; Liberty, Ohio; Flint, Michigan; San Antonio, Texas; Aurora, Illinois; Casselberry, Florida; and Bridgewater, New Jersey.[8] This list is by no means complete. Hindu temples have become a regular feature of the American landscape.

The Mainstreaming of Hinduism in America: Major Hindu Events

In addition to their temple building activities, Hindus in America have increasingly staged large public events of a religious nature. The fact that Hindus in America have felt sufficiently secure and empowered to stage these events shows the degree of acceptance Hinduism in America has received in the later decades of the twentieth century, especially compared with the "bad old days"—the period of the Bellingham Riots and the Asiatic Exclusion League.

Examples of large events which have contributed to the mainstreaming of Hinduism, and of Indian culture more broadly, in America include the 1987 staging of Peter Brook's nine-hour production of the *Mahabharata* in Brooklyn. This production was later made into a film. Cultural festivals of India are now annual events in many American cities. The first festival "took place in the summer on the grounds of Middlesex County College in Edison, New Jersey. The festival attracted some 40,000 people every weekend for a month."[9] In 1993, "the Gayatri Pariwar in India sponsored a three-day '1008 Kundi Ashwamedha Yagna' in a huge parking lot of Cerritos College in Norwalk, California. 1008 sacred fires were kindled as the individuals, couples, and families sponsoring the event made offerings into the fire pits or kundis."[10] Also in 1993, the one-hundredth anniversary of the coming of Swami Vivekananda to America was celebrated in several venues, including "Global Vision 2000," held in Washington, DC, and attracting roughly 10,000 Hindus, and centennial gathering of the World Parliament of Religions held, appropriately, in Chicago, near the site of the first parliament where Vivekananda spoke.

> Hindu teachers and speakers at the Parliament included many with U.S. centres: Swami Chidananda of the Divine Life Mission; Swami Satchidananda of Yogaville, Virginia; Satguru Sivaya Subramuniswami of Hawaii; Sadguru Keshavdas of the Temple of Cosmic Religion, California; and Mother Amritanandamayi of Castro Valley, California.[11]

At the same time, despite the widespread acceptance, or at least tolerance, for Hinduism of which these major events provide evidence, the dual reaction of Americans to Hinduism—openness from some and strong resistance from others—continues to characterize even the last few decades. It is not uncommon, for example, for efforts to build Hindu temples to be resisted—sometimes in quite pointedly exclusionary terms—by local zoning boards.

Prominent Hindu Traditions in the United States

Near the end of this book, the reader will find an Appendix listing Hindu temples and other organizations in the United States. This list includes approximately 325 temples and is probably not exhaustive. It does give a sense, though, of the number and the variety of Hindu communities in the United States, as well as the distribution of Hindus across the country. Some states, such as California, have over a dozen Hindu temples. A handful have none, or at least none that were captured by the methodology through which this list was generated: a survey of temple websites. There are some small temple communities that do not have websites (although this is fairly rare, particularly given the high level of involvement of Indian Americans in the information technology industry). The Vedanta Society of Central Pennsylvania, for example, utilizes an e-mail list but has not developed, as of this writing, an internet presence. It may be, then, that even states under which no temples are listed actually have a few, and it is likely that states under which temples are listed have a few more beyond those in the list.

A glance at the list shows that certain Hindu traditions are particularly prominent or well represented in the United States, in terms of temples and other facilities. A comprehensive survey of these would require an entire book of its own. In an introductory textbook like this one, we shall simply give an overview of a few representative traditions to give the reader a sense of the variety, as well as the points of commonality, of Hindu traditions in America.

The next few sections of this chapter will offer brief overviews of several such traditions: the Chinmaya Mission (a largely educational organization developed to pass Hinduism on to the next generation of American Hindus), Swaminarayan Hinduism (an increasingly prominent Hindu movement, with temples in many different states, based originally in Gujarat), the Pushti Marg (a movement of Krishna devotion, also based originally in Gujarat), and the Shirdi Sai Baba tradition (yet another tradition with a large following which, interestingly, includes both Hindu and Muslim adherents). A glance at the list will also show large numbers of temples based on southern Indian traditions, such as Venkateshvara temples, like the one in Pittsburgh. It will also show a presence of organizations with large non-South Asian followings, like ISKCON and the Vedanta Society.

The Chinmaya Mission

A particularly strong concern, frequently expressed by diasporic Hindus, is the need to pass Hindu thought and practice accurately to the next generation. A less frequently expressed concern, at least in the experience of this author, but certainly one which diasporic Hindus are quite happy to advance, is to educate the wider American public about Hinduism. When the latter concern is expressed, it typically does not take the form not of a desire to proselytize—and indeed many Hindus would say that religious proselytizing is a form of violence, linked closely in their minds with the colonial experience. It is instead expressed as the belief that, if Americans understood Hinduism better, they would be less likely to feel prejudice toward Hindus. Even the desire to educate non-Hindus about Hinduism, then, is ultimately connected to concern for the well-being of the next generation of Hindus.

One particularly popular educational venture among Hindus in America is the Chinmaya Mission. According to its website:

> Chinmaya Mission follows the Vedic teacher-student tradition (guru-shishya parampara) and makes available the ageless wisdom of Advaita Vedanta, the knowledge of universal oneness, providing the tools to realise the wisdom in one's life. Vedanta, the essential core of Hinduism, is the universal science of life, relevant to all people of all backgrounds and faiths. Vedanta inspires seekers to understand their own faith better. Thus, although Chinmaya Mission is a Hindu organisation, it

> does not seek to convert other religious practitioners. As a spiritual movement that aims for inner growth at individual and collective levels, the mission offers a wide array of Vedanta study forums for all ages, promotes Indian classical art forms, and operates numerous social service projects.[12]

Swami Chinmayananda, a disciple of Swami Sivananda—and so a brother-monk of Swami Vishnudevananda—brought the Chinmaya Mission to America in 1975. He had initially established it in India in 1953, where it continues to be an active organization. Swami Chinmayanada traveled widely, gave lectures, and sponsored summer youth camps and family camps in America until his death in 1993, and Chinmaya Mission summer youth and family camps continue to be offered to the present. There are Chinmaya Mission centers in many American cities.[13] Its reach, however, is even larger than the number of its centers might suggest, because the Chinmaya Mission also provides books and other curricular materials to Hindu temples for use in their Sunday schools.

Swaminarayan Hinduism

A relatively new Hindu movement with deep roots in the Indian state of Gujarat has also found a home in America. This is the Swaminarayan movement. This Hindu movement is based on devotion to and practice of the teachings of Sahajanand Swami, also known as Swaminarayan (1781–1830). This movement is especially popular in Gujarat, but it has become global with the emigration of Gujaratis out of India to various parts of the world, including the United States. The movement, broadly speaking, is not a formally organized one, but an organization exists internal to the movement: the Bocāsanvāsī Akṣar Puruṣottam Swāmīnārāyaṇ Sansthā (or BAPS). The first Swaminarayan temple in America was consecrated on August 3, 1977, in Flushing, New York.

After 1977, this movement grew rapidly with new Gujarati immigration and within twenty-five years had over fifty centers and eight temples in the United States. As of this writing, however, there are approximately twenty BAPS temples in the United States. The number of BAPS temples in the United States has more than doubled, in other words, since the year 2000.

The temples of the Swaminarayan movement are quite elaborate and speak to the financial resources of the community that supports it. The Los Angeles Swaminarayan temple is particularly impressive, in that, in addition to its massive size and the elaborate carvings that adorn it, it is also earthquake-proof, incorporating technology from Japan designed for this purpose.

A central teaching of the Swaminarayan movement is the importance of *seva* or selfless service to God in the form of living beings in need. This helps to account for the strong spirit of volunteerism that one finds in this movement—as evidenced, again, by the resources its members have been willing to put into their temple-building activities. Although Swami Vivekananda is known for having promoted the ideal of *seva* in the modern Hindu tradition, Swaminarayan's ideal of seva predates Vivekananda's

FIGURE 29 *BAPS Swaminarayan Temple, Atlanta, Liburn, Georgia (Photo by Qwiddler via Wikimedia Commons).*

by nearly a century. Swaminarayan is believed in this tradition to be an incarnation of Krishna or avatar. Swaminarayan's image is the central *mūrti* housed in all temples of this tradition. According to Hinduism scholar Raymond Williams: "The group teaches that one reaches Purushottam [the Supreme Being] most effectively by means of contact with the personal manifestation of the akshar [the infinite Brahman]."[14]

The Pushti Marg

Another Gujarati Hindu tradition centered on devotion to Krishna that has made a home for itself in America is the Pushti Marg or "Path of Prosperity." This tradition has been most popular among Gujarati merchant communities. This tradition was established by the Vaishnava Vedanta teacher, Vallabha (1479–1531).

Vallabha's teaching is known as *Śuddhādvaita* or "Pure Non-Dualism." It teaches that all souls are ultimately one with Krishna. Strong emphasis is placed on bhakti and cultivating a personal relationship with Krishna as his servant, friend, parent, or lover—which is a theme of many Vaishnava traditions. Special emphasis is given in this tradition on giving honor to Krishna as a divine child. The specific image of Krishna that is most adored in this tradition, and found in the Pushti Marg temples in the United States, is a replica of an original that is in a Krishna temple in Nathdwara, in Gujarat, which is a very popular Vaishnava pilgrimage site, especially for the Pushti Marg tradition.

Vallabha, a south Indian Brahmin who relocated to Gujarat and made many pilgrimages to Vrindavan, where Krishna spent his youth, is held by adherents of his tradition to be an incarnation of Krishna. Not an ascetic tradition, the gurus of the Pushti Marg are direct male descendants of Vallabha.

The Shirdi Sai Baba Tradition

The list of Hindu temples in the United States at the end of this book includes fifteen temples of the Shirdi Sai Baba tradition, which is distinct from the Satya Sai Baba tradition mentioned previously. The reader may recall that Satya Sai Baba (1926–2011) is seen by his devotees as a reincarnation of Shirdi Sai Baba (1838–1918). Sai Baba resided in the village of Shirdi, in the present-day state of Maharashtra. Quite similarly to Sri Ramakrishna, Sai Baba taught a nonsectarian spiritual path. He rejected distinctions of caste and even of religion, and it is not even entirely clear if he was a Hindu or Muslim. During his lifetime he had, and continues to have, a following of both Hindu and Muslim devotees. His Hindu devotees regard him as an avatar and his Muslim devotees regard him as a great saint. His teachings emphasize contentment and doing one's duty with detachment.

FIGURE 30 *Painting depicting Sai Baba of Shirdi (Photo by Godong/Universal Images Group via Getty Images).*

The Gurus Keep Coming

The coming of the Hindu diaspora to the United States did not slow the flow of gurus from India, willing to take on both American and Indian disciples. Indeed, since the emergence of the Hindu diaspora in America in the latter part of the twentieth century, it is increasingly the case that one finds Hindu-inspired organizations started by teachers from India that are made up of Indian and non-Indian devotees.

In 1981, Swami Prakashananda Saraswati established the International Society of Divine Love, a bhakti movement devoted to Lord Krishna. He established his first ashram in Philadelphia in 1984. The movement now has nine centers in America and dedicated a large temple complex in Austin, Texas, in 1994 to serve as its home base.[15]

In 1981, Bhagwan Shree Rajneesh (1931–1990), who was later known as "Osho," started a new ashram—"Rajneeshpuram"—near the town of Antelope, Oregon. By 1984 the community, made up largely of European and American devotees, was thriving. However, "the ashram disintegrated amidst internal dissent and legal controversy in l985."[16] Born a Jain, Rajneesh was known for his iconoclastic teachings, much in the spirit of Jiddu Krishnamurti, but with tāntric elements as well.

In 1985, Swami Dayananda Saraswati (1930–2015)—not to be confused with the founder of the Ārya Samāj in the nineteenth century—established the Arsha Vidya Gurukulam in the Pocono Mountains in Pennsylvania to promote Hindu thought and practice in America. The ashram offers courses in Sanskrit and Indian philosophy, with a strong emphasis on classical Advaita Vedanta.

Swami Dayananda Saraswati is also the founder of the Hindu Dharma Ācārya Sabhā (or "Assembly of Hindu Religious Leaders"). The Hindu Dharma Ācārya Sabhā has a membership of over 100 *ācāryas* or leaders of *saṃpradāyas* (Hindu religious traditions). It was established as an attempt to bring greater institutional cohesion to Hinduism to advance a number of interests and concerns shared across many *saṃpradāyas*. Particularly noteworthy actions of the Hindu Dharma Ācārya Sabhā include a 2008 summit between the Sabhā and the Chief Rabbis of Israel in order to facilitate dialogue between Hinduism and Judaism and proclamations that condemn proselytizing as a form of cultural violence against indigenous religions.

A Hindu Temple in the United States: HARI (The Hindu American Religious Institute)

Hindu temples, again, have gradually become a regular, if not exactly common, part of the American landscape—and Hindu traditions an increasingly accepted part of the American *religious* landscape. Hindu temples in America are remarkably diverse—no less so, as they grow in number, than Hindu temples in India. While certain generalizations can be made about them, no two are exactly alike. Having gotten an overview of the diasporic Hindu community in the United States, let us now take a closer and more intimate look at two representative American Hindu temples.

The Hindu American Religious Institute—or HARI—temple is located on a two-lane road that winds through the woods of rural central Pennsylvania. Unlike many Hindu temples in North America, the building does not immediately strike one as distinctively Hindu in its appearance. It looks somewhat like a large, two-story house, with a parking lot in the front and an American flag flying in the breeze near the entrance. The only clearly Hindu architectural feature is the large gate through which one enters the property. This gate has the holy mantra *Om* written at the top in the Devanagari script of Sanskrit, and the names of the two holiest couples in the Vaishnava tradition—*Sita Ram* and *Radha Krishna*—written in the Roman alphabet on the sides.

Entering the temple on a Sunday morning, the first sight to meet one's eyes is that of three brightly clothed and highly decorated *mūrtis*, or images, of three Hindu deities in the central altar of the temple, directly facing the front entrance. At the center is Ram or Rama (as he is known in Sanskrit). Just to his left (the right, from the perspective of the viewer) is his wife, Sita, and to his right is his brother and "right-hand man," Lakshman or Lakshmana. Before leaving the lobby area and entering the temple proper, one turns to the left and enters a room where shoes are kept on wooden shelves (as well as on the floor, despite the efforts of temple management to get devotees to keep their shoes on the shelves).

After removing one's shoes—a gesture of respect that is observed not only in temples, but in Hindu homes as well—one climbs a half staircase and enters the main sanctuary of the temple. Devotees who enter may touch the floor at the top of the staircase, as they reach the top, and then touch their foreheads, also a gesture of respect and reverence.

Because it is a Sunday morning, the temple is not a quiet place. On the contrary, there is a great deal of activity taking place. At the far left of the sanctuary, there is a performance stage where cultural events are held. At the moment, a group of elementary school children are sitting cross-legged in a semicircle around an Indian woman playing a harmonium—a German instrument with some resemblance to an accordion that has been adapted to the playing of Indian music. The woman is teaching the children to sing *bhajans* or devotional songs.

At the far right of the sanctuary, there is a bearded man who is not Indian but is wearing a *kurtā* and *pajāma*, a traditional Indian long shirt and loose pants. He is showing another, smaller group of slightly older children, around middle-school age, how to play a sitar.

Scattered throughout the sanctuary are smaller groups of adults—mostly but not entirely of South Asian ethnic origin—engaged in quiet conversation. Seated in front and slightly to the side of the central images of Ram, Sita, and Lakshman is one of the two priests who serve at the HARI temple. We approach the central images and make a *praṇām*, or gesture of respect, by bringing the palms of both our hands together, raising them to the level of the face, and bowing slightly. This specific gesture is also called *añjali*. Before doing this, one might also ring a large brass bell that hangs from a rope suspended from the ceiling. The ring of the bell does not disturb any of the activity already occurring in the sanctuary. At this point, the priest, unless he is already engaged in conversation with another devotee, will smile at one warmly and say, "Namaste! Aap kaise hain?" In Hindi, this means "Hello! How are you?" Not everyone in the temple community speaks Hindi. Many come from parts of India where other languages are predominant, and a handful are not South Asian. But most of the discourse in the temple seems to occur in either Hindi or English (or some combination of the two).

After exchanging pleasantries with the priest, one will walk around the central altar in a clockwise direction, a ritual of respect and devotion known as *pradakshina* or circumambulation. When doing *pradakshina*, one keeps the main images to one's right and walks around them in a clockwise direction. Most devotees at HARI do this once, but some do it more than once. This author once observed a devotee at HARI perform 108 *pradakshinas*.

At HARI, as one does *pradakshina*, one passes through a small corridor, the walls of which are decorated with two-dimensional portraits of Hindu deities and saints from Hindu history. One notes that these images include Mahavira, the twenty-fourth *Tirthankara*, or enlightened teacher of Jainism, and Guru Nanak, the founder of Sikhism. After circumambulating the central altar, one holds out one's right hand to the priest and is given a few drops of water mixed with the oil of the *tulsī* plant—a variety of basil sacred to the Hindu deity Vishnu. After one drinks this water from the palm of one's hand, one again extends one's right hand and is given a mixture of nuts and sugar cubes. This is *prasād*—food that has been offered to the deities and is then returned to devotees as a form of divine blessing.

Inset into the back wall of the sanctuary, extending to either side of the central altar, are smaller altars that house the images of other Hindu deities. From left to right, moving toward the central altar, one sees Saraswati, goddess of wisdom; the divine couple, Śiva and Parvati; and a large image of Mahavira, who is adorned in keeping with Shvetambara Jain tradition. From right to left, moving one's gaze away from the central altar, one sees another divine couple—Krishna and Radha; Durga, the Divine Mother, having ten hands and riding a lion; and then finally Balaji, or Venkateshvara, whom we have encountered previously in this chapter: a popular southern Indian image of Vishnu, the original of which is in a famous temple and pilgrimage site in the southern Indian city of Tirupati.

The presence of the Jain *mūrti* in a Hindu temple may seem surprising, given that Jainism is a distinct religious tradition from Hinduism. Jainism, Buddhism, and Sikhism, however, have a number of close affinities with Hinduism, both conceptually and in terms of shared history. As discussed in an earlier chapter, all four originated in India. They are sometimes categorized as "Dharma traditions," sharing, like the Abrahamic traditions, many basic concepts and practices.

When both Jains and Hindus began immigrating to America in large numbers after 1965, both communities were still sufficiently small that they found it worked well to pool their resources and share worship spaces. There are prominent Hindu-Jain temples in both Pittsburgh and New Jersey.

The Hindu-Jain temple of Pittsburgh also has a copy of the *Guru Granth Sahib*, the sacred scripture of the Sikh tradition, and Sikhs use the facility as well.

Returning one's gaze to the central altar, one sees, on the pedestal on which Ram stands, a bright red "*Oṃ*," beneath which is a small bronze image of a baby Krishna. At Lakshman's feet is a small image of Hanuman, the ape deity who assisted Rama in his quest to rescue Sita from the demonic Ravana in the sacred epic poem, the *Ramayana*. A similar-sized image of the elephant-headed Ganesha is at Sita's feet. Just to Ganesha's left is a gray stone abstract symbol of Shiva—the liṅgam—which is being closely guarded by an image of Nandi, the bull—Shiva's animal vehicle or *vahana*—which is made from the same type of gray stone.

The sanctuary as a whole is a large, simple, and functional room, with little in the way of adornment, apart from the images themselves—which are brilliantly decorated. On the floor is a dark red carpet, except for a square roughly one meter to a side in the midst of the right half of the room, which is bare stone. Directly above this bare spot is a vent. This space is for the lighting of a small fire (held in a metal container placed on bricks) in order that a Vedic *havan*, or ritual offering to the sacred fire, might be performed. *Havan* is held once a month at the temple and on New Year's Day. If one goes downstairs, one will find a large communal dining room and kitchen, as well as restrooms, an apartment for the family of one of the priests (the other priest lives nearby), and a storage space for chairs and tables, which are set up and taken down as needed. There are also classrooms, and because it is Sunday morning, these are filled with children who are learning Indian languages and taking religion classes from volunteers from the community.

At noon, classes end, and all of the children gather in the center of the sanctuary directly in front of the central images. Their parents and teachers sit to the sides. Almost everyone sits on the carpeted floor, though there is a row of chairs along the back wall for the elderly or anyone who does not feel like sitting on the floor. The head of the Sunday school stands at the front and makes announcements, as well as inviting the children to tell the community something that they learned that day. If any of the children has had a birthday in the past week, the community applauds them. Then everyone stands for *āratī*.

Āratī is a ritual that one of the priests performs at the temple daily, at both noon and seven o'clock at night, regardless of whether or not any devotees are present. Small oil lamps sitting on metal plates are lit and waved in front of the images of the deities to the accompaniment of communal singing. The traditional *āratī* song at HARI temple, as at many North American Hindu temples, is *Om Jaya Jagadisha Hare*, or "Victory to Hari (Viṣṇu), Lord of the Universe." This song was popularized by the Hindi singer, Lata Mangeshkar. After *āratī*, everyone heads downstairs for lunch, which is provided by volunteer families from the community.

HARI is a type of temple that is quite common in the Hindu diaspora—a "universal temple": that is, a nonsectarian temple that does not cater exclusively to any *saṃpradāya* or denomination of Hinduism but is open to all. The goal of the temple community is to provide a place of worship and cultural experience for as wide a cross-section of Hindus as possible. Though the Vaishnava presence is considerable—the central deity is, after all, Ram; the song sung at *āratī* is a Vaishnava song; and one of the priests is a Sri Vaishnava from Andhra Pradesh, in southern India—the temple is not Vaishnava in an exclusive way. Mahashivaratri, Durga Pūjā, Saraswati Pūjā, and Ganesh Chaturthi are celebrated with as much fanfare and devotion in the temple as Krishnajanmashtami and Ramanavami. And, of course, the HARI community also includes Jains, with Mahavir Jayanti being a festival on the temple calendar of no less importance than the celebrations of the various Hindu deities already mentioned.

Some of the festivals just mentioned—and the deities they celebrate—are more prominent in some parts of India than in others. The pūjās, or rituals of worship, for the goddesses Durga and Saraswati, for example, are celebrated with particular fanfare and devotion in Bengal, while the birthday of the elephant-headed deity, Ganesha, is special to Hindus in Maharashtra. The HARI community, though, is made up of people from all parts of India, plus a few non-Indians who have been drawn to Hinduism either through being married to a Hindu or because of their own personal interest, or both. When a festival that is particularly sacred to a given subgroup of this community occurs, families from that sub-community typically take the lead in the cooking for the day, putting on a cultural program featuring music or dance from that part of India, and so on.

Bengali families therefore sponsor the Saraswati and Durga Pūjā events, Marathi families the Ganesh Chaturthi celebration, Jain families the Mahavir Jayanti observance, etc. The monthly *havan*, or fire ritual, is frequently performed and sponsored by north Indian families with affiliation to the aniconic Ārya Samāj, a nineteenth-century reform movement that emphasizes the ancient Vedic rites such as *havan* over the *mūrti*- or image-centered pūjās of the dominant traditions. That being said, I have seen members of these families participating in the *ārati* and other temple events involving *mūrtis* without any apparent hesitation or discomfort.

On Friday evenings, devotees of Lord Krishna—mostly from the local branch of ISKCON, known as the "IOHU," or "Institute of Higher Understanding"—use the temple facilities for singing *bhajans* and holding a discourse in English based upon the teachings of their tradition—the Gauḍīya Vaishnava saṃpradāya.

Of the two priests employed by the temple, one is from northern India—specifically from Ahmedabad, in the state of Gujarat—while the other, as mentioned earlier, is from southern India—Hyderabad, in Andhra Pradesh. The distinctive northern and southern styles of pūjā are therefore both available to devotees, who are able to hire the priests to perform rituals either in the temple or in their homes.

The HARI community is thus a microcosm of the global Hindu community—many distinct traditions with specific cultural forms and a variety of theological perspectives all sharing a space and the common label *Hindu*. Membership does not require that one be affiliated to a specific sect or adhere to any specific view. The temple's web site states it simply:

> The mission of the Hindu American Religious Institute (HARI) is to serve as a centre for Hindu worship, to promote spiritual development, and conduct cultural and educational activities for the benefit of the Hindu community … The vision of the

Hindu American Religious Institute (HARI) is to bring together people of Hindu faith coming from various parts of the world so as to promote the Hindu way of life and to preserve and protect the rich Hindu cultural heritage in our present and future generations.[17]

The last of the concerns mentioned is particularly central to the HARI community—preserving the Hindu cultural heritage for future generations. Passing Hinduism on to their children is the central preoccupation of the families making up this community: a typical concern of Hindus in America.

The Sunday school and activities associated with it are only the most obvious manifestation of this concern. Children are also central to all of the cultural programs that the temple sponsors, and conversations with adults about the purpose of the temple always include some mention of the youth as a primary motivator in participating in temple activities, since temple attendance is not required in most Hindu traditions, and most families perform worship at home. A contrast with India is often made as well. In the words of Lakshmi, a community member, "In India, Hinduism is everywhere. It's in the air you breathe. But in this country, you need to work to keep it alive. You need to have a special place for it." For its members, the HARI temple is one such special place.

Hinduism being a highly decentralized tradition, the HARI temple is not affiliated with any larger organization—no "Hindu Church." It is independent and is run entirely by volunteers. It has a governing body consisted of an executive committee (in charge of day-to-day administration) and a board of trustees (in charge of policies and finances), both elected from the membership.

Washington Kali Temple

In the words of its web site, "Washington Kali Temple is not just another temple. It is a Bengali religious and cultural centre where you will find many opportunities to deepen your spiritual experience and to participate in community events and gatherings."[18] In a clear contrast with the HARI temple, the Washington Kali Temple—actually in Burtonsville, Maryland, just north of suburban Washington, DC, between Washington and Baltimore—strives to maintain the Hindu traditions of a specific part of India: Bengal. Both its full-time priest and his assistants are Bengali Hindus. The Sanskrit in which the prayers accompanying rituals are chanted is pronounced with a strong Bengali accent and the deities and festivals that it celebrates are those most prominent in Bengal. Like HARI, it is not exclusive. One can meet devotees at the Washington Kali Temple from all parts of India, as well as a handful of non-Indians. The atmosphere, like that of HARI, is friendly and welcoming. The goal does not appear to be to create a "Bengali only" setting. Nobody seems unwelcome. But the temple nevertheless quite consciously sustains a distinctively *Bengali* atmosphere and cultural environment.

The temple, first of all, has a more distinctively Hindu appearance than HARI but shares with HARI a basically functional nature, consisting primarily of two large rooms—one, like the HARI basement, for communal dining, and a large sanctuary. On entering the sanctuary, one's first sight is a large and brightly adorned image of Durga in her form as *Mahishasuramardini* or "Slayer of the Buffalo Demon." Having ten arms and hands and riding upon a lion, she is impaling the fierce Buffalo Demon while at the same time smiling benevolently at her devotees. She is flanked by images of her children. To her immediate right (to her left, from the vantage point of the viewer) is Lakshmi, goddess of prosperity and good fortune, and just beyond Lakshmi is the elephant-headed Ganesha, remover of obstacles. To Durga's immediate left is Saraswati, goddess of wisdom, and Karttikeya, warrior deity and divine general. Each of these deities is accompanied by his or her animal vehicle—Ganesha by a mouse, Lakshmi by an owl, Saraswati by a swan, and Karttikeya by a peacock. Durga, of course, is riding her lion. All five of these deities are lined up along an entire wall of the sanctuary and are the main focus of attention during the ten-day festival of Durga Pūjā.

During the rest of the year, however, most of the ritual activity takes place to the right of the sanctuary entrance. The central deity of the Washington Kali Temple—as one may gather from its name—is Kali, the Mother Goddess in her fiercest form, as the protector of Her devotees and destroyer of evil. Of all the Hindu deities, Kali's appearance is probably the most striking—and disturbing—to those not familiar with Hindu traditions. Her bright red tongue is protruding from Her mouth, in striking contrast with Her black skin. In Her upper left hand, She holds a fierce-looking, bloody, curved sword. Her lower left hand holds the severed head of a demon by the hair. Her upper right hand, however, is raised in a gesture of benediction—the *abhaya mudrā*, a gesture, which literally means "Do not be afraid." Her lower right hand is lowered, with the palm outward—a gesture called *dana mudrā*, which symbolizes generosity and divine grace. She is standing upon the body of Her husband, Shiva, though Shiva is largely obscured at the Washington Kali Temple by the robes and other finery, which have been draped lovingly over the image of the goddess as a sign of devotion and reverence.

Interestingly, at the feet of Kali, to Her right (to the viewer's left), is a photograph of Sri Ramakrishna, and on the opposite side, to Kali's left, is a photograph of Ma Sarada Devi, the wife and spiritual companion of Sri Ramakrishna, known to devotees as the Holy Mother.

The Washington Kali Temple is not a Vedanta Society, and it has no affiliation with either the Ramakrishna Order or the Ramakrishna Mission in India. Ramakrishna is held in high regard by many Bengali Hindus, however, and is known for his profound devotion to Kali.

The priest of the Washington Kali Temple holds Sri Ramakrishna in great reverence, as do many Bengali Hindus. But the bond between this priest and Sri Ramakrishna is special, due to the fact that both are priests of Kali who also reside on the premises of her temple. In an interview, this priest spoke of aspiring to the level of *bhakti*, or devotion, that he saw exemplified in the life of Sri Ramakrishna. In Bengali Hindu tradition, as in other Hindu traditions, it is believed that if the priest in a temple has sufficient devotion, the image of the central deity of the temple will be "awakened," intensifying the power of the spiritual experience of devotees who visit it.

To the left of the image of Kali is an image of Durga known as *Jagaddhatri*, the "Protector of the World." This image is smaller than the one on the far wall and has eight, rather than ten, arms, and is not depicted in the act of slaying the Buffalo Demon. To Kali's right (left, from the perspective of the viewer) is a large Shiva liṅgam, above which hangs a two-dimensional painting of Shiva as Yogeshvara, or Lord of Yoga, sitting in a calm posture of meditation (in contrast with his other popular depiction as Nataraja or Lord of the Cosmic Dance of creation and destruction). A little distance beyond the Shiva liṅgam, closer to the wall near which Durga and Her children are housed, is the divine couple, Krishna and Radha. To their right is a smaller image of Hanuman.

Adjacent to and accessible from the main sanctuary is a smaller sanctuary that houses the images of the *Navagraha* or Nine Astrological Bodies. One typically sees this term translated as "nine planets." This is somewhat inaccurate, however, as the Navagrahas do not correspond with the nine planets of the physical solar system—or eight planets, given the demotion of Pluto to the status of a planetoid—though there is some overlap among them. The Navagrahas are better seen as deities with the power to influence the course of human events.

The Navagrahas are the "planets" of Hindu astrology: the Sun, the Moon, Mercury, Venus, Mars, Jupiter, Saturn, and Rahu and Ketu, the latter two being seen as the causes of solar and lunar eclipses. One pays devotion to the Navagrahas in order to maximize the positive benefits—or, especially in the cases of Saturn, Rahu, and Ketu, to neutralize or ward off the negative effects—of their astrological energies. Just outside the main temple is also a smaller temple devoted to Shiva. The main image in this temple is of a seated Shiva—again, in his form as Yogeshvara—as well as a set of Shiva liṅgams modelled upon liṅgams located at sacred sites across India. By visiting this temple one can, in effect, undertake a pilgrimage to all of these various sites and experience some of the spiritual merit of such a journey.

If one visits the Washington Kali Temple on any given day, one will find a fairly small group of devotees present. The numbers are larger if one visits on Amavasya, the day of the new moon. New moon nights are especially sacred to Kali, and a Kali Pūjā is performed on this day monthly by many devotees. (Devotees of Viṣṇu similarly have a special Satyanarayana Pūjā on *Pūrṇimā*, the full moon day.) The *āratī* performed at the Kali Temple is a sharp contrast with that performed at HARI. In both, lit oil lamps are waved in front of the images of the deities as divine blessings are invoked. But rather than a communal singing of *Om Jaya Jagadisha Hare*, Kali's *āratī* involves the ringing of bells, the clashing of cymbals, and the pounding of drums, all of which are accompanied by the blowing of conch shells and the making of eerie (at least to non-Bengali ears) ululations by the women who are present. The sound can be quite loud, and its intention is to dispel all negative forces from the sacred space at the moment when blessings are invoked. It is also celebratory, and many of the devotees—especially children and young people—clearly have a good deal of fun banging the cymbals and drums.

During the ten-day festival of Durga Pūjā, however, the Washington Kali Temple becomes heavily crowded. (The same is true of the HARI temple during Diwali, the feast of the goddess Lakshmi and of Rama's victory over Ravana.) The very large numbers of people—combined with the drumming, bell ringing, and chanting—make for an intense and exciting atmosphere that strives to re-create the experience of Durga Pūjā in Bengal.

HARI and the Washington Kali Temple Compared and Contrasted

The contrast between HARI and the Washington Kali Temple is essentially that between a temple designed to accommodate as wide a swath of the American Hindu community as possible and a temple designed to replicate, as closely as possible, the experience of being immersed in one specific Hindu culture (or subculture). Although a superficial examination might suggest the two institutions are at cross-purposes, closer analysis shows that this is not necessarily the case. The two temples being only about an hour-and-a-half drive apart from one another, many Bengali Hindu families in the region are members of both and participate in the services of both. Bengali Hindus in the Harrisburg area of Pennsylvania will thus typically be members of the HARI temple and participate in its regular events—having their children attend Sunday school, for example, and going for activities such as Satyanarayana Pūjā and the festivals of the various other deities. They will also put a great deal of time and energy into celebrating those festivals that are special to their subcommunity—like the aforementioned Durga and Saraswati Pūjās—at HARI, so the entire community can participate. If time permits, however, they also participate in the longer and more elaborate celebrations of the Kali Temple. (The HARI Durga Pūjā is typically held on only one of the ten days of the festival, while the Kali Temple has events on all of the ten days. HARI also tends to hold many of its festival observances on Sunday mornings, whereas the Kali Temple tends to observe its events on Saturday evenings, making participation in both possible.) In interviews on this issue, Harrisburg area Bengali Hindus, speaking of their participation in HARI events, spoke mainly in terms of "loyalty" to their local temple and the convenience of having a temple nearby. As one person said, "This is where our children go to Sunday school." But when speaking about the Washington Kali Temple, there were frequent references to a desire—both for themselves and their children—to experience a "real" or "authentic" Bengali Durga Pūjā. Nostalgia for India in general, but for Bengal in particular, seemed a prominent emotion connected to the Kali Temple, whereas HARI was connected more with a commitment to Hinduism and passing Hindu traditions on to the next generation. Children were mentioned more often in reference to HARI, whereas the interviewees' own childhood memories played a greater role in the discussion of the Kali Temple.

At the same time, however, there are many respects in which these two temples have far more in common than either does with Hindu temples in India. Both are centers of community activity aimed at preserving traditions, beliefs, and practices that are not at all predominant in their larger, North American context. In contrast with India, where it can be said that Hinduism is, in the words of one person, "in the very air that you breathe," in America, a Hindu space is something that must be consciously cultivated, nurtured, and preserved. Both place considerable emphasis on education and hold classes in which Hindu children can receive not only religious instruction in a conventional sense, but also instruction in music, dance, and languages (although the focus of language teaching at the Washington Kali Temple is on Bengali and Sanskrit, whereas at HARI it includes Gujarati, Tamil, Hindi, and other Indian languages as well, so long as instructors with the necessary skills are willing to share their time and expertise). Both are largely functional spaces, with a minimum of traditional decoration—unlike large North American Hindu temples that try to replicate the more elaborate Indian temple styles. In both cases, interviewees said that this was a matter of both time and financial expense, the more elaborate, traditional styles of temple taking far more time and money to construct than the more basic buildings that these communities have elected to utilize. And in both cases, interviewees said that "it would be nice" at some later point to renovate their buildings in a more traditional style, should the resources become available to do so.

Hindu-Inspired or Hindu?

As will be discussed in more detail in the next chapter, Hindu-inspired organizations that were established by gurus who came to America and took on American followers—beginning with Swami Vivekananda in 1893—generally have a distinctly different atmosphere from the temples of the Hindu diaspora. Diasporic Hindu temples often appear "chaotic" to non-Indian Americans. A Self-Realization Fellowship or Siddha Yoga meditation center, on the other hand, will be orderly and serene. The programming in such organizations will also tend to focus more upon meditation and talks on Vedanta philosophy rather than rituals and cultural programs. Increasingly, however, this is a distinction that is breaking down in practice, particularly as more diasporic Hindus come to America and join Hindu-inspired organizations.

The membership of many Vedanta Societies, for example, is made up largely of diasporic Hindus—and often, specifically Bengali Hindus, given Sri Ramakrishna and Swami Vivekananda's Bengali heritage, and their status, in addition to their religious and philosophical significance, as Bengali cultural heroes. Vedanta Societies increasingly include programs such as performances of Indian classical music and the singing of *bhajans*. A sharp distinction between a Hindu temple and the center of a Hindu-inspired organization is thus becoming increasingly difficult to make.

Hinduism in Canada

Today, there are about half a million Canadian Hindus. These Hindus make up 1.5 percent of the Canadian population. There are thus roughly a fifth the number of Canadian Hindus as there are American Hindus; but because Canada has a smaller population than the United States,' Hindus make up a larger percentage—almost twice as much—of the population of Canada as they do of the United States.

The history of Hinduism in Canada in many ways parallels that of Hinduism in the United States. In Canada, Indians—Hindu, Sikh, and Muslim—have faced both racism and other difficulties related to resistance from the majority population toward Hindus, and Indians more generally. The early Indian immigrants in Canada were, like Indian immigrants to the United States in the same period, largely male and working class. While allowed to work in Canada, Indians were not given voting rights until 1947: the same year that India was granted its independence from the British Empire. As long as India was a subjugated nation under the rule of the Empire, its people did not have full rights of citizenship anywhere else in the Empire, even as far from India as Canada. With independence, however, India came to be seen by Britain and its former colonies as a sovereign nation and Indians as "proper" immigrants. The status of Indians thus improved in Canada after 1947, much as it did in the United States after 1965.

During the late nineteenth and early twentieth centuries, when racism against Indians in the United States was particularly virulent, much the same could be said of Canada. There were attempts to restrict Indian immigration, and the Canadian analogue of the Asiatic Exclusion League was a movement called "White Canada Forever."

As Peter Ward recounts, and we have seen previously in regard to the United States, Indian men took up work in the logging industry on the west coast of Canada:

> In the decade before World War I successive outbursts of racial animus marked relations between East Indians and whites in British Columbia. Predisposed to racial hostility by their fear of racial pluralism, whites emphatically rejected the East Indian immigrant. The first outburst occurred in Vancouver during the summer of 1906, the torrent loosed by the sudden arrival of several hundred immigrants. Once again west coast nativists called for a white Canada while civic officials did what they could to discourage immigration. Later in the year, as the rate of immigration fell, agitation ceased. In 1907, however, heavy Asian immigration and resurgent racial tension once more raised the question of migration from India.[19]

The situation in 1907 became so difficult for the Indians that many left Canada and went south, to the United States, and began to work in the state of Washington. They encountered similarly fierce racism there, however, culminating in the notorious Bellingham riots of the same year, discussed earlier. Many Indians—as mentioned previously, primarily Sikh men—continued to move south, eventually settling in California. Many married Mexican women giving rise to a Punjabi Mexican American community.[20]

The status of Indians in Canada, again, improved after 1947. Despite the history of racism and ongoing reality of racism in both countries, Canada, very much like the United States, has long been a home to refugees. Because of its longstanding relations with other Commonwealth nations, it has been easier for refugees from these nations to travel to Canada. As a result, Canada has been seen as a more "natural" place to go for Hindus seeking refuge from persecution, even after the lifting of the immigration restrictions, which had limited Indian immigration to the United States. Hindus have fled from Commonwealth states such as Fiji and Sri Lanka to Canada when they faced persecution in these respective places: from the majority Christian population in Fiji and the majority Buddhist population in Sri Lanka.

Sikhs, too, fleeing persecution from Hindus in India after the violent events of 1984—the Khalistan movement for Sikh independence and the subsequent storming of the Golden Temple in Amritsar by the Indian army, the assassination of Prime Minister Indira Gandhi, and anti-Sikh riots in Delhi—often made their way to such Canadian cities as Vancouver, Toronto, and Montreal.

In fact, the Sikh population of Canada is almost the same size as the Hindu population. As of this writing, Hindus make up 1.5 percent of the population of Canada, while Sikhs make up 1.4 percent.[21]

Hindu Temple Societies developed in Canada somewhat earlier than in the United States: quite understandably, given the long period of immigration restrictions in the latter country. There are today roughly one thousand Hindu temples in Canada: many more than in the United States, despite the number of Hindus in the United States being larger. Much like temples in the United States, Canadian Hindu temples serve not only as places of worship, but also as community centers. Some even provide schooling to Hindu children, beyond the "Sunday Schooling" found in many US Hindu temples. Many of the same Hindu organizations have also gone to Canada as have gone to the United States, such as ISKCON, the Vedanta Society, the Chinmaya Mission, and Swaminarayan. The largest Canadian temple is the Swaminarayan temple in Toronto.

Canada has also had a similar experience to the United States in terms of persons whose native religion is not Hindu wishing to convert to Hinduism or to join specific Hindu-inspired or Hindu-based organizations based on the teachings of Indian gurus. Both ISKCON and the Ārya Samāj have substantial presences in Canada, and some Canadians have availed themselves of the possibility that the Ārya Samāj allows, with its ritual of conversion, for persons to join the Hindu community through a Vedic ritual. This ritual is a variant of the investiture with the sacred thread, or *upanayanam*, by which young Hindus leave childhood and enter the first stage of life: the stage or *āśrama* of *brahmacharya*, also known as the student stage. Many of the Canadians who convert to Hinduism in this way are also in the process of marrying a Hindu spouse. As in the United States, relations between Hindus and mainstream Canadian society have slowly improved through the years.

Hinduism in the Caribbean Region: Resilience and Dignity in the Face of Adversity

The Caribbean region has a Hindu population of roughly 280 thousand—over a quarter of a million—making up just over 1 percent of the population of this region. The number of Hindus in the Caribbean countries is thus slightly larger than that in Canada and makes up a similar portion of the total population: between 1 and 2 percent.

The ancestors of most Caribbean Hindus were brought to this region under conditions little different from those of African slaves brought to the United States in the same period. As Murali Balaji vividly describes:

> On May 5, 1838, the Whitby, a British ship docked in British Guiana (now known as Guyana) with 249 human cargo after a nearly three-month voyage from the Port of Calcutta in India. Along the way, many of those on board were abused by the ship's crew, and five died.
>
> The Whitby was the first of many chartered ships that would bring Indians—mostly poor Hindus from rural northern India—to work on the sugar cane plantations in the British West Indies. Over the next 80 years, more than 500,000 Indians would make the trip to the Caribbean as indentured servants, primarily to places such as Guyana and Trinidad. Their story—shaped by the trauma of Transatlantic migration, struggles in a new environment, and eventually the triumph of forging a distinct identity—continues to be an overlooked part of colonial history.[22]

To again cite Vinay Lal, the circumstances of the Hindus shipped to the Caribbean in the nineteenth century could not be more different from those of the second wave of Indian immigration into the United States after 1965. Even to use the same term—diaspora—to describe both groups seems to stretch the meaning of this word, creating the sense of a unity at the expense of effacing the massive gulf that separates their experiences. As Lal explains:

> Perhaps the word "diaspora" flattens too much and fails to distinguish between … diasporas that have arisen under circumstances of extreme repression and diasporas that suggest more benign histories of ambition, self-improvement, economic advancement, or sheer adventure.[23]

Among the Caribbean nations, Trinidad and Tobago have the largest Indian population. In fact, Indians make up "just under half" of the country's population.[24] Hindus make up "some 24 per cent of the total population (about 60 percent of all Indians)."[25] As Vertovec says, "The Hindu community has generally been at the bottom of the society's ethnically-determined status hierarchy since the original immigrants arrived as indentured laborers between 1845 and 1917."[26]

The story of Hindus in the Caribbean, though, is not one of unmitigated tragedy, but of a singular triumph. In the face of the intense pressures which they faced, the Hindus in the Caribbean region were forced to differentiate what was essential to their traditions—what had to be preserved at all costs—and what was expendable. Many features of Indian village Hinduism, like observance of caste strictures and patriarchy, were cast aside by Hindus in the Caribbean. As Balaji recounts:

> Hindu reform movements such as Ārya Samāj, which encouraged women priests, became widely embraced by Hindus in Guyana and Trinidad, as well as in Suriname, a former Dutch colony that neighbors Guyana. Moreover, the idea of caste, which had

> been formalized in the Indian subcontinent by 1850 with the implementation of the colonial census, was marginalized and ultimately eliminated by Indo-Caribbean Hindus by the early 20th century. Many Caribbean Hindus embraced a practice that blended Vedic Hinduism with the devotional strength of the Bhakti movement, particularly the Vaishnavism (devotion to Vishnu) inspired by the 16th century Hindu saint Chaitanya. Others embraced the ideas of the Bharat Sevashram Sangh established by Swami Pranavananda in the early 20th century and spread to Guyana and Trinidad.[27]

Regarding the Ārya Samāj presence in the Caribbean, which is considerable, relative to other parts of the Hindu world, Vertovec notes:

> The first Ārya Samāj missionary to Trinidad arrived in 1910, followed by others in 1914, 1917, 1928, and 1933. The earliest ones established a sustained presence (though no great following), while the latter two (Pundits Mehta Jaimani and Ayodhia Prasad) were renowned for their sophistication and scholarship. Of widening significance in the late 1920s and early 1930s, the Ārya Samājis held popular public forums on the greatness of Indian civilization, the importance of the Vedas, the futility of idol worship, the equality of women, the merits of education, and more. Even those who were not motivated to convert to their brand of Hinduism were moved to reflect upon, and take pride in, the grand heritage of India.[28]

As a minority community, and not a very privileged one in terms of the social hierarchy in the Caribbean, the pressure upon Hindus in the Caribbean to convert to Christianity has historically been intense, with a good deal of evangelical missionary activity being targeted specifically at the Hindus. But most managed to resist this pressure and have continued to sustain their distinctive practice of Hinduism.

Some Hindus who have converted to Christianity have nevertheless managed to maintain ties to their Hindu traditions. Anjali, an American Hindu who migrated with her parents to the United States from Guyana, has a Hindu mother and a Christian father (who is of Indian descent). Her father's parents had converted to Christianity, but they continued to celebrate major Hindu festivals with the wider Hindu community, and they did not object when their son wanted to marry a Hindu girl. Anjali self-identifies as Hindu, but she also notes that "I love my multi-religious heritage. I enjoy being involved in both Hinduism and Christianity. For me, Jesus is an avatar. All religions teach love."

Today, many Caribbean Hindus have migrated to the United States. The regions in the United States that have fairly strong concentrations of Caribbean Hindus include New York, Maryland, Florida, and Minnesota. One Minnesota-based Hindu from Trinidad, Anantanand Rambachan, is a scholar of Hinduism and a respected Hindu theologian who does constructive work in his chosen tradition of Advaita Vedanta. Rambachan notes that the first Hindu temple in the United States was actually in the home of a Caribbean Hindu who migrated to the United States—specifically, to Minnesota—in the middle to late nineteenth century, well before Swami Vivekananda's arrival in America or his famous speech at the first World Parliament of Religions.[29]

Clearly, Hinduism in America, like Hinduism as a whole, is too varied and vast to fit into a simple, linear narrative.

Study Questions

1. Why are Hindus in America, in particular, concerned to ensure that their traditions are passed on to the next generation?
2. What role does the home shrine play in Hinduism in America?
3. What are the main points of contrast and similarity between the HARI temple and the Washington Kali Temple?
4. How are the Canadian and Caribbean experiences of Hinduism both similar to and different from the experiences of Hindus in the United States?

Suggestions for Further Reading

Corinne Dempsey, *The Goddess Lives in Upstate New York* (New York: Oxford University Press, 2005).

Diana Eck, *On Common Ground: World Religions in America* (New York: Columbia University Press, 2002).

Mahalingum Kolapen, *Hindu Temples of North America* (Orlando, FL: Hindu University of America, 2008).

P. Pratap Kumar, *Contemporary Hinduism* (New York: Acumen, 2013).

Karen Isaken Leonard, *Making Ethnic Choices: California's Punjabi Mexican Americans* (Philadelphia: Temple University Press, 1992).

Gurinder Singh Mann, Paul Numrich, and Raymond Williams, *Buddhists, Hindus, and Sikhs in America: A Short History* (Oxford: Oxford University Press, 2008).

W. Peter Ward, *White Canada Forever: Popular Attitudes and Public Policy toward Orientals in British Columbia* (Third Edition) (Montreal: McGill-Queen's University Press, 1978).

Raymond Williams, *An Introduction to Swaminarayan Hinduism* (Cambridge: Cambridge University Press, 2001).

6

Non-Indian Practitioners, Yoga, Vegetarianism, and Religious Pluralism

Chapter 6 Summary and Outline

This chapter will turn to the phenomenon of adopters of Hinduism—Hindus by choice—Hindu-inspired meditation movements, and the broader influence of Hinduism and India in American culture: vegetarianism, yoga, religious pluralism.

Adopters of Hinduism

As discussed near the beginning of this book, among the roughly 2.23 million Americans who identify themselves as Hindu, 9 percent do not self-identify as Asian—2 percent of American Hindus self-identify as "mixed," 4 percent as "white," 2 percent as African American, and 1 percent as Hispanic. Although Hinduism continues to be seen by many as a way of life to which one must be born, inheriting it from and being acculturated to it by one's family, it is increasingly coming to be seen as a religion, like Christianity, that one can *adopt*. This reflects the Protestant sensibility which informs American culture—a sensibility that perceives religion not so much as a way of life, but as a set of *beliefs*: beliefs one has the freedom to *choose* to accept or reject. At the same time, to be Indian and Hindu is seen as "normal," whereas a non-Indian self-identifying as Hindu is unusual.

The issue of adopters of Hindus, though—particularly "white" Hindus—is contentious, not only among some Hindus, but also among scholars of Hinduism, some of whom continue to repeat the claim that one must be born Hindu. For most Hindus, Hinduism is a precious heritage which they desire very strongly to pass on to their children. Spiritual seekers for whom Hinduism is not a matter of heritage, and particularly who are willing to experiment creatively with rituals and other practices, may not necessarily be welcome in an environment like a Hindu temple, which can be seen not only as a place of religious activity, but as a cultural refuge, where the sounds, smells, and flavors of one's upbringing can be experienced and shared with one's children.

The white community in particular—from which sprang the imperial rulers and colonizers of the past, as well as the racists and religious bigots who, even today, express their disapproval of the Hindu presence in their midst—can quite understandably be viewed with suspicion. This suspicion is expressed in strong terms by Deepak Sarma, who writes:

> It is ironic that, while so many Diasporic Hindus mimic imaginary archetypes of "white" American culture in order to assimilate, to deny their colonized and oppressed histories, to (futilely) self-blanch, and to be accepted by the dominant white Christian privileged culture, a select group of white Americans do the opposite. They claim to have "converted" to Hinduism and concurrently mimic their imaginary (and often Orientalist) archetypal "Hindu" in order to reverse-assimilate, to deny their colonial histories, to (futilely) color their lives, and paradoxically, to be marginalized.[1]

To be sure, most non-Indians who have attended a Hindu temple have remarked on what a warm, welcoming place it is—warmer and friendlier, some will even say, than certain churches they have attended.[2] But a sentiment on the part of South Asian Hindus of feeling "invaded" would certainly be understandable, one might argue, and perhaps even warranted, given the historical sufferings Hindus have experienced at the hands of Europeans and their descendants, both in India and in America. Sarma questions whether the warm welcome that is given to "white converts" by many Diasporic Hindus is sincere. "Or is it merely proof that Diasporic Hindus still suffer from post-traumatic, post-colonial, servile disorder?"[3]

Whatever the answer to this question may be, there are many Hindus who at least express happiness when persons from the majority community in America take a strong and sincere interest in Hindu traditions. It is likely that, given the experience of racism, as well as rejection on a purely religious basis (the belief that Hinduism is a "heathen" faith from which Hindus ought to convert to Christianity, a view still found, or that all religion is "backward" and should be abandoned, the secular version of this view), it is with a sense of relief that some Hindus encounter non-Indians who have a positive view of Hindu thought and practice. Indeed, there are non-Indians—adopters of Hinduism—who have been given roles of leadership in Hindu traditions and who are regarded by inheritors of Hinduism as authorities in their particular traditions. Such "home-grown gurus" are an increasingly prominent feature of the Hindu tradition in America.[4]

The first "white Hindu" to take up a leadership role in a Hindu tradition was Satguru Sivaya Subramuniyaswami (1927–2001). Born as Robert Hansen, he was preceded by the white members of the Ramakrishna Order, such as Sister Nivedita, and white disciples of Paramahansa Yogananda who succeeded him in the leadership of the Self-Realization Fellowship. However, it is important to note that, in neither the Ramakrishna tradition nor that of Yogananda, is there an emphasis on being *Hindu*. Indeed, we have seen that Swami Vivekananda clearly stated that he was not seeking converts to Hinduism, and that Vedanta, at least as he understood it, was to be seen as a universal philosophy undergirding all religions. These may be better seen as "Hindu-Inspired" traditions.

Subramuniyaswami, however, embraced the terms *Hindu* and *Hinduism* from a very early period as appropriate descriptors for the tradition he had adopted. Subramuniyaswami's guru, a Shaiva master from Sri Lanka, named Śiva Yogaswami (1872–1964), passed the mantle of spiritual succession to Subramuniyaswami in 1949. This event marked the establishment of what came to be called the Śaiva Siddhanta Church. Śaiva Siddhanta is an ancient Shaiva tradition, rooted in Tamil traditions of southern India. Subramuniyaswami's mission, though, was to bring it to the Western world. He "returned to the US, practiced intense meditation, and began his active teaching in 1957. The first headquarters of the Śaiva Siddhanta Church was in Kauai, Hawaii."[5]

In 1979, Subramuniyaswami began the publication of a quarterly journal, *Hinduism Today*, which is seen by many Hindus globally as an authoritative source of authentic knowledge about Hinduism. And as the leader of his particular Shaiva saṃpradāya, Subramuniyaswami was also a member of Swami Dayananda Saraswati's Hindu Dharma Acharya Sabha. In short, his credentials as a legitimate Hindu, and indeed a legitimate Hindu leader, were beyond reproach from the point of view of the Hindu community. His ethnicity was not seen as a bar to this level of acceptance.

The consistent observation that I have made in my own research, and which other scholars and scholar-practitioners have noted as well, is that, in order to be accepted as truly Hindu, converts need to demonstrate sincerity: that they are not simply passing through a "phase" or "shopping" for an easy spiritual path. Sincerity is demonstrated by showing commitment through in-depth study and devoted practice. And of course taking monastic vows represents the height of commitment.[6]

For many inheritors of Hinduism, being Hindu and being Indian are practically the same thing. For some, the idea of "white Hindus"—or "African American Hindus" or "Latino Hindus"—is an oxymoron. It may even be seen as deeply disrespectful to an ancient and dignified heritage that these Hindus regard as uniquely their own. White Hindus, in particular, might be seen as one more wave of colonialism, seeking to appropriate a culture without fully understanding it, causing untold disruption and destruction in the process. One might identify as a Hindu without an understanding of what this means or involves for many of those who have grown up as such—or even, like other cultural appropriators, while showing disrespect for certain elements or aspects of the tradition. For some inheritors of Hinduism, the local temple can serve as a refuge from the dominant society. In a North American context, white practitioners could well be seen as invaders of this cherished and private cultural space, particularly if they do not behave with proper humility and respect.

Hinduism and Multiple Religious Belonging

There is a pull in a very different direction, though, for many non-Indians drawn to Hindu spirituality. Often, it is precisely the openness and non-boundedness of Hinduism that appeal to many Westerners who are put off by religious dogma and exclusivism. Many of the Hindu teachers who have come to the West have encouraged this view as well, such as Swami Vivekananda, who explicitly endorsed either an inclusivist or pluralistic view of religions: many rivers wending their way to the same ocean. Paramahansa Yogananda, too, emphasized the idea of Christ as the great yogi. The aim of these teachers, again, was not so much to promote Hinduism—at least not by that name—but what they took to be a universal philosophy and way of life capable of incorporating all of the world's great traditions into its vast vision.

In a similarly pluralistic vein, Ma Jaya Sati Bhagavati was "a Brooklyn-born guru whose spiritual journey was guided by Christ, Swami Nityananda, and her guru Neem Karoli Baba" who established an ashram in Florida that has become "an interfaith religious community of service."[7] For many seekers who are drawn to Hindu thought, and for many Hindu spiritual teachers, to be excessively preoccupied with labels is itself a sign of spiritual immaturity. The point of the path is not to take on a label, but to be liberated from all such limitations: to attain moksha.

Hindu: To Be or Not to Be?

The question is sometimes raised whether the non-Indian members of organizations and movements like the Vedānta Society, the Self-Realization Fellowship, Transcendental Meditation, and Siddha Yoga are properly designated as *Hindus*. If one defines Hinduism as something into which one must be born, then all Hindus must by default be South Asian or of South Asian descent. It would be oxymoronic, from this view, to speak of "non-Indian Hindus" or adopters of Hinduism.

Lola Williamson makes a distinction between those who were raised in a Hindu tradition and those who have taken up a Hindu or Hindu-inspired spiritual practice, pointing out that "there is a qualitative difference between people who have been raised in a tradition in which the rituals, the foods, the prayers, and the ethics are second nature, and people who have incorporated only parts of a tradition into their religious style."[8]

On the other hand, although Williamson's observations about the differences between the somewhat chaotic atmosphere of a Hindu temple—such as HARI and the Washington Kali Temple—and the highly serene atmosphere of a Hindu-inspired meditation hall—such as that of a Vedanta Society—do justify making some kind of distinction between the types of practitioner that gravitate to these spaces, might variations upon Hindu thought and practice that incorporate elements of the broader American cultural environment—like having quiet halls with rows of seats facing a central altar—end up being perceived, in the long run, as just one more way of being Hindu? Surely the differences between traditional Hinduism and Hindu-inspired meditation movements are no more nor less stark than those between a highly formal Roman Catholic mass said in the Vatican and an evangelical revival meeting in Appalachia. Yet most scholars would not hesitate to designate the latter two as instances of a single phenomenon called Christianity. Particularly as more second- and third-generation Indian American Hindus have grown up practicing their traditions in a North American cultural environment, with its predominantly Protestant Christian ethos, the distinction between an "ethnic" Hinduism and "Hindu-inspired" movements is already becoming increasingly tenuous. The point is not that non-Indian adherents of Hindu-inspired movements ought or ought not be called *Hindu*, but that this distinction may simply be losing its relevance.

This issue is a somewhat contentious one, particularly among the non-Indian practitioners whose "Hinduness" is in question. On the one hand, many practitioners do not wish to identify themselves as Hindu because they do not identify their practice with the totality of Hindu practice, but with one specific school of thought. Hinduism historically includes elements such as caste and patriarchy repugnant to the progressive sensibilities of many spiritual seekers, many of whom are rebelling against these very things in their native traditions. At the same time, it could be replied that there are many born Hindus who do not agree with these things either. Caribbean Hindus, as we have seen, do not often observe caste, for example. Are they not "real" Hindus? This would appear to be a dangerous direction in which to take the discourse. Indeed, Hinduism is such a vast tradition, with such a great variety of systems of belief and practice, that it is hard to conceive of anyone in a single lifetime practicing it "in its totality," whatever that might even mean.

But there is also a tendency among practitioners of Hindu or Hindu-based paths to see their practices not as religious—and so localized in a faith community—but as "scientific" and universal. This tendency has been facilitated by the founding figures of these paths. For example, Swami Vivekananda, on numerous occasions, claimed that the Vedanta that he taught was not a religion, but the philosophy underlying all religions—including, but not limited exclusively to, Hinduism. Hinduism, for Vivekananda, was something particular to India and to the people of India. Vedanta, though, is universal, prompting Sarvepalli Radhakrishnan to write that Vedanta "is not a religion, but religion itself in its most universal and deepest significance."[9] On this understanding, one could be a Hindu Vedantin, or a Christian Vedantin, or a secular Vedantin. It is not uncommon, even today, to encounter practitioners of Vedanta who identify themselves either with no religious label at all, or with the label with which they grew up (if their Vedanta has not led to a break with their native tradition). I have met self-identified Catholic Vedantins, Presbyterian Vedantins, and Jewish Vedantins—as well as, of course, Hindu Vedantins. Similarly, both Maharishi Mahesh Yogi and Swami Muktananda presented Transcendental Meditation and Siddha Yoga, respectively, not as Hindu or Hindu-based spiritual paths, but as universal practices, available in principle to anyone. If they were not for everyone, why go to the trouble of teaching them in America?

In the words of Jean MacPhail, a former nun of the Ramakrishna Order (formerly known as Pravrajika Gayatriprana):

> Vedanta is my belief system and what I am trying to live in practice. Does it make me a Hindu? In my own mind, the answer is no. I think of myself as a Vedantist, in the sense in which Swami Vivekananda used the word. The word does not imply any specific forms of religious observance. Swami Vivekananda himself felt that Vedanta is of universal significance, because it is a map, as it were, of the whole range of spiritual possibilities, covering the dualist through non-dualist positions, including all levels of consciousness which humanity has as yet manifested, and open to all possible forms of depth inquiry, including contemporary science.[10]

On the other hand, there are non-Indian practitioners of Vedanta and other Hindu-inspired systems of thought and practice who *do* identify themselves as Hindu. These practitioners will point to the Hindu provenance of their practices and beliefs and express a suspicion of unconscious racism and other holdovers from a colonial mentality in the strong insistence of some non-Indian practitioners that they not be thought of or referred to as Hindu. The fact that some of those non-Indian practitioners who self-identify as Hindu have been accepted by many born Hindus suggests that it would be arbitrary to insist that they are not Hindu because they were not born as such.

For a scholar, the question is not "Who is really a Hindu?" or "Who is not really a Hindu?" Rather, the category of *Hindu* is a scholarly tool. The fact that some people, not of Indian descent, choose to identify themselves with this term, while others, who are engaged in the same practices and even inhabit the same organizations as those who do so identify themselves, make the opposite choice, is simply another interesting piece of data. It further heightens the awareness that the term *Hindu* is itself a slippery and imperfect category for describing a highly complex set of phenomena.

The fact that Western practitioners of ostensibly Hindu or Hindu-based spiritual paths tend to avoid self-identifying as Hindu seems to relate to broad three issues: the general Western trend of avoiding *any* religious self-identification out of preference for a self-identification as "spiritual," the tendency of the category of *Hinduism* to be constructed in ways that are incompatible with the self-understanding of particular saṃpradāyas—specifically, the Gauḍīya Vaishnava saṃpradāya, as represented in the West by ISKCON, and finally the concern to avoid identification with militant Hindu political movements in India, which place great emphasis on the label *Hindu*.

Regarding the first issue, identifying oneself as "spiritual" rather than "religious" stems from a sense that religious self-identification of any kind is overly limiting. Practitioners who share this sensibility often perceive themselves as in rebellion against religious institutions that they take to be oppressive, while seeing their own belief and practice—despite its historical basis in Hinduism—in non-sectarian, universal terms.

Regarding the second issue, the category of "Hinduism" has generally been constructed in a way that privileges Advaita Vedanta, as taught by many gurus who have come to America, such as Swami Vivekananda. Practitioners in intensely devotional lineages that emphasize bhakti, such as that of ISKCON, therefore sometimes see their beliefs and practices as distinct from Hinduism.

Third, the term *Hindu* has come to be identified by many—particularly in the scholarly community—with militant Hindu politics, with which many Western practitioners do not wish to identify themselves (though which some Western practitioners who do self-identify as Hindu also embrace).

In short, some Western practitioners of Hindu and Hindu-based traditions self-identify as Hindu and some do not. The former could be called "non-diasporic Hindus": Hindus by choice, who adhere to their tradition as a religious belief and way of life to which they have converted. In the latter case, self-identifications vary and are to be respected—as people have the right to define themselves—even as the Hindu provenance of many of their beliefs and practices is acknowledged.

Non-diasporic Hindus who have been interviewed about this question have tended to give answers that are either pragmatic in nature or that express their zeal and pride in being associated with a tradition which has changed their lives in many profound ways. On the pragmatic side, one interviewee says:

> I follow Vedanta. That's my religious belief and practice. What does that make me? I'm not a Muslim. I'm not a Buddhist. I'm not a Christian anymore, at least not in any way that my old church would recognise or accept. So what else do I say? I'm Hindu. Most people in America have no idea what the word "Vedanta" means and would look at you like you were from another planet if you said that was your religion. They do that with "Hindu," too, but at least they have some idea of what it means.

On the "Hindu pride" side, there is the interviewee who said:

> I love being a Hindu! It connects me with an ancient wisdom tradition—the most ancient in the world—and a vibrant and beautiful culture like no other. I'm a proud Hindu!

Another non-diasporic Hindu who had his self-identification challenged on social media by born Hindus in India who, it turned out, were much younger than himself, responded in the following way to their claim that he could not be a true Hindu: "I told them, 'I've been a Hindu longer than you've been alive!'"

Practitioners in Hindu or Hindu-based traditions who chose not to identify as Hindu largely responded to this question as discussed above: that they took *Hindu* to be an ethnic designation to which one must be born, that they did not want to show disrespect to their diasporic Hindu friends, that they were spiritual but not religious, or that the word *Hindu* has become too tainted by Indian politics.

Hinduism and Vegetarianism

Beyond those Americans who have either converted to Hinduism and now self-identify as Hindu and those who do not self-identify as Hindu but who adhere to a way of life rooted in Hindu traditions, there is a much wider penumbra of Americans who have assimilated specific practices and beliefs that are typical of Hinduism, and that often have Hindu roots, but that have come to be seen as simply part of the fabric of American society. In many cases, this has often been due to the influence of the countercultural movements of the sixties and seventies.

One such Hindu-inspired, but now more mainstream American, practice is vegetarianism. Vegetarianism in the West certainly has its own roots, and the reasons given for it typically focus either on compassion for animals or on physical health. This parallels Hinduism and the related Buddhist and Jain traditions, which also argue for vegetarianism on the basis of compassion, but also because meat is considered "tamasic" and not conducive to mental clarity such as that needed for the practice of meditation.

According to scholar Julia Hauser, vegetarians in Europe during the early modern period often cited other cultures, such as that of India, in favor of their arguments:

> In order to buttress what was then a fringe lifestyle, vegetarians in Europe made frequent reference to meat abstention in other parts of the world. Particularly the figure of the "merciful Hindoo," as John Oswald, author of one of the first tracts on vegetarianism, put it in 1791, loomed large in the vegetarian imagination.[11]

In 1891, when Mohandas Gandhi was still studying law in London, he and another Indian law student, T.T. Majumdar, joined the London Vegetarian Society. The fact that Westerners were drawn to vegetarianism on an ethical basis made a deep impression on Gandhi. His attention was first drawn to European vegetarianism by Theosophists in London.[12]

According to Hauser's account, vegetarianism presents an interesting case in which there were mutual influence and mutual reinforcement between India and the West. Members of both societies (albeit far more in India than in the West) felt drawn to vegetarianism, and both used the arguments of the other to support their own practice, with Westerners drawing inspiration from Indians and vice versa.

Vegetarianism is an important component of many forms of Hinduism. To be sure, not all Hindus practice vegetarianism. According to a 2006 survey, only 31 percent of India's population is vegetarian.[13] That 31 percent is not made up entirely of Hindus, as there are non-Hindus who practice vegetarianism in India as well: Jains, of course, but members of other communities, too. Informal polling, taking into consideration not only India, but the Hindu diaspora as well, suggests that roughly one in three Hindus practices pure vegetarianism, avoiding not only meat (including fish), but items such as eggs. Roughly 55 percent of Brahmins in India are vegetarian.[14] Brahmins are, of course, the priestly community of Hinduism, tasked with preserving the *Vedas* and passing the wisdom of the tradition to the next generation, as well as performing religious ceremonies.

In terms of religious ceremonies, though, even some Hindu deities are offered meat. Goats are regularly offered to the goddess Kali in Bengal, and meat offerings are common in Nepal.[15] Snehesh, a Nepali Hindu, says, "In Nepal, some of the *prasād* always has to be non-veg [non-vegetarian]." The vast majority of food offerings to the Hindu deities today, though, are vegetarian in nature. This author has witnessed, for example, offerings of gourds, cucumbers, and bananas being made to Kali at worship services in both the United States and India, despite the fact that this goddess is seen as fierce and is widely associated with animal sacrifice.

Hindu vegetarianism developed gradually. In ancient times, there were Hindus who ate meat, and meat was part of many religious rituals, including some of the ancient Vedic sacrifices. Gradually, however, a movement toward vegetarianism, and toward disapproval of the offering of animals in sacrifice, began to change the larger Hindu sensibility. Jainism and Buddhism were an important part of this conversation, as both Mahāvīra and the Buddha rejected animal sacrifice.

The *ideal* of vegetarianism is an important one, even for those Hindus who do not observe it, or who observe it with various compromises (such as the custom of many Bengali Hindus of eating fish). There are major Hindu texts that condemn the violence required by meat-eating. One of the foundational texts of the Vaishnava tradition, where vegetarianism is particularly strong, the *Bhāgavata Pūrāṇa*, condemns violence against animals that is committed in order to feed oneself, as does the *Varaha Pūrāṇa*.[16] A common epithet of Krishna is *Gopāla*, or Gopal, which literally means "protector of cows." The *Manusmṛti*, one of the *Dharma Śāstras*, or legal texts, of Hinduism also states: "Whoever does violence to harmless creatures out of a wish for his own happiness does not increase his happiness anywhere, neither when he is alive nor when he is dead."[17]

Hinduism and Yoga: A Case Study

Yoga, as discussed previously, was transmitted to the West primarily by Hindu masters, some of whom presented it as part of a total spiritual path and some of whom focused more upon its physical health dimensions. Some also innovated and incorporated particular postures and approaches which they adapted from the West. Just as Indian and Western vegetarians have drawn from and supported one another's practices, and continue to do so today, there is also now a mutual flow of yogic knowledge between India and the West, although the practice began in India.

The question of the relationship between yoga and Hinduism has become a hotly contested topic in the contemporary world. Many Hindus believe the Hindu roots of yoga have been erased by Western yoga practitioners—many of them Americans—who are focused wholly on the physical side of the practice without regard for its spiritual dimensions and who are making an enormous amount of money off of this Indian spiritual heritage in the process. This is the basis, for example, of the Hindu American Foundation's "Take Back Yoga" campaign:

> As the multi-billion dollar yoga industry continues to grow with studios becoming as prevalent as Starbucks and $120 yoga pants, the mass commercialization of this ancient practice, rooted in Hindu thought, has become concerning. With proliferation of new forms of "yoga," the underlying meaning, philosophy, and purpose of yoga are being lost. Take Back Yoga aims to bring to light yoga as a life-long practice dedicated to achieving *moksha*, or liberation/union with God.[18]

Scholars note, however, that yoga has never been an exclusively Hindu practice, if by the term *Hindu* we are referring exclusively to the Vedic family of traditions. Yogic practice has also been an integral element of both Jainism and Buddhism. Sufis in medieval India participated in yogic traditions as well, both adopting and adapting the practice to their own spiritual path. Hindu traditions have certainly been a massive part of yoga's history, but not to the exclusion of others.[19]

Many American yoga practitioners received this practice, often from Indian masters, as a secular, non-sectarian mode of achieving and sustaining health and peace of mind. Aware of the resistance that a presentation of yoga as Hindu might evoke in their Western students with strong Christian beliefs, or that a presentation of yoga as religious at all might evoke in their students who are not religious, they prefer to present the practice in what they see as neutral terms.

Below follows the case study of Judith, a long-time yoga practitioner and yoga instructor who was asked a variety of questions about her practice in an effort to discern how a serious American yoga practitioner might respond to issues of the kind under discussion here. As we shall see, like many American yoga practitioners, Judith's practice began as a health practice. This has led, however, to a deepened interest in and appreciation for dimensions of yoga that many Hindus would recognize as its more "spiritual" side, including the aspiration for moksha.

How did you first become interested in yoga?

> In my mid-thirties I was slowly developing more pain in my spine. (Later it was discovered a car accident at eighteen created this slow undoing of body, mind and spirit for me.) Many unsuccessful doctor visits led me to a woman who was trained in acupuncture by her grandfather. She was fortunately also an American trained physician, so after two treatments she sent me for an MRI of my cervical spine (neck) and found a massive herniated disc. It was described as all the toothpaste

was out of the tube, not good. Two surgeries followed with months of recovery. Realising that I needed to not only heal physically but emotionally and mentally as well, a friend suggested I try yoga with her. Because I had been a triathlete, I was enthusiastic about the challenge of Bikram Yoga. This practice helped me gain self-confidence that had been lost, lift my mood, feel physically stronger and more integrated within myself.

How did you go about exploring yoga?

My husband would say I read everything I could about yoga once the fire was ignited. But I first was interested in postures (asanas), then breath (pranayama), then meditation (dhyana) and the spiritual components of practice. I found the Yamas and Niyamas to be gems of wisdom, I loved a book by Deborah O'Dell. I had her come to lead a seminar at my studio! Delightful! Shortly after I found yoga, I needed more than reading to answer my questions and I started formal yoga training. My first yoga teacher training/certification program was in hot yoga, followed by certification in Hatha Yoga, then Yin Yoga. Most recently, I completed a 500-hour teacher training program with Gary Kraftsow, founder of Viniyoga. I currently read Pantajali's *Yoga Sutras* every day, practice with them in many ways, and study from many texts. I have oodles of books by my bedside and around the house on topics like the Vedas, Tantra, Ayurveda, and Meditation. A few authors that help me prepare practices to teach are Gary Kraftsow, Jack Kornfield, David Frawley, and Judith Lassater. I chant with CDs daily, practice integrated practices that provide care for my spine, mind and heart.

[The authors whom Judith mentions in answer to this question are eclectic in their orientations. Jack Kornfield, for example, is an American Buddhist and a well-known author on this tradition, and David Frawley is an American Hindu teacher and Ayurveda expert who has a considerable following among both adopters and inheritors of Hinduism. He also frequently comments upon contemporary Indian politics, making him a somewhat controversial figure, although Judith did not seem aware of this. Judith's eclecticism is quite typical of Americans, and Westerners generally, who are drawn to Hindu traditions. We shall see this in the case of George Harrison as well.]

How long have you practiced yoga?

Almost a decade.

Are you associated with any school of yoga? With a particular lineage or philosophy?

I am grateful to be a student of Gary Kraftsow's, and am connected to the Krishnamacharya lineage through Gary, who was a student of his and his son, T.K.V. Desikachar. While I am influenced by all my teachers and training, I teach primarily from the Viniyoga tradition.

Are you a certified Yoga teacher? Where did you receive your certification?

I have a number of certifications. My yoga certifications currently are listed behind my name are: E-RYT200; RYT500; 200-hour Hatha Yoga, local teacher training program; 200-hour hot yoga, completed in FL and NY; 50-hour Yin Yoga, completed in Vancouver, BC; 500-hour Viniyoga, completed at Yogaville, Virginia. I am currently studying David Frawley's Ayurveda and Yoga online program.

What are your thoughts on certification, qualifications, authenticity, etc.? In other words, would you see yoga as a field in which there should be maximum freedom of creative expression, or do you see yoga as something that can be done correctly or incorrectly, and that it is important to be doing and teaching yoga the "right" way?

When trained with an authentic teacher connected to a rich history and tradition of a lineage, there is a path to becoming a reputable and well-educated teacher. Very few exceptional programs exist in the states with what I would call a master teacher. I feel a bit uncomfortable sharing that publicly, as it is not a popular view, but I have experienced the poor training of yoga teachers that surround me. There are definitely correct ways yoga should be taught, either for safety reasons, philosophical reasons or therapeutic reasons. It is much more a science than an art. Examples are proper ways to sequence asanas, proper ways to prepare students for pranayama and meditation, and certain yoga tools can be contra-indicated for certain conditions. While yoga is meant to be applied to the individual, the teacher must understand a complete range of tools, how they can be integrated, what the affects can be to offer the student a meaningful practice that changes their condition. There is a method to creating a beautiful practice, and a good teacher honors this with regular practice of their own. Gary frequently reminds us, "You can't teach what you don't have." From our tradition, we teach for ourselves and practice for our students.

From your perspective as a practitioner of yoga, how would you describe the relationship between yoga and Hinduism? Do you see the two as deeply connected or as completely separate and distinct from one another?

For myself, I have not had a path to a Hindu community to connect with, so I have only begun to understand the relationship between the two intellectually. In my personal practice, I am aware of elements that have meaning for me as a yoga practitioner that are deeply rooted in the Hindu tradition.

What are some of the issues that arise for you, as a teacher, in imparting yoga to your students? Is there resistance to the "Hindu-ness" or "Indian-ness" of the practice?

As a teacher, and a studio owner, I find I need to carefully offer deeper teachings slowly. I would describe my approach to be like quietly knocking on a door. My students have become more receptive to pranayama, chanting, mantra, chakra, and

> Sutra study and the spiritual components of yoga as they have grown to trust me. Students are primarily coming to yoga to "move and breathe." Many have tight hamstrings or lower back issues and are carrying stress in their neck and shoulders, but beyond that yoga doesn't have a role in their lives. Fortunately, my students appreciate that I am a serious student of yoga and often go away for training. Upon returning home they are curious what I was studying. Over time, my studies have become more focused on yoga creating opportunities for personal transformation. Hence, I can introduce these ideas gently, quietly knocking. Recently I have begun study in Ayurveda as another means to open doors to discussing diet and lifestyle from this ancient perspective.

She adds:

> Even though I might say in class something like, "ultimately yoga creates an opportunity for us to recognize patterns that don't serve us, remove these obstacles or limitations and move closer to our true nature," I don't think [the students] generally have a deep faith or an understanding of what yoga can really do for them psychologically, emotionally, and spiritually. Private sessions are often a more open exchange with an individual student about many tools of yoga. At times, I fault myself for not sharing more with my group classes. I have realized that, like my students, I too am setting my own path as a yoga student, and until I wanted to know what this yoga journey could truly be, I wasn't ready. When the student is ready the teacher appears (in many forms)!

If you had to, how would you define yoga?

> Yoga is a path to liberation (moksha) that each individual can explore uniquely, with or without the support of a teacher. From my own experience, I do believe it needs to be done with eagerness, discipline and consistency.

Hinduism and Religious Pluralism

The first statistic that Lisa Miller notes in her 2009 editorial, "We Are All Hindus Now," is the fact that 65 percent of Americans believe that "many religions can lead to eternal life." The association of Hinduism with religious pluralism is a strong one in the American consciousness, going back to Swami Vivekananda's first address at the World Parliament of Religions where he characterizes Hinduism as a religion of "not only tolerance, but universal acceptance."

The term *religious pluralism* is sometimes used to refer to the simple fact that there are a great many religions in practice. In a theological sense, though, religious pluralism is the idea that there are many *true* religions that can lead their practitioners to ultimate reality: to some form of *salvation*, or ultimate fulfillment.

In this area, as with vegetarianism and yoga, it is possible to trace mutual influences which flow between Hinduism and Western culture. The pluralistic roots of Hinduism run quite deep. From the *Shiva Mahimna Stotra*: "As the different streams having their sources in different places all mingle their water in the sea, so, O Lord, the different paths which people take through different tendencies, various though they appear, crooked or straight, all lead to Thee." From the *Bhagavad Gītā*: "Whosoever comes to Me, through whatsoever form, I reach them; all are struggling through paths which in the end lead to Me." And from the *Ṛg Veda*: "Truth is One, though the wise speak of it in various ways."

In the modern period, too, there are the words of prominent Hindu figures such as Gandhi:

> Religions are different roads converging upon the same point. What does it matter that we take different roads so long as we reach the same goal? In reality there are as many religions as there are individuals. I believe in the fundamental truth of all great religions of the world. I believe that they are all God-given, and I believe that they were necessary for the people to whom these religions were revealed. And I believe that, if only we could all of us read the scriptures of different faiths from the standpoint of the followers of those faiths we should find that they were at bottom all one and were all helpful to one another.[20]

And in the words of Sri Ramakrishna:

> I have practiced all religions—Hinduism, Islam, Christianity—and I have also followed the paths of the different Hindu sects. I have found that it is the same God toward whom all are directing their steps, though along different paths. He who is called Krishna is also called Shiva, and bears the name of the Primal Energy, Jesus, and Allah as well—the same Rama with a thousand names.[21]
>
> God can be realised through all paths. All religions are true. The important thing is to reach the roof. You can reach it by stone stairs or by wooden stairs or by bamboo steps or by a rope. You can also climb up a bamboo pole ... Each religion is only a path leading to God, as rivers come from different directions and ultimately become one in the one ocean ... All religions and all paths call upon their followers to pray to one and the same God. Therefore, one should not show disrespect to any religion or religious opinion.[22]

Pluralistic ideas of this kind found a ready audience in the Unitarian movement, who would pave the way for the assimilation of even more Hindu ideas into the American consciousness in the form of the Transcendentalist movement. There was a universalist undercurrent in Unitarianism which encouraged the kind of receptivity to other traditions that the Transcendentalists exhibited. One may recall that this universalism led to a split in the Unitarian movement for a period time, which was eventually healed when Unitarians reunited as the Unitarian Universalist Association.

In the meantime, though, the teachings of Swami Vivekananda, Paramahansa Yogananda, and other Hindu masters who presented their ideas in a universalist form, as a knowledge available from within all traditions, began to pervade American society through the work of intellectuals in the Vedanta movement and other Hindu-inspired organizations. Huxley, influenced by his guru in the Vedanta Society, Swami Prabhavananda, wrote *The Perennial Philosophy*, and Prabhavananda himself authored a commentarial work on the teachings of Jesus entitled *The Sermon on the Mount According to Vedanta*.[23]

Religious pluralism finally found its way into mainstream Christian theology through the work of philosopher of religion, John Hick (1922–2012). Although his views were long resisted by more conservative theologians, they have gradually become more accepted. Some thinkers, such as the Christian process theologians John Cobb and David Ray Griffin, even argue that Hick's model of pluralism does not go far enough. Hick asserts, in much the same spirit as Ramakrishna and Gandhi, that many religions can lead to the same ultimate goal of unification with "the Real."[24] Griffin and Cobb, however, assert that there can be not only multiple valid paths, but also multiple valid ultimate goals.[25] This is a far cry from the exclusivism which is traditionally found in many older, and in the more conservative evangelical, Christian theologies of religions.[26] Hick's views were shaped by his reading of works by Sarvepalli Radhakrishnan and Sri Aurobindo.[27]

Study Questions

1. What are some of the issues involved when someone who is not born Hindu self-identifies as such?
2. What are some of the reasons that some practitioners in Hindu-inspired traditions do not choose to self-identify as Hindu?
3. What are the pros and cons involved in "taking back yoga"?

Suggestions for Further Reading

C.R. Brooks, *The Hare Krishnas in India* (Princeton: Princeton University Press, 2014).
David Ray Griffin, ed., *Deep Religious Pluralism* (Westminster, KY: John Knox Press, 2005).
John Hick, *An Interpretation of Religion: Human Responses to the Transcendent* (New Haven: Yale University Press, 1989).
Andrea Jain, *Selling Yoga: From Counterculture to Pop Culture* (New York: Oxford University Press, 2014).
Paul F. Knitter, *Introducing Theologies of Religion* (Maryknoll, NY: Orbis Books, 2014).
Jeffery D. Long, *A Vision for Hinduism: Beyond Hindu Nationalism* (London: I.B. Tauris, 2007).
Swami Prabhavananda, *The Sermon on the Mount According to Vedanta* (Hollywood: Vedanta Press, 1964).

Mattew Remski, *Practice and All Is Coming: Abuse, Cult Dynamics, and Healing in Yoga and Beyond* (Rangiora, New Zealand: Embodied Wisdom Publishing, 2019).
Holly Roberts, *The Vegetarian Philosophy of India: Hindu, Buddhist, and Jain Sacred Teachings* (Sequim, WA: Anjeli Press, 2006).
Mark Singleton, *Yoga Body: The Origins of Modern Posture Practice* (New York: Oxford University Press, 2010).

7

Hindu and Indian Influence in American Popular Culture

Chapter 7 Summary and Outline

This chapter will explore Hindu and broader Indian influences in American popular culture, with a particular emphasis on the Beatles (especially George Harrison) and the *Star Wars* films created by George Lucas, as well as the ongoing struggle to overcome stereotypes of Indians and Hinduism in the popular media.

The Two Georges: Harrison and Lucas

Hindu thought continues to pervade and influence American culture in ways of which many Americans are unaware, just as American culture reshapes Hinduism as this tradition finds a new home in the American environment. This process of mutual influence will no doubt continue to unfold in new and unpredictable ways.

Two figures have played particularly strong roles in the process of transmitting Hindu ideas and assumptions into the Western world in the latter half of the twentieth century. My reasons for focusing on these figures in particular are also twofold. First, these two figures have been involved in two of the most powerfully transformative cultural phenomena that the Western world has seen in the modern period: namely, the Beatles and the *Star Wars* franchise. It is hard to exaggerate the importance of either of these two phenomena in recent and contemporary Western culture. These two figures, whom I call "the two Georges," are George Harrison, of the Beatles, and George Lucas, the creator of the *Star Wars* universe.

Another reason for focusing on these two figures is that they represent two very different ways in which Hindu ideas and practices have come to infuse the Western world: one which is very conscious and deliberate, and one which is more unconsciously evocative of Hinduism than it is directly and clearly inspired by it, and indeed draws upon Buddhism no less than Hinduism.

Harrison—although it is not clear that he ever actually used this term to describe himself—is the quintessential Western Hindu: devout, yet eclectic, and also willing to go against the dominant trends of his society in order to affirm his allegiance to the spiritual traditions of India. Lucas has, to my knowledge, no specifically Hindu affiliations, but it is known that he was inspired to craft the *Star Wars* films, in part, by his interactions with Joseph Campbell, a scholar and popularizer of comparative religion and mythology who *did* have a close connection with Hinduism. Campbell had strong ties to the Vedanta Society. He even assisted Swami Nikhilananda, of the Ramakrishna-Vivekananda Center of New York, with his translation of *The Gospel of Sri Ramakrishna*. The thought of Sri Ramakrishna pervades Campbell's work to such a degree that Pravrajika Vrajaprana makes the observation that "no reader of Joseph Campbell can escape Sri Ramakrishna."[1]

The Hindu influence upon Harrison is crystal clear and obvious, being directly included in his use of Indian instrumentation and musicians in many songs, and in many of his lyrics: "Hare Krishna, Hare Rama." "The Lord is awaiting on you all to awaken and see."[2] "All that matters to me is to touch your lotus feet."[3] In the case of Lucas, the Hindu influence is subtle. It needs to be teased out of a close viewing (or better yet, multiple close viewings) of his films: the very idea of the Force; the teachings of Yoda; and the theme of detachment which runs throughout the tragic story of the rise, fall, and redemption of Anakin Skywalker.

George Harrison: The Paradigmatic Western Hindu

George Harrison's Hindu connections and commitments were quite open and well known. Starting with the brief sitar passages in the Beatles' "Norwegian Wood," then moving on to the reflections found in *Sgt. Pepper's Lonely Hearts Club Band*'s "Within You without You," and culminating in the Krishna devotion of "My Sweet Lord," from 1970s *All Things Must Pass*, and continuing to the end of his life, the evidence of Hindu influence on Harrison is abundant, and has become one of the most distinctive features of this artist (though the other Beatles were not without these influences, as one can find in songs like Lennon's "Tomorrow Never Knows" and "Across the Universe," and more subtly in McCartney's "The Fool on the Hill" or in the title of his 2001 instrumental on the album *Driving Rain*, "Riding into Jaipur"), as well as his vegetarianism.

George Harrison can be called the paradigmatic Western Hindu because, apart from those aspects of his story which stem from his being a member of the most successful and popular rock band in history, his journey in many ways mirrors those of numerous spiritual seekers who have found themselves drawn to a Hindu, Hindu-infused, or Hindu-inspired way of life.

The pattern of the Western seeker drawn to Hinduism is that of, first, experiencing a sense of deep disenchantment with the conceptual and spiritual resources provided by Western society. This disenchantment can arise from a personal tragedy (like the loss of a parent at a young age).

But it can also arise from a feeling that many of the goals and aspirations Western society tends to value—such as financial success and fame—are ultimately empty without a wider framework to give one's life a sense of meaning and purpose.

This was certainly the case for Harrison, who rose to the pinnacle of fame and fortune via the success of the Beatles, only to find that he was no happier or more fulfilled than he was in his youth—and in some ways, much *less* happy.

Second, not having been raised in a Hindu tradition, the Western seeker is often eclectic, sampling a variety of spiritual traditions before settling upon one that "works"—and even then, often continuing to draw on varied spiritual resources. And given that many Hindu traditions that have come to the West typically do not disallow eclecticism or pluralism, and often actively promote it, this does not prove to be a difficulty, and may even be a factor in attracting the seeker to identify more closely with Hinduism. It gives the seeker "permission" to be eclectic, yet grounded.

Finally, the Western seeker who settles into a Hindu tradition becomes dedicated to it for life, and is not a mere dabbler. It is often the case, as we have discussed earlier in this chapter, that born Hindus are suspicious of Western seekers because many are seen as "dabbling," or passing through a "phase" before returning to a more conventional Western way of living and thinking. The serious Western Hindu, though, makes no such "U turn," although it may certainly be the case over the course of a person's lifetime that that person might experience the occasional lapse into older patterns of thought and behavior, or reach a compromise that some may accept as being compatible with a Hindu way of life while others may not.[4]

Adding to the complexity of this issue is also the fact that many Westerners who are drawn to Hinduism are simultaneously repelled by an excessive emphasis on labels, and may not even use the term *Hindu* to describe themselves or their practice, even while much of this practice is derived from traditions that scholars (and most Hindus) would typically identify as such.

Harrison's life story can quite readily be seen to fit the pattern just described. First, his awakening to a Hindu spiritual path was precipitated by the existential crisis brought on by the fame of the Beatles, and catalyzed by his experiences with the drug LSD.

Second, Harrison drew from a variety of Hindu traditions and teachers before finally settling on a particular one (the Gauḍīya Vaishnava-based tradition of ISKCON—, more popularly known as the Hare Krishnas). But he was neither exclusive nor rigidly orthodox in his ISKCON adherence.

Harrison's desire not to be "boxed in" to a singular adherence is illustrated by the fact that he wore only two rows of tulsi beads, rather than the traditional three of a full ISKCON initiate. It was explained to me by a friend from this tradition who knew Harrison, that, by wearing two rows of beads, Harrison was indicating his allegiance, but also "keeping his options open."[5]

Finally, while continuing to be eclectic and open-minded, Harrison nonetheless maintained his affiliation to the end of his life, chanting the name of Krishna on his deathbed, surrounded by friends from the tradition who maintained a constant vigil and ensured that a spiritual atmosphere was preserved. His wife, Olivia Harrison, notes, near the close of Martin Scorsese's beautifully moving, excellent documentary on Harrison's life and journey, *Living in the Material World*, that, at the moment of his passage from his body, he "lit up the room." "George was at peace and ready. There was a great light in the room when he passed."[6]

Existential Crisis

The Beatles' rapid rise to enormous fame and fortune was, of course, their collective dream come true. They had, for many years, aspired to become "the toppermost of the poppermost," in the words of John Lennon, playing long hours in the clubs of Hamburg, Germany, and their native Liverpool.

By 1965, however—two years after the rise of "Beatlemania" in Britain, and its transmission in the following year to the United States and around the world—the group had become jaded and exhausted. It is truly remarkable that Lennon, the ostensible leader of this incredibly successful band, was not writing songs about how wonderful fame and fortune were, but rather penning pieces with morose titles like "I'm a Loser" and "Help!"—the latter of which is, as its title indicates, a cry for help from someone whose independent, carefree existence has slipped away. Harrison says of the Beatles' relationship with the rest of the world during this time, "It was a very one-sided love affair. People gave their money and they gave their screams, but the Beatles gave their nervous systems, which is a much more difficult thing to give."[7]

During this same year, Harrison's interest in India—specifically, in Indian music—had been aroused while the band was filming their second movie—also entitled *Help!*, like the song of the same name.

Help! is, ironically, a parody of Hinduism. This is ironic given Harrison's later seriousness about this tradition. The plot, such as it is, involves the band fleeing for their lives from a group of Kali worshipers who are intent on sacrificing the wearer of a sacred ring. The ring has become stuck on Ringo's finger. International hijinks ensue as the cult members chase the Beatles not only throughout England, but also to exotic locales such as the Austrian Alps and the beaches of the Bahamas. A mad scientist, consulted by the band in the hope that he can help remove the ring, is also chasing them. The scientist, played by the hilarious Victor Spinetti, has concluded, "With a ring like that I could—dare I say it?—rule the world!" The soundtrack includes Beatles' songs, but also Indian sitar music, the sound of which immediately caught Harrison's attention. He would later say of Indian music that it "made more sense" to him than anything else he had ever heard.

While filming the scenes from *Help!* which were set in the Bahamas, the Beatles were met by Swami Vishnudevananda Saraswati, who gave each member of the band a copy of his *Complete Illustrated Book of Yoga*. Swami Vishnu's ashram—the Swami Sivananda Ashram, named after his guru—is located in the Bahamas, on Paradise Island. It is not far from where the Beatles were filming. This book was Harrison's first direct exposure to Hindu thought and practice.

Later that same year, Harrison and Lennon were at a small, private party at which they were given LSD by their host. Frightened when told by their host what he had done, the two Beatles left the party with their wives and went to a club, and then later returned to Harrison's home. As it does for many who try it, this drug elicited a deeply spiritual experience in Harrison. "I had such an overwhelming feeling of well-being, that there was a God, and I could see him in every blade of grass," he said, "It was like gaining hundreds of years of experience in twelve hours."[8]

Eclecticism

Combined with his interest in Indian music, this dramatic experience drew Harrison toward the spiritual path. He would soon set aside drug use in favor of a more natural and sustainable route to spiritual experience, through meditation. In addition to studying the sitar directly under the able guidance of the maestro, Ravi Shankar (whose music would also be popularized by his association with Harrison), Harrison began to study Hindu philosophy in earnest. After the Beatles stopped their frenzied touring and started to focus on crafting their music in the recording studio, all four members of the group had an opportunity to pursue other interests. John Lennon took up acting, appearing in the highly surrealistic anti-war film, *How I Won the War*, by Richard Lester. Paul McCartney wrote the soundtrack to a British television series called *The Family Way*. Ringo Starr bought a house.

George Harrison, on the other hand, went to India. On his first visit, after the Beatles' last tour of America, in 1966, he stayed with his wife Patti (his first wife) in a houseboat in Kashmir. He took with him two books: Swami Vivekananda's *Raja Yoga* and Paramahamsa Yogananda's *Autobiography of a Yogi*. Influences from both these Hindu masters can be discerned in Harrison's interviews and song lyrics for the rest of his life.

Yogananda, in particular, seems to have held an especially strong fascination for Harrison during this time. Yogananda and the organization he established—the Self-Realization Fellowship—have been, for many Westerners, especially those with a strong Christian background, relatively easy "gateways" to Hinduism, given the prominent role Jesus plays in Yogananda's thought.

In the teachings of Yogananda, as in many other modern Hindu movements, Jesus is seen as an avatar and a great, enlightened teacher. Yogananda even encourages devotion to Jesus as a spiritual path. When the Beatles were in the process of designing the cover for their 1967 album, *Sgt. Pepper's Lonely Hearts Club*—widely viewed as a masterpiece—they settled upon the idea of depicting the faces of figures who had influenced them. The figures include actors and fellow musical artists, such as Bob Dylan, but also major literary figures and philosophers—such as Edgar Allan Poe and Carl Gustav Jung. Beyond the figures on whom the group agreed, each member was also allowed to select four figures of special interest to himself.[9] Harrison chose Yogananda, Yogananda's guru (Sri Yukteswar Giri), Yogananda's guru's guru (Lahiri Mahasaya), and Babaji, the figure to whom Yogananda ultimately traced his lineage: an ancient yet youthful-appearing Himalayan sage who is believed by many to still be alive.

Vivekananda's influence can be seen in Harrison's enduring eclecticism and in comments about the spiritual path that he would continue to make until his death. In a recorded conversation with the founder of ISKCON, A.C. Bhaktivedanta Swami Prabhupada—a conversation which also included John Lennon and Yoko Ono—Harrison seems to differ with Prabhupada on the exclusive spiritual efficacy of the Hare Krishna mantra, emphasizing pluralism, and that the intent behind a mantra is a decisive factor in determining its efficacy. These are ideas found in Vivekananda's teaching.[10]

It is also worth noting that a series of home movies made by Harrison during his trips to India, parts of which are included in Scorsese's documentary, shows Harrison visiting the Kali temple at Dakshineshwar, the residence of Vivekananda's renowned guru, Sri Ramakrishna.

In late 1967, the Beatles began their association with the Maharishi Mahesh Yogi, founder of the Transcendental Meditation movement. This well-documented association culminated with a trip to Rishikesh, India, in 1968, to the Maharishi's ashram, where the Beatles continued their studies of meditation. Each would become, in succession, disillusioned with the experience to one degree or another. Ringo Starr left the ashram first, citing stomach complaints and issues with the food at the ashram. Then Paul McCartney returned, eager to get on with recording new songs.

Lennon and Harrison stayed the longest, until Lennon became disillusioned upon hearing rumors of misconduct by the Maharishi and feeling dissatisfied at the Maharishi's response after confronting him about it. (In complete fairness to the Maharishi, all Lennon apparently told the Maharishi was that they were leaving. When the Maharishi asked why they were leaving, Lennon apparently believed that the Maharishi should already know, due to his psychic powers. In a later recorded conversation, during the Beatles' *Let It Be* sessions, when the story is recounted, Yoko Ono sagely tells Lennon of the Maharishi, "You expected too much from him.")

It is not clear that Harrison himself ever felt disillusioned with the Maharishi, although he departed Rishikesh with Lennon to return to England and begin recording songs for the album *The Beatles* (best known as the "White Album," because of its simple white cover). In 1992, he played at a benefit concert for the Natural Law Party, the political party established by members of the Maharishi's Transcendental Meditation movement. That he was not disillusioned by meditation, or by Hindu spirituality as such, is quite clearly evidenced by the fact that, in 1969, he entered into a much closer and more enduring association with ISKCON. His support for this tradition was so strong that, when the group was having difficulty finding land to build a temple in London, he very happily and spontaneously donated one of his own houses to them for this purpose.

Enduring Commitment

Harrison's devotion to Krishna endured long beyond his initial association with ISKCON, lasting to the very end of his earthly life, on November 29, 2001. References to this devotion specifically and to Hindu philosophy more broadly (including the pluralism of the Vivekananda tradition) are present in his song lyrics, starting during the time of the Beatles themselves, and culminating with prayer to Lord Shiva at the end of his last album, *Brainwashed*, which he knew would only be released posthumously, as he was fighting cancer while he recorded it. The most famous reference to Krishna in Harrison's work is, of course, in his first major hit song after the Beatles' breakup: 1970s "My Sweet Lord." In the chorus of this celebrated song, he popularized the Hare Krishna mantra and brought a Hindu tradition closer to the Western mainstream. "My Sweet Lord" was the best-selling single by a former Beatle in the seventies.

The Significance of George Harrison for Hinduism in America

In his life and music, George Harrison—both as a member of the Beatles, but even more so during his solo career—served to infuse Hindu thought and practice into Western culture. Such a famous and celebrated member of Western society had not so openly embraced Hindu ideas since the time of Ralph Waldo Emerson and Henry David Thoreau. George Harrison was far from being alone, as a member of the counterculture of the 1960s and 1970s, in this embrace. But few, if any, other representative of this culture had his cultural power and enduring impact.

More Hindu Rock: From Prog to Krishnacore

Again, though, Harrison was far from alone, either in the counterculture or in the world of Western popular music, to embrace Hinduism and to incorporate Hindu lyrical themes, or Indian musical elements, or both, into his work.

During the "psychedelic period," centered around 1967, many rock artists drew upon aspects of Hinduism as part of the general aesthetic of the time. Jimi Hendrix, somewhat notoriously, had himself and his band members depicted, on the cover of their second album, *Axis: Bold As Love*, as the cosmic form of Krishna, revealed to Arjuna in the eleventh chapter of the *Bhagavad Gītā*. The Rolling Stones, who, until 1968, had a tendency to imitate the Beatles' various innovations in their music, incorporated the sitar into their 1966 hit, "Paint It, Black" (following the Beatles' use of the sitar in a popular song from their 1965 album, *Rubber Soul*, "Norwegian Wood (This Bird Has Flown)"—which was George Harrison's first use of Indian instrumentation in a Beatles' song). The sound of the sitar, as well as ethereal, psychedelic lyrics, was present in the music of many artists at this time. An especially elaborate example is the epic, "Inheld 'Twas in I," by the band Procol Harum (best known for their hit, "A Whiter Shade of Pale"). This song, which closes Procol Harum's second album, includes a spoken word portion which tells the story of a pilgrim who goes to ask the Dalai Lama the meaning of life. This is, of course, a Buddhist reference. As we have seen, Buddhism and Hinduism were often seen as part of the whole package of "Eastern wisdom" by Western seekers in the sixties. Buddhist themes—including the Dalai Lama—occur in the early songs of David Bowie in this period, such as in "Silly Boy Blue," about the young Dalai Lama.

One of the most clearly Hindu-influenced albums of this period was by the Moody Blues. In 1968, the Moody Blues released *In Search of the Lost Chord*. The Moody Blues were pioneers of the "concept album." Usually attributed to having been started by the Beatles with *Sgt. Pepper's Lonely Hearts Club Band*, a concept album is an album of songs either unified by a common theme or arranged in such a way that they tell a story. The "lost chord," we learn at the end of *In Search of the Lost Chord*, is the sacred mantra, *Om*:

I know why
The skies all cry
Om
Om
Heaven ...[11]

With their fondness for concept albums, spiritually themed lyrics, and lush orchestration, with a generous helping of influence from Western classical music, the Moody Blues helped to spearhead a sub-genre of rock, which would reach its peak in the seventies, known as "Progressive" or simply "Prog" rock. One of the features of progressive rock is a tendency to have lyrics laden with philosophical meaning, often evoking science-fiction, fantasy, and ancient mythology. (One particularly favorite prog-rock influence is J.R.R. Tolkien, also referenced by Led Zeppelin, who, though not technically regarded as a prog band, were certainly at the periphery of this movement.)

Jon Anderson, the lead singer of one the most prominent prog-rock bands of the seventies, Yes, has been a longtime devotee of Paramahansa Yogananda. *Tales from Topographic Oceans*, an album released by Yes in 1973, is based on the story of creation presented by Yogananda in his classic work, *Autobiography of a Yogi*, which was one of Anderson's major inspirations.[12]

From roughly the mid-seventies, although with earlier antecedents, a movement emerged in the world of rock that reacted against the increasingly elaborate and excessive aura surrounding rock music. With a desire to return to the basics—to make music that could be made in someone's garage, and with a minimum of musical training, and infused with the rebellious attitude that was at the heart of the genre from its beginning—punk rock exploded onto the music scene. Prog rock was, in fact, one of the targets of at least some of the early punk rockers, along with the Beatles and the entire earlier generation of rock stars.

The punk sensibility was not, however, immune to Hindu influence. Punk has itself split into subdivisions, including alternative and hardcore. Joseph Mascis (better known as J Mascis), a guitarist and founding member of the hardcore band Dinosaur Jr., is a devotee of the south Indian guru, Mata Amritanandamayi, better known as Amma, or "mother," the "hugging saint." Hindu themes can be found in his music, most prominently on his 2005 album *J and Friends Sing and Chant for Amma*.

There is an entire sub-genre of hardcore known as *Krishnacore*, which while its music is basic punk rock, its lyrical content and the ethos it promotes are drawn from the Gauḍīya Vaishnava tradition and ISKCON. The band Shelter is widely regarded as the original band in this category. Krishnacore has ties with a sub-set of the punk movement known as "straightedge." Straightedge embraces punk's search for authenticity, but rejects certain aspects of youth culture, such as sexual promiscuity and drug usage. In this sense, it resonates with ISKCON itself, which, in its origins in the 1960s, became a refuge for many young people who had suffered from addiction and other issues and who were seeking not only an alternative to the lifestyles of their parents, but also an alternative to some of the more self-destructive aspects of the counterculture.[13] Indeed, it is one of the interesting aspects of Hindu influence in Western culture that much of it came through the counterculture of the 1960s, but that it continues into succeeding generations which are critical of the excesses of the counterculture.

Raghunath Cappo speaks of his journey, via punk rock, to Vaishnava spirituality:

> I've been on a spiritual quest in this life! From my teens I started a punk/hardcore band called *Youth of Today*, which championed the principles of clean living, vegetarian diet, and self-control [straightedge]. By the time I was 21, my band had tens of thousands of fans around the world. I was shocked. I started Revelation Records, an indy record label with my high school buddy and signed 20 bands with a similar belief and ethics. As exciting as this was, there was a growing void in my heart I knew only Spirit could fill. I got into spirituality, metaphysics, and mysticism; eagerly consuming spiritual classics, my hunger only increased. This eventually manifested as a strong desire to go deeper. I split and quit the band. Gave the label to my partner. The teachings of India drove me East and at age 22, I ended up on an ashram floor in the holy village of Vrindavan [believed in the Vaishnava to be the place where Krishna spent his youth, and a deeply sacred place of Vaishnava pilgrimage]. That was 1988—and one of the best choices I made in my life.[14]

Finally, British musician Crispian Mills represents a second-generation Hindu sensibility. His mother is a member of ISKCON, a tradition with which he grew up. The music of his band, Kula Shaker, as well as another of his bands, the Jeevas (named after the *jīva*, or soul, in Hinduism) that he formed while Kula Shaker were on hiatus, is replete with Hindu themes. With song titles like "Govinda," "Tattva," and "Narayana," the music is a blend of Western and Indian influences.

George Lucas

Let us turn now to the other George—George Lucas. In terms of Hindu influence in Western popular culture, the case of Lucas is quite different from that of HarrisonAlthough he has apparently practiced Transcendental Meditation since the 1970s and has cited the Maharishi Mahesh Yogi as an inspiration for the character of Yoda, the Hindu themes that one can discern in his work are arguably as much a reading into the text of his cinematic oeuvre as they are a result of discernible influence, although the intellectual influence of Joseph Campbell, a scholar deeply immersed in the Vedanta tradition of Hinduism, cannot be completely discounted.[15] It is certainly possible—indeed likely—that any element of Hindu thought one can find in *Star Wars* is there purely to create an entertaining story, and may even be coincidental.

In some cases, it may not even be Hindu but Buddhist. Hinduism and Buddhism overlap a great deal in their basic worldviews, ethical teachings, and spiritual practices, and are often hard for Westerners to distinguish from one another. The eclecticism of both Western seekers and, in at least some cases, teachers of Asian traditions themselves—like Alan Watts and Yogananda—can make it difficult to differentiate between the two. The histories of Hinduism and Buddhism in America parallel one another quite closely, and the two traditions often appealed to the same group of people, who would often have no problem with blending elements of many traditions.

This does not, however, render *Star Wars* irrelevant as part of the larger story of how Hindu ideas and practices came to infuse Western culture in the second half of the twentieth century. Literary theorist Roland Barthes, writing in 1967 of the "death of the author," argued that once a text has been created, its meaning is not fixed. Even the text's creator has no authority over how it is to be interpreted. Each reader (or viewer, in the case of a visual text like the *Star Wars* films) has the ability and the authority—the "right"—to interpret the text in whatever way she sees fit.

Unlike the case of George Harrison, the Hindu influences on George Lucas are not obvious or overt, and may even be unconscious, though again, such influence is not to be discounted entirely. But one can nevertheless find deep resonances between Hindu thought and the *Star Wars* universe if one examines it attentively.

The Force

The most obvious point of contact between Hindu philosophy and the *Star Wars* universe is, of course, the Force. We are first introduced to the Force in the original *Star Wars* film, *A New Hope* (later revealed to be the fourth chapter of the *Star Wars* saga as a whole). Luke Skywalker—who is the archetypal hero, in Joseph Campbell's sense, of this epic—asks his mentor, Obi Wan Kenobi, how his father died. Kenobi explains that Luke's father, a great Jedi Knight, was killed by a young Jedi named Darth Vader, who was "seduced by the dark side of the Force." The Jedi are essentially warrior monks. For millennia, they were the guardians of peace and justice in the galactic republic which has, by the time of *A New Hope*, fallen, becoming an evil galactic empire.

When Luke asks Obi Wan what the Force is, Obi Wan explains to him, "The Force is what gives a Jedi his power. It's an energy field created by all living things. It surrounds us and penetrates us; it binds the galaxy together."[16] The Force certainly has resonance with the Daoist concept of *qi*, or *chi*: an energy that exists within and manifests as all things. *Qi* itself, though, has resonances with Hindu concepts, such as *prāṇa*, which literally means "breath," but which is the energy or "force" within all living things. According to the *Upaniṣads*, this breath of life is one of the pre-eminent manifestations of *Brahman*. "Breath" is also the original meaning of *spirit*.

In the scene immediately following this one, the Force is again the focus of discussion, but in a very different setting. On board the Death Star, a superweapon in the form of a spherical space station which houses a laser with the ability to destroy an entire planet, imperial officials are in a heated debate about how to proceed because the rebels against the empire have stolen the plans to the Death Star and are likely planning to destroy it. Among these officials is Darth Vader, whom we have already met at the start of the film, when he was pursuing the rebels who had stolen the Death Star plans.

A fearsome figure, Vader is the archetypal villain: physically imposing, dressed in black armor, his face concealed behind a mask and his head covered in a shiny black helmet that has a strong (and not coincidental) resemblance to the flared helmet of a samurai warrior. One of the officials arrogantly defies Vader, mocking Vader's "sad devotion" to the "ancient religion" of the Jedi, and his faith in the Force, which Vader insists is more powerful even than the Death Star.

As the skeptic continues to taunt Vader, he suddenly begins to choke and turn blue, as if an invisible hand were crushing his throat. Vader, meanwhile, is holding his thumb and forefinger together. The lead imperial official, Governor Tarkin, grows impatient with the bickering of the group and says, "Vader, release him!" "As you wish," Vader replies, and the choking official slumps to the table in relief as Vader's invisible grip vanishes.[17]

The most obvious comparison between the Force and something in Hindu philosophy is with the omnipresent Brahman: the infinite being, consciousness, and bliss that is the true nature of reality, according to the teaching of Advaita (or non-dualist) Vedanta.[18] Both entities can be likened to an all-pervasive energy field. The Force, however, has a "dark side," whereas Brahman is the highest good in Hindu thought. Significantly, though, many Hindu deities, the preeminent forms of Brahman in the relative realm of space and time, do have destructive aspects that do not easily fit into morally dualistic Western ideas of "good" and "evil." The Force and Brahman also bear resemblances to the Chinese concept of the Dao, the reality from which all things arise: the infinite reality beyond the capacity of words to express.[19]

Another way to look at the question of the dark side is that Brahman, in and of itself, is the ultimate good; but for as long as we suffer from the state of cosmic ignorance known as *māyā*, we will project onto Brahman attributes which do not belong to it, properly speaking. In other words, Brahman is itself beyond our relative notions of good and evil, but appears to us in forms based on the relative good and evil in our own consciousness. One can also find resonances here with the Tibetan Buddhist *Bardo Thodol* (or *Tibetan Book of the Dead*)—also an inspiration of the Beatles' song, "Tomorrow Never Knows"—where the same entities can appear as benevolent Buddhas and Bodhisattvas or as malevolent, demonic beings, depending on the consciousness of the observer.

This occurs because the reality we experience, according to Advaita Vedānta and Yogācāra Buddhism, is of the nature of consciousness. It is shaped by consciousness. If the consciousness of the observer is filled with compassion, the observer will then experience compassion. If it is filled with fear, the observer's fears will manifest. This is how karma works. As Matthew Bortolin explains, "Presumption skews our perception of reality, giving us an impression that is entirely wrong."[20] This imposition, or *adhyāsa*, may explain what *appears* to us as the dark side of the Force. More evidence for this interpretation emerges in the next *Star Wars* film.

The Wisdom of Yoda

The Jedi master Yoda, probably the *Star Wars* character most obviously rooted in Asian spiritual traditions, is introduced in the second *Star Wars* film (part five of the entire saga): *The Empire Strikes Back*. In *A New Hope*, Luke's guide—the character playing the mythic mentor role, in terms of Joseph Campbell's archetypes—is Obi Wan Kenobi. Obi Wan, however, is struck down in his duel with Vader: or rather, he merges with the Force, his physical form vanishing, much to Vader's bafflement. This provides a distraction that allows Luke and his band of friends to escape from the Death Star (from which they have rescued the epic's chief heroine, Princess Leia) and go to the hidden rebel base. In the climactic scene of the film, Luke destroys the Death Star with the help of the Force, guided by Obi Wan's disembodied voice.

In *The Empire Strikes Back*, Obi Wan again appears to Luke, not only as a voice, but with a visible form as well (which fans refer to as a "Force ghost"). He advises Luke to go to the planet Dagobah to be instructed by Yoda, "the Jedi master who instructed me."[21] It is interesting to note that, in Sri Lanka, a "dagoba" is a stupa—a Buddhist shrine—and *yoḍha*, in Sanskrit, means "warrior." In other words, Luke is to go to a sacred place to meet a warrior.

Yoda, in many ways, fills the archetypal role of the eccentric teacher whose divine madness serves to uproot the limiting preconceptions of the student and open the student's mind to higher spiritual realities. "You must unlearn what you have learned," Yoda tells Luke in one scene.[22] And unlearn he does. When Luke first encounters Yoda, Luke's X-wing Starfighter has crash-landed in the swampy environment of Dagobah.

Yoda is a tiny figure—roughly three feet tall—with green skin and large, pointed ears that extend from the sides of his head. He is also ancient—over nine hundred years old—and lives in a humble hut on a world that Luke unkindly characterizes at one point as a "slimy mud hole." "Mud hole! Slimy! My home this is!" Yoda replies, using the subject-object-verb word order typical of such languages as Sanskrit and Japanese: a verbal idiosyncrasy for which this character has become famous (or rather, this character famous for which has become). Upon Luke's arrival, Yoda offers to help him find his friend, to which Luke replies, "I'm not looking for a friend, I'm looking for a great warrior." Yoda's reply to this is instructive, "Ah! Wars not make one great." This is also interesting in light of the Sanskrit meaning of Yoda's name—*yoḍha*, or *warrior*.[23]

Once Luke actually realizes that this eccentric little figure is the very Yoda he seeks, he becomes his earnest—though often frustrated—student. The initial interactions between Luke and Yoda are, in many ways, reminiscent of the first encounters between the young Narendranath Datta—later to be Swami Vivekananda—and his master, Sri Ramakrishna. Naren, too, thought his master-to-be was, at first, a madman, only later coming to see him as a great enlightened teacher—and even then, still challenging him with doubt and skepticism. The job of the guru in both the Advaita Vedānta and Zen traditions is to deconstruct the ego and the false conceptions in the mind of the student, to enable the student's true, divine potential to shine through: to purify the student's consciousness.[24]

This is what Yoda does for Luke Skywalker. At one point, Yoda takes Luke to a cave that is strong with the dark side of the Force: a place of evil. Luke asks Yoda what is in the cave, to which Yoda replies, "Only what you take with you." He also tells Luke that Luke will not need his weapons in the cave. Still skeptical, Luke takes his weapons with him. In the cave, he encounters Darth Vader—or rather, an apparition of Vader. The two duel with their light sabers (swords with a blade made up of a coherent energy beam). Luke strikes Vader down, beheading him. Vader's mask is broken and Luke beholds the face behind it. The face is his own.

This scene strongly suggests that the Force—and reality itself—is shaped by our perceptions: by the impositions of our own fears and expectations upon it. This is a major theme of Vedanta.

Finally, there is the scene which could be called the "*Bhagavad Gita*" moment of *Star Wars*. One can see *Star Wars* as a modern American version of the kind of epic found in ancient cultures, which embody and express the values of those cultures. The two great epics of Hinduism are, of course, the *Rāmāyaṇa* and the *Mahābhārata*. Many parallels can be seen between *Star Wars* and these two epics—parallels which have been well documented in Steven Rosen's work, *The Jedi in the Lotus*.[25]

The *Bhagavad Gītā*, or "Song of God," is a dialogue which occurs in the midst of the action of the *Mahābhārata*—indeed, just as the climactic battle of the epic is about to begin. The *Gītā* is an interlude, in which the events of the larger epic fade into the background, and the focus becomes the spiritual path, which Lord Krishna explains to the hero Arjuna as he is about to lead his forces into battle against the rival forces of the Kaurava clan. Similarly, Yoda engages Luke in a series of dialogues in which he communicates to his student the knowledge he will need in order to win his own battle against the Empire.

The most profound dialogue between Luke and Yoda occurs as Luke's Starfighter sinks fully into the waters of the swamp, effectively stranding him on Dagobah as the war between the rebellion and the empire rages in the space beyond. This dialogue is worth replicating in full:

Luke: "Oh, no. We'll never get it out now."

Yoda: "So certain are you. Always with you it cannot be done. Hear you nothing that I say?"

Luke: "Master, moving stones around is one thing. This is totally different." [Yoda had just been teaching Luke to use the Force to move stones with his mind.]

Yoda: "No! No different! Only different in your mind. You must unlearn what you have learned."

Luke: "All right, I'll give it a try."

Yoda: "No! Try not. Do. Or do not. There is no try." [This is probably the most famous of Yoda's lines in the *Star Wars* films.]

Luke extends his hand, closes his eyes, and the ship begins to emerge from the waters, but then it sinks again and Luke opens his eyes and lowers his hand in frustration (and apparent exhaustion).

Luke: "I can't. It's too big."

Yoda: "Size matters not. Look at me. Judge me by my size, do you? And well you should not. For my ally in the Force. And a powerful ally it is. Life creates it, makes it grow. Its energy surrounds us and binds us. Luminous beings are we, not this crude matter. [As he says this, he pinches Luke's shoulder, underscoring that the Self is not the physical body.] You must feel the Force around you. Here, between you, me, the tree, the rock: everywhere! Yes, even between the land and the ship!"

Luke: "You want the impossible."

Yoda then closes his eyes and turns toward the ship, extending his clawed hand. The ship starts to rise from the water and floats to the dry land, where it lands gently.

Luke: "I don't ... I don't believe it."

Yoda: "That is why you fail."[26]

Space, time, size, extent, causation itself: none of these things are ultimately real, according to Advaita Vedanta. The reality is Brahman: infinite being, consciousness, and bliss. Time, space, and causation are impositions of the mind upon reality. Yoda challenges Luke to see well beyond our normal concepts of time, space, and causation, which are completely upended by the sight of the diminutive Yoda, eyes closed, clawlike hand outstretched, making the X-wing float up out of the swamp to rest on the dry land.

This scene is reminiscent of a similar moment in *The Matrix*, when the guru character of Morpheus asks the hero, Neo: "Do you think that's air that you're breathing?" The phenomena that we normally experience and take to be real are manifestations of a deeper consciousness. One who becomes attuned to that consciousness has the power to shape these phenomena. In fact, we are doing this all of the time, though without any awareness (or with only very little or occasional awareness) of the process involved. "Using the Force" involves becoming better attuned to this deeper consciousness: to the Self (Atman), or the Brahman within.

Vasudha Narayanan also notes this conceptual connection between *Star Wars*, the *Matrix* films, and Vedanta: "For example, 'the Force' in *Star Wars* has parallels with Hindu philosophical ideas such as 'Brahman,' the Supreme, the ultimate principle of the universe, as does the illusory overlay [*adhyāsa*] in *The Matrix*, with 'Maya,' the wondrous illusory power."[27]

The Power (and Peril) of Attachment

After being instructed by Yoda and beginning to have visions of the future in which he sees his friends suffering—visions not unlike the *siddhis*, the "perfections" or paranormal powers that arise in meditative practice—Luke rushes off to save his friends, even though Yoda and Obi Wan warn him that his training is not yet complete. Siddhis can lead one to stray from one's path. Luke ends up facing Darth Vader in combat and (here is the biggest spoiler alert of all time) discovering the terrible truth that Vader did not, literally speaking, kills his father. Vader *is* his father. The great Jedi, Anakin Skywalker, became consumed by the dark side of the Force. The final film of the original *Star Wars* trilogy (part six of the saga as a whole), *Return of the Jedi*, narrates Vader's redemption. Luke, confident that there is still good in his father, refuses to kill him in a final confrontation orchestrated by the Emperor: the dark lord whom Vader serves and who has enslaved the galaxy under his rule. The Emperor, seeing that it will not be possible to sway Luke to the dark side, assaults him with his Force powers, shooting lightning bolts from his hands. Luke cries out to his father for help, and the divine spark within Vader finally asserts itself. He tosses the Emperor into a nearby pit. Anakin Skywalker has come back. He dies, however, from the wounds inflicted in his battle with Luke and from the lightning of the Emperor. Luke, full of unconditional love for his father, tries to rescue him from the new Death Star, where the confrontation with the Emperor has happened, and which is about to be destroyed by the rebel fleet. "I've got to save you!," Luke tells his father, who replies, "You already have, Luke."

The idea of a dualistic battle between good and evil is very Western, probably originating with Zoroastrianism, and its presence in *Star Wars* is understandable, given that Lucas originally conceived of his films as an American myth. The idea that there is a core of divinity—of essential goodness—in all beings, though, is also strongly present in Hindu traditions. It was this core of divinity that Mahatma Gandhi sought to evoke in his opponents when he used nonviolent methods of opposing oppression. Luke, in tossing aside his light saber and refusing to kill his father, by this nonviolent act, evokes the good from him. The good, divine core of Vader—Anakin—reasserts itself and the Emperor—representing ego and delusion—is destroyed.

Of course, another major difference between Asian and Western thought is that there is no final battle, no ultimate defeat of evil, in such traditions as Hinduism and Buddhism. There is for the individual who attains liberation from the cycle of rebirth. But within the cycle, good and evil are constantly waxing and waning, ebbing and flowing. If we see the end of the *Return of the Jedi* as the final defeat of evil in the *Star Wars* universe—through a Christian lens—we miss this point. It is interesting to note, though, that the recent resumption of the *Star Wars* saga, with the release of *The Force Awakens*, shows us that all evil was not, in fact, defeated in *Return of the Jedi*. The war continues to rage, as the Empire seeks to be reborn through the help of a fanatical and fascistic group known as the First Order. And if one rumor circulating among fans turns out to be true in future films, a Hindu reading of *Star Wars* will become even more plausible. This is the rumor that the character of Rey, introduced in *The Force Awakens*, may actually be the reincarnation of Anakin Skywalker/Darth Vader. This would help to explain why this completely untrained young woman is both an outstanding pilot and instinctively adept in the use of the Force, not only resisting Kylo Ren's powerful mind probe but even turning it back against him.

Returning to Anakin Skywalker: how does he become Darth Vader in the first place? This is the story of the first three *Star Wars* films (in terms of the chronology of the *Star Wars* universe, but released in theatres as "prequels" many years after the release of the original films). *The Phantom Menace, Attack of the Clones*, and *Revenge of the Sith* together narrate the rise and fall of Anakin Skywalker, the fall of the Jedi and the Republic, and the rise of the Galactic Empire.

The story of Anakin's fall expresses another deeply Hindu theme (also present in other Asian traditions, like Buddhism): the theme of the perils of attachment. In the *Star Wars* universe, we are all basically good (except, perhaps, for the Emperor). As in Hinduism, the soul is essentially pure. It turns to evil because of avidya, or ignorance of its true nature. Thinking itself limited, it comes to feel fear. And in the words of Yoda, "Fear is the path to the dark side. Fear leads to anger. Anger leads to hate. Hate leads to suffering."[28] Anakin's original fear is for the loss of his mother. He is separated from her in the first film when he goes, as a young boy, to join the Jedi order.

Between the first and second film, Anakin has no contact with his mother for several years. In the second film, he begins to see premonitions of her death. Fearing for her, he rushes off to his home planet of Tatooine to find he is too late. Having been attacked by a group of desert bandits known as Tusken Raiders, or Sandpeople, she dies in his arms. Filled with fury, he uses his warrior skills to destroy the entire Tusken village, sparing not even the children. This is his first turn toward the dark side.

Also in the second film, Anakin violates his Jedi vows, falling in love with and marrying the princess Padme. *Padma* means *lotus* in Sanskrit, and the lotus flower is a symbol for spiritual awakening in Indian religious traditions. *Padme* is the vocative form of *Padma* and is part of the popular Tibetan Buddhist mantra *Oṃ maṇi padme huṃ*.

The Palpatine, the Chancellor of the Republic (who is soon to become the Emperor from the original films) begins to tempt Anakin by telling him the dark side will give him the ability to save the ones he loves from death. Anakin has begun to have premonitions of Padme's death, just as he did of his mother. When the Chancellor is finally revealed to be an evil Sith lord (the dark side analogue of the Jedi), Anakin sides with him, taking the Sith name of Darth Vader and helping the Emperor to, as Obi Wan narrated to Luke in *A New Hope*, hunt down and destroy the Jedi. Anakin/Vader is also responsible for Padme's death, using his Force powers to choke her in anger when she does not wish to join him on his new path. She dies later, secretly giving birth to twins who will become Luke Skywalker and Princess Leia. The children are hidden and their identities kept from them and Obi Wan watches over Luke from a distance as he grows into the hero that he will eventually become.

How is love different from attachment? Love is the experience of the unity of all souls as finally one with the divine Self, or Atman. Attachment, though, is rooted in ego and avidya: in our sense of being separate individuals that can be threatened and experience loss. In our experience, the two are often mixed up together, and are often difficult to disentangle. But the difference between the two could not be more stark. One is life-affirming, while the other leads, unchecked, to death and destruction.

Like all great works of art, *Star Wars* is subject to many interpretations. Each interpretation has its strengths and its limits. A Hindu reading is not the only possible reading. But the fact that *Star Wars* does lend itself to such a reading, on so many levels, makes it part of the larger story of the infusion of Hindu thought and practice into Western culture, especially when one takes into consideration the relationship between Lucas and Campbell, and Campbell's close connections to the Vedanta Society.

Hinduism and Buddhism in *Lost*

The popular, and unconventional, science fiction television series *Lost*, which originally aired from 2004 to 2010, displays a number of Hindu and Buddhist influences as well. The series involves a variety of unexpected connections among its various characters, who have suffered a plane crash on a remote island in the general vicinity of Indonesia. (The series was filmed almost entirely in Hawaii, however, on the island of Oahu.) There are strong implications throughout the series of concepts such as karma and the deeper oneness and interconnectedness of all existence, as well as the harmony of religions, which comes to the fore in the series finale and is depicted in one scene through a stained glass window that includes symbols from most of the world's major religions.

The most obvious nod to Indian religious traditions is a shadowy organization known as "the DHARMA Initiative." Dharma is of course a pervasive term in Hinduism and Buddhism. We have seen that, in Hinduism, *dharma* refers to the fundamental order of existence, as well as the duties and responsibilities of living beings within that larger cosmic and social order. In the modern period, it has also come to mean something close to *religion*. In Buddhism, it refers to the teachings of awakened beings (Buddhas) and to the fundamental components of experience. The DHARMA Initiative engages in experiments on the cutting edge of science, including experiments with time travel and travel between parallel universes. These become a major plot point.

Although it has never been suggested by the creators of the series or in the literature or fan commentary on the internet, the DHARMA Initiative seems like a nod to the Esalen Institute. One of the scholars connected with the Esalen Institute was the psychologist, B.F. Skinner:

> [Skinner] founded a school of research psychology called the experimental analysis of behaviour, which is reflected in the DHARMA experiments including those with the polar bears [which appeared in the series]. Setting up a reward system with food after completing tasks tied into Skinner's theories of reinforcing consequences, as did the observation of the button pressing every 108 minutes.[29]

The pressing of the button to which this quotation from the *Lost Encyclopedia* refers occurs in one of several DHARMA research stations located all over the island. This particular station is called the Swan station. One of the characters in the series is required to push a button that is located in this station every 108 minutes, having been told that if this is not done, the world will be destroyed. The number 108 is a sacred number in Indian traditions: Hinduism, Buddhism, and Jainism. Its symbolism is explained in a variety of ways. One of these explanations is that 108 represents the manifestation of creation from the original unity of existence, because it equals $1^1 \times 2^2 \times 3^3$. It is common in meditation practice to silently recite one's mantra in rounds of 108.[30] When this experiment is first revealed in the series, at the beginning of the second season, it is one of the first indications of the presence of Indic religious themes in the series. It is worth noting that the station where the 108 experiment occurs is called the Swan station. The Sanskrit word for *swan* is *haṃsa*, or hansa. One might note that this word figures in the title of certain prominent Hindu religious figures, such as Sri Ramakrishna Paramahansa and Paramahansa Yogananda. *Paramahansa* means "great swan," and refers to a sage who has risen above the dualities of conventional existence. The logo of the DHARMA Initiative's Swan station is quite reminiscent of the logo of the Ramakrishna Mission, or Vedanta Society, as it is known in the Western world. One of the founders of the DHARMA Initiative is also said to be a Danish industrialist named "Alvar Hanso."[31] The Āḷvars were bhakti poets of southern India in the medieval period whose works are viewed in the Śri Vaiṣṇava tradition of Hinduism as the "fifth *Veda*." Hanso, of course, is similar to *hansa*, and also sounds somewhat like *hansa* in its Bengali pronunciation (in which the name Sri Ramakrishna Paramahansa sounds like "Sri Ramkrishna Poromhongsho"). Finally, members of the DHARMA Initiative all greet one another with the traditional Hindu, "Namaste," which indicates respect for the divinity dwelling within each person.

The members of the DHARMA Initiative are depicted as scientists who are immersed in the counterculture of the sixties. Many are fans of a fictitious rock band Geronimo Jackson, who sound vaguely like the Grateful Dead and whose hits include a song called "Dharma Lady," which can be found on the soundtrack to the series, along with songs by other artists of period, such as the Who, Derek and the Dominoes (led by Eric Clapton), and the Flying Burrito Brothers.

In terms of Buddhist influence on the DHARMA Initiative, the *Lost Encyclopedia* says the following:

> The word Dharma has several meanings and significances in different religious and spiritual beliefs, all of which relate to the DHARMA Initiative beliefs, practices, and causes.
>
> In Buddhism, Dharma mostly refers to the wisdom and teachings of the Buddha. It also refers to a basic unit of existence and/or experience called a "phenomenon." A core concept of Buddhism is that all phenomena are interlinked and interdependent.
>
> Buddhists believe that only through the practice of Dharma will they discover the greatest peace, happiness, and fulfilment. While there are many different schools of Buddhism that focus on individual aspects of what the Buddha taught, the concept of Dharma unites them all. The [founders of the DHARMA Initiative] infused that idea into the heart of their DHARMA Initiative experiment that was created to unite many different scientific disciplines and research schools of thought together on the island with one united goal.[32]

This wholistic aim of "uniting many different scientific disciplines and research schools of thought" is certainly reminiscent of the integral approach of Sri Aurobindo, which was of course a major influence on the founders of the Esalen Institute.

Struggling with Stereotypes: Indiana Jones, Apu, and Raj Koothrappali

As the foregoing discussions of George Harrison, Hindu themes in rock music, *Star Wars*, and *Lost* suggest, Hinduism has been a major source of inspiration for many contributors to pop culture in the West: sometimes overtly and openly acknowledged, sometimes less obviously.

A criticism to which much of this influence might be subject has to do precisely with the extent to which it is unacknowledged, particularly when this is juxtaposed with the ways in which India and Indians are often portrayed in explicit ways in Western popular culture. Just as, in the early twentieth century, there were Americans who eagerly embraced Hindu spirituality and such practices as meditation and yoga, while actual Indians were being physically attacked, harassed, and finally expelled and banned from the United States, similarly, one can note the infusion of the concepts of Hinduism in such film series as *Star Wars* and *The Matrix*, while finding that actual Indians are portrayed either as helpless victims or as objects of ridicule. It is both deeply ironic and tragic that the ideals and practices of a culture could be found to have intrinsic appeal, but that the adoption of these could occur in tandem with such poor treatment of the people of that culture.

One of the most egregious offenders in this regard is the film *Indiana Jones and the Temple of Doom*. Often regarded as the weakest film in an otherwise popular and beloved series (or the second weakest, given the poor reception of the last film in the series, *Indiana Jones and the Cave of the Crystal Skull*), *Indiana Jones and the Temple of Doom* features Harrison Ford in his iconic role as the swashbuckling adventurer and archaeologist, Indiana Jones, rescuing enslaved Indian children from an evil human sacrifice cult centered on the goddess Kali.

We have encountered Kali previously. She is the goddess to whom Sri Ramakrishna was a faithful devotee and priest. She is also the goddess to whom animal sacrifices are still offered in Bengal to the present day, although vegetarian offerings have become the norm in her worship in America. We have also seen that a cult of human sacrifice devoted to Kali was featured in another film—the Beatles' *Help!*—albeit their depiction there was for comedic purposes. We have also seen that George Harrison was nevertheless able to see beyond this depiction, to the real Indian culture.

Kali is most certainly the goddess whom non-Hindus are likely to have greatest difficulty understanding. Relating to the absolute devotion and worship that she evokes, particularly among Bengali Hindus, is made difficult because her iconography presents her in a way that Americans are likely to find frightening, and perhaps even demonic. Herself a demon slayer, Kali is presented in the midst of combat. One of her two left hands is holding a wicked-looking scimitar upraised, while her other left is grasping the severed head of a demon by the hair. Both of the right hands of this four-armed, four-handed goddess, though, are upraised in the *abhāya mudrā*, a gesture that means "do not be afraid," or "have no fear." Her tongue is sticking out in a way that may remind Westerners of the Gorgon or Medusa of Greek mythology. She is standing on the body of Shiva.

The story of Kali is that she is actually the gentle goddess Parvati, or Shakti, the wife of Shiva. The earth was once attacked by a demonic being known as Raktabija, whose name means "blood seed." Whenever a drop of the Raktabija's blood touched the earth, an entirely new form of Raktabija would appear. An army of gods and humans sought to subdue him, but whenever he was struck by their weapons and bled on the ground, more Raktabijas would appear. Soon, the earth was being overrun by a growing army of Raktabijas.

The beings of the earth called out for help, and the goddess Parvati, hearing the cries of her children, the living beings of the earth, grew incredibly angry. Who could be harming her children to make them cry out so? Her form became fierce and she leaped into battle, slaying the Raktabijas. In order to keep the blood of these beings from creating more of the same kind, she quickly lapped it up, hence her extended bloody tongue. This fierce form of Parvati is called Kali.

Kali's husband, Shiva, fearing that, in her frenzy to destroy the demons, she might destroy the earth as well, lay down on the ground in front of her. Kali leaped on top of Shiva, but suddenly remembered her true nature, as Parvati. This was accomplished by Shiva, who knew that touching a respected person with one's foot is deeply disrespectful in Indian culture. The foot is considered an impure part of the body, because it touches the ground and becomes dirty. The head is the purest part of the body. Hindus often show respect to elders and teachers, and to images of deities, by touching the feet of these persons and then touching their own forehead, as a way of showing that these persons are "above" them, and pure.

A wife would never typically stand on top of her husband or touch him with her feet at all, and vice versa. When Kali realizes she is standing on Shiva, she comes to her senses. She thinks, "What am I doing? I am standing on my husband!" She may also fear that she has accidentally slain him, given that he is lying on the ground. This, of course, was Shiva's plan all along to save the earth from Kali's wrath.

Kali, in short, is a protective deity who is fierce in order to protect her children—humanity—from evil. Fierce, protective deities, who may look, from a Western sensibility, demonic, are not at all uncommon in Asian religious traditions. Such protectors are common in Buddhist temples.

The symbolism of Kali is also important. The multiple arms (and sometimes, heads and faces) of many Hindu deities represent multiple powers or aspects of that particular divinity. They are not to be taken literally, but as revelatory of that deity's nature. The head represents the ego, so Kali's demon-decapitating sword, and the head she is holding, both symbolize the destruction, or transformation, of the ego that is required on the spiritual path. Kali is a purifier, taking on all impurity upon herself, which is represented by her bloody tongue.

When Sri Ramakrishna had his experience of Kali, he saw her not in her fierce iconic form, but as "a limitless, infinite, effulgent Ocean of Consciousness."[33] This is, one could say, Kali's true form, according to her devotees. The fierce, demon-slaying goddess is best viewed as a way of conceptualizing the interaction of the "limitless, infinite, effulgent Ocean of Consciousness," or Brahman, with the human ego, with all its petty vanities and self-preoccupcations, well symbolized by the demons that are "slain" in the moment of the awakening of transcendental consciousness.

Kali, as depicted in *Indiana Jones and the Temple of Doom*, is not a benevolent mother or a protector from evil or a remover of ego and impurity. She is depicted as a fierce, evil goddess who demands human sacrifice. To be sure, there was a quite notorious cult of human sacrifice in nineteenth-century Bengal, to which this film is no doubt alluding: the *ṭhags*, or *ṭhagi*, from which the English word "thug" is derived. It was a criminal cult, whose members were rounded up and imprisoned during the period of the British Raj.[34] It was not even remotely mainstream, though, or representative of Hinduism of that, or of any, period. In the film, though, the thugs have a massive temple—the "temple of doom"—where they not only perform an elaborate ritual of human sacrifice, presided over by the wicked Mola Ram, but also enslave children in a mine. Indiana Jones, the "white savior," of course liberates the children and defeats the evil cult—with the help of British soldiers, who arrive at the end of the film. In the final showdown between Indiana Jones and Mola Ram, Jones is assisted with the help of some glowing sacred stones, dedicated to the god Shiva. It is strongly implied that Shiva is the "good" god who is opposed to Kali. Nowhere is it mentioned that Shiva and Kali are husband and wife!

More than the distortion of the Hindu religion, though, Indians who discuss the film often object most strongly to the outrageous food which the villains are depicted as eating in their palace. They are shown dining on such dishes as "chilled monkey brains" and a soup with eyeballs floating in it. These bear no resemblance whatsoever to actual Indian cuisine. Some of the most famous Indian dishes are, in fact, vegetarian; for, as discussed previously, although not all Indians practice vegetarianism, many do, and it is seen as an important virtue by many. Madhu, an Indian American who saw this film, said, "That was the worst! What rubbish! Indian food is nothing like that."

It should be noted that this film and *Help!* have not been the only representations of Kali in the Western media that have played upon the idea that she is a force for evil. *Song of Kali*, by horror and fantasy author, Dan Simmons, is based on this same deep cultural misunderstanding.[35] The cover of the book describes it as "a chilling voyage into the squalor and violence of the human condition." The book includes extensive and explicit depictions of poverty in the city of Kolkata (Calcutta). The idea of India as a land of poverty is also central to *Slumdog Millionaire*.

The 2008 *Slumdog Millionaire*, another popular film set in India, has also been a target of criticism by many Indians and Indian Americans. Its vivid depictions of poverty in the slums of Mumbai, while not inaccurate, have been argued to convey a one-sided picture of life in India. More than whether or not the film is accurate in its depiction, the question has been raised as to why this subject is fascinating to many Americans. It has been derided by some as "poverty porn." Ramesh, an Indian

American professional, says, "Films like this make white people feel better that they live in such a great country and can show generosity to their little brown brothers." The problem is not the desire to help others so much as the condescending and patronizing attitude with which this is often expressed. Sheela, another Indian American professional, says, "Films like this, sadly, are not empowering at all. The hero succeeds by winning on a game show. What kind of message is that supposed to send?"

Two very popular and beloved characters that are also rooted in problematic stereotypes, on which the humor they produce often depends, are the character of Apu from the long-running animated series, *The Simpsons*, and Raj Koothrappali, from *The Big Bang Theory*.

Both *The Simpsons* and *The Big Bang Theory* are comedy series which often serve to draw attention to stereotypes and social issues of various kinds, but that also do so by utilizing some of these very same stereotypes. Apu has been an object of considerable criticism from many in the Indian American community. Apu, whose full name is Apu Nahasapeemapetilon, is the owner of a convenience store, the Kwik-E-Mart, in the American town of Springfield, where *The Simpsons* is set. His last name, which is entirely fictitious, gives a sense of how many non-Indian Americans perceive Indian names: as long and difficult to pronounce.

Apu is frequently depicted as being engaged in dishonest business practices—like leaving the hot dogs that he sells in his store out too long—and as generally unscrupulous. In one episode, where Apu is part of an increasingly popular barber shop quartet, he is told by his manager that he will have to change his last name, to which Apu replies, "It is a great dishonour to my heritage and my God, but okay!" Later in the same episode, when asked by a reporter if he is Indian, he replies. "By the many arms of Vishnu, I swear it's a lie!" No Hindu says, "By the many arms of Vishnu."

Indian American comedian, Hari Kondabolu has made a documentary, *The Problem with Apu*, on why, precisely, this character is problematic, in which many South Asians talk about the kinds of prejudice and stereotyping they have experienced based on the Apu character. There is also the fact that the character is not actually voiced by an Indian person. Hank Azaria, the voice actor who portrays Apu, and many other characters on *The Simpsons* as well, has responded in a sympathetic way to the objections raised against the character, saying in an interview with Stephen Colbert that he would be "willing to step aside" from the role of Apu. He then added that "the most important thing is to listen to Indian people and their experience with it ... I really want to see Indian, South Asian writers in the writers' room, genuinely informing whichever direction this character takes."[36]

Another controversial Indian character is Rajesh Koothrappali, from *The Big Bang Theory*. Rajesh, or Raj, is a shy, sexually repressed astrophysicist, and part of a group of "nerds"—scientists working at Caltech with strong interests in science fiction, fantasy, super heroes, and so on—whose nerdishness is the source of much of the show's humor. The show is replete with stereotypes, not only of Indians, but of Jews (another of the characters, Howard Wolowitz, is Jewish) and southern white evangelical Christians (the most outrageous character of all, Sheldon Cooper, being from an evangelical Christian family in Texas). The identification of Indianness with nerdishness in Raj's character marks a shift in stereotypes of Indian Americans, from owners of motels and convenience stores, along the lines of Apu, to engineers, scientists, doctors, IT professionals, and so on.

Additional elements of Raj's character, particularly his shyness (in the early seasons of the series he could not speak to a woman unless he was drunk) and sexual repression are certainly harmful stereotypes. Like Apu, Rajesh's last name is fictitious, although Koothrappali sounds much more like an actual South Asian name than Nahasapeemapetilon. He has also been given the unheard-of middle name *Ramayan*, presumably after the *Rāmāyaṇa*. The character is also played by an actual Indian actor, Kunal Nayyar. But, as may be expected, Nayyar has received criticism for what some perceive to be his role in perpetuating racism.[37]

Another Alternative: Mindy Kaling and *The Office*

Not all of the representations of Indians in the American media are negative, including in the realm of comedy. One South Asian actress who has shown that one does not need to stoop to demeaning stereotypes in order to evoke humor is Mindy Kaling, whose full name is Vera Mindy Chokalingam. Kaling's character, Kelly Kapoor, in the long-running American version of what was originally a BBC series, *The Office*, does not behave in a stereotyped "Indian" fashion. In fact, she is probably one of the most believable Indians on American television: certainly in comparison with Apu and Raj Koothrappali.

The character of Kelly does not hide from or in any way seek to downplay her Indianness. In fact, one episode of the series focuses on the celebration of the Hindu holy day, Diwali, which she emphasizes as being a time for fun and getting dressed up in one's best clothes (which is also how one often hears Hindu holidays described informally). But her Indianness is not her dominant characteristic as a human being. Her character is flirtatious, competitive, and highly, highly, highly talkative: characteristics that could be possessed by any person, of any culture. Kelly is, in other words, a human being, who happens to be an Indian American Hindu.

Another feature of *The Office* helps make its representations, not only of Indian Americans but of several minority communities, more authentic and less stereotyped than those in either *The Simpsons* or *Big Bang Theory*. (The show features two African American characters as well, Darryl and Stanley, who are very different from one another, as well as a gay Hispanic character, named Oscar.)

This feature has to do with the nature of the gaze of the audience that is assumed to be the case by each of these series. *The Simpsons* and *The Big Bang Theory* presume that their audiences will find racial stereotypes to be funny. Apu and Raj are taken to be funny, in large part, *because of* the fact that they are Indian. Their Indianness is integral to what is believed to make them funny. *The Office*, on the other hand, presumes that its audience finds people who traffic in stereotypes to be funny. The main buffoon in *The Office* is not Kelly, Darryl, Stanley, or Oscar. And when any of these characters is funny, it is typically due to personal characteristics other than race. It is the boss, Michael Scott, played brilliantly by Steve Carrell, who is the main buffoon, and much of his buffoonery, particularly in early seasons, is a direct function of his belief in both ethnic and gender stereotypes, which places him in a variety of hilarious situations in which he is the butt of the joke.

At the same time, part of the ethos of *The Office* seems to be compassion. *The Office*, in other words, does not come across as "revenge" against white males who engage in stereotyping. The character of Michael is also handled with great compassion, and he evolves considerably over the course of the series. And none of this occurs at the expense of the humor of the show.

It probably does not hurt that Kaling herself is one of the lead writers of the series. To be fair, Kunal Nayyar has also been involved in the writing for Raj in *The Big Bang Theory*. Because Nayyar, though, did not create this character, but must operate within the constraints of the way in which this character has already been presented, his agency, one could argue, has been less than that of Kaling in *The Office*.

From Comedy to Commentary: The Growing Indian Presence in American Media

Another positive development in terms of the representation of Indian Americans in the American media is the emergence of the Indian American expert. Indian Americans are becoming increasingly prominent as commentators on topics like medicine, politics, and international affairs. Dr. Sanjay Gupta, a neurosurgeon at Grady Memorial Hospital in Atlanta, Georgia, and assistant professor of neurosurgery at Emory University has served for many years as a reporter on medical issues. He is probably best known to most Americans as a medical expert who speaks regularly on CNN.

Another well-known CNN expert, Mumbai-born political scientist, Fareed Zakaria, has his own series—*Fareed Zakaria GPS*—which Zakaria says stands for "Global Public Square." Zakaria is widely respected on international issues whose series regularly attracts renowned experts in a variety of fields to discuss contemporary events.

Neera Tanden is also a regular commentator on MSNBC. Tanden is the president of the Center for American Progress, a public policy "think tank" in Washington, DC. Very active in the Democratic Party, Tanden is an example of the topic to which we shall turn in our next chapter: the growing presence of Indian Americans, and of Hindu Americans in particular, in American political life.

Study Questions

1. What are some examples of Hindu themes that can be discerned in the *Star Wars* films?
2. How might the attraction of Hinduism for Western celebrities such as George Harrison be explained?
3. In what senses does the increasing representation of Indians in the American media represent an advance for the community? In what senses is such representation problematic?

Suggestions for Further Reading

The Beatles, *The Beatles Anthology* (San Francisco: Chronicle Books, 2000).
Matthew Bortolin, *The Dharma of Star Wars* (Somerville, MA: Wisdom Publications, 2005).
Joshua Greene, *Here Comes the Sun: The Spiritual and Musical Journey of George Harrison* (Hoboken, NJ: John Wiley and Sons, 2006).
George Harrison, *I, Me, Mine* (San Francisco: Chronicle Books, 2007).
Steven Rosen, *The Jedi in the Lotus: Star Wars and the Hindu Tradition* (Budapest: Arktos Media, 2011).
Dan Simmons, *Song of Kali* (New York: Open Road Integrated Media, 2010).
Paul Terry and Tara Bennett, *Lost Encyclopedia* (New York: Dorling Kindersley, 2010).
Lao Tzu (Victor Mair, trans.), *Tao Te Ching: The Classic Book of Integrity and the Way* (New York: Bantam Books, 1990).
Martine van Woerkens, *The Strangled Traveler: Colonial Imaginings and the Thugs of India* (Chicago: University of Chicago Press, 1995).

8

Identity and Engagement: Hinduism in America Finds Its Voice

Chapter 8 Summary and Outline

This chapter will explore the emergence, as the twentieth century has ended and the twenty-first century begun, of an increasingly assertive, socially, and politically active American Hinduism. It will end with some concluding reflections on what has been explored in this book.

Responding to Indignities

In the late 1990s, a growing number of Hindus began to respond to incidents in which they believed they or their traditions had been disrespected. One early response involved the formation, in 1997, of "American Hindus Against Defamation." Incidents in which Hindus felt singled out included the distribution in 1999 by the Southern Baptist Convention—on Diwali, a major Hindu festival—of "thirty thousand copies of a prayer guide for converting Hindus" to Christianity.[1] There were also incidents in which Hindus found themselves to be victims of Islamophobia:

> After the tragic events of September 11th, 2001, Hindus across America found themselves the victims of hate crimes. For example, during the week following the attacks, two Hindu temples, one in Medinah, Illinois, and the other in Matawan, New Jersey, and a convenience store owned by a Hindu man from Gujarat, India in Somerset, Massachusetts, were all firebombed.[2]

Such incidents call to mind the early twentieth century, when all Indian immigrants were referred to without distinction as "Hindoos," regardless of whether they were Hindu, Muslim, or Sikh.

In 2002, Hindus went to court in a case in which many felt they had been deceived in regard to food they had taken to be vegetarian:

> McDonald's apologised to Hindus for having failed to inform them that their French fries contained beef flavouring. McDonalds also stated that they would pay ten million dollars to Hindus, vegetarian and other groups. In a similar case three years earlier in 1999, Taco Bell settled a lawsuit with Hindu, Mukesh K. Rai, after they served him a beef burrito instead of a vegetarian bean burrito.[3]

These cases, as well as the spread of vegetarianism in America, have led to changes in the practices of many restaurants in regard to their handling of vegetarian food.

Case Study: The Hindu American Foundation

Hindu American activism can be placed in a long lineage of activism by immigrant groups throughout the history of the United States who have sought, in the words of Prema Kurien, "a place at the multicultural table."[4] Hindu American activism is an effort by a minority community to be recognized by the majority and to be afforded the same dignity in civil society that previous generations of immigrants to the United States have sought.

We have seen that, after the lifting in 1965 of the Asian Exclusion Act of 1924—which had banned almost all immigration from India to the United States, with the exception of a handful of students—growing numbers of Hindus moved to the United States for both employment and education. Hindus from India and from other parts of the world began, in the seventies, to build temples and to become a regular part of the social fabric of America. The tech boom of the nineties increased this trend.

Coinciding with this influx of Hindus who had been born into and who grew up practicing Hindu traditions, there also emerged a growing fascination with Hinduism and Hindu thought and practice among the majority population. Practices such as meditation, yoga, nonviolence, and vegetarianism, as well as concepts like reincarnation and religious pluralism, held a great appeal for many Americans, especially those involved in the counterculture of the sixties, but for many since that time as well.

By the middle of the 1990s, a sufficient number of Americans identified themselves as Hindu for American Hindus to see themselves as a distinct group within the larger American societies, with distinctive interests and concerns. Prominent among these was the representation of Hindu thought and practice in academic writing that was emerging from American colleges and universities, as well as in middle school and high school textbooks.

After the terror attacks of September 11, 2001, which were followed by a massive wave of Islamophobia which has yet to abate fully, there was also a concern in the minds of many Hindu Americans to differentiate Hindus and Hinduism, in the perception of the average American, from Islam.[5]

It was in this context that the Hindu American Foundation (HAF) was established on September 3, 2003, in Fremont, California. The vision of this organization, as expressed on its website, is "To sustain a leading institution of Hindu American advocacy for the promotion of dignity, mutual respect, and pluralism." The identity of HAF is further elaborated in its mission statement:

> The Hindu American Foundation (HAF) is an advocacy organization for the Hindu American community. The Foundation educates the public about Hinduism, speaks out about issues affecting Hindus worldwide, and builds bridges with institutions and individuals whose work aligns with HAF's objectives. HAF focuses on human and civil rights, public policy, media, academia, and interfaith relations. Through its advocacy efforts, HAF seeks to cultivate leaders and empower future generations of Hindu Americans.[6]

The organization does not align with any specific Hindu group, but presents itself as being at the service of all American Hindus:

> The Hindu American Foundation is not affiliated with any religious or political organizations or entities. HAF seeks to serve Hindu Americans across all sampradayas (Hindu religious traditions) regardless of race, colour, national origin, citizenship, caste, gender, sexual orientation, age and/or disability.[7]

The activism of HAF has been directed at a variety of issues that the organization takes to be of central concern to Hindus. These have included the aforementioned issues of representation of Hinduism in school textbooks, but also human rights abuses that have been suffered by Hindus globally, domestic American issues related to the separation of church and state (like attempts to erect displays of the Ten Commandments on public property, or anti-Hindu comments by persons running for office), abuses that are related to casteism in India, and the representation of yoga as an exercise routine with no relation to Hinduism or Hindu spirituality (controversially called, as noted in the previous chapter, the "Take Back Yoga" campaign).

The issues on which HAF has taken a stand cut across the political spectrum, in both the Indian and American contexts. In its advocacy for revisions of school textbooks that present Hinduism in a negative light (while maintaining a fairly positive image in their representations of other religions), as well as in its "Take Back Yoga" campaign, the interests of HAF and what could be called a conservative approach to Hinduism coincide quite closely.

At the same time, in its extensive critique of casteism, HAF found itself running afoul of many of those same Hindus who had cheered its activism in the textbook cases. Its advocacy for separation of church and state in the US places it firmly on the side of political progressives who consistently challenge attempts to transform the United States into a "Christian nation." The reality of HAF is clearly a complex one, not reducible to a single factor or ideological orientation.

The question is sometimes raised why HAF focuses specifically on Hindu issues and not on the wider issues affecting all Indian Americans. In answer to the interview question, "Why a Hindu American Foundation and not an Indian American Foundation?" the answers included the following:

> The question could be asked—why a Federation of Indian American Christian Organizations of America, or an Indian American Muslim Council, or a Sikh Coalition or a Jain Foundation? Religion is primary and supreme in the American consciousness and in the political, cultural and social arenas, and being a majority Christian country, minority Hindus need to become agents for informing the rest of society about the Hindu faiths, philosophies, traditions, and cultures so that we can respond both positively in constructing and sustaining a diverse society but also step in to protect and defend the rights of Hindus in their new homeland.

Another respondent, Rajesh, said,

> I think many Hindus born and raised in the United States care more about their identity formation in the United States than in India. Moreover, I think Hindus as a diverse religious minority in the American social fabric need to be identified as such. It also is a disservice to the hundreds of thousands of Indian-Americans who are *not* Hindu.

And in the words of Mala, who is of Indian descent but born in the United States:

> I don't think Indian American defines me the way that Hindu American does. Indian and American are at times identities that are at odds with each other. I simply can't wear jeans and a sari at the same time. On the other hand, I've never once felt like my Hindu identity competed with my American ethics. The Indian identity is something that my parents owned and passed down, while the Hindu identity is something I've developed myself and come to own.

The vast majority of Hindus in America are also ethnically South Asian. There are thus many issues on which most Hindu Americans can and do unite with the greater

Indian American community. In many instances, for example, in which both Hindus and Sikhs face harassment or physical violence in the United States, this is due to Islamophobia on the part of their attackers, who typically do not differentiate among these groups, and may not even be aware of their separate existence.

This is because an American bigot who is bent on harassing or attacking someone different from themselves will not usually be sufficiently knowledgeable to differentiate between a person with brown skin who is Muslim and one who is Hindu or Sikh. Being a bigot, such a person will also be unlikely to care one way or the other, as we have seen from earlier periods of history, when the religious identity of "Hindoos" was perceived as a confused jumble of Hinduism, Sikhism, and Islam. This appalling phenomenon of racist attacks is clearly a strong reason for Indian Americans to work as a united group, across religious boundaries. An attack on one is an attack on all. Shefali, however, an employee of HAF, points out that:

> Nothing stops a Hindu of Indian descent from supporting the work of the HAF and at the same time supporting and participating in the work of organizations of South Asian or Indian Americans as well. None of these organizations demands exclusive allegiance. And HAF has condemned all religious violence, not only violence against Hindus. In many ways, HAF models itself on Jewish advocacy in the US, focusing mainly, but not exclusively, on the rights of one community.

In Their Own Words: HAF Members Speak for Themselves

How do HAF members respond to questions about their organization, its ideology, and its aims? The persons whose words are presented below included persons who were born and grew up in India and migrated to the United States as adults, persons who were born in India but who migrated with their families in early childhood, persons whose parents are from India but who were born and have lived their lives in the United States, and one white American Hindu. The ages of the persons interviewed ranged from their early twenties to seventies. Importantly, the interview group included a roughly equal number of men and women.

In response to the question, "What drew you to work for (or to help establish) the Hindu American Foundation?" the following answers are of particular interest:

> I was born in the US, and though my parents have worked hard to help me understand and develop my Indian and Indian-American identity, I've always felt a lot more comfortable with the Hindu piece of my identity, because it actually describes who I am, what I practice, and what I believe. Since it's the strongest piece of my identity, and one that's made me a better person, I was drawn to HAF and the idea of helping other Hindus develop pride in their identity. I've been very frustrated of late with

> peers who take a very passive approach to developing that pride and scoff when others try to help others develop theirs, and through HAF I've found a group of like minded people who work hard to give the community said pride.

This respondent affirms the distinction between an Indian identity and a Hindu identity. Both are parts of who she is, but she is most comfortable with, as she says, the Hindu piece of her identity. This answer is also significant in affirming the fact that we all have multiple identities. None of us is simply reducible to ethnicity or to a religion; and in American context, a religious identity, as a thing chosen and reaffirmed by the individual, as opposed to an accident of birth, can be more central than one's ethnicity in one's self-understanding.

Yet another respondent came to HAF through her pursuit of grassroots level interfaith work. Her response highlights the character of the Hindu community as a minority community in the American context:

> In early 2005, I was in the midst of a controversy over the National Day of Prayer in my hometown. The city was going to exclude or segregate faith communities for its annual National Day of Prayer ceremonies. I was on the front page of major newspapers, as the Hindu woman who spoke out against exclusion from this event ... The numerous calls we had during the following years as I became an interfaith activist and speaker for the Hindu community made me understand the importance of HAF's advocacy work, and also realize how much I needed like-minded Hindus who understood the challenges. Interfaith dialogue as it stands right now is dominated by Abrahamic traditions, and more about finding common ground between "People of the Book." People speaking about Hinduism would say things that are not necessarily based on fact or knowledge of Hinduism as a lived religion, based on normative Hindu practices, and some—within interfaith circles—also misrepresented, demeaned or diminished the tradition. I also had children who went to middle school and high school during these years, and saw them go through the same kind of frustration I had gone through during my childhood. My father, now a retired English professor and writer, had advised me during the same time that Hinduism was being seen through a western lens, and taught me how to explain our practice of Sanatana Dharma. I found that the leaders of HAF ... all used similar language and had a similar understanding of the challenges we faced with exclusion and misrepresentation of Hinduism, and knew how to speak up with the nuance required.

In response to the question, "Why do you feel that Hindus, specifically, need advocacy of this kind?" one interviewee said,

> Lots of people ask questions, which temple leadership doesn't always have answers to. What is the Hindu position on abortion, care of the environment, animal rights, etc.? HAF and its leaders have written about various issues and provided both official policy level briefs as well as the diversity of Hindu perspectives on issues

> including abortion, gay marriage, gun rights, animal rights, caste, religious freedom, and proselytization/conversion. Temples and other Hindu institutions can reference these documents. The viewpoints are also helpful to Hindus who may not be affiliated with any organization or institution but want an articulate way of explaining the issues. My daughter in 9th grade was told by her teacher that the Abrahamic faiths were the original monotheists. Long story short, she reached out to HAF leadership, the Academic Advisory Council and others in the community to explain the misunderstanding—that Hinduism is both polytheistic and monotheistic, and that the western way of looking at or describing, and the history around the study of Hinduism comes from a place that often diminishes the tradition. Having role models at HAF as well as the resources and connections available through HAF will help her and other young Hindus be strong in their pursuit of dharma.

This person also spoke of the tendency for Indian political issues to be brought into the American arena of discourse, saying,

> There are [also] negative forces at play—[some] in the Muslim community who speak loudly about the rights of minority religious groups in India, certain Sikh leaders who want to lay the violence against Sikhs in India in 1984 at the door of all diasporic Hindus, and Christians who didn't like my questions regarding predatory proselytizing. A strong and strategic Hindu voice that is reasoned and respectful, expecting mutual understanding and fair treatment, is needed to advocate against these negative forces and promote pluralism.

Another respondent to this question spoke of the need for fair representation and inclusion in American society,

> Every group of people in the United States deserve a voice, and HAF is ours. That said, we are in more dire need than other faith groups, because we are incredibly misunderstood. The average American's piecemeal picture of a Hindu is exotic and hard to relate to. We have much work to do before people understand the very basics of our faith, and that we aren't so very foreign after all.

Because parallels are sometimes drawn between the Hindu American and Jewish American experiences, I asked the question, "Do you see parallels between the work of HAF and the situation of Hindus in the US and the work of organizations such as the Anti-Defamation League and the situation of the Jewish community in the US?" The answers to this question included the following, "I believe there are certainly parallels between any group that's been misunderstood and discriminated against on the basis of beliefs. The Jewish community has done a stupendous job of taking control of their own narrative, and the Hindu community must learn from them and apply their successes." A quite provocative response to this question was, "HAF's work is critical to reduce Hinduphobia—similar to what the Jewish and other minority religious groups face. Hindu self-loathing similar to Jewish self-loathing is also an unspoken reality, something I see even when I am at the temple. In fact, people who follow what I see as Hindu practices—both those in and out of the temple—rarely like to call themselves Hindu, based on my experiences."

Regarding the phenomenon that this respondent characterizes as "self-loathing," which manifests as persons who follow Hindu practices and adhere to a Hindu worldview not wishing to identify themselves as Hindu, in some cases, this phenomenon does indeed appear to be a result of a kind of self-loathing, or shame, resulting from the experiences of marginalization and ridicule to which many Hindus are subjected. In other cases, though, a desire not to self-identify as Hindu arises from impulses internal and integral to particular forms of Hindu thought toward identifying not with a limited concept from the realm of *nāma-rūpa*, or "name and form," but with the *ātman*, or universal self. Out of such philosophies arise the phenomenon in which many people who might otherwise be regarded as Hindu instead make statements like, "My religion is nonviolence" or "My religion is truth." A similar philosophical orientation characterizes the distinct but related phenomenon of the "Spiritual but Not Religious" movement in the United States: a sense of any identification with a finite identity—ethnic, national, or religious—as an impediment on the spiritual path. Given this deeper reality, a desire not to self-identify as Hindu should not always be taken as evidence of "self-loathing," even if this may sometimes be the case.

There is also an aversion among many to the kind of politicization to which Hindu identity has been subjected in India, such that identification as Hindu becomes conflated with adherence to the Hindutva or Hindu nationalist movement. For many, it is better to set aside the term *Hindu* than to be identified with such an ideology.

How do members of HAF respond to this concern? In response to the question, "What is your response to the criticism that the Hindu American Foundation is an extension of the Hindu nationalist movement into the American political scene, and that HAF is a Hindutva front organization?" a number of interesting responses were provided. One respondent said,

> It is interesting that Indian Christian, Muslim, Jain, and Sikh organizations are not asked if they are fronts for proselytizing, monopolistic, and other enterprises, including political ones. Those who took the initial lead to support and speak for Hindus happened to include members of the RSS and the VHP and given the fact that those two organizations had already been demonized in India by a whole host of Indian political and religious groups, it was easy to label Hindu activists here as Hindutva activists.

Another said, "It's laughable, so it's not worth a response. I think there has been a concerted effort to attach a stigma to the word Hindu." According to another,

> The first time I was accused of being a Hindu nationalist or Hindutva, I had to ask my husband, who was raised in Hyderabad, what it meant. I could sense it was

> derogatory, based on how it was used. I had been engaged in building community and seeking social justice for many years prior to joining HAF, wanting people to stop "othering." I had nothing to do with any kind of politics. It was all about my local and regional community, and helping weave the various aspects of who I am and what I come from, into my own identity. I am not Hindutva and neither is HAF a Hindutva front organization, if by that one means [it] seeks to make all Indians Hindu, or make India a 100% Hindu nation ... Several of us at HAF have been involved in various Hindu organizations—we work with people in these organizations due to an interest in the mission of that organization. None of the work that we do as part of these other organizations is related to or seeks to influence Indian politics. Just as HAF is non-partisan and critical of any elected official or public figure in the United States who says something in contradiction to our vision to promote pluralism and advocate for the Hindu community, we use the same rules when it is relevant to speak about issues in India or elsewhere in the world.

Finally, another said, "The Hindu American Foundation has no interest in the creation of a Hindu nation, which is what I understand a 'nationalist' movement to be, and nothing that we have said or done comes anywhere near implying we would ever be in support of such a thing."

HAF has pursued a number of initiatives, such as its study on caste and its statement in support of marriage equality, which have placed it at odds with at least some portions of the Hindu nationalist movement.[8] Regarding initiatives such as these, HAF members have said, "Hindu American Foundation clearly has a strong track record of taking independent positions—leftists and radicals throw the label Hindutva at HAF, and right-wing Hindus call HAF knee-jerk liberals! Yet the reality is that HAF is neither. The team at HAF thinks through positions that have nothing to do with the usual left-right paradigm present in India or the U.S., and therefore HAF rejects any labels."

The HAF report on caste—*Hinduism: Not Cast in Caste*—released in 2011, evoked quite a considerable backlash from many Hindus who saw it as an attack on Hinduism and who argued that HAF was a front group for anti-Hindu forces in the United States—an ironic charge when one takes into account allegations from the other end of the political spectrum that HAF is a front for Hindu nationalism, due to its involvement in the school textbook issue.

The brief on homosexuality, issued more recently, provoked much less backlash, although the issue of gay rights had emerged as a major dividing line in the Indian context. This more muted reaction was attributed by one HAF member whom I interviewed to the fact that Hindu acceptance of homosexuality has a stronger foundation in Hindu scriptures than the arguments advanced in the previous report on caste. Another noted humorously that those who might have otherwise been outraged by the report on homosexuality had in any case already given up on HAF after the caste report.

HAF exists within an American cultural and political milieu in which religious communities routinely advocate for acceptance and inclusion in American society, and in which minority religious communities, in particular, routinely argue for and affirm the values of tolerance and pluralism on which the United States was founded, but which it has embodied only imperfectly at each phase of its history: a prime example of what Jürgen Habermas calls the "incomplete project of modernity."[9]

Other Examples of Hindu Political Engagement in America

HAF is merely one example, although a particularly prominent one, of American Hindus becoming more deeply engaged in the American political system. It also illustrates the fact that what are regarded as "Hindu" issues can span the political spectrum.

Another prominent Hindu organization is the Sadhana Coalition. Sadhana—named after the Sanskrit term for spiritual practice—is dedicated to promoting progressive political causes from a Hindu perspective. Its mission and vision are rooted in the idea that Hindu values are inherently progressive:

> Since, 2011, Sadhana has been building a progressive Hindu movement. We practice our *sadhana*, or faith in action, by advocating for those social justice principles we believe are at the heart of Hinduism.[10]

The Hindu values on which Sadhana's vision is based are listed on its website as:

> *Ekatva*: Oneness of all
> *Ahimsa*: Nonviolence
> *Seva*: Service[11]

Sadhana Coalition is reflective of the fact that most Hindu engagement in American politics has occurred at the progressive end of the US political spectrum. Of the four American Hindus who have been elected as representatives to the US Congress—Tulsi Gabbard, Pramila Jayapal, Ro Khanna, and Raja Krishnamoorthi—all are members of the Democratic Party and three—Gabbard, Jayapal, and Khanna—are members of the Congressional Progressive Caucus. Jayapal is one of the Caucus's co-chairs. Jayapal, Khanna, and Krishnamoorthi are Indian American Hindus, whereas Gabbard, from Hawaii, is of "mixed" Irish American and Samoan American heritage. Her mother adopted a Vaiṣṇava Hindu tradition when Gabbard was a child. She was the first Hindu to be elected to Congress, taking her oath of office on a copy of the *Bhagavad Gītā*. As of this writing, she has recently announced her candidacy for the presidency of the United States. Significantly, while much of Hindu political activity in America has been, again, on the progressive end of the political spectrum, some Hindu activists and politicians—including Gabbard—have nevertheless been criticized for their perceived closeness to Hindu nationalist organizations in India. Whether such perceptions are fair or are an example of guilt by association is a matter of heated debate.

The emergence of assertive Hindu voices in American politics marks a new phase in the history of Hinduism in America. Hindus are increasingly asserting their agency and speaking for themselves. Even before the emergence of this trend, as we have seen, Hinduism had shaped the national consciousness of America in many and varied profound ways. Assuming this trend of engagement continues, Hindus will no doubt continue to shape the character of American life into the future, in ways yet unforeseen.

Study Questions

1. Why have some criticized the Hindu American Foundation for being a *Hindu* organization and not an Indian organization?
2. That stances has the Hindu American Foundation taken that clash with the ideology of Hindu nationalism?
3. Why do you think that American Hindus who have become involved in politics tend to identify with the progressive side of the American political spectrum?

Suggestions for Further Reading

Hindu American Foundation, "Coalition against Genocide: A Nexus of Hinduphobia Unveiled." http://www.hafsite.org/sites/default/files/Coalition_Against_Genocide_A_Nexus_of_HinduphobiaUnveiled.pdf, accessed September 18, 2016.

Hindu American Foundation, "HAF Policy Brief: Hinduism and Homosexuality." http://www.hafsite.org/media/pr/haf-policy-brief-hindusim-and-homosexuality, accessed September 18, 2016.

Hindu American Foundation, "Hinduism: Not Cast in Caste." http://www.hafsite.org/media/pr/hinduism-not-cast-caste-full-report, accessed September 18, 2016.

Hindu American Foundation, "Who We Are." http://www.hafsite.org/about-us/who-we-are, accessed September 18, 2016.

Pew Research Center. "How Racially Diverse Are US Religious Groups?" http://www.pewresearch.org/fact-tank/2015/07/27/the-most-and-least-racially-diverse-u-s-religious-groups/ft_15-07-23_religiondiversityindex-1/, accessed September 18, 2016.

Sadhana Coalition, "Our Mission, Vision, and Values." https://www.sadhana.org/mission-vision

Khyati Joshi, *New Roots in America's Sacred Ground* (New Brunswick, NJ: Rutgers University Press, 2006).

Vamsee Juluri, *Rearming Hinduism* (Chennai: Westland, 2014).

Prema Kurien, *A Place at the Multicultural Table* (New Brunswick, NJ: Rutgers, 2007).

Krishnan Ramaswamy, ed., *Invading the Sacred* (Kolkata: Rupa & Company, 2007).

John Zavos, ed., *Public Hinduisms* (Thousand Oaks, CA: Sage, 2012).

9

Conclusion

Chapter 9 Summary and Outline

This chapter consists of concluding reflections on the material that this book has explored. Having looked at its past and present, what might the future hold for Hinduism in America? What issues are Hindus in America likely to continue to face? And what contributions will they make to the consciousness of American society at large?

Hinduism and Hindus in America: Paradoxical Perceptions, Complex Realities

Despite the emergence of the phenomena that are explored in this book—a growing Hindu community of immigrants and converts, inheritors and adopters, Hindu-based organizations, the popularity of Hindu beliefs and practices, and the rise of an assertive Hindu voice in American political and social life—it is probably fair to say that Hinduism is one of the most misunderstood religions in America.

When coming across the terms *Hindu* and *Hinduism*, stereotyped images of "caste, cows, and curry"[1] spring to the minds of many Americans. Characteristics associated in the minds of many with Hinduism are negative—poverty, illiteracy, superstition, and an oppressive, exploitative priesthood. Many of these associations have long been promoted by Christian missionary groups seeking to advance conversion to Christianity in India. But they have also been promoted in the secular media, through films like *Slumdog Millionaire* and *Indiana Jones and the Temple of Doom*.

Because, as discussed earlier, the vast majority of the world's Hindus—93.2 percent—live in India, associations between Hinduism and India are strong. Perceptions of and attitudes toward the Hindu religion, therefore, often match closely with perceptions of and attitudes toward India. India is widely seen in America as a land of poverty. Many Americans' mental associations with India come from television ads that seek to raise money for Indian poverty relief. Many also think of the work of missionaries, such as Mother Theresa of Calcutta, and see Indians—and so Hindus—as poor, and as potential objects of charity and sympathy. Often, the blame for this situation is placed upon Hinduism, which, with its many deities and poorly understood customs, is seen as backward. Such perceptions are further fuelled by images in the popular media, such as the "white savior"—think of *Indiana Jones and the Temple of Doom*—who must rescue Hindus from themselves.

There is also a tendency among those Americans who know little about religions other than their own to conflate or confuse Hinduism with other traditions, such as Islam and Sikhism, which also have large South Asian followings. Often accompanied by racial bias, such a conflation also involves projecting onto Hindus and Sikhs many of the stereotypes and anxieties that are projected onto Islam: stereotypes of Muslims as violent and prone to terrorism. Both Hindus and Sikhs have been victims of hate crimes motivated by Islamophobia.[2]

Anti-Hindu bias, however, is not only found among the uneducated, or among the elements in American society from whom one might expect anti-minority violence to erupt. Many negative perceptions of Hinduism, or profound ignorance about it, can be found even among those who may be relatively open to Indian culture or to non-Western culture as a whole. Indeed, many Americans who have negative perceptions of Hinduism have a positive view of Buddhism, associating it with peace, nonviolence, wisdom, and a range of practices with scientifically proven benefits to mental and physical health, such as meditation and mindfulness. Yet Hindus and Buddhists share a great many common views and practices, and these two traditions are arguably far more alike than they are different, particularly when they are viewed against the background of the dominant Protestant Christian religious culture of the United States. The historical process through which stereotypes of religious traditions come to be widely held has resulted, it seems, in the case of Hinduism, in a more negative set of perceptions, and in the case of Buddhism, in largely positive ones. This is in spite of the extensive overlap which these two traditions share in belief, practice, and imagery.

To be sure, not all the perceptions of India and Hinduism are negative. India is also seen by some as a land of deep spirituality and ancient wisdom. It is fairly well known that the popular practice of yoga has its roots in India. Indian cuisine, textile arts, and jewelry are also popular, particularly in the more urban and cosmopolitan regions of America. India has also come to be seen, correctly, as an emerging economy, and Indians themselves as hardworking individuals who are dedicated to success. America's capitalist economy and Protestant traditions value these kinds of characteristics. At the same time, even "positive" stereotypes put pressure on Indian Americans, such as on students to be super intelligent and focused exclusively on academic success.

Often, positive perceptions of India are combined with a romanticizing attitude known as *orientalism*. This also has its problems. As conceived of by scholar Edward Said, orientalism is a way of projecting onto another group of people or another culture various anxieties that one has about oneself. One projects onto the other either positive things that one feels are lacking in one's own society, or negative things which *are* present, but which one wants to deny.[3] This is not, however, simply a matter of Westerners giving themselves emotional comfort. The discourses to which orientalism gives rise have profound implications for those on whom this projection occurs. And this, indeed, is its purpose. As Richard King notes, "Orientalism refers to those particular discourses that, in conceptualizing the Orient, render it susceptible to control and management."[4] Such discourses are not only a relic of the nineteenth century. They are very much alive and well in the American popular media and educational system.

Nonetheless, a recent Pew survey suggests that Americans generally hold a positive view of most major religions. And the differences in perceptions of Hinduism and Buddhism are shown to be relatively slight, with 60 percent of Americans viewing Buddhism positively and 58 percent viewing Hindu traditions positively. Interestingly, according to the same survey, a mere 61 percent of Americans view Evangelical Christianity positively—only 3 percent higher than Hinduism, and 1 percent higher than Buddhism. Atheism and Islam both fare the worst in this survey, with only 50 percent of Americans perceiving Atheism favorably and 48 percent—fewer than half—perceiving Islam favorably. The best regarded religions, according to this survey, are Judaism, with 67 percent approval; Roman Catholicism, at 66 percent; and mainline Protestantism, at 65 percent.[5]

The greatest paradox of the American perception of Hinduism rests with the fact that, in spite of some negative stereotypes or complete ignorance about it among many Americans, Hindu views and attitudes have come to infuse American culture over the course of the last century, of the kind Miller mentions in her essay, "We Are All Hindus Now." Growing numbers of Americans meditate and practice yoga, both practices with strong connections to Hinduism.[6]

Author Philip Goldberg has chronicled the infusion of Hindu concepts and practices into American consciousness in his book, *American Veda: From Emerson and the Beatles to Yoga and Meditation—How Indian Spirituality Changed the West*. With even greater precision than Miller, Goldberg identifies the following, specific teachings of Vedanta, the dominant system of modern Hindu philosophy, as having been adapted and absorbed, albeit often in new forms, into Western thinking:

1. Ultimate reality is both transcendent and immanent, both one and many; God can be conceived in both personal and non-personal terms, that is, as formless Absolute and in numerous forms and manifestations.
2. The infinite divine, while ineffable, has been given any number of names (Brahman, Allah, Lord, et cetera), descriptions, and attributes. A line from the *Ṛg Veda* (1.64.46) is frequently cited in this context: *Ekam sat bahudha vipra vadanti*, typically translated as "Truth is one, the wise call it by many names" and sometimes summarized as "One Truth, many paths."

3. The Ground of Being is also the essential nature of the Self. In the *mahavakyas* (great utterances) of the Upanishads [later Vedic scriptures] we read: *Ayam Atma Brahma*, or "This Self is Brahman," and *Tat Tvam Asi*, or "Thou art That."
4. Our innate unity with divinity is obscured by ignorance: we identify with our individual egos, when our true identity is the transcendent Self (which is Atman, which is Brahman).
5. Individuals can awaken to their divine nature through any number of pathways and practices: no single one is right for everyone.
6. Spirituality is a developmental process, moving through a progressive series of stages; tangible benefits—joy, compassion, wisdom, peace—accrue in each.
7. Fully realizing one's true nature brings an end to suffering in the state of liberation or enlightenment called *moksha*.[7]

Clearly, the average American has not adopted Sanskrit terminology—words such as *Atman* and *Brahman* and *moksha*—or taken to citing the *mahāvākyas* of the Upaniṣads. But, as Goldberg explains, these ideas have been translated into the following set of attitudes, again, as demonstrated in a wide array of opinion polls from highly reputed organizations, "such as Gallup, Harris, and Pew; academic institutions like Princeton's Center for the Study of Religion … and media outlets from *Newsweek* to Beliefnet.com":

1. *Spiritual independence*. One Gallup survey asked, "Do you think of spirituality more in a personal and individual sense or more in terms of organized religion and church doctrine?" Almost three-quarters opted for "personal and individual."
2. *Direct experience*. A 2005 Newsweek/Beliefnet survey asked respondents, "Why do you practice religion?" The most frequent answer (39 percent) was "To forge a personal relationship with God."
3. *Tolerance*. Exclusivism is in decline; pluralism is in the ascendancy. A 2008 Pew Research Center survey found that [65] percent of Americans agreed that "many religions can lead to eternal life."
4. *Fluidity*. Princeton sociologist Robert Wuthnow has identified a shift from a "dwelling spirituality," in which "a spiritual habitat defines one's relationship to God," to a "seeking spirituality," where "we seek God in many different venues."
5. *Nonliteralism*. Wuthnow says that the number of people who believe the Bible is the literal word of God has "dropped remarkably since the 1960s."
6. *A different kind of God*. Over 80 percent of Americans check "yes" when asked if they believe in God. But increasingly they see God as an abstract, non-personal force or intelligence, as opposed to an anthropomorphic deity.[8]

America is, of course, a large country, with a highly diverse population, and, as one might expect, a correspondingly diverse set of attitudes. Thus, American interest in and openness to Indian ideas have co-existed with often bitter racism against actual Indians.

Indian immigration to the United States in the nineteenth century was relatively limited. It increased, though, near the century's end, and in the early years of the twentieth century. Most of the Indian immigrants to the United States—much as in the Caribbean region—came to America to work as laborers, particularly in the state of California. It is believed that most of these immigrants were, in fact, Sikh, but they were referred to as "Hindoo," with this term acting as an ethnic designation.

There was a racist backlash against immigrants from Asian countries—not only India, but also China and Japan—early in the twentieth century. Bias against Indian immigrants, in particular, was reflected in the notorious Bellingham Riots of 1907. The backlash against Asian immigrants culminated with the Asian Exclusion Act of 1924. This act greatly curtailed Indian immigration, permitting only a handful of students and scholars to enter the country. The Asian Exclusion Act was finally lifted only in the 1960s, with the passage by the US Congress of the Immigration and Nationality Act of 1965 (an act which actually took effect in 1968). The passage of this act can be seen as part of the broader cultural shift that was also reflected in the Civil Rights Act of 1964.

Interestingly, the passage of the Civil Rights Act, which ended the racial segregation laws of the American south, would likely not have happened without the efforts of the African American Civil Rights movement, led by Martin Luther King, Jr. King's renowned movement of nonviolent social protest was directly inspired by the nonviolent movement for Indian independence from the British Empire, led by Mohandas K. Gandhi—known as Mahatma, or "Great Soul," to his admirers. King's movement, inspired by a Hindu, helped to create the conditions which made it possible for Hindus once again to come to America.

It was after 1968, with the lifting of immigration restrictions, that relatively large numbers of people from India began to settle in North America, thus laying the foundations for today's Hindu American community. The 1960s were, of course, also a period which was marked by a strong interest in Hinduism among many Americans, due to the rise of the counterculture.[9] This led to yet another cultural shift, in which Hindus could be embraced as part of American life. In the 1970s, construction of Hindu temples began in many US cities, a process which accelerated in the 1980s. Such temples are increasingly accepted as a regular feature of the American landscape.

How well have Hindus fit into North American society and culture? Despite stereotypical associations of Hinduism with poverty, American Hindus make up one of the wealthiest religious communities in the United States, second only to the Jewish community.[10] American Hindus are also one of the best educated communities in the United States, with roughly 48 percent holding postgraduate degrees.[11] American Hindus are also increasingly taking leadership roles in political and cultural spheres. There are currently four Hindu members of the United States House of Representatives, one of whom—Tulsi Gabbard, a Democrat from Hawaii—is running for president.

It can therefore be said that, despite certain struggles—such as hate crimes, and ever-present concerns about possible anti-immigrant backlashes, as well as religious prejudice against minority traditions in general—the American Hindu community has been, on the whole, quite successful at assimilating and finding a home in America. At the same time, doubts have been raised by some as to whether this assimilation has come at the price of a surrendering of identity, a "domestication" of Indianness to fit in with dominant white American sensibilities.

As primarily a community of immigrants, American Hindus, in many ways, fit the ideal of a "model minority"—highly successful in both the economic and academic arenas. Indeed, a newer set of stereotypes of Hindus in America—and of Indians more generally—is based on the reality of everyday encounters with Indian doctors, computer experts, and business professionals: the Indian as hyper-intelligent overachiever. Although, in some ways, an improvement over older stereotypes of ignorance and poverty, these newer stereotypes carry with them their own pressures, and their own destructive effects on the people who are thus stereotyped. The "model minority" concept, as pointed out by Vijay Prashad, is also used to oppress other minorities, like African Americans, who are viewed as something less than a "model":

> The "model minority" thesis ... says that some "minorities" are able through their own efforts (that is, without state support) to be socially mobile, whereas others seem to be constitutionally unable to do so. In the mid-1960s, the former included east Asians and the latter the blacks. The Chinese, once fundamentally oppressed by white supremacy, are transformed in the context of the Black Liberation movement into a pliant and worthy "minority." Chinatown was a colony prior to the 1960s, not an ethnic arcade for tourists. Only when the Chinese became a "model" did Chinatown itself become a place to eat and stroll.[12]

Essentially, being designated a "model minority" means that a particular ethnic group has managed to assimilate itself to the dominant (white) society of the United States, without creating the kind of discomfort elicited when minority groups stand up for their rights, as in the case of the Black Liberation movement to which Prashad refers. There is also an irony in Indian Americans being designated a "model minority," precisely because many young Indian Americans do not so much identify with the dominant white culture as with African American popular culture:

> Some young desis [people of Indian origin] ... do not find the model minority category useful in their social lives. Children of the technoprofessionals are expected to identify with white, bourgeois values, but, says Uttam Tambar, if you hail from the working class or urban petty bourgeoisie, "you identified with black culture." Ravi Dixit, a young desi from Boston who attended the Youth Solidarity Summer of 1997, noted that "for many South Asians, myself included, city life and culture have been the most welcoming and adaptable culture in the United States. Of course, Hip-Hop is definitely more of a medium of living and expression for people of color and I, being Indian, feel more like a person of color than white."[13]

Hindu Identity and Hindu Influence

Certainly, the experiences of Hindu immigrants in America and of American seekers drawn to Hinduism are distinct cultural worlds, and have generally been treated as such in the scholarship of those who have taken up this field of study. Studies of the Indian diaspora rarely have occasion to mention, except perhaps in passing, the phenomenon of non-Indians who take up Hindu practice, or who follow Hindu-based or Hindu-inspired ways of life. Similarly, the studies of communities centered around particular yoga practices, or the teachings of charismatic figures of Indian origin—communities that typically have a largely non-Indian membership—rarely engage with phenomena such as Hindu temples or Hindu communities in America made up largely of diasporic Indians.

Not only are these cultural worlds distinct; they also sometimes clash. People who wish to preserve an ancient tradition (its inheritors) and people who want to explore and experiment (its adopters)—even if this means going against the dominant views and customs of the society in which they were raised—often have very different temperaments and goals. Inheritors of a tradition are concerned with preserving a culture. Adopters of a tradition—and this is certainly the case of many adopters of Hinduism in America—are often engaged in a countercultural move, especially if the tradition they adopt is seen as far from the mainstream of their culture of origin.

The convergence of worlds this book has explored has not always been a smooth, easy, or harmonious process. There are plenty of stories of insensitive Western seekers who have outraged or offended Hindus by birth by treating certain ideas or practices in a way indicative of arrogance and disdain, thus leading to a situation in which such seekers are regarded, quite rightly, with suspicion. There are also plenty of stories of Western seekers who have found their spiritual quest stymied in settings where the focus was not so much on philosophy or meditation as the correct performance of ritual, or the preservation of cultural forms like language, song, and dance.

While distinct, however, the phenomena of diasporic Hinduism and of Westerners inspired by Hinduism are not altogether unrelated. Both could be seen as iterations of the larger, complex phenomenon of Hinduism in America, and of the transformation of American society and culture by the presence in it both of Hindus and of Hindu ideas and practices which have gained purchase far beyond the community that goes by this name. While specific studies on diasporic Hindus and Hindu-inspired practitioners generally remain distinct, the North American Hinduism unit of the American Academy of Religion has long sponsored panel discussions on both, thus acknowledging that this field encompasses and includes both of these phenomena. While they are clearly distinct, they are not entirely separable.

"Hinduism in America," therefore, as it has been understood in this book, does not refer solely to the ideas and practices of those who identify themselves as Hindu. These form, one could say, the core or center of the topic under discussion. But it also refers to the totality of ideas and practices that can be traced, ultimately, to Hindu traditions, whether or not those who adhere to these ideas and practices identify themselves with the label *Hindu*.

It also refers to the wider Indian American experience. Hindus, as mentioned earlier, make up about 70 percent of Americans who identify as Indian, or *Asian Indian* (a terminology coined in the United States census to differentiate persons of South Asian origin from Native Americans, who are also referred to as *Indians*). The experiences of most American Hindus are experiences shared by those American Muslims, Christians, Sikhs, Jains, and others who have come from India. More broadly speaking, they are the experiences of minorities and people of color more broadly who daily have to navigate the realities of American life.

How to approach the topic of Hinduism in America is a potentially sensitive issue because, as with all discussion of religion, it touches upon questions of identity. My aim in this book has not been to appropriate people into a religious identity they do not wish to claim for themselves: to say that "We're all Hindus now." It is, rather, to acknowledge the religious provenance of ideas and practices which have come to define the American cultural landscape in ways that resonate far beyond the community of those who identify themselves as Hindu. Although not all people who adhere to these ideas and practices identify themselves as Hindu, they nonetheless participate, to varying degrees, in the larger phenomenon of Hinduism in America under discussion here.

The approach I have taken, although it will certainly not satisfy everyone involved in this conversation, is an attempt to accommodate both sides of what has become a polarizing issue in regard to Hindu thought and practice in the Western world. On the one hand, there is the view of many Western practitioners that the teachings and practices to which they adhere are not Hindu, in the sense of belonging to a particular community or culture, but are universal, and available for everyone to experience, explore, and, in some cases, experiment with. Many Indian masters who brought their teachings to America, beginning with Swami Vivekananda in 1893, presented these teachings as a universal philosophy, available to all, and not as something specifically Hindu or meant only for Hindus.[14] Their disciples have continued in this vein. On the other hand, there is the view that the Westerners who take up these ideas and practices without acknowledging their traditional sources are engaging in *cultural appropriation*. Such appropriation—taking up practices and ideas in which one finds value from another culture and identifying them as one's own without acknowledging the source of these ideas, and possibly even treating that source with contempt or disdain—is a form of neo-colonialism, an ongoing act of violence by the West against other cultures.

The approach adopted in this book acknowledges the freedom of practitioners to adopt and interpret ideas and practices as they see fit, while simultaneously acknowledging the fact that many ideas and practices that are now widespread in contemporary American society are Hindu in origin, or at least that one can discern elements of Hinduism in their genealogies. The attempt is to avoid the erasure of Hinduism that characterizes cultural appropriation, while honoring the freedom of people to adopt a practice or a worldview that suits them. Denying Hindu ties to yoga, for example, is cultural appropriation, and is mistaken. But there are also no "yoga police" tasked with ensuring that yoga be done in a Hindu fashion—whatever that might mean—nor should there be (although it could certainly be argued that there are plenty of people who see themselves as yoga police, or who aspire to this role). Insisting that all those who practice yoga are, in some sense, Hindu, is to do violence to their right to define themselves religiously and culturally, and also to deny the many contributions of other traditions, like Jainism and Buddhism, to the development of yoga through the centuries.

At the same time, though, seeking to downplay, or even to erase, the fact that many of the ideas and practices in question either originated in or have been deeply shaped by Hindu traditions does a disservice not only to the Hindu communities whose traditions are being thus appropriated, but also to Western practitioners themselves, who thereby miss out on the historical, cultural, and spiritual depth of the practices they are seeking to appropriate. Why would someone *not* want to have as rich and in-depth an understanding of the sources of one's practice as possible, and thereby deprive oneself of a potential deepening of one's experiences? What could be behind such a move?

It is a move that is not only puzzling, but that raises questions of political motivation. What lies behind attempts to downplay or disregard Hindu contributions to many popular ideas in the West? Is it racism? Or a paternalistic or supremacist attitude toward those who are still regarded by some as practicing a "heathen" religion? Or is it a suspicion of religion and religious labels in general? Or is it some combination of all of these? Finally, just like identifying all who take up these ideas and practices as Hindu when they are not, erasure or denial of the Hindu origins of or contributions to these ideas and practices results in a factually inaccurate and impoverished picture of reality. It does not help that there are supremacist ideologies operating on both "sides" of this conversation: those who downplay or seek to erase Hinduism and those who wish to promote it *exclusively*.

Similarly, and as already noted, many practitioners of yoga traditions brought to America by Indian Hindu masters do not regard themselves as Hindu. They either accept the widespread identification of being Hindu with being Indian and do not wish to show disrespect, or identify themselves as "spiritual" rather than "religious," seeing *Hindu* as a religious label. Some might question why a book on Hinduism in America deals with non-Indians at all, if *Hindu* equals *Indian*. Non-Indian practitioners in various Hindu-inspired lineages might also wonder why their beliefs and practices have been included in this book.

Some traditions described in this book which have non-Hindu adherents are nevertheless derived or drawn from specific and identifiable Hindu traditions, and have typically had founders who did identify as Hindu, even as they presented their teachings as universal, and in some cases, as scientific. We have categorized such traditions as "Hindu-Inspired Meditation Movements" or "HIMMs," following Lola Williamson's coinage of this term, who developed it precisely to draw a distinction between these traditions and Hinduism—for they are, indeed, distinct.[15]

These traditions, though, have been included in this book because, even as one maintains the distinction between them and what may be called Hinduism proper, HIMMs nevertheless form an important part of the cultural context in which Hinduism in America exists. The reception of immigrant Hindus in America—the willingness or unwillingness of a community to, for example, accept the construction of a Hindu temple in its midst—has been, to some extent, shaped by prior perceptions of Hinduism as mediated by HIMMs: perceptions of yoga, chanting of mantras, vegetarianism, and so on. In other words, even if HIMMs are not, technically speaking, part of Hinduism per se (based upon the self-identifications of their adherents), they *are* part of the phenomenon of Hinduism in America taken in its totality, which is the subject of this book.

HIMMs have also been included in this book because, even as one might wish to maintain and respect the distinction between these movements and Hinduism as traditionally understood, and as important as this distinction is to the self-understandings of both Hindus and adherents of HIMMs, it is a distinction that is increasingly collapsing in practice.

Why is this the case? This is because growing numbers of second- and third-generation Indian Hindu Americans are turning to non-Indian teachers and Hindu-inspired organizations with large non-Indian followings for their understanding of authentic Hindu thought and practice. At the same time, more non-Indian adherents of these traditions are embracing the term *Hindu*. So an excessively sharp distinction between what is Hindu and what is Hindu-inspired seems to be misplaced. The increasingly common fact, furthermore, of intermarriage between South Asian Hindus and Westerners drawn to Hinduism is also leading to a gradual erasure of any kind of sharp or absolute distinction between the inheritors of Hinduism and Western seekers or adopters of this tradition. An excessive focus on who is Indian and who is Western, or who is Hindu and who is "Hindu-inspired," can lead to categorizations to which many practitioners simply cannot relate, and which run the risk of doing violence to their subjectivity: their understanding of themselves both as complex human beings and as participants in a spiritual tradition.

As with Hinduism globally, a too-excessive focus on defining groups of people in mutually exclusive terms is, in this case, misguided. Worlds are converging, and people define themselves and their traditions in myriad ways in the process. In the words of Mahatma Gandhi, "In reality, there are as many religions as there are individuals."[16] All of these can be respected even as the process itself is treated as a singular phenomenon.

Concluding Reflections

Having reflected on the past and present of Hinduism in America, what might we be able to say about its future? We have seen, in this book, that the American response to Hinduism has been characterized by ambivalence. On the one hand, there are Americans who have enthusiastically welcomed their Hindu neighbors, and some who have taken up Hindu-inspired practices, or who have adopted a Hindu religious identity, making the American Hindu community increasingly a multi-ethnic one. Indians more broadly have at the same time experienced vicious racism, even to the point of being excluded from the country and having their citizenship stripped from them. The violence Indians have suffered in America has ranged from brutal physical attacks to the subtler, but nonetheless destructive, stereotypes perpetuated in the popular media.

One suspects that, much like other ethnic and religious minorities, Hindus in America will still struggle for acceptance in the future, but that this struggle will be rewarded as Hindus come to be seen by most Americans as a natural part of the American cultural and religious environment, as other minorities have found acceptance as well. It is possible that an American Hindu president will be a reality at some point in the future. While Tulsi Gabbard has not, as of this writing, risen to the status of a frontrunner, the fact that a Hindu has emerged as a candidate for the nomination of one of the two major American political parties is certainly a sign of progress. Just as Barack Obama's presidency did not mark the end of the struggles of African Americans—but was still an important moment in the nation's history, as it was shown that an African American *could* rise to this coveted role—even a Hindu president would not mark the end of prejudice against either Hindus or Indians. It would show, though, the resilience and adaptability of Hinduism, as not a tradition confined to just one country, but as a truly global tradition, and of America, as a country where ideals such as openness and acceptance, even if they are often not fully realized, nevertheless continue to play an important role in shaping the trajectory of its history.

Mention was made in our discussion of an emerging political activism among Hindus of Jürgen Habermas's concept of the "incomplete project of modernity."[17] One can hope that Hindu Americans, drawing upon Hindu ideals such as those espoused by the Sadhana Coalition, will help to bring the modern project ever closer to completion: to embody the ideals of freedom, equality, and community. But might the presence of Hinduism in America lead to a transformation even more profound than this?

Ann Gleig and Scott Mitchell, in their respective writings on Buddhism in America, have conceptualized the emergence of American Buddhism in terms of wider questions of modernity and postmodernity.[18] At their most basic modernity and postmodernity, as well as premodernity, are modes of being based on differing ideas of what counts as knowledge. In the premodern mode, knowledge is typically based upon the authority of something external to oneself: a sacred text or institution or authoritative teacher. Medieval Europe can be characterized as a premodern society, in which the Church was the ultimate arbiter of what was true and what was false. Modernity, which is often characterized as a reaction to premodernity, locates knowledge in reason reflecting on experience, represented paradigmatically by the scientific method. It is modernity which has given risen to modern science, constitutional democratic government, and concepts such as human rights. Postmodernity is seen either as a critical, questioning moment within modernity, or as an entirely new paradigm, in which the sovereignty of reason over all aspects of life has come into question, particularly in light of a technocratic civilization which can be insensitive to the needs of living human beings, or even worse, put in the service of projects like colonialism and genocide.

What Gleig and Mitchell both suggest, in different ways, about Buddhism in America can certainly be said of Hinduism in America as well: that this emergent tradition, drawing from the elements of multiple civilizations, might not only contribute to, but also challenge, deepen, and transform such notions as *modern*, *premodern*, and *postmodern*, pointing to new ways of being human and expressing human creativity and freedom.

At the heart of both Hinduism and Buddhism, as at the heart of Western thought at its best, is an aspiration for freedom, for liberation from the limitations which bind us, be they political, social, or spiritual. And freedom has of course long been upheld as a central American ideal—even, again, when it has not been fully realized, or even militated against by forces of racism, patriarchy, and privilege. The convergence of the worlds of immigrant Hindus, bringing with them the ideals and values that have shaped Indian civilization, and Western seekers, chafing against the limits of their inherited traditions—and yet indelibly shaped by those same traditions—has already led to the creative transformation of both worlds, as well as involving challenges and struggles. What may the future hold? Perhaps a hint can be found in the words of Swami Vivekananda, "This freedom that distinguishes us from mere machines is what we are all striving for. To be more free is the goal of all our efforts, for only in perfect freedom can there be perfection."[19]

Appendix: Hindu Temples and Organizations in the United States

It is likely that this list is incomplete, given the pace at which Hindu communities are emerging in the United States, and the fact that Hindu organizations can range from small gatherings in homes of devotees to massive temples with thousands of members. This list was compiled by means of a lengthy and in-depth internet search carried out by my research assistant, Loretto Taylor, as well as through my own interactions with some of the smaller organizations that do not yet have a web presence. It does give a fairly good sense of which states have the highest concentrations of Hindu temples and Hindu-inspired organizations. Based on our research, only two states in the United States—North Dakota and Wyoming—have no Hindu temples, although further research could prove that temples or temple communities exist that we have overlooked in these states, due to their not having had a web presence at the time our research was done.

Alabama

BAPS Shri Swaminarayan Mandir, Birmingham
Birmingham Hindu Temple and Cultural Center
Hindu Cultural Center of North Alabama

Alaska

Sri Ganesha Mandir of Alaska

Arizona

Arizona Hindu Temple, Scottsdale
BAPS Shri Swaminarayan Mandir, Phoenix
Ekta Mandir
Hindu Temple of Arizona
Maha Ganapati Temple of Arizona
Shirdi Saibaba Temple, Arizona
Sri Venkatakrishna Kshetra Temple

Arkansas

Hindu Association of Northwest Arkansas

California

Balaji Temple, San Jose
BAPS Shri Swaminarayan Mandir, Los Angeles
East Bay Hindu Community Center
Hare Krishna Temple of San Jose
Hare Krishna Temple of Soquel (Santa Cruz)
Hayward Hindu Temple
Hindu Temple of Antelope Valley
Hindu Temple of Fresno
Hindu Temple of Kern County
Hindu Temple, Ventura County
Kali Mandir in Laguna Beach
Krishna Valley Temple
Malibu Hindu Temple
Mandir, Irvine, California
Nithyanandeshwara Hindu Temple, Los Angeles
Pasadena Hindu Temple
Pittsburg, California Hindu Temple
Sanatan Mandir, San Bruno
Santa Barbara Temple, Vedanta Society of Southern California
Saratoga Hindu Temple and Community Center
Shiva Murugan Temple
Shiva-Vishnu Temple, Livermore
Shri Lakshmi Narayan Mandir
Shri Nand Shiv Durga Mandir
Sri Satyanarayana Swamy Devasthanam
Sri Siddhi Vinayaka Cultural Center, Sacramento
Sunnyvale Hindu Temple and Community
Vallejo Hindu Temple
Valley Hindu Temple, Northridge
Vedanta Society of Northern California, San Francisco
Vedanta Society of Southern California, Hollywood
Vedic Dharma Samāj, Fremont Hindu Temple

Colorado

Hindu Temple and Cultural Center of the Rockies
Hindu Temple of Colorado
Sanatan Mandir Colorado, Hindu Temple, Cultural and Community Center
Shirdi Sai of Rockies

Shiva Sai Mandir
Sri Venkateswara Temple of Colorado

Connecticut

Connecticut Valley Hindu Temple Society
Hindu Cultural Center
ISKCON Connecticut
Shri Shirdi Sai Temple of Connecticut
Vaishnav Parivar of Connecticut
Wilton Hindu Temple

Delaware

Hindu Temple of Delaware

Florida

Alachua Hare Krishna Temple
Hindu Devi Temple
Hindu Society of North East Florida
Hindu Temple of Central Florida
Hindu Temple of Florida
Hindu Temple of Southwest Florida
Miami Lakshmi Narayan Mandir
Palm Beach Hindu Mandir
Sanatan Mandir, Tampa
Shivadham Hindu Temple, Orlando
South Florida Hindu Temple
Sri Shirdi Sai Society of North East Florida
Vedic Cultural Society Hindu Temple of Fort Pierce
Vishnu Mandir, Tampa

Georgia

Ambaji USA Shree Shakti Mandir
BAPS Shri Swaminarayan Mandir, Atlanta
Cartersville Ram Mandir
Columbus Indian Temple
Ganesha Temple in Atlanta
Hare Krishna Temple of Atlanta
Hindu Temple of Atlanta
Hindu Temple of Dunwoody Parivaar
Hindu Temple of Georgia, Atlanta Darpan
Hindu Temple Society of Augusta
North American Shirdi Sai Temple of Atlanta

Sanatan Mandir Atlanta
Shiv Temple
Sri Hanuman Mandir
Sri Mahalakshmi Temple of Atlanta
Sri Sai Ram Temple

Hawaii

Hawaii Hindu Temple
Kauai's Hindu Monastery and Himalayan Academy
New Navadvipa Dhama, Temple of the Pancatattva

Idaho

Hare Krishna Temple and Vedic Cultural Center

Illinois

Balaji Temple, Sri Venkateswara Temple
BAPS Shri Swaminarayan Mandir, Chicago
Chicago SVS Hindu Temple, Aurora
Hanuman Temple of Greater Chicago
Hindu Mandir of Lake County
Hindu Temple and Cultural Society of Central Illinois
Hindu Temple of Greater Chicago
ISKCON Chicago, Hare Krishna Temple
ISKCON Temple of Greater Chicago, Naperville
Manav Seva Mandir Temple, Hindu Sanatan Mandir in Chicago
Sai Samsthan of Central Illinois
Shivalya Hindu Cultural Center
Shree Swaminarayan Temple
Sri Venkateswara Temple
Vaishnav Samāj of Midwest
Vedanta Society of Chicago

Indiana

BAPS Shri Swaminarayan Mandir, Indianapolis
Bharatiya Temple and Cultural Center of Greater Lafayette
Bharatiya Temple of Northwest Indiana
Hindu Society of Southern Indiana
Hindu Temple of Central Indiana
Hindu Temple of Michiana
Omkaar Temple
Sathya Sai Baba Center of Indianapolis
Sri Venkateswara Temple
Tri State Hindu Temple, Newburgh

Iowa

Hindu Temple and Cultural Center
Hindu Temple Association of Eastern Iowa
Sri Devi Mandir

Kansas

BAPS Shri Swaminarayan Mandir, Kansas City
Hindu Temple and Cultural Center of Kansas City
Hindu Temple of Greater Wichita

Kentucky

Bharatiya Temple and Cultural Center
Hindu Temple of Kentucky

Louisiana

Bharatiya Temple and Cultural Center of Greater Lafayette
Datta Temple
Hindu Temple of New Orleans
Hindu Vedic Society, Baton Rouge
ISKCON New Orleans
Sadhu Vaswani Hindu Cultural Center and Hindu Temple

Maine

Maine Hindu Temple

Maryland

Greater Baltimore Temple
Greater DC Vedanta Society
Murugan Temple of North America
Hindu Temple of Metropolitan Washington
Shri Mangal Mandir
Shri Radha Krishna Mandir
Sri Bhaktha Anjaneya Temple
Sri Siva Vishnu Temple, Lanham
Washington Kali Temple, Burtonsville

Massachusetts

Global Network of BAPS Mandirs in USA, Fall River
Hindu Temple of Massachusetts
ISKCON Boston
NESSP—A Community at the Shirdi Sai Baba Temple and Mission

Ramakrishna Vedanta Society, Boston
Sarva Dev Mandir
Shivalaya Temple of Greater Boston
Shree Umiya Mataji Mandir
Shri Dwarkamai
Shri Gurusthan-Shri Shirdi Sai Temple
Shri Sai Chavadi
Siddha Lalitha Peetham
Springfield Temple
Sri Chinmaya Maruti Temple
Sri Lakshmi Temple
Sri Radha Bhakti
Vedanta Centre, Cohasset

Michigan

Bharatiya Temple of Lansing
Bharatiya Temple of Metropolitan Detroit
Hindu Temple of Canton
ISKCON Michigan
Kasi Temple of Flint
Parashakthi Amman Temple in Pontiac
Sri Shirdi Saibaba Temple
Sri Venkateswara Temple and Cultural Center
Tri-City Hindu Temple
West Michigan Hindu Temple

Minnesota

Hindu Samāj Temple, Minnesota
Hindu Temple of Minnesota
Minnesota Hindu Dharmic Sabha, Vishnu Mandir Minnesota
Sri Saibaba Mandir
Sri Venkateswara (Balaji) Temple

Mississippi

BAPS Shri Swaminarayan Mandir, Jackson
Hindu Temple Society of Mississippi
ISKCON New Talavan Farm Community

Missouri

BAPS Shri Swaminarayan Mandir, St. Louis
Hindu Temple of St. Louis

Shanthi Mandir
Vedanta Society of Kansas City
Vedanta Society of St. Louis

Montana

Hindu Society of Montana

Nebraska

Balvihar of Omaha
Hindu Temple of Omaha
Sai Nebraska

Nevada

Hindu Temple of Las Vegas
Hindu Temple of Northern Nevada
ISKCON of Las Vegas
Las Vegas Hindu-Jain Temple

New Hampshire

Hindu Temple of New Hampshire

New Jersey

Adyapeath USA, Dakshineswar Ramkrishna Sangha Adyapeath
BAPS Shri Swaminarayan Mandir, Robbinsville
Hindu Samāj Temple of Mahwah
India Temple Association, Berlin
ISKCON of New Jersey
Shirdi Sai Cultural and Community Center
Shree Ram Mandir
Shree Swaminarayan Temple
Shri Krishna Vrundavana, Edison
Sri Guruvayurappan Temple
Sri Venkateswara Temple
Vaikunth Hindu Jain Temple

New Mexico

Amma Center of New Mexico
Hindu Temple Society of New Mexico
Neem Karoli Baba Ashram

New York

Asa'Mai Hindu Temple
Bhakti Center
Bharatiya Mandir, Middletown
Hindu Center Temple, Flushing
Hindu Cultural Society of Western New York
Hindu Mandir of Central New York
Hindu Temple and Cultural Center, Albany
Hindu Temple of Rochester
Hindu Temple, Staten Island
Mahavallabha Ganapathi Devasthanam
Mandir, Holi New York
New York Kali Mandir
Radha Govind Dham, New York
Ramakrishna-Vivekananda Center, New York (Upper East Side)
Shirdi Saibaba Temple, Flushing
Shiva Mandir
Tulsi Mandir
Vedanta Society of New York (Upper West Side)

North Carolina

BAPS, Shri Swaminarayan Mandir, Raleigh
Hindu Bhavan of Fayetteville
Hindu Center of Charlotte
Hindu Society of North Carolina (HSNC) Temple
Hindu Temple of Triad
ISKCON NC, New Goloka
Mata Hindu Temple
Mount Soma, North Carolina Vedic Community
Prabhupada Village
Sri Sathya Sai Baba Center (Greensboro)
Sri Shirdi Sai Baba Mandir of North Carolina
Sri Venkateswara Temple of North Carolina

North Dakota

None currently listed.

Ohio

BAPS Shri Swaminarayan Mandir, Columbus
Bharatiya Hindu Temple
Columbus Indian Temple

Hindu Temple of Canton
Hindu Temple of Dayton
Hindu Temple of Toledo
Jain Center of Central Ohio
Nithyananda Vedic Temple
Shiva Vishnu Temple of Greater Cleveland
Shree Swaminarayan Temple, Strongsville
Sree Venkateswara (Balaji) Temple
Sri Lakshmi Ganapathi Temple and Hindu Cultural Center of Ohio
Sri Lakshmi Narayan (SLN) Temple, Youngstown
Sri Sai Baba Mandir
Sri Sai Baba Temple of Greater Cincinnati

Oklahoma

BAPS, Shri Swaminarayan Mandir, Oklahoma
Hindu Temple of Oklahoma City
Oklahoma Nithyanandeshwara Hindu Temple

Oregon

Arsha Vijñana Gurukulam-Arsha Vijñana Mandiram
Global Network of BAPS Mandirs in USA, Portland
International Society for Krishna Consciousness, Portland
Portland Balaji Temple
Portland Hindu Temple
Portland Shirdi Saibaba Temple
Swaminarayan Hindu Temple
Vedanta Society of Portland

Pennsylvania

BAPS Shri Swaminarayan Mandir, Harrisburg
Bharatiya Temple
Bhavani Temple
Hindu American Religious Institute (HARI) Temple
Hindu Jain Temple of Pittsburgh
ISKCON Harrisburg
ISKCON Philadelphia, Mt. Airy Radha Krishna Temple
Lehigh Valley Hindu Temple Society, Allentown
Organization for Hindu Religion and Culture (Bhutanese Hindu Temple), Harrisburg
Sai Temple PA
Samarpan Hindu Temple
Sarada Sangha, Philadelphia (Vedanta Society)
Sri Venkateswara Temple, Pittsburgh

Sringeri Vidya Bharati Foundation (SVBF), Stroudsburg
Vedanta Society of Central Pennsylvania
Vedanta Society of Pittsburgh
Vraj Mandir, Schuylkill Haven

Rhode Island

Rhode Island Hindu Temple Society
Vedanta Society of Providence

South Carolina

BAPS Shri Swaminarayan Mandir, Orangeburg
Hindu Temple and Cultural Center of South Carolina
Vedic Center of Greenville

South Dakota

Hindu Temple of Siouxland

Tennessee

BAPS Shri Swaminarayan Mandir, Nashville
Hindu Temple of Chattanooga
Regional Indian American Community Center
Sanatan Mandir
Sri Ganesha Temple (Hindu Cultural Center and Temple), Nashville

Texas

Austin Hindu Temple and Community Center
BAPS Shri Swaminarayan Mandir, Houston
Chinmaya Mission, Beaumont
DFW Hindu Temple Mandir, Ekta Mandir, Irving
Flower Mound Hindu Temple
Fort Worth Hindu Temple and Community Center
Hindu Association of West Texas
Hindu Society of Brazos Valley
Hindu Temple of Amarillo
Hindu Temple of Central Texas
Hindu Temple of Frisco
Hindu Temple of Lubbock, Texas
Hindu Temple of San Antonio
Hindu Temple of the Woodlands
Hindu Worship Society, Houston
Karya Siddhi Hanuman at Frisco

Lakshmi Narayan Mandir of North Houston
North Texas Hindu Mandir
Radha Kalachandji, Hare Krishna Temple
Radha Krishna Mandir
Radha Krishna Temple in Dallas-Hindu Temple in Dallas
Radha Madhav Dham
Sai Durga Shiva Venkateswara Temple
Sanatan Shiv Shakti Mandir
Shirdi Sai Center of Texas
Shirdisai Sannidhi, North Texas Hindu Society
Shiva Vishnu Temple of Texas
Shri Nanak Center
Shri Radha Krishna Temple
Sri Ganesha Temple, Hindu Temple of North Texas
Sri Govindaji Gaudiya Matha, Hindu Vaishnava Temple in Houston
Sri Guruvayurappan Temple of Dallas
Sri Lakshmi Ganapathi Temple
Sri Meenakshi Temple Society
Sri Shirdi Sai Baba Temple of Austin
Sri Venkateswara Temple, Corpus Christi
Sri Venkateswara Temple of Austin

Utah

India Cultural Center
Radha Krishna Temple in Utah
Sri Ganesha Hindu Temple of Utah

Vermont

Vermont Hindu Temple

Virginia

BAPS Shri Swaminarayan Mandir, Virginia Beach
Durga Temple of Virginia
Hindu Center of Virginia
Hindu Temple of Hampton Roads
Hindu Temple of Virginia (Balaji Temple)
Murugan Temple of North America
Rajdhani Mandir, Chantilly
Richmond Hindu Temple
Shantiniketan Temple
Sri Venkateswara Lotus Temple
Vedic Temple of Virginia

Washington

Bellevue Hindu Temple
Hindu Society of Eastern Washington
Kent Hindu Temple
Lakshmi Venkateswara Temple
Nithyanandeshwara Hindu Temple
Veda Temple
Vedanta Society of Western Washington, Seattle

Washington, DC

BAPS Shri Swaminarayan Mandir, Washington, DC
ISKCON of DC

West Virginia

Hindu Religious and Cultural Center, Morgantown
New Vrindaban, The Land of Krishna (ISKCON)

Wyoming

None currently listed.

Glossary

ācārya/acharya teacher; the founder or leader of a Hindu religious lineage

Ādi Śaṅkarācārya "the first teacher of the lineage who is named Śaṅkara"; formal title of Śaṅkara, the founder of the Advaita Vedānta tradition; the later leaders of this tradition are also called *Śaṅkarācārya*, as part of their title, with the term *Ādi*, or "first," being used to distinguish the founder

Advaita Vedānta non-dualist system of Vedanta, established by Shankara in the ninth century CE; teaches that all that truly exists is Brahman, the absolute and ultimate reality; view held by many Hindu teachers who have gone to America, beginning with Swami Vivekananda

Agni fire; the Vedic deity, or deva, associated with fire, particularly the sacred fire into which ritual offerings are made; cognate with the English word "ignite"

ahiṃsā nonviolence in thought, word, and deed; the first moral rule that is affirmed in Hindu, Jain, and Buddhist teaching; the first of the yamas, or moral restraints, taught in Patañjali's *Yoga Sūtra*; part of sādhāraṇa dharma, or universal morality

ānanda bliss, joy; a characteristic of Brahman; this word is suffixed to the names of many Hindu monks, or swamis; Vivekananda, for example, means the bliss of discernment (*viveka*)

ananta/anantaram (uh-nuhn-tuh/ uh-nuhn-tuh-ruhm) infinity, infinite; a characteristic of Brahman

Āraṇyakas "forest texts"; commentaries on the *Vedas*, composed during the period between, or overlapping, the composition of the *Brāhmaṇas* and the *Upaniṣads*

Arjuna heroic character in the *Mahābhārata* and one of the conversation partners in the dialogue recounted in the *Bhagavad Gītā*

āsana literally "seat"; the correct posture for the practice of meditation in Patañjali's Yoga system; a more extensive system of postures was developed in the later Haṭha Yoga system, although this may be based on more ancient precedents; āsana has become central in modern yoga in America

asparśa "untouchable"; term used of persons with hereditary duties regarded as impure; these "untouchable" persons are today referred to as Dalits, or "the oppressed," and have struggled for equal treatment in modern India, where caste prejudice is today illegal but still present

āśrama/ashram place of spiritual retreat and study, traditionally in a forest setting; also, a stage of life in the system of stations and stages of life (varṇāśrama) taught in the *Dharma Śāstras*; the āśramas are the student, householder, retirement, and renunciation stages, respectively

asteya non-stealing; one of the yamas (moral restraints) of the Yoga system of Patañjali; part of sādhāraṇa dharma (universal morality)

Atharva Veda fourth of the *Vedas* to be composed; contains rituals a householder may perform without the aid of the Brahmin priesthood, as well as some philosophical reflections; some of the rituals focused on healing contain information that develops into medical science in India (Āyur Veda)

ātman Self; in Vedanta philosophy, the true, divine Self in contrast with the empirical personality or ego; ultimately identical to Brahman, according to Advaita Vedanta

avatar "descent"; divine incarnation, of whom there have been many, according to Vaishnava traditions; prominent avatars include Rama, Krishna, and Buddha; some devotees of modern gurus take these gurus to be avatars—such as, for example, Sri Ramakrishna

Āyur Veda "science of [long] life"; traditional Indian medicine; based in part on the *Atharva Veda*

Bhagavad Gītā "Song of the Blessed Lord"; philosophical dialogue in the *Mahābhārata* between the characters Arjuna and Krishna (that latter of whom is *Bhagavān*, the "Blessed Lord," or God); regarded as having comparable authority to the *Upaniṣads* and part one of the three texts that form the "triple foundation" of Vedānta philosophy

Bhagavān "Blessed Lord"; God; typically refers to Vishnu

bhakti devotion; absolute faith in and devotion to a personal form of divinity; in theistic forms of Vedanta, such as that of Rāmāṇuja, bhakti is constitutive of liberation, much as knowledge (jñāna) is constitutive of liberation in Advaita Vedānta; a central principle of the Hare Krishna tradition, promoted by ISKCON (International Society for Krishna Consciousness)

bhakti yoga a path to liberation from the cycle of rebirth; consists of the cultivation and expression of bhakti

brahmacharya restraint of the senses, with special emphasis on sexuality; usually implies celibacy; one of the yamas of the Yoga tradition, and so part of sādhāraṇā dharma (universal morality); the first stage of the āśrama system of stages of life found in the *Dharma Śāstras*; as such it is the first, student stage, in which one is a celibate student of the *Vedas* before moving to marriage and the stage of the householder; in some monastic traditions, like the Ramakrishna Order, brahmacharya is the stage prior to taking the full vows of renunciation (sannyāsa)

Brahman the absolute, the ground of all being, according to Vedanta philosophy; infinite being, consciousness, and bliss; in early Vedic literature, the power behind creation

Brāhmaṇas "Priestly Texts"; first set of commentaries written on the *Vedas*; part of the *Karma Kāṇḍa*, the ritualistic "Action Portion" of the Vedic literature

Brahmanirvāṇa "absorption in Brahman"; the highest state, leading to liberation from the cycle of rebirth; a prominent term in the *Bhagavad Gītā*

Brahmin the priestly varṇa or "caste"; typically understood to be a matter of birth, although portions of the *Upaniṣads* and of Buddhist literature take this title to be earned—a matter of character rather than of birth; Brahmins are traditionally responsible for performing Vedic ritual and passing on the Vedic tradition to the next generation

Brahmo Samāj "Community of Brahman"; organization inspired by the work of Ram Mohan Roy, although it was actually first presided over under this name by Debendranath Tagore; the first modern Hindu reform organization, aimed at "restoring" an original Vedic ideal of Hinduism; in the time of Ram Mohan Roy, it was called the Brahmo Sabhā.

Bṛhadāraṇyaka Upaniṣad often regarded as the oldest of the *Upaniṣads*, this text introduces important key concepts of Vedanta and of later Indian philosophy generally, including the identity of Brahman and ātman, the cycle of karma and rebirth, the role of desire in fuelling this process, and the importance of renunciation in ending it

Buddha literally, "awakened"; a being who has achieved the state of perfect awareness that leads to liberation and has done so entirely through self-effort; *the* Buddha refers to the historical founder of the Buddhist tradition, Siddhārtha Gautama.

cakra/chakra "wheel"; energy center located in the subtle body according to Tantra; there are seven cakras, each associated with a different set of spiritual qualities

Chaitanya (1485–1533), Sri Chaitanya Mahaprabhu Vedantic ācārya, founder of the Acintya Bhedābheda system of Vedanta; Chaitanya's teaching has a very strong emphasis on bhakti as constitutive of liberation; ISKCON (the International Society for Krishna Consciousness) looks to Chaitanya as an important founding figure

Chāndogya Upaniṣad major *Upaniṣad*, and of relatively early composition; includes the famous teaching *tat tvam asi*, or "You are That"

cit/citta pronounced "chit"; consciousness

citta-vṛtti-nirodha Patañjali's definition of yoga in the *Yoga Sūtra*, "calming the modifications of consciousness"

Dalit "oppressed"; preferred term for members of those castes traditionally regarded as "low" or "impure," to reflect their sense of exclusion from mainstream Indian society and their desire for social justice

darśana/darshan view, viewpoint, worldview, perspective; a system of philosophy; also, the act of viewing (and being viewed by) an image of a Hindu deity, usually housed in a temple, as a source of spiritual edification

deva "shining one"; deity

Devī goddess; feminine form of *deva*; often used as a name of the Mother Goddess, Śakti, wife of Shiva, also known as Umā, Parvatī, Durgā, and Kālī

dharma (DHAR-muh) cosmic order; the social and moral duties of human beings, and as such, one of the four aims of human life; religion; goodness

dhyāna meditation; the seventh stage of Patañjali's system of Yoga

dīkṣā/diksha initiation; the ritual by which one formally undertakes a spiritual discipline under the guidance of a guru, or teacher

Dvaita Vedānta dualistic Vedanta; established by the ācārya Madhva as a response to the Advaita Vedānta of Shankara; emphasizes the essentially distinct and separate natures of Īśvara and the individual jīvas, or souls, in the universe; such distinction is essential to the relationship of bhakti, which Madhva, along with the other non-Advaita Vedānta philosophers, sees as constitutive of liberation

Eckankar Hindu-inspired movement started by Paul Twitchell in 1965, teaching Vedāntic ideas such as karma and the ultimate unity of the human and divine.

Govinda "cow-finder"; an epithet of Krishna

guru teacher, usually a spiritual teacher or guide; in some traditions, this relationship has been formalized, such that one's guru is the person from whom one receives initiation and who confers one with a mantra to use in meditation practice

Hanuman major character in the *Rāmāyaṇa*; an intelligent ape who is deeply devoted to Rama and aids him in his struggle with the demonic entity, Rāvaṇa; Hanuman is a deity in his own right in Hinduism, associated with strength and protection from evil.

Haṭha Yoga "yoga of force"; system of yoga particularly known for its use of physical postures (āsanas) in cultivating a physical and mental state conducive to meditation; highly popularized in North America in the modern period

Integral Yoga modern system of yoga developed by Sri Aurobindo based upon his reflections on both Indian and Western philosophy and his yogic experiences while imprisoned by the British

involution term coined by Swami Vivekananda and further elaborated by Sri Aurobindo to refer to the process, first described in the *Upaniṣads* and in the Sāṃkhya philosophy of Hinduism, by which spirit enters into the realm of matter; Vivekananda and Aurobindo see this process as complementary to (and the spiritual side of) the process of evolution described in modern science, in which consciousness emerges and evolves from matter

iṣṭa-devatā/ishta-devata preferred deity, chosen deity, beloved deity; term used by Patañjali and subsequently in the Vedanta tradition to refer to the idea that one might conceive of the Supreme Being in whatever way one chooses, as best suits one's spiritual temperament, and then use that conceptual image of divinity as one's object of contemplation; extended by many modern Hindu teachers in the West to encompass the deities of all religions

Īśvara the Supreme Lord; God, understood as the creator, preserver, destroyer, and re-creator of the universe through each cosmic cycle, though not the creator of everything from nothing, as in classical Western theism; in the Sāṃkhya and Yoga philosophies, Īśvara is a passive, perpetually liberated soul on whom one meditates in order to achieve liberation oneself

Īśvara-praṇidhāna contemplation of God; one of the niyamas, or moral injunctions, listed in the *Yoga Sūtra* as a practice conducive to the attainment of the goal of the Yoga system—samādhi, or contemplative absorption, culminating in liberation from the cycle of rebirth; part of sādhāraṇā dharma, or universal morality

Jaina/Jain adherent of Jainism; follower of the Jinas

Jainism ancient Indic tradition which has a minority following in India to the present day; Jains are also part of the wider Indian diaspora in America and other parts of the world.

jāti "birth"; "sub-castes" which make up the varṇas, or castes, of Indian society; typically seen as a matter of birth; birth-caste; conceptually not unlike the concept of ethnicity

jīva/jīvātman life-force; soul; that which reincarnates from one lifetime to the next; the Self on the individual level, in contrast with the paramātman (Supreme Self, or "Oversoul," as translated by Emerson, which is the divine Self in all beings)

jñāna knowledge; the knowledge that constitutes liberation, according to the Sāṃkhya, Yoga, and Advaita Vedānta systems of Hindu philosophy

jñāna yoga the path to liberation which consists of cultivating knowledge through scriptural study and contemplative practice; characteristic of many systems of Vedanta and Yoga in America

Kali Yuga current, degenerate phase of history, after which the cosmos will regenerate itself and return to a purer, better mode of existence

kāma pleasure, sensory enjoyment, one of the four aims of human life

Kāma Sūtra text authored by Vātsyāyana in the second or third century CE; known for its frank discussion of sexuality

Kamarpukur village in West Bengal; birthplace of Sri Ramakrishna

karma literally, "work," "action"; the law of cause and effect governing all action

karma yoga either selfless performance of rituals out of a sense of duty or selfless service to living beings without any desire for reward; conceived either as a purifying practice in preparation for liberation or, in modern Vedanta, as a path to liberation in its own right

Krishna/Kṛṣṇa/Śrī Kṛṣṇa in some Hindu texts, an avatar, or incarnation, of the deity Vishnu; in other Hindu texts, the Supreme Being; character in the *Mahābhārata* whose instruction to Arjuna constitutes the *Bhagavad Gītā*

Kṣatriya member of the warrior varṇa, or "caste"

kuṇḍalinī śakti "coiled power"; the energy field coiled at the base of the spine in the subtle body, according to Tantra; much Tāntric practice is aimed at tapping into and raising this power latent in all living beings; a manifestation of the Mother Goddess, Shakti, in her role as the energy which powers all of creation; important concept in Tāntric traditions that have been brought to America, such as Siddha Yoga

Lakshmana in the *Rāmāyaṇa*, brother of Rama who accompanies him into his exile and aids him in his conflict with the wicked Rāvaṇa; often depicted standing to the right of Rama in temples in both India and America, including the Hindu temples of Lamont, Illinois (in the Chicago suburbs) and at the HARI Temple in New Cumberland, Pennsylvania

Lakshmi goddess of prosperity; wife of Vishnu; in Vaishnava theology, Lakshmi embodies Lord Vishnu's grace; Lakshmi and Vishnu are sometimes said to constitute a single composite being, known as Lakshminarayana, or Shrinarayana, or Shrilakshminarayana

Madhva (1238–1317) founder of the Dvaita, or dualistic, system of Vedanta, which sees the distinctions among beings as their essential defining characteristics; like the other non-Advaita forms of Vedanta, sees bhakti as constitutive of liberation, and the relationship between a distinct Lord and devotee as essential to the existence of bhakti

Mahābhārata *Great Tale of the Bhāratas*; along with the *Rāmāyaṇa*, one of two major historical epics of Hinduism; includes the *Bhagavad Gītā*

mahātma "great soul"; a title that is given to highly revered figures in Hindu traditions, the most famous of the modern period being Mohandas K. Gandhi

mahāvākya "great statement"; in Advaita Vedanta, statements found in the *Upaniṣads* that are to be taken literally as communicating the core truth of the *Vedas*, such as *prajñānaṃ brahma* ("Brahman is consciousness"), *ayam ātmā brahma* ("This Self is Brahman"), *tat tvam asi* ("You are That"), *aham brahmāsmi* ("I am Brahman"), and *sarvaṃ khalvidaṃ brahma* ("All this, indeed, is Brahman")

Mahāvīra (499–427 BCE or 599–527 BCE) "great hero"; best-known epithet of Vardhamāna Jñātṛputra; twenty-fourth Tīrthaṅkara of Jainism, who established the current Jain community, re-establishing the teachings of the previous twenty-three Tīrthaṅkaras of this cosmic era

mantra sacred verse or prayer repeated silently during meditation, usually focused on the name of a deity; originally, the hymns of the *Ṛg Veda* were referred to as *mantras*.

Manusmṛti *Sacred Text of Manu*; also translated as *The Laws of Manu*; one of the *Dharma Śāstras* outlining human moral and social obligations according to the principles of varṇāśrama—or stations and stages of life; one of the first Hindu texts translated into English (by Indologist Sir William Jones)

māyā appearance; the creative power by which the Lord manifests the world out of Himself, out of His own nature as Brahman; sometimes translated as "illusion," for it is said to conceal the true nature of reality as simply Brahman; in Vaishnava theology and Tantra, *māyā* is seen positively, as concealing but also revealing the nature of reality

mokṣa/moksha liberation, specifically from the cycle of death and rebirth; the ultimate good, according to most systems of Indian philosophy; "salvation," in a religious sense; one of the four aims of human life, typically seen as the ultimate aim

Mughal third dynasty, after the Mauryas and Guptas, to rule most of India; Mughals were Muslim, whose attitudes toward indigenous Indian traditions varied greatly, from hostility to appreciation; they reigned from 1526 to 1857, although they experienced a decline after the death of the emperor Aurangzeb in 1707.

mūrti image; form; a physical image of a deity used in worship, to cultivate and to express bhakti (devotion) and to interact with the deity

mūrti pūjā "image worship"; worship which uses physical images in order to cultivate and express devotion and to interact with the deities these images represent; some early modern Hindu reformers, such as Ram Mohan Roy, objected to this practice, which has also been criticized by Muslim and Christian missionaries as "idolatry," for it is a practice banned in these two religions; the practice is so central to Hindu spirituality that reform movements which have rejected it have generally failed to acquire a mass following.

nāmakaraṇa saṃskāra Vedic ritual by which a baby is given a name; in modern Hinduism, also used to give a Hindu name to a convert to the tradition, particularly in the Ārya Samāj

Nānak/Guru Nānak (1469–1539) spiritual leader in the Punjab region of northwestern India in the Mughal period; rejected boundaries which divided people according to caste, class, or sect and famously taught, "There is no Hindu, there is no Muslim"; established a community of disciples, or *Sikhs*, which became a distinct group from both Hindus and Muslims; known to Sikhs as Guru Nānak; first of the ten Sikh gurus, or teachers

nirvāṇa absorption (when a flame returns to a potential state when it is blown out); refers to the cessation of suffering and the cravings which lead to it; term most often associated with Buddhism, but also used in Jain and Hindu traditions with the same essential meaning; the *Bhagavad Gītā* elaborates on it with the term *brahmanirvāṇa*, or "absorption in Brahman"

niyama restraint; a set of five moral injunctions, and the second of the eight stages of Patañjali's Yoga system; a set of five habits one must cultivate on the path to liberation; along with the five yamas, the five niyamas make up sādhāraṇā dharma, or universal Hindu morality

Oṃ (or AUM) sacred syllable, or mantra, utilized in Hindu, Buddhist, and Jain mantras; the ultimate bīja, or seed, mantra; believed to be the original sound, from which all other sounds have emerged; in Vedānta, Brahman in the form of sound

Pāṇḍavas five brothers who, in the *Mahābhārata*, are in contention with their cousins for rulership of the Kuru kingdom in ancient northern India; the heroes of the epic, one of whom is Arjuna, the friend of Krishna, with whom he engages in dialogue in the *Bhagavad Gītā*

paramātman supreme self; the ātman; the soul shared by all beings; God; translated by Emerson as "Oversoul"

Patañjali author of the *Yoga Sūtra*; traditionally regarded as the founder of Yoga, though likely a compiler of the views and practices of an already existing and more ancient tradition

prāṇayama breath control; fourth of the eight stages of Patañjali's Yoga system; breathing correctly for the practice of meditation

pūjā worship; a way of expressing and cultivating bhakti, or devotion to the divine

Pūrāṇas "ancient lore"; collections of stories and reflections focused on the deities of Hinduism; composed from the first millennium of the Common Era and extending into the second, though using source materials which may be as early as, or even older than, the *Vedas*

Rāma/Rama/Ram hero of the *Rāmāyaṇa*; warrior prince of Ayodhya, son of King Daśaratha; husband of Sita; according to Vaishnava theology, an avatar or incarnation of Vishnu; a highly popular deity; Mahatma Gandhi called out his name in prayer at the moment he was assassinated

Ramakrishna Mission educational and relief organization established in the name of his spiritual master by Swami Vivekananda in 1897

Ramakrishna Order order of monks established by Swami Vivekananda in 1897

Rāmāṇuja (1077–1157) founder of the Viśiṣṭādvaita system of Vedanta; affirms both the duality and non-duality between the world and entities composing it, on the one hand, and Brahman, on the other; affirms the necessity of some distinction between God and God's devotees in order for bhakti to exist; sees bhakti as constitutive of liberation

Rāmāyaṇa *The Life of Rāma*; along with the *Mahābhārata*, one of the two major historical epics of Hinduism

Ṛg Veda the oldest of the *Vedas*, consisting mainly of hymns to deities, most of whom are tied to natural phenomena

sādhana spiritual practice; discipline aimed at liberation

sādhāraṇā dharma universal dharma; duties that apply to all people; general moral principles, in contrast with svadharma, or the duties applying only to certain groups; often identified with the yamas and niyamas (moral restraints) of the Yoga tradition

Sāma Veda one of the original three *Vedas*, focused on the correct singing and intonation of Vedic chants; important source for the tradition of Indian classical music

samādhi absorption; becoming completely identified with the object of one's meditation; eighth of the eight stages of Patañjali's system of Yoga; Sri Ramakrishna is believed to have been able to attain this state spontaneously

Sāṃkhya "enumeration"; Vedic system of philosophy focused on the duality of matter and spirit; closely aligned with the Yoga system; influential upon Vedanta as well, as many of its teachings are contained in texts such as the *Upaniṣads* and the *Bhagavad Gītā*

saṃpradāya denomination; sect; a tradition of thought and practice, often focused on a specific deity, such as Vishnu, Shiva, or Shakti

sannyāsa renunciation; the fourth stage, or āśrama, of life, in the system of life stages and stations presented in the *Dharma Shastras*; in the *Upaniṣads*, this is taken to be, at least for most persons, a prerequisite for liberation; leaving behind worldly life for a life focused on the spiritual path

Sanskrit "cultured," "perfected"; the formal language of much of Indian philosophy and of Hindu sacred literature and ritual

Saraswati goddess of wisdom, revered by both Hindus and Jains; also, the river that ran roughly parallel to the Indus during the period of the Indus Valley Civilization which dried up around 1900 BCE, helping to precipitate the decline of this civilization and its dispersal further into the Indian subcontinent; also one of the ten orders of renouncers established by Ādi Śaṅkarācārya. Both the nineteenth-century and late twentieth- and early twenty-first-century swamis with the name Dayananda Saraswati were members of this order, hence the inclusion of this title in their names.

śāstra/shastra authoritative text on a specific topic, such as *Dharma Śāstra* or *Artha Śāstra*

seva service; selfless service; strong emphasis of modern Vedanta; karma yoga

Shaiva of or referring to the deity Shiva; a devotee of Shiva; an adherent of a school of thought and practice that takes Shiva to be Īśvara, the Supreme Being.

Shakta of or referring to the deity Shakti, the Mother Goddess; a devotee of Shakti; an adherent of a school of thought and practice that takes Shakti to be the Supreme Being

Shakti primal energy, power of creation; also, the Mother Goddess and wife of Śiva

Shiva literally, "benevolent one"; supreme deity; in Shaiva traditions, identical to Īśvara (God)

siddha "perfected one"; a fully enlightened or liberated being

Siddha Yoga "spiritual discipline of perfection"; Tāntric Shaiva lineage of Hindu practice brought to America by Swami Muktananda, who was later succeeded by Gurumayi as head of this lineage

siddhi "perfection"; a paranormal ability resulting from advancement in meditation

Siddhārtha Gautama (c. 490–410 BCE) the historical Buddha

Sikh student, disciple; adherent of Sikhi, the tradition established by Guru Nānak (1469–1539), widely known in the West as Sikhism

Sita (Sītā) in the *Rāmāyaṇa*, wife of Rāma, abducted by the wicked Rāvaṇa and rescued by Rāma with the help of his brother, Lakshmana, the intelligent ape general Hanuman, and an army of apes and other animals

smṛti "that which is remembered"; sacred tradition; authoritative Hindu texts whose authority is derivative from the more authoritative śrūti, or "heard" literature, consisting of the *Vedas*; a category encompassing a vast array of texts, and including the *Rāmāyaṇa*, *Mahābhārata*, *Pūrāṇas*, and the various *Śāstras* (*Dharma*, *Artha*, *Kāma*, and *Mokṣa*)

Soma a Vedic deva or deity associated with the moon, mind, and memory; associated with Shiva; personification of a psychedelic substance used in ancient times by the Brahmins, taken from a leafy plant and mixed with milk to produce a potent drink; used as a term for a psychedelic drug in Aldous Huxley's novel, *Brave New World*

śrūti "heard"; the *Vedas*, understood either as an eternal, authorless truth perceived by the Vedic seers or as the word of God spoken to these same seers

sūtra "thread," the root text of a system of philosophy; sometimes synonymous with *śāstra*

svadharma "own-duty"; the duties for which one is responsible as a member of a certain social station and during a certain stage of one's life, in contrast with universal duty, which all persons are obligated to uphold; enumerated in the *Dharma Śāstras*

swami "master"; honorary title taken by many Hindu renouncers

Swaminarayan (Sahajanand Swami) (1781–1830) Hindu renouncer and spiritual teacher who established a community of followers in Gujarat in the early nineteenth century; in many ways he was a modern reformer who prefigured Swami Vivekananda's emphasis on seva (social service); his movement has a massive following today, particularly among Gujarati Hindus

Tantra form of spiritual practice that uses the senses and material energies in order to achieve transcendence; appears in Hindu and Buddhist varieties, exerting some influence upon Jainism as well; based on texts also known as *Tantras*; focused primarily in the Shaiva and Shakta traditions of Hinduism; Tāntric systems brought to America include Siddha Yoga and Kashmir Shaivism.

Tāntric Tāntrika; an adherent of Tantra; of or relating to Tantra

tat tvam asi "That you are"; "You are That"; you are Brahman; one of the "great statements" (mahāvākyas) of the *Upaniṣads*, according to Advaita Vedanta, summarizing Vedic teaching

tattva "thatness"; nature; essence; the truth of a thing; essential principle

Theravāda "teaching of the elders"; the one early Buddhist tradition which has survived to the present day, having been transmitted to Sri Lanka and Southeast Asia prior to the invasions which destroyed Buddhism in most of India; emphasizes fidelity to the teachings of the Buddha as found in the Pāli *Tripiṭaka*, the oldest *Tripiṭaka* to survive in its original form; taken up by Henry Steel Olcott, of the Theosophical Society, in the nineteenth century; Olcott wrote a *Buddhist Catechism* based on his understanding of this tradition; Anagarika Dharmapala, who disagreed with Olcott's interpretation, represented the Theravāda Buddhists of Sri Lanka at the First World Parliament of Religions.

upanayanam Vedic ritual in which a young person is presented with a sacred thread which is then worn as a symbol of that person's social status; the ceremony marks the entry of the youth into the first stage of the āśrama system—the student stage; it usually occurs around the age of thirteen; a ritual traditionally reserved from males, in the modern period, and especially among Hindus in the United States, it has become increasingly common to perform it for young women as well.

Upaniṣads "secret doctrine," teaching given while one is sitting near to one's teacher; the last portion of the *Vedas* to be composed, containing the philosophy of Vedanta; most likely composed in the first millennium BCE

Vaishnava of or pertaining to Vishnu, the supreme deity according to traditions that go by this name; one of the major theistic Hindu traditions

varṇa "color"; refers not to skin-color, but to a system of categorization of people into four basic occupational categories—priest, warrior, common person, and servant; later known as "caste"

Veda literally, wisdom; the most sacred literature of Hindu traditions, also written in the plural as *Vedas* when referring to the entire collection of texts

Vedānta/Vedanta end of the *Vedas*, end or goal of wisdom; the philosophy of the *Upaniṣads*; the dominant system of Indian philosophy over the course of the last millennium; strong influence on Hinduism in America

Vedanta Society educational and religious organization first established by Swami Vivekananda in 1894; the Western branch of the Ramakrishna Mission (though technically established first)

Vishnu/Viṣṇu literally, "omnipresent," the supreme deity, the preserver of the cosmic order; identical to Īśvara according to Vaishnava traditions, also called *Bhagavān*

Viśiṣṭādvaita Vedānta system of Vedanta developed by Rāmāṇuja in the eleventh to twelfth centuries CE; meaning "non-duality with difference," it seeks to bring together the ideas of duality and non-duality found in the Vedic scriptures, teaching that there are real distinctions between God, the world, and the souls inhabiting the world, but that all of these together, as a collective totality, make up Brahman, which is the organic unity of everything

Vivekananda, Swami (1863–1902) the chief disciple of Sri Ramakrishna (1836–86); first Hindu monk to travel to the West and teach Vedānta; established the Vedanta Society in the United States in 1894 and then the Ramakrishna Mission and Ramakrishna Order in 1897, after returning to India; major influence on modern Vedānta

Yajur Veda one of the original three *Vedas*; this text focuses on how to do rituals; exists in two versions, the "white" and the "black," the former being less detailed the latter more so

yama/Yama restraint; the five moral rules of Patañjali's Yoga system, making up the first stage of his eight-stage path; along with the five niyamas, the five yamas make up sādhāraṇā dharma, or universal morality; as a proper name, the Vedic lord of death, so named because he carries a noose to catch and restrain the souls of those whom he carries off to his abode at the time of their death

yoga/Yoga literally, "yoke"; generically, a system of spiritual discipline; formally, the name of the system of spiritual thought and practice attributed to the seer Patañjali and elaborated in his *Yoga Sūtra*; widely assimilated set of physical exercises in the Western world, derived from the yoga traditions of India

Yoga Sūtra root text of the Yoga system of philosophy, attributed to Patañjali

yogi/yogin/yogini a practitioner of yoga; *yogin* is masculine and *yogini* is feminine; *yogi* is *yogin* in the Sanskrit nominative case, when the word is functioning as the subject of a sentence.

Zoroastrianism a religious tradition originating in ancient Iran with historical ties to Hinduism. Many Zoroastrians today live in India. Popular guru Meher Baba (1894–1969) and rock vocalist Freddie Mercury (1946–91) were both Zoroastrian.

Notes

Prologue

1 *Bhagavad Gita: As It Is*, with translation and commentary by A.C. Bhaktivedanta Swami Prabhupada (Los Angeles: Bhaktivedanta Book Trust, 1972), 21–4. The original verses are *Bhagavad Gita* 2:11b–13.

2 Mohandas K. Gandhi, *The Story of My Experiments with Truth* (Boston: Beacon Press, 1957), 265.

3 The consonant combination "jñ" found in words such as *jñāna* has a pronunciation that varies from one region of India to the next. The pronunciation one most frequently hears for "jña" is "gya." It can also be pronounced as though the "j" is silent: so "ña," or "nya." It is *not* pronounced "ja-na" or "ja-ña," but is always a single syllable.

4 I have discussed the childhood traumas that prompted my journey and that led to my "discovery" of the *Bhagavad Gītā* in some depth in other publications. For the most in-depth account, see Jeffery D. Long, "'Never Was There a Time …' Crossing Over to Hinduism through the *Bhagavad Gītā*," in Jennifer Howe Peace, Or Rose, and Gregory Mobley, eds., *My Neighbor's Faith: Stories of Interreligious Encounter, Growth, and Transformation* (Maryknoll, New York: Orbis Books, 2012), 93–9.

5 India, like the United States, is divided into states. Gujarat is a state on the western coast of India. In addition to being the home state of my friends, it is also the home state of Mahatma Gandhi.

Introduction

1 Central Intelligence Agency, *The World Factbook*. https://www.cia.gov/library/publications/resources/the-world-factbook/geos/xx.html, accessed February 9, 2019.

2 The numbers of religiously unaffiliated persons globally are likely inflated in most surveys because many in the People's Republic of China list themselves as unaffiliated, due to concerns about government disapproval of religion, while in fact having a private religious practice.

3 Ibid., and Office of the Registrar General & Census Commissioner, India, "Distribution of Population by Religion." http://censusindia.gov.in/Census_And_You/religion.aspx, accessed February 9, 2019. Regarding adherents of other religions, not listed here, it can probably be said that every religion, or nearly every religion, in the world has adherents in India. In addition to the traditions listed, there are, for example, adherents of traditional Chinese religions, such as Daoism and Confucianism, due to the existence of pockets of ethnic Chinese who live in large metropolitan areas like Delhi and Kolkata. See Zhang Xing, "Who Is a Chinese-Indian: Search for the Cultural Identity of the Chinese-Indians of Kolkata, Sihui, and Toronto" and Kwai Yum

Li, "Shifting Worlds and Changing Identities: The Reshaping of the Chinese-Indian Communities in India after the 1962 'Sino-Indian Incident,'" in Jayanti Bhattacharya and Coonoor Kripalani, eds., *Chinese and Indian Immigrant Communities: Comparative Perspectives* (London: Anthem Press, 2015), 219–34, 281–90.

4 Given the co-existence of the nation-state called the Republic of India with other nations in this region, like Pakistan, Nepal, Bangladesh, Bhutan, Afghanistan, and Sri Lanka, the older convention of referring to the entire region as India, or the Indian subcontinent, has largely been superseded in scholarly work by the term *South Asia*.

5 Scholar Asko Parpola traces the first known usage of the word *Hindu* to the sixth-century BC Persian emperor, Darius the Great. See Asko Parpola, *The Roots of Hinduism: The Early Aryans and the Indus Civilization* (New York: Oxford University Press, 2015), 3.

6 Tim Cooke, ed., *National Geographic Concise History of World Religions: An Illustrated Time Line* (Washington, DC: National Geographic, 2011), 15.

7 The word *imagined* is significant here; for recent scholarship on the early histories of other religious traditions, such as Christianity, suggests that most traditions are made up of heterogenous elements from the beginning, and that there were, in fact, many "Christianities" in the early days of the tradition, rather than a singular community only later developing into branches such as Roman Catholicism, Eastern Orthodoxy, and Protestantism, as earlier scholarship tends to suggest. See, for example, Elaine Pagels, *The Gnostic Gospels* (New York: Random House, 1979).

8 See Christopher R. Cotter and David G. Robertson, eds., *After World Religions: Reconstructing Religious Studies* (New York: Routledge, 2016).

9 For an example of a reaction of this kind to the scholarly focus on the variety that underlies both Hinduism and Indian culture more broadly, see Rajiv Malhotra and Aravindan Neelakandan, *Breaking India: Western Interventions in Dravidian and Dalit Faultlines* (Bhopal: Manjul Publishing House, 2012).

10 Sarvepalli Radhakrishnan, *The Hindu View of Life* (New York: Macmillan, 1973).

11 David N. Lorenzen, "Who Invented Hinduism?," in J.E. Llewellyn, ed., *Defining Hinduism: A Reader* (London: Equinox, 2005), 53–8. It should be noted that Lorenzen is critical of this view, and his article is an argument against it.

12 See Andrew Nicholson, *Unifying Hinduism: Philosophy and Identity in Indian Intellectual History* (New York: Columbia University Press, 2010).

13 This is the approach taken by, among others, Wendy Doniger. See Wendy Doniger, *The Hindus: An Alternative History* (Oxford: Oxford University Press, 2009).

14 See Lorenzen.

15 Julius Lipner, "Ancient Banyan: An Inquiry into the Meaning of 'Hinduness,'" in Llewellyn, ed., *Defining Hinduism: A Reader* (London: Equinox, 2005), 32.

16 This is why one of my teachers, Paul J. Griffiths, refers to the religions of the world as "semi-fictional entities." See Paul J. Griffiths, *An Apology for Apologetics: A Study in the Logic of Interreligious Dialogue* (Maryknoll, NY: Orbis Books, 1991), 5.

17 Brian Pennington, *Was Hinduism Invented? Britons, Indians, and the Colonial Construction of Religion* (Oxford: Oxford University Press, 2005), 4.

18 Ibid.

19 Nicholson, 2–3.

20 Pew Research Center, "How Racially Diverse Are US Religious Groups?" http://www.pewresearch.org/fact-tank/2015/07/27/the-most-and-least-racially-diverse-u-s-religious-groups/ft_15-07-23_religiondiversityindex-1/, accessed February 9, 2019.

21 Khyati Y. Joshi, *New Roots in America's Sacred Ground: Religion, Race, and Ethnicity in Indian America* (New Brunswick, NJ: Rutgers University Press, 2006), 96.

22 Diana Eck, *Darśan: Seeing the Divine Image in India* (Delhi: Motilal Banarsidass, 2007), 64.

23 Vasudha Narayanan, "Americans May Not Know It, but They've Long Been Embracing Hindu Philosophy," February 6, 2018. https://qz.com/india/1199543/americas-long-and-complex-relationship-with-hinduism/, accessed February 9, 2019.
24 Central Intelligence Agency, *The World Factbook.*
25 See Robert L. Winzeler, *Popular Religion in Southeast Asia* (Lanham, MD: Rowman and Littlefield, 2016).
26 Veena R. Howard, ed., *Dharma: The Hindu, Jain, Buddhist, and Sikh Traditions of India* (London: I.B. Tauris, 2017), 1–37.
27 Pankaj Jain, *Dharma and Ecology of Hindu Communities: Sustenance and Sustainability* (New York: Routledge, 2016), 25.
28 Steven Vertovec, *The Hindu Diaspora: Comparative Patterns* (London: Routledge, 2000), 141.
29 Ibid., 142.
30 Ibid.
31 Ibid., 142–5.
32 Ibid., 148.
33 Ibid., 153–6.
34 See Murali Balaji, ed., *Digital Hinduism: Dharma and Discourse in the Age of New Media* (Lanham, MD: Lexington Books, 2018) and Juli L. Gittinger, *Hinduism and Hindu Nationalism Online* (New York: Routledge, 2019).
35 The Commonwealth of Nations is described by *Encylopedia Britannica* as "a free association of sovereign states comprising the United Kingdom and a number of its former dependencies who have chosen to maintain ties of friendship and practical cooperation and who acknowledge the British monarch as symbolic head of their association." https://www.britannica.com/topic/Commonwealth-association-of-states, accessed September 18, 2016.
36 Central Intelligence Agency, *The World Factbook.*
37 Ibid.
38 Ibid.
39 Personal communication with members of ISKCON. See also http://centers.iskcondesiretree.com/mexico/, accessed September 18, 2016.
40 Richard Beeman, *The Penguin Guide to the United States Constitution: A Fully Annotated Declaration of Independence, U.S. Constitution and Amendments, and Selections from The Federalist Papers* (New York: Penguin Books, 2010).
41 Pew Research Center, "How Racially Diverse Are US Religious Groups?"
42 Democratic Congresswoman and, as of this writing, presidential candidate, Tulsi Gabbard, is probably the best-known American Hindu of "mixed" descent, but neither of her parents is South Asian. She is of Irish and Samoan descent.
43 Ibid.
44 Ibid.
45 John Hick, "Religious Pluralism," in Philip L. Quinn and Charlies Taliaferro, eds., *A Companion to Philosophy of Religion* (Cambridge, MA: Blackwell Publishers, 1997), 610.
46 Swami Dayananda Saraswati, "Conversion Is an Act of Violence." http://www.swamij.com/conversion-violence.htm, accessed January 24, 2018.
47 See, for example, Satguru Sivaya Subramuniyaswami, *How to Become a Hindu: A Guide for Seekers and Born Hindus* (Kauai, HI: Himalayan Academy Publications, 2000). Even prior to Subramuniyaswami, in the nineteenth century, Swami Dayananda Saraswati, founder of the Ārya Samāj, had established a ritual for the conversion of non-Hindus to Hinduism, although this seems originally to have been focused on Indian Muslims and Christians whose ancestors had been Hindu, and so was seen essentially as a "re-conversion" or "homecoming"—*ghar wapsi*, as this kind of conversion is known in Hindi.

48 See, for example, the articles contained in Lola Williamson and Ann Gleig, *Homegrown Gurus: From Hinduism in America to American Hinduism* (Albany: State University of New York Press, 2013).

49 This periodical is mentioned by Vertovec as an instance of "diaspora" as a form of cultural production. Vertovec, 156.

50 See Sri Dharma Pravartaka Acharya's website. http://dharmacentral.com, accessed September 18, 2016.

51 Amanda J. Lucia, *Reflections of Amma: Devotees in a Global Embrace* (Berkeley: University of California Press, 2014), 187, 195.

52 Lola Williamson, *Transcendent in America: Hindu-Inspired Meditation Movements as New Religion* (New York: New York University Press, 2010), 4.

53 Lisa Miller, "We Are All Hindus Now," *Newsweek* (August 15, 2009).

54 *Ṛg Veda* 1.164: 46c.

55 *Bhagavad Gītā* 4:11.

56 See, for example, Jim Tucker, *Return to Life* (New York: St. Martin's Griffin, 2015).

57 The "classic" in the genre of books exploring past life regression is certainly Brian Weiss, *Many Lives, Many Masters* (Bellefonte, PA: Fireside, 1988).

58 *Ahiṃsā* is the virtue of nonviolence in thought, word, and deed.

59 See the "Pronunciation Guide" between the Acknowledgments and the Prologue of this book.

Chapter 1

1 John Cort, *Jains in the World: Religious Values and Ideology in India* (Oxford: Oxford University Press, 2001), 15.

2 Nancy Auer Falk, *Living Hinduisms: An Explorer's Guide* (Belmont, CA: Thomson Wadsworth, 2006).

3 See Howard, 1–37.

4 William Dalrymple, "The Great Divide: The Violent Legacy of Indian Partition," in *The New Yorker*, June 22, 2015.

5 Parpola, 2015, 3.

6 Vinayak Damodar Savarkar, *Hindutva* (1923) in S. Hay, ed., *Sources of Indian Tradition, Volume Two* (New York: Columbia University Press, 1988), 83–131.

7 Pravrajika Vrajaprana, *Vedanta: A Simple Introduction* (Hollywood, CA: Vedanta Press, 1999), 1.

8 This is the case for many Jains whom I interviewed regarding questions of Jain identity for my second book, *Jainism: An Introduction* (London: I.B. Tauris, 2009).

9 This is in Article 25(2)(b) of the Constitution of India. P.M. Bakshi, *Constitution of India: Selective Comments* (New Delhi: Universal Law Publishing Company, 2006), 41.

10 The porosity of religious boundaries in India has been the topic of many studies. Two that are particularly helpful are John Cort, ed., *Open Boundaries: Jain Communities and Cultures in Indian History* (Albany: State University of New York Press, 1998) and Peter Gottschalk, *Beyond Hindu and Muslim: Multiple Identity in Narratives of Village India* (Oxford: Oxford University Press, 2000).

11 The numerous controversies surrounding the dating and the origin of the earliest Vedic texts are well documented in Edwin Bryant's, *The Quest for the Origins of Vedic Culture: The Indo-Aryan Migration Debate* (New York: Oxford University Press, 2004).

12 There are also varied views about the historicity of these texts, with many Hindus being more inclined to see them as metaphorical accounts pointing to deep truths of spirituality, rather than as straightforward accounts of past events.

13 One popular medium by which Hindus both in India and America become acquainted with the smṛti literature is through the *Amar Chitra Kathā* comic book series. A more recent trend has been the novelization of texts such as the *Rāmāyaṇa* in a manner akin to popular fantasy novels, such as *The Lord of the Rings.* Two especially popular authors in this regard are Ashok Banker, whose *Prince of Ayodhya* series is a retelling of the *Rāmāyaṇa*, and Amish Tripathi, whose series, *The Immortals of Meluha*, sets the biography of the Hindu deity Shiva in the period of the Indus Valley Civilization, which was apparently known by its inhabitants as Meluhha.

14 See Ayon Maharaj, "Sarvamukti: Sarvepalli Radhakrishnan's Aporetic Metaphysics of Collective Salvation," in *Philosophy East and West*, 70 (1):136–54 (2020).

15 See Eileen Gardiner, *Hindu Hell: Visions, Tours, and Descriptions of the Infernal Underworld* (New York: Italica Press, 2013).

16 Arvind Sharma, *Gandhi: A Spiritual Biography* (New Haven and London: Yale University Press, 2013), 3–4.

17 For in-depth discussion of the relative levels of religious violence in the histories of Asian and Western religions, see Nicholas F. Gier, *The Origins of Religious Violence: An Asian Perspective* (Lanham, MD: Lexington Books, 2016).

18 See Nicholson, 2010.

19 See, for example, Vrajaprana, 1999, 37–47.

20 See Doniger, 103–34.

21 See *Dhammapāda*, chapter 26 and *Chāndogya Upaniṣad* 4.4–9.

22 See Ramdas Lamb, *Rapt in the Name: The Ramnamis, Ramnam, and Untouchable Religion in Central India* (Albany: State University of New York Press, 2002).

23 *Bhagavad Gītā* 9:23.

24 Joyce Burkhalter Flueckiger, *Everyday Hinduism* (Oxford: Wiley Blackwell, 2015), 15.

25 Ibid., 15.

26 *Dalit Nation.* https://dalitnation.com, accessed December 5, 2019.

27 Swami Vivekananda, *Complete Works*, Volume Five (Mayawati: Advaita Ashrama, 1979), 22–3.

28 Flueckiger, 44–5.

29 Patañjali, *Yoga Sūtra* 1:2, Patañjali (Edwin Bryant, trans.), *The Yoga Sūtras of Patañjali: A New Edition, Translation, and Commentary* (New York: North Point Press, 2009).

30 See Parpola; see also Jonathan Mark Kenoyer, *Ancient Cities of the Indus Valley Civilization* (Oxford: Oxford University Press, 1998), Gregory L. Possehl, *The Indus Civilization: A Contemporary Perspective* (Lanham, MD: Rowman and Littlefield, 2002), and Jane McIntosh, *A Peaceful Realm: The Rise and Fall of the Indus Civilization* (Boulder, CO: Westview Press, 2002).

31 See Tony Joseph, *Early Indians: The Story of Our Ancestors and Where We Came From* (New Delhi: Juggernaut, 2018).

32 Nicholson 2010 chronicles the gradual rise and coalescence of the "six orthodox systems of philosophy" in Indian thought, traced through doxographical writings, or writings that delineate the views of various schools of thought.

33 John Keay, *India: A History* (New York: HarperCollins, 2010), 231–61.

34 Richard Gombrich, *What the Buddha Thought* (London: Equinox, 2009).

35 See Jenny Rose, *Zoroastrianism: An Introduction* (London: I.B. Tauris, 2014).

36 For the Jewish example, see Nathan Katz, *Who Are the Jews of India* (Berkeley: University of California Press, 2000), 59–66.

Chapter 2

1 Keay, 2010, 383–508.
2 See Shubhra Chakrabarti and Utsa Patnaik, eds., *Agrarian and Other Histories: Essays for Binay Bhushan Chaudhuri* (Chennai, India: Tulika Books, 2017).
3 Shashi Tharoor, "Viewpoint: Britain Must Pay Reparations to India," BBC News, July 22, 2015. https://www.bbc.com/news/world-asia-india-33618621, accessed September 18, 2016 and John MacKenzie, "Viewpoint: Why Britain Does Not Owe Reparations to India," BBC News, July 28, 2015. https://www.bbc.com/news/world-asia-india-33647422, accessed September 18, 2016.
4 Matthew 28:19.
5 Gandhi, 1957.
6 Rudyard Kipling, "The White Man's Burden," in *The White Man's Poet: Selected Works by Rudyard Kipling* (London: Blurb, 2017).
7 See Bipan Chandra, Mridula Mukherjee, Aditya Mukherjee, K.N. Panikkar, and Sucheta Mahajan, *India's Struggle for Independence* (New York: Penguin, 2016).
8 Ashis Nandy, *Intimate Enemy: The Loss and Recovery of Self under Colonialism* (London: Oxford University Press, 2009).
9 Samaren Roy, *The Bengalees: Glimpses of History and Culture* (New Delhi: Allied Publishers, 1999), 164–6.
10 Glyn Richards, ed., *A Source-book of Modern Hinduism* (Surrey, UK: Curzon Press, 1985), 1.
11 Charles A. Howe, *For Faith and Freedom: A Short History of Unitarianism in Europe* (Boston: Skinner House Books, 1997), 2.
12 Keshub Chunder Sen, cited in Richards, ed., 43–4.
13 Swami Nikhilananda, trans., *The Gospel of Sri Ramakrishna* (New York: Ramakrishna-Vivekananda Center, 1942), 60.
14 Sri Ramakrishna, cited in Richards, ed., 65.
15 The Pluralism Project, Harvard University, "Hinduism in America." http://pluralism.org/timeline/hinduism-in-america/, accessed September 18, 2016.
16 Ibid.
17 John Adams, cited in Thomas A. Tweed and Stephen Prothero, *Asian Religions in America* (New York: Oxford University Press, 1999), 48.
18 Michael J. Altman, *Heathen, Hindoo, Hindu: American Representations of India, 1721–1893* (Oxford: Oxford University Press, 2017), 1.
19 Ibid., xxi–xxii.
20 Pluralism Project.
21 Robert Gordon, *Emerson and the Light of India*, cited by Philip Goldberg, *American Veda: From Emerson and the Beatles to Yoga and Meditation—How Indian Spirituality Changed the West* (New York: Three Rivers Press, 2010), 31.
22 Translation mine, adapted from that of George Thompson.
23 *Bhagavad Gītā*, 18:66a; translation mine.
24 Pluralism Project.
25 Ibid.
26 Henry David Thoreau, *Walden and Civil Disobedience* (Signet Classics, 2012), 50.
27 Walt Whitman, *Song of Myself and Other Poems by Walt Whitman* (Berkeley: Counterpoint, 2010), 71.
28 Helena Petrovna Blavatsky, *The Key to Theosophy: A Simple Exposition Based on the Wisdom-Religion of All Ages* (Pasadena: Theosophical University Press, 1889), 39.
29 Peter van der Veer, *Imperial Encounters: Religion and Modernity in India and Britain* (Princeton: Princeton University Press, 2001), 55.

30 George Bond, *The Buddhist Revival in Sri Lanka: Religious Tradition, Reinterpretation, and Response* (Columbia: University of South Carolina, 1988), 48–3.
31 Gandhi, 1957, 233.
32 Nandy.
33 Leela Gandhi, *Affective Communities: Anticolonial Thought, Fin-de-Siécle Radicalism, and the Politics of Friendship* (Durham, NC: Duke University Press, 2006), 2.
34 Goldberg, 47–8.
35 William James, *The Varieties of Religious Experience* (New York: University of Virginia Press, 1929), 92–3.
36 See, for example, Altman, xv–xvi.
37 See Swami Shuddhidananda, ed., *Vivekananda as the Turning Point: The Rise of a New Spiritual Wave* (Mayawati: Advaita Ashrama, 2018).

Chapter 3

1 Goldberg, 2010, 76.
2 Interestingly, Dharmapala eventually broke with Olcott for reasons similar to the reasons Swami Dayananda Saraswati had done so. He did not approve of the theosophical conflation of Hinduism and Buddhism. Unlike the Hindu Dayananda, Dharmapala's objections, of course, came from the Buddhist side of the conversation.
3 Vivekananda, *Complete Works*, Volume One, 4–5.
4 Sister Nivedita (Sankari Prasad, ed.), *Letters of Sister Nivedita*, Volume Two (Calcutta, India: Nababharat, 1982), 661.
5 Ibid., 3.
6 Ibid., 4.
7 Pluralism Project.
8 Vivekananda, *Complete Works*, Volume One, 24.
9 Radhakrishnan, 1973, 18.
10 Pluralism Project.
11 Joseph Lelyveld, *Great Soul: Mahatma Gandhi and His Struggle with India* (New York: Vintage Books, 2012), 50.
12 As of this writing, the minister in charge of the Vedanta Society of New York is Swami Sarvapriyananda and the minister in charge of the Ramakrishna-Vivekananda Center is Swami Yuktatmananda.
13 Pluralism Project.
14 See Christopher Isherwood, *Ramakrishna and His Disciples* (Hollywood: Vedanta Press, 1965).
15 Aldous Huxley, *The Perennial Philosophy* (New York: Harper and Row, 1944), vii.
16 *Bhagavad Gītā* 2: 13–14; translation mine, adapted from that of George Thompson.
17 Goldberg, 2010, 26.
18 Pluralism Project.
19 Ibid.
20 Jiddu Krishnamurti, "The Dissolution of the Order of the Star: A Statement by J. Krishnamurti," *International Star Bulletin*. (Eerde, Ommen, the Netherlands: Star Publishing Trust), 3.
21 Pluralism Project.
22 Ibid.
23 Ibid.

24 Joseph S. Alter, "Shri Yogendra: Magic, Modernity, and the Burden of the Middle-Class Yogi," in Mark Singleton and Ellen Goldberg, eds., *Gurus of Modern Yoga* (Oxford: Oxford University Press, 2014), 60.
25 Pluralism Project.
26 Ibid.
27 See David Godman, *The Power of the Presence (Part One)* (Lithia Springs, GA: New Leaf Distributing Company, 2000).
28 Somerset Maugham, *The Razor's Edge* (New York: Vintage Books, 1943).
29 See, for example, Andrew Cohen, *Embracing Heaven and Earth.*
30 See, for example, Ken Wilber, *A Theory of Everything: An Integral Vision for Business, Politics, Science, and Spirituality* (Boston: Shambhala, 2001).
31 Pluralism Project.
32 Ibid.
33 Ibid.
34 Vivekananda, *Complete Works*, Volume One, 11.
35 Altman, 2017, xv.
36 Anya P. Foxen, *Biography of a Yogi: Paramahansa Yogananda and the Origins of Modern Yoga* (Oxford: Oxford University Press, 2017).
37 Wendell Thomas, *Hinduism Invades America* (New York: Beacon Press, 1930), 253–4.
38 Vinay Lal, *The Other Indians: A Political and Cultural History of South Asians in America* (New Delhi: HarperCollins, 2008), 1–2.
39 Sanjoy Chakravorty, Devesh Kapur, and Nirvikar Singh, *The Other One Percent: Indians in America* (New York: Oxford University Press, 2017), 4–5.
40 Ibid., 5.
41 Pluralism Project.
42 Chakravorty et al., 6.
43 Ibid., 5.
44 Padma Anagol, *The Emergence of Feminism in India, 1850–1920* (Aldershot, UK: Ashgate, 2005), 57.
45 Deborah A. Logan, "America, the Superlative, and India, the Jewel in the Crown: Religious Ideologies, Transnationalism, and the End of the Raj," in Lavanya Vemsani, ed., *Modern Hinduism in Text and Context* (London: Bloomsbury, 2018), 109.
46 Ibid., 6.
47 Ibid.
48 Ibid., 8.
49 Lal, 20–1.
50 Chakravorty et al., 9.
51 *Mohammedan* is of course a term for Islam which inaccurately reflects an Islamic understanding of the role of the Prophet Mohammed in the religion.
52 Chakravorty et al., 10.
53 Ibid., 11.
54 Ibid.
55 Miriam Schneir, "The Statute Aimed at Julian Assange: For more than a century, the US government has used the Espionage Act to restrict speech, imprison activists and whistle-blowers, and dismantle progressive organizations," in *The Nation*, July 1/8, 2019, 23.
56 Ibid., 12.
57 Ibid.

Chapter 4

1 Paul Oliver, *Hinduism and the 1960s: The Rise of a Counter-Culture* (London: Bloomsbury, 2014), 5.
2 Ibid.
3 Pluralism Project.
4 See Mark Singleton, *Yoga Body: The Origins of Modern Posture Practice* (New York: Oxford University Press, 2010).
5 Pluralism Project.
6 Ibid.
7 Oliver, 5.
8 Jiddu Krishnamurti, "You Are the World." chapter 1, October 18, 1968, First Public Talk at Brandeis University. http://www.jkrishnamurti.org/krishnamurti-teachings/print.php?tid=19&chid=68560, accessed September 18, 2016.
9 Jeffrey J. Kripal, *Esalen: America and the Religion of No Religion* (Chicago: The University of Chicago Press, 2007), 60.
10 Vivekananda, *Complete Works*, Volume One, 124.
11 Kripal, 60.
12 Ibid., 30.
13 Ibid.
14 Personal communication.
15 "Natural Law Party." http://www.natural-law.org, accessed September 18, 2016.
16 Mark Wallgren, *The Beatles on Record* (New York: Simon and Schuster, 1982), 63.
17 Ibid.
18 "The Movement Center." http://www.themovementcenter.com/bio/, accessed September 18, 2016.
19 Pluralism Project.
20 Helen Crovetto, "Building Tantric Infrastructure in America: Rudi's Western Kashmir Shaivism," in Ann Gleig and Lola Williamson, *Homegrown Gurus: From Hinduism in America to American Hinduism* (Albany: State University of New York Press, 2013), 42.
21 Pluralism Project.
22 Ibid.
23 Oliver, 5.
24 I know of one example, for instance, in which, on the date the monk was alleged to have committed the abuse, at a center in the United States, he was in fact in India.
25 See Ana Guinote and Theresa K. Vescio, *The Social Psychology of Power* (New York: Guilford Press, 2010).
26 See Robert Jay Lifton, *The Nazi Doctors: Medical Killing and the Psychology of Genocide* (New York: Basic Books, 1988).
27 Oliver, 33.
28 Bob Dylan, "Subterranean Homesick Blues," *Bringing It All Back Home* (New York: Columbia Records, 1965).
29 Ibid., 34.
30 Oliver.

Chapter 5

1 Gurinder Singh Mann, Paul Numrich, and Raymond Williams, *Buddhists, Hindus, and Sikhs in America: A Short History* (Oxford: Oxford University Press, 2008), 43–4.

2 Ibid., 62.
3 Flueckiger, 2015, 40.
4 Ibid., 41–2.
5 Pluralism Project.
6 Ibid.
7 Ibid.
8 Ibid.
9 Ibid.
10 Ibid.
11 Ibid.
12 Chinmaya Mission. http://www.chinmayamission.com/who-we-are/the-mission/, accessed September 18, 2016.
13 Pluralism Project.
14 Raymond Williams, *An Introduction to Swaminarayan Hinduism* (Cambridge: Cambridge University Press, 2001), 97.
15 Ibid.
16 Ibid.
17 HARI Temple, "About HARI." http://www.haritemple.org/abouthari.htm, accessed September 18, 2016.
18 Washington Kali Temple. http://kalitemple-washington.org/, accessed September 18, 2016.
19 W. Peter Ward, *White Canada Forever: Popular Attitudes and Public Policy toward Orientals in British Columbia* (Third Edition) (Montreal: McGill-Queen's University Press, 1978), 86.
20 See Karen Isaken Leonard, *Making Ethnic Choices: California's Punjabi Mexican Americans* (Philadelphia: Temple University Press, 1992).
21 Central Intelligence Agency, *World Factbook*.
22 Murali Balaji, "The Hindus of the Caribbean: An Appreciation," *Huffington Post*, February 13, 2015 (updated April 15, 2015). https://www.huffingtonpost.com/murali-balaji/the-hindus-of-the-caribbe_b_6680036.html, accessed February 9, 2019.
23 Lal, 2008, 1–2.
24 Vertovec, 2000, 67.
25 Ibid.
26 Ibid.
27 Balaji, 2015.
28 Vertovec, 2000, 69.
29 Anantanand Rambachan, personal communication.

Chapter 6

1 Deepak Sarma, "White Hindu Converts: Mimicry or Mockery?" *Huffington Post*, November 15, 2012 (updated January 14, 2013). https://www.huffpost.com/entry/mimicry-or-mockery-white_b_2131329, accessed August 6, 2019.
2 This is a common comment from students whom I take on field trips to the local Hindu temple.
3 Sarma.
4 See Williamson and Gleig, 2013 for a variety of examples of this phenomenon.
5 Pluralism Project.
6 See, for example, C.R. Brooks, *The Hare Krishnas in India* (Princeton: Princeton

University Press, 2014). Brooks argues that white Hare Krishna devotees have been accepted as, for all intents and purposes, Brahmins, even taking up the role of officiating temple worship, by Hindus in India who are impressed with their clearly sincere devotion.

7 Pluralism Project.

8 Williamson, 2010, 4.

9 Radhakrishnan, 1973.

10 "The Indians Are Coming," in *Hinduism Today*, July/August/September 2008.

11 Julia Hauser, "Vegetarianism between Europe and India: An Entangled History." *Food, Fatness and Fitness: Critical Perspectives.* http://foodfatnessfitness.com/

12 Ibid.

13 "The Food Habits of a Nation," *The Hindu*, August 2006 (updated March 22, 2012). https://www.thehindu.com/todays-paper/the-food-habits-of-a-nation/article3089973.ece, accessed February 9, 2019.

14 Ibid.

15 Sanjukta Gupta, "The Domestication of a Goddess: *Caraṇa-tīrtha* Kālīghāṭ, the *Mahāpīṭha* of Kālī," in Rachel Fell McDermott and Jeffrey J. Kripal, eds., *Encountering Kālī: In the Margins, at the Center, in the West* (Delhi: Motilal Banarsidass, 2005), 73; Margo DeMello, *Animals and Society: An Introduction to Human-Animal Studies* (New York: Columbia University Press, 2012), 317–19.

16 Holly Roberts, *The Vegetarian Philosophy of India: Hindu, Buddhist, and Jain Sacred Teachings* (Sequim, WA: Anjeli Press, 2006), 41.

17 *Manusmṛti* 5: 41. See Doniger, 1991, 103.

18 Hindu American Foundation, "Take Yoga Back: Bringing to Light Yoga's Hindu Roots." https://www.hafsite.org/takeyogaback, accessed February 9, 2019.

19 See Andrea R. Jain, *Selling Yoga: From Counterculture to Pop Culture* (Oxford: Oxford University Press, 2015) and Andrew Nicholson, "Is Yoga Hindu? On the Fuzziness of Religious Boundaries," in *Common Knowledge Symposium: "Fuzzy Studies," Part 6* (August 2013).

20 Cited in Richards, 1985, 156–7.

21 Swami Nikhilananda, 1942, 60.

22 Cited in Richards, 1985, 65.

23 Swami Prabhavananda, *The Sermon on the Mount According to Vedanta* (Hollywood: Vedanta Press, 1964).

24 John Hick, *An Interpretation of Religion: Human Responses to the Transcendent* (New Haven: Yale University Press, 1989).

25 David Ray Griffin, ed., *Deep Religious Pluralism* (Westminster, KY: John Knox Press, 2005).

26 Paul F. Knitter, *Introducing Theologies of Religion* (Maryknoll, NY: Orbis Books, 2014).

27 Sharada Sugirtharajah, personal communication. An outstanding scholar in her own right, Sugirtharajah was also a student and friend of John Hick.

Chapter 7

1 Pravrajika Vrajaprana, "Vedanta in America: Where We've Been and Where We Are." https://vedanta.org/2000/monthly-readings/vedanta-in-america-where-weve-been-and-where-we-are/, accessed February 9, 2017.

2 George Harrison, "Awaiting on You All," *All Things Must Pass* (London: Apple Records, 1970).

3 George Harrison, "Stuck Inside a Cloud," *Brainwashed* (Dark Horse Records, 2002).
4 The use of the term *U turn* to denote the choice of a Westerner who has explored Hinduism to return to a Western religious tradition seems to have been started by Rajiv Malhotra, who develops the idea into a fairly elaborate theory about Western psychology.
5 Joshua Greene, *Here Comes the Sun: The Spiritual and Musical Journey of George Harrison* (Wiley, 2006), personal communication.
6 Dave Masko, "George Harrison Died Peacefully Discloses Widow, Olivia, and How to Do It." http://www.huliq.com/10282/george-harrison-died-peacefully-discloses-widow-olivia-and-how-do-it, accessed February 9, 2017.
7 The Beatles, *The Beatles Anthology* (San Francisco: Chronicle Books, 2000), 354.
8 Legs McNeil and Gillian McCain, "The Oral History of the First Two Times the Beatles Took Acid." https://www.vice.com/en_us/article/ppawq9/the-oral-history-of-the-beatles-first-two-acids-trips-legs-mcneil-gillian-mccain, accessed February 9, 2017.
9 Philip Goldberg, personal communication.
10 "Dialogue (Excerpts): 1969–09/11; Tittenhurst Park, London, UK," (Apple Records, 1969).
11 The Moody Blues, "Om," in *In Search of the Lost Chord* (Deram Records, 1968).
12 "Jon Anderson Gets Chatty about Carrying On," *Independent Ethos*, November 8, 2013, https://indieethos.wordpress.com/2013/11/08/jon-anderson-of-yes-gets-chatty-about-carrying-on-full-interview-in-miami-new-times/, accessed February 9, 2019.
13 Mike Dines, "The Sacralization of Straightedge Punk: Nada Brahma and the Divine Embodiment of Krishnacore," in *Musicological Annual* (Department of Musicology, Faculty of Arts, University of Ljubljana), 147–56.
14 Raghunath Cappo, "My Story." https://www.raghunath.yoga, accessed February 9, 2019.
15 George Lucas, Star Wars, and Transcendental Meditation. http://goldendome.org/lucas/, accessed September 18, 2016.
16 *Star Wars: A New Hope* (Lucasfilm, 1977).
17 Ibid.
18 Narayanan, 2018.
19 Daoism scholar Victor Mair actually raises the possibility that the *Daodejing* was influenced by both Vedanta and Yoga traditions from India. See Victor Mair, trans., *Tao Te Ching: The Classic Book of Integrity and the Way* (New York: Bantam Books, 1990), 140–8.
20 Matthew Bortolin, *The Dharma of Star Wars* (Somerville, MA: Wisdom Publications, 2005), 50.
21 *Star Wars: The Empire Strikes Back* (Lucasfilm, 1980).
22 Ibid.
23 There is also a female Jedi knight named Shaak Ti. Shakti is, of course, the mother goddess of Hinduism and the underlying creative energy or power behind existence: "the Force."
24 See Leesa S. Davis, *Advaita Vedānta and Zen: Deconstructive Modes of Spiritual Inquiry* (London: Continuum, 2010).
25 Steven Rosen, *The Jedi in the Lotus* (Budapest: Artktos Media, 2011).
26 *Star Wars: The Empire Strikes Back* (Lucasfilm, 1980).
27 Narayanan, 2018.
28 *Star Wars: The Phantom Menace* (Lucasfilm, 1999).
29 Paul Terry and Tara Bennett, *Lost Encyclopedia* (New York: Dorling Kindersley, 2010), 109.
30 It may also be worth noting that the section of the *Lost Encyclopedia* that discusses the DHARMA Initiative starts on page 108.

31 Terry and Bennett, 2010, 109.
32 Ibid.
33 Nikhilananda, 1942, 14.
34 See Martine van Woerkens, *The Strangled Traveler: Colonial Imaginings and the Thugs of India* (Chicago: University of Chicago Press, 1995).
35 Dan Simmons, *Song of Kali* (New York: Open Road Integrated Media, 2010).
36 "Hank Azaria Ready to 'Step Aside' from *Simpsons* Apu Role," BBC News, April 25, 2018. https://www.bbc.com/news/entertainment-arts-43892039, accessed February 9, 2019.
37 Jinal Bhatt, "I Wrote Most of the Scene: Kunal Nayyar Responds after Being Called 'Racist' for a TBBT Clip," *Storypick*, November 13, 2017. https://www.storypick.com/kunal-nayyar-racist-tbbt-clip/, accessed February 15, 2019.

Chapter 8

1 Pluralism Project.
2 Ibid.
3 Ibid.
4 Prema Kurien, *A Place at the Multicultural Table: The Development of an American Hinduism* (New Brunswick, NJ: Rutgers University Press, 2007).
5 I recall in this connection a conversation that was recounted to me by one HAF member who was meeting members of the US Congress in order to educate them about Hinduism and Hindu issues. The first question that one Congressman asked her was "What is the difference between Sunni Hindus and Shia Hindus?"
6 http://www.hafsite.org/about-us/who-we-are
7 Ibid.
8 http://www.hafsite.org/media/pr/hinduism-not-cast-caste-full-report and http://www.hafsite.org/media/pr/haf-policy-brief-hindusim-and-homosexuality
9 Jürgen Habermas, "Modernity: An Incomplete Project," in Hal Foster, ed., *The Anti-Aesthetic: Essays on Postmodern Culture* (New York: The New Press, 2002), 3–15.
10 Sadhana Coalition, "Our Mission, Vision, and Values." https://www.sadhana.org/mission-vision, accessed August 6, 2019.
11 Ibid.

Chapter 9

1 The coinage of this phrase is generally attributed to Hindu American activist, Rajiv Malhotra.
2 Hindu assault victims whose attackers took them to be Muslim include Srinivas Kuchibotla and Sureshbhai Patel. Sikh victims include Prabhjot Singh, whose assailants called him "Osama," and, most notoriously, the victims of the mass shooting at the Sikh gurdwara in Oak Creek, Wisconsin in 2012. https://www.nytimes.com/2017/06/09/us/indian-immigrants-kansas-hate-crime.html?mcubz=0, http://www.cnn.com/2015/02/12/us/alabama-police-beating/index.html, http://indiatoday.intoday.in/story/sikh-professor-at-columbia-university-called-osama-attacked-in-us/1/311224.html, and http://www.nytimes.com/2012/08/06/us/shooting-reported-at-temple-in-wisconsin.html?mcubz=0.

3 Edward Said, *Orientalism* (New York: Vintage Books, 1979).
4 Richard King, *Orientalism and Religion: Postcolonial Theory and the "Mystic East"* (London: Routledge, 1999), 82.
5 Pew Research Center, "Americans Express Increasingly Warm Feelings toward Religious Groups." http://www.pewforum.org/2017/02/15/americans-express-increasingly-warm-feelings-toward-religious-groups/
6 Vasudha Narayanan, "How Americans Came to Embrace Meditation, and with It, Hinduism," February 2, 2018. https://theconversation.com/how-americans-came-to-embrace-meditation-and-with-it-hinduism-90081, accessed February 9, 2019.
7 Philip Goldberg, *American Veda: From Emerson and the Beatles to Yoga and Meditation—How Indian Spirituality Changed the West* (New York: Three Rivers Press, 2010), 10–11.
8 Ibid., 21–2.
9 See Oliver, 2014.
10 Pew Research Center, "How Income Varies among US Religious Groups." http://www.pewresearch.org/fact-tank/2016/10/11/how-income-varies-among-u-s-religious-groups/
11 Pew Research Center, "Demographic Profiles of Religious Groups." http://www.pewforum.org/2015/05/12/chapter-3-demographic-profiles-of-religious-groups/.
12 Vijay Prashad, *The Karma of Brown Folk* (Minneapolis: University of Minnesota Press, 2000).
13 Ibid.
14 See Narayanan, 2018.
15 Ibid.
16 Cited from Richards, 1985, 156.
17 Habermas, 2002, 3–15.
18 Ann Gleig, *American Dharma: Buddhism beyond Modernity* (New Haven: Yale University Press, 2019) and Scott A. Mitchell, *Buddhism in America: Global Religion, Local Contexts* (London: Bloomsbury, 2016).
19 Vivekananda, Volume One, 342.

Bibliography

Michael J. Altman, *Heathen, Hindoo, Hindu: American Representations of India, 1721–1893* (Oxford: Oxford University Press, 2017).

Padma Anagol, *The Emergence of Feminism in India, 1850–1920* (Aldershot, UK: Ashgate, 2005).

Sri Aurobindo, *The Life Divine* (Pondicherry, India: Sri Aurobindo Ashram, 2010).

P.M. Bakshi, *Constitution of India: Selective Comments* (New Delhi: Universal Law Publishing Company, 2006).

Murali Balaji, ed., *Digital Hinduism: Dharma and Discourse in the Age of New Media* (Lanham, MD: Lexington Books, 2018).

The Beatles, *The Beatles Anthology* (San Francisco: Chronicle Books, 2000).

Gwylim Beckerlegge, *The Ramakrishna Mission* (Oxford: Oxford University Press, 2001).

Richard Beeman, *The Penguin Guide to the United States Constitution: A Fully Annotated Declaration of Independence, U.S. Constitution and Amendments, and Selections from The Federalist Papers* (New York: Penguin Books, 2010).

Jayanti Bhattacharya and Coonoor Kripalani, eds., *Chinese and Indian Immigrant Communities: Comparative Perspectives* (London: Anthem Press, 2015).

Helena Petrovna Blavatsky, *The Key to Theosophy: A Simple Exposition Based on the Wisdom-Religion of All Ages* (Pasadena, CA: Theosophical University Press, 1889).

George Bond, *The Buddhist Revival in Sri Lanka: Religious Tradition, Reinterpretation, and Response* (Columbia: University of South Carolina, 1988).

Matthew Bortolin, *The Dharma of Star Wars* (Somerville, MA: Wisdom Publications, 2005).

C.R. Brooks, *The Hare Krishnas in India* (Princeton: Princeton University Press, 2014).

Edwin Bryant, *The Quest for the Origins of Vedic Culture: The Indo-Aryan Migration Debate* (New York: Oxford University Press, 2004).

Patañjali (Edwin Bryant, trans.), *The Yoga Sūtras of Patañjali: A New Edition, Translation, and Commentary* (New York: North Point Press, 2009).

Sarah Caldwell, "The Heart of the Secret: A Personal and Scholarly Encounter with Siddha Yoga," in *Nova Religio: The Journal of Alternative and Emergent Religions*, 5:1 (October 2001), 9–51.

Shubhra Chakrabarti and Utsa Patnaik, eds., *Agrarian and Other Histories: Essays for Binay Bhushan Chaudhuri* (Chennai, India: Tulika Books, 2017).

Sanjoy Chakravorty, Devesh Kapur, and Nirvikar Singh, *The Other One Percent: Indians in America* (New York: Oxford University Press, 2017).

Bipan Chandra, *India's Struggle for Independence* (New York: Penguin Books, 2012).

Tim Cooke, ed., *National Geographic Concise History of World Religions: An Illustrated Time Line* (Washington, DC: National Geographic, 2011).

John Cort, *Jains in the World: Religious Values and Ideology in India* (Oxford: Oxford University Press, 2001).

Christopher R. Cotter and David G. Robertson, eds., *After World Religions: Reconstructing Religious Studies* (New York: Routledge, 2016).

William Dalrymple, "The Great Divide: The Violent Legacy of Indian Partition" (*The New Yorker*, June 22, 2015).

Leesa S. Davis, *Advaita Vedānta and Zen: Deconstructive Modes of Spiritual Inquiry* (London: Continuum, 2010).
Swami Dayananda Saraswati, "Conversion Is an Act of Violence." http://www.swamij.com/conversion-violence.htm, accessed January 24, 2018.
Margo DeMello, *Animals and Society: An Introduction to Human-Animal Studies* (New York: Columbia University Press, 2012).
Corinne Dempsey, *The Goddess Lives in Upstate New York* (New York: Oxford University Press, 2005).
Wendy Doniger, trans., *The Laws of Manu* (New York: Penguin Books, 1991).
Wendy Doniger, *The Hindus: An Alternative History* (Oxford: Oxford University Press, 2009).
Diana Eck, *On Common Ground: World Religions in America* (New York: Columbia University Press, 2002).
Diana Eck, *Darśan: Seeing the Divine Image in India* (Delhi: Motilal Banarsidass, 2007).
Ralph Waldo Emerson, *Essential Writings* (New York: Modern Library Classics, 2000).
Gavin Flood, *An Introduction to Hinduism* (Cambridge: Cambridge University Press, 1996).
Joyce Burkhalter Flueckiger, *Everyday Hinduism* (Oxford: Wiley Blackwell, 2015).
Thomas Forsthoefel, ed., *Gurus in America* (Albany: State University of New York Press, 2005).
Hal Foster, ed., *The Anti-Aesthetic: Essays on Postmodern Culture* (New York: The New Press, 2002).
Anya P. Foxen, *Biography of a Yogi: Paramahansa Yogananda and the Origins of Modern Yoga* (Oxford: Oxford University Press, 2017).
Leela Gandhi, *Affective Communities* (Durham, NC: Duke University Press, 2006).
Mohandas K. Gandhi, *The Story of My Experiments with Truth* (Boston: Beacon Press, 1957).
Eileen Gardiner, *Hindu Hell: Visions, Tours, and Descriptions of the Infernal Underworld* (New York: Italica Press, 2013).
Nicholas F. Gier, *The Origins of Religious Violence: An Asian Perspective* (Lanham, MD: Lexington Books, 2016).
Juli L. Gittinger, *Hinduism and Hindu Nationalism Online* (New York: Routledge, 2019).
Ann Gleig, *American Dharma: Buddhism beyond Modernity* (New Haven: Yale University Press, 2019).
David Godman, *The Power of the Presence (Part One)* (Lithia Springs, Georgia: New Leaf Distributing Company, 2000).
Philip Goldberg, *American Veda: From Emerson and the Beatles to Yoga and Meditation—How Indian Spirituality Changed the West* (New York: Three Rivers Press, 2010).
Richard Gombrich, *What the Buddha Thought* (London: Equinox, 2009).
Peter Gottschalk, *Beyond Hindu and Muslim: Multiple Identity in Narratives of Village India* (Oxford: Oxford University Press, 2000).
Joshua Greene, *Here Comes the Sun: The Spiritual and Musical Journey of George Harrison* (Hoboken, NJ: Wiley, 2006).
David Ray Griffin, ed., *Deep Religious Pluralism* (Westminster, KY: John Knox Press, 2005).
Paul J. Griffiths, *An Apology for Apologetics: A Study in the Logic of Interreligious Dialogue* (Maryknoll, NY: Orbis Books, 1991).
Ana Guinote and Theresa K. Vescio, *The Social Psychology of Power* (New York: Guilford Press, 2010).
Brian Hatcher, *Bourgeois Hinduism, or Faith of the Modern Vedantists* (Oxford: Oxford University Press, 2007).
Julia Hauser, "Vegetarianism between Europe and India: An Entangled History," *Food, Fatness and Fitness: Critical Perspectives*. http://foodfatnessfitness.com/

S. Hay, ed., *Sources of Indian Tradition, Volume Two* (New York: Columbia University Press, 1988).
John Hick, *An Interpretation of Religion: Human Responses to the Transcendent* (New Haven: Yale University Press, 1989).
John Hick, "Religious Pluralism," in Philip L. Quinn and Charlies Taliaferro, eds., *A Companion to Philosophy of Religion* (Cambridge, MA: Blackwell Publishers, 1997), 607–14.
Veena R. Howard, ed., *Dharma: The Hindu, Jain, Buddhist, and Sikh Traditions of India* (London: I.B. Tauris, 2017).
Charles A. Howe, *For Faith and Freedom: A Short History of Unitarianism in Europe* (Boston: Skinner House Books, 1997).
Aldous Huxley, *The Perennial Philosophy* (New York: Harper and Row, 1944).
Christopher Isherwood, *Ramakrishna and His Disciples* (Mayavati: Advaita Ashrama, 1969).
Carl T. Jackson, *The Oriental Religions and American Thought* (Westport, CT: Greenwood Publishing Group, 1982).
Carl T. Jackson, *Vedanta for the West: The History of the Ramakrishna Movement* (Bloomington, IN: Indiana University Press, 1994).
Andrea R. Jain, *Selling Yoga: From Counterculture to Pop Culture* (Oxford: Oxford University Press, 2015)
Pankaj Jain, *Dharma and Ecology of Hindu Communities: Sustenance and Sustainability* (New York: Routledge, 2016).
William James, *The Varieties of Religious Experience* (New York: University of Virginia Press, 1929).
Tony Joseph, *Early Indians: The Story of Our Ancestors and Where We Came From* (New Delhi: Juggernaut, 2018).
Khyati Joshi, *New Roots in America's Sacred Ground* (New Brunswick, NJ: Rutgers University Press, 2006).
Vamsee Juluri, *Rearming Hinduism* (Chennai, India: Westland, 2014).
Nathan Katz, *Who Are the Jews of India?* (Berkeley: University of California Press, 2000).
John Keay, *India: A History* (New York: HarperCollins, 2010).
Jonathan Mark Kenoyer, *Ancient Cities of the Indus Valley Civilization* (Oxford: Oxford University Press, 1998).
Richard King, *Orientalism and Religion: Postcolonial Theory and the "Mystic East"* (London: Routledge, 1999).
Rudyard Kipling, "The White Man's Burden," in *The White Man's Poet: Selected Works by Rudyard Kipling* (London: Blurb, 2017).
Paul F. Knitter, *Introducing Theologies of Religion* (Maryknoll, NY: Orbis Books, 2014).
Mahalingum Kolapen, *Hindu Temples of North America* (Orlando, FL: Hindu University of America, 2008).
Jeffrey J. Kripal, *Esalen: America and the Religion of No Religion* (Chicago: The University of Chicago Press, 2007).
Jeffrey J. Kripal, *Esalen: America and the Religion of No Religion* (Chicago: University of Chicago Press, 2008).
Jiddu Krishnamurti, "The Dissolution of the Order of the Star: A Statement by J. Krishnamurti," in *International Star Bulletin* (Eerde, Ommen, Netherlands: Star Publishing Trust).
P. Pratap Kumar, *Contemporary Hinduism* (New York: Acumen, 2013).
Prema Kurien, *A Place at the Multicultural Table* (New Brunswick, NJ: Rutgers, 2007).
Vinay Lal, *The Other Indians: A Political and Cultural History of South Asians in America* (New Delhi: HarperCollins, 2008).
Ramdas Lamb, *Rapt in the Name: The Ramnamis, Ramnam, and Untouchable Religion in Central India* (Albany: State University of New York Press, 2002).

Jeffrey D. Lavoie, *The Theosophical Society* (Irvine, CA: Brown Walker Press, 2012).
Joseph Lelyveld, *Great Soul: Mahatma Gandhi and His Struggle with India* (New York: Vintage Books, 2012).
Karen Isaken Leonard, *Making Ethnic Choices: California's Punjabi Mexican Americans* (Philadelphia: Temple University Press, 1992).
Robert Jay Lifton, *The Nazi Doctors: Medical Killing and the Psychology of Genocide* (New York: Basic Books, 1988).
J.E. Llewellyn, ed., *Defining Hinduism: A Reader* (London: Equinox, 2005).
Jeffery D. Long, *Jainism: An Introduction* (London: I.B. Tauris, 2007).
Jeffery D. Long, *A Vision for Hinduism: Beyond Hindu Nationalism* (London: I.B. Tauris, 2007).
Jeffery D. Long, *Historical Dictionary of Hinduism* (Lanham, MD: Scarecrow Press, 2011).
Jeffery D. Long, "'Never Was There a Time…' Crossing Over to Hinduism through the *Bhagavad Gītā*," in Jennifer Howe Peace, Or Rose, and Gregory Mobley, eds., *My Neighbor's Faith: Stories of Interreligious Encounter, Growth, and Transformation* (Maryknoll, NY: Orbis Books, 2012), 93–9.
Jeffery D. Long, "Hindu Dharma," in Veena Howard, ed. *Dharma: The Hindu, Jain, Buddhist, and Sikh Traditions of India* (London: I.B. Tauris, 2017), 38–102.
Lisa Lowe, *Immigrant Acts: On Asian American Cultural Politics* (Durham, NC: Duke University Press, 1996).
Amanda J. Lucia, *Reflections of Amma: Devotees in a Global Embrace* (Berkeley: University of California Press, 2014).
Ramana Maharshi, *The Spiritual Teaching of Ramana Maharshi* (Boulder, CO: Shambhala Publications, 2004).
Victor Mair, trans., *Tao Te Ching: The Classic Book of Integrity and the Way* (New York: Bantam Books, 1990).
Rajiv Malhotra and Aravindan Neelakandan, *Breaking India: Western Interventions in Dravidian and Dalit Faultlines* (Bhopal: Manjul Publishing House, 2012).
Gurinder Singh Mann, Paul Numrich, and Raymond Williams, *Buddhists, Hindus, and Sikhs in America: A Short History* (Oxford: Oxford University Press, 2007).
Somerset Maugham, *The Razor's Edge* (New York: Vintage Books, 1943).
Rachel Fell McDermott and Jeffrey J. Kripal, eds., *Encountering Kālī: In the Margins, at the Center, in the West* (Delhi: Motilal Banarsidass, 2005).
Jane McIntosh, *A Peaceful Realm: The Rise and Fall of the Indus Civilization* (Boulder, CO: Westview Press, 2002).
Gita Mehta, *Karma Cola: Marketing the Mystic East* (New York: Fawcett Columbine, 1990).
Lisa Miller, "We Are All Hindus Now," *Newsweek* (August 15, 2009).
Scott A. Mitchell, *Buddhism in America: Global Religion, Local Contexts* (London: Bloomsbury, 2016).
Ashis Nandy, *Intimate Enemy: The Loss and Recovery of Self under Colonialism* (London: Oxford University Press, 2009).
Vasudha Narayanan, "How Americans Came to Embrace Meditation, and with It, Hinduism." February 2, 2018. https://theconversation.com/how-americans-came-to-embrace-meditation-and-with-it-hinduism-90081.
Andrew Nicholson, *Unifying Hinduism: Philosophy and Identity in Indian Intellectual History* (New York: Columbia University Press, 2010).
Swami Nikhilananda, trans., *The Gospel of Sri Ramakrishna* (New York: Ramakrishna-Vivekananda Center, 1942).
Sister Nivedita (Sankari Prasad, ed.), *Letters of Sister Nivedita*, Volume Two (Calcutta: Nababharat, 1982).

Paul Oliver, *Hinduism and the 1960s: The Rise of a Counter-Culture* (London: Bloomsbury, 2015).
Barbara L. Packer, *The Transcendentalists* (Atlanta: University of Georgia Press, 2007).
Asko Parpola, *The Roots of Hinduism: The Early Aryans and the Indus Civilization* (New York: Oxford University Press, 2015).
Brian Pennington, *Was Hinduism Invented? Britons, Indians, and the Colonial Construction of Religion* (Oxford: Oxford University Press, 2005).
Gregory L. Possehl, *The Indus Civilization: A Contemporary Perspective* (Lanham, MD: Rowman and Littlefield, 2002).
Swami Prabhavananda, *The Sermon on the Mount According to Vedanta* (Hollywood: Vedanta Press, 1964).
A.C. Bhaktivedanta Swami Prabhupada, *Bhagavad Gita: As It Is* (Los Angeles: Bhaktivedanta Book Trust, 1972).
Vijay Prashad, *The Karma of Brown Folk* (Minneapolis: University of Minnesota Press, 2000).
Vijay Prashad, *Uncle Swami: South Asians in America Today* (New York: The New Press 2012).
The Pluralism Project, Harvard University, "Hinduism in America." http://pluralism.org/timeline/hinduism-in-america/, September 9, 2017.
Sarvepalli Radhakrishnan, *The Hindu View of Life* (New York: Macmillan, 1973).
Krishnan Ramaswamy, ed., *Invading the Sacred* (Kolkata, India: Rupa & Company, 2007).
Mattew Remski, *Practice and All Is Coming: Abuse, Cult Dynamics, and Healing in Yoga and Beyond* (Rangiora, New Zealand: Embodied Wisdom Publishing, 2019).
Glyn Richards, ed., *Sourcebook of Modern Hinduism* (Surrey, UK: Curzon Press, 1985).
Holly Roberts, *The Vegetarian Philosophy of India: Hindu, Buddhist, and Jain Sacred Teachings* (Sequim, WA: Anjeli Press, 2006).
Jenny Rose, *Zoroastrianism: An Introduction* (London: I.B. Tauris, 2014).
Steven Rosen, *The Jedi in the Lotus* (Budapest: Artktos Media, 2011).
Samaren Roy, *The Bengalees: Glimpses of History and Culture* (New Delhi: Allied Publishers, 1999).
Edward Said, *Orientalism* (New York: Vintage Books, 1979).
Arvind Sharma, *Gandhi: A Spiritual Biography* (New Haven: Yale University Press, 2013).
Swami Shuddhidananda, ed., *Vivekananda as the Turning Point: The Rise of a New Spiritual Wave* (Mayavati: Advaita Ashrama, 2018).
Dan Simmons, *Song of Kali* (New York: Open Road Integrated Media, 2010).
Mark Singleton, *Yoga Body: The Origins of Modern Posture Practice* (New York: Oxford University Press, 2010).
Mark Singleton and Ellen Goldberg, eds., *Gurus of Modern Yoga* (Oxford: Oxford University Press, 2014).
David Smith, *Hinduism and Modernity* (London: Wiley-Blackwell, 2003).
Leonard Smith, *The Unitarians: A Short History* (Ashland, OR: Blackstone Editions, 2008).
Eleanor Stark, *The Gift Unopened: A New American Revolution* (Portsmouth, NH: Peter E. Randall, 1988).
Satguru Sivaya Subramuniyaswami, *How to Become a Hindu: A Guide for Seekers and Born Hindus* (Kauai, HI: Himalayan Academy Publications, 2000).
Anne Taylor, *Annie Besant: A Biography* (Oxford: Oxford University Press, 1992).
Paul Terry and Tara Bennett, *Lost Encyclopedia* (New York: Dorling Kindersley, 2010).
Wendell Thomas, *Hinduism Invades America* (Whitefish, MT: Kessinger Publishing, 2003).
George Thompson, trans. *Bhagavad Gītā: A New Translation* (New York: North Point Press, 2008).

Henry David Thoreau, *Walden and Civil Disobedience* (New York: Signet Classics, 2012).

Jim Tucker, *Return to Life* (New York: St. Martin's Griffin, 2015).

Thomas Tweed and Stephen Prothero, *Asian Religions in America: A Documentary History* (New York: Oxford University Press, 1999).

Peter van der Veer, *Imperial Encounters: Religion and Modernity in India and Britain* (Princeton: Princeton University Press, 2001).

Lavanya Vemsani, ed., *Modern Hinduism in Text and Context* (London: Bloomsbury, 2018).

Martine van Woerkens, *The Strangled Traveler: Colonial Imaginings and the Thugs of India* (Chicago: University of Chicago Press, 1995).

Steven Vertovec, *The Hindu Diaspora: Comparative Patterns* (London: Routledge, 2000).

Swami Vivekananda, *Complete Works* (Mayawati: Advaita Ashrama, 1979).

Pravrajika Vrajaprana, *Vedanta: A Simple Introduction* (Hollywood, CA: Vedanta Press, 1999).

Mark Wallgren, *The Beatles on Record* (New York: Simon and Schuster, 1982).

W. Peter Ward, *White Canada Forever: Popular Attitudes and Public Policy toward Orientals in British Columbia* (Third Edition) (Montreal: McGill-Queen's University Press, 1978).

Brian Weiss, *Many Lives, Many Masters* (Bellefonte, PA: Fireside, 1988).

Walt Whitman, *Song of Myself and Other Poems by Walt Whitman* (Berkeley: Counterpoint, 2010).

Ken Wilber, *A Theory of Everything: An Integral Vision for Business, Politics, Science, and Spirituality* (Boston: Shambhala, 2001).

Raymond Williams, *An Introduction to Swaminarayan Hinduism* (Cambridge: Cambridge University Press, 2001).

Lola Williamson, *Transcendent in America: Hindu-Inspired Meditation Movements as New Religion* (New York: New York University Press, 2010).

Lola Williamson and Ann Gleig, *Homegrown Gurus: From Hinduism in America to American Hinduism* (Albany: State University of New York Press, 2013).

Robert L. Winzeler, *Popular Religion in Southeast Asia* (Lanham, MD: Rowman and Littlefield, 2016).

John Zavos, ed., *Public Hinduisms* (Thousand Oaks, CA: Sage, 2012).

Index